AF680005

Fixed
or
Flexible Exchange Rates?

History and Perspectives

Marin Muzhani
CDI College, Canada

Vernon Series in Economics

VERNON PRESS

Copyright © 2018 Vernon Press, an imprint of Vernon Art and Science Inc, on behalf of the author.

All rights reserved. No part of this publication may be reproduced, stored in a retrieval system, or transmitted in any form or by any means, electronic, mechanical, photocopying, recording, or otherwise, without the prior permission of Vernon Art and Science Inc.

www.vernonpress.com

In the Americas:
Vernon Press
1000 N West Street,
Suite 1200, Wilmington,
Delaware 19801
United States

In the rest of the world:
Vernon Press
C/Sancti Espiritu 17,
Malaga, 29006
Spain

Vernon Series in Economics

Library of Congress Control Number: 2017935187

ISBN: 978-1-62273-177-0

Product and company names mentioned in this work are the trademarks of their respective owners. While every care has been taken in preparing this work, neither the authors nor Vernon Art and Science Inc. may be held responsible for any loss or damage caused or alleged to be caused directly or indirectly by the information contained in it.

Table of Contents

Introduction

After the Second World War, the United States of America became the financial center of the West. Most of the international agreements after the war, such as the *Bretton Woods* or the *Marshall Plan* in Europe, endorsed the position of prominence of the United States and at the same time tried to avoid monetary and trade tensions that had characterized the years following 1945. With the agreement of *Bretton Woods* the convertibility of US dollar was 35 dollars per "ounce" in fixed exchange rates; the main scope of this agreement was the pledge of all participants to put into effect the full convertibility of their currencies and the gradual abolition of foreign exchange controls created after the great depression during the thirties.

The system of fixed exchange rates or "dollar-gold" standard was constituted by a combination of laws, commitments and conventions by which the United States (inner country) fixed its currency to gold and the outer countries fixed their currencies to the US dollar, either directly or indirectly through another currency (such as the pound sterling, the mark or the franc). All these elements quickly restored a world-wide system of free exchange, while the Marshall Plan helped with financing the reconstruction of West, creating at the same time an open market for the United States products.

The *International Monetary Fund (IMF)*, which grew out of *Bretton Woods*, became an international institution invested with the power of regularizing the international monetary system in order to prevent liquidity, scarcity and competitive devaluation. Until the 1970s the United States carried out the role of a central bank which created currency and regularized credit expansion. The dollar became a universal currency accepted for international payments, therefore the exchange rate stability and international flow of goods and capitals depended on the dollar's stability. The United States in many aspects had acquired the position of Great Britain in the 19th century.

In the last forty years, international organizations such as IMF and World Bank have taken on important weight in global monetary decisions, although there were likewise other national and interregional organisms like Federal Reserve in the United States, and later the foundation of the European Central Bank in Europe to which all EU members gave up their monetary sovereignty for the creation of monetary union.

The debate about fixed or flexible exchange rates began in the early 1950s when Milton Friedman wrote his first influential paper, "The Case for Flexible

Exchange Rates" (1953). It developed further in the 1960s when the *Bretton Woods* system was in crisis, and the prevalent opinion moved in favor of flexibility of exchange rates. Furthermore, the publication of *Optimized Currency Areas Theory* by Robert Mundell (1961) opened another front on the debate about the exchange rates as never seen before. Although more than six decades have passed, the debate about fixed or flexible exchange rates is still relevant today as it was in the 1950s.

The aim of this work is to reconsider at length the monetary debate on fixed versus flexible exchange rates, and theories regarding the optimum currency areas.

The Bretton Woods System

In July 1944, before the Great War ended, an international conference took place at Bretton Woods, New Hampshire (USA) that had its main mission to carry out the creation of the International Monetary Fund (IMF) an international organization which was supposed to be created after WWII to manage the control of international payments. The *Bretton Woods* system was developed by two important protagonists of that time, the American minister of state in the U.S. treasury, Harry Dexter White, and the renowned British economist, John Maynard Keynes.

According to the White's plan, an International Bank for Reconstruction (today the World Bank) and an International Stabilisation Fund (later the IMF) were to be established in order to help different countries reconstruct their damaged economies and ease the problem of balance of payments. Keynes, in general, agreed on this plan although he had another idea. Keynes wanted to vest the IMF with possibilities to create money and with the authority to take actions on a much larger scale on the stabilisation of international finance. In case of balance of payments imbalances, Keynes suggested that both sides, debtors and creditors, should reach an accord and adjust their strategies to achieve the equilibrium in the foreign trade. In few words, countries with payment surpluses should enhance their imports from the deficit countries and in so doing generate foreign trade equilibrium. Harry Dexter White, alternatively saw the imbalance of payments as an issue only for the deficit country. However, Keynes' plan was not taken into consideration as it was not realistic and participants of the Bretton Woods' conference agreed on the White's plan.

The new monetary order created after the Great War was quite different from the pre-war situation. Exchange rates continued to be fixed. Alignments without the previous consensus of the IMF were forbidden. The newly created IMF was provided with its own financial resources in order to guarantee that countries in difficulty with their balance of payments had access to alternative solutions to devaluation. The exchange rates demanded the official declaration of fixed parity as a central value based on the gold unit or the U.S. dollar and all monetary authorities were expected to maintain the market value of their currencies within 1% of the central parity. The United States fixed the price of gold but the new system was not a real international gold standard, and the *Bretton Woods* agreement represented a compromise between gold standard and dollar standard in which both dollar and gold were used as reserves.

The controls on exchange rates and custom tariffs were admitted as a temporary solution to the post-war situation. In reality, the full convertibility of European currencies came only in 1958 although most of the underdeveloped countries did not have convertible currencies and still held the control over capital flows. Officially all currencies were convertible in gold terms. At the end of the Second World War, the U.S. held 70% of all gold reserves and was the only country sufficiently credible for fixing a parity with gold. Gold remained the principal standard although all the currencies were linked to gold through the dollar. The system therefore was based on the ability of the U.S. to maintain the declared fixed parity of $35 per ounce of gold. The use of the dollar as a currency for international transactions implied that the U.S. must continue its deficit balance of payments in order to supply liquidity to other countries.

The volume of financing of international exchanges depends, according to the *Bretton Woods* agreement, on gold production not absorbed from private uses and price variations. The impossibility of financing the increasing volume of international trade with the flow of new "monetary" gold and the opposition of the United States to devaluate the dollar, aggravated the American deficit balance of payments.

At the end of the 1960s and the beginning of the 1970s the increase of American public expenditures for the war in Vietnam and the extension of charitable and social security programs accelerated economic growth and at the same time worsened the deficit payments. Some industrialized western countries were skeptical about the benefits of the international monetary system and made known their protests. Much criticism was aimed at the American government for the monetary policy of seigniorage in order to finance the economic growth and the war efforts in Vietnam. The U. S. policy was overly expansionist. During the first half of the 1960s, the French government decided to exchange US dollars with gold for increasing the inventory of gold. In fact, the French gold stock increased from 3.7 to 5.2 billion dollars between 1964 and 1966. The international markets took into consideration this fact and pressed the monetary authorities of many countries of the *Gold Pool* (Belgium, Holland, Switzerland, Italy, West

Germany, United Kingdom and the USA), to sell gold in order to maintain the parity of 35 dollars per ounce. Rather than bring on a total collapse of the system, the countries changed their mode of operation.

However, the reduction of official gold reserves was accelerated, and the gold pool countries went out from the international gold market and declared that they would change gold to the official price only between themselves but not from private agents. On the free market, the gold was changed to a much higher price than the official one. The internal tension of Gold Pool countries grew until President Nixon's historic decision, on August 15, 1971, to suspend the parity of the dollar with gold. That decision ended the Bretton Woods system.

The Exchange Rates Policy after Bretton Woods

The collapse of the *Bretton Woods* system was an initial manifestation of the growing contradiction between the intrinsic tendency of the productive forces to develop on a global scale and the nation-state system.

The slide to flexible exchange rates in 1971, after systemic crises and the inconvertibility of the dollar, did not come as a result of international conference agreement (as in the case of Bretton Woods) or IMF decision but was a unilateral action of the United States when President Nixon took the dollar off. Then the major western countries took their currencies off the dollar. Although, from a political standpoint the agreement to move to a flexible exchange rate was a decision made in 1973 by three men, George Schultz, US Secretary of the Treasury, Giscard d'Estaing, Minister of Finance in France, and Helmut Schmidt, Minister of Finance in Germany. George Schultz was a distinguished labor economist and had been a colleague of Milton Friedman at the University of Chicago in the 1960s, and later become Secretary of Treasury in Nixon's cabinet (Mundell, R. A., 2001, 15).

Milton Friedman was one of the first economists to assert that the only motivation behind variations of exchange rates was the differential of inflation and that flexibility was necessary in order to maintain the Purchasing Parity Power (PPP). If the hypothesis of Purchasing Parity Power was verified and the variations of exchange rates compensated for the differential of inflation, we would have a relatively constant real exchange rate or at least exchange rates characterized by a regular course. But in reality, things seem to be different, the cause of exchange rate variation is often connected to competitive structural changes in the economy. From an economic standpoint, the real exchange rate in equilibrium changes, but these changes are not very frequent and sometimes continue for a long time. This indicates that the real exchange rate does not always correspond to fundamental structural changes. These oscillations can be also presented as the product of monetary forces or *overshooting*. The thesis against fixed rates proves that we do not really know the exact value of the exchange rate. This implies that those who are called to address the exchange rates of one country do not always have a solid basis for fixing and defending the right parity. The overvaluation or undervaluation of fixed exchange rates is often a result of political pressures; an argument that in the absence of a clear rule for the fixation of the parties, monetary authorities probably base their decisions on political convenience.

A prominent Nobel-prize economist, Robert Mundell, agreed that Bretton Woods was not perfect because big countries did not follow the rules of adjustment formally introduced by the system from the beginning. For example, Britain and the United States in the 1960s automatically sterilized reserve losses, throwing the burden of adjustment on other countries. The period from 1950 to 1970 was a period of rapid growth for all the western countries and Japan. Many countries, during this period, simply did not follow the rules of a fixed exchange rate system due to the problems with their monetary system. The developing countries tried to use the inflation tax as an instrument of financing economic growth.

According to Mundell[1], there are at least two main reasons for the collapse of Bretton Woods System: the first one is the undervaluation of the gold anchor. The price of gold was politically decided by President Roosevelt administration at $35 per ounce since 1934, and had become obsolete and undervalued especially after the rise of inflation between 1959 and 1970 and during the Korean and Vietnam War[2]. Most of the consumer prices were more than doubled and the price of gold was undervalued.

---

[1]"One World, One Money" Robert Mundell and Milton Friedman debate the virtues – or not – of fixed exchange rates, gold, and a world currency. *The Canadian Financial Post*, 14 November- 14 December 2000, conceived and organized by editor-in-chief Terence Corcoran. Re-printed in Mundell R. and Friedman M. (2001), "One World, One Money", *Policy Options* (May), 20.

[2] For political reasons the two biggest producers of gold in the World were South Africa and Soviet Union. South Africa during 1970s was doing a noxious policy of apartheid against the principles of democracy; meanwhile Soviet Union was the historical enemy of the west during the cold war. At this time the credibility of US was at stake so the US rejected the Bretton Woods solution, provided by the IMF *Articles of Agreement*, for a reduction in the par value of currencies, raising the price of gold. At the beginning of 1970s the US lose more than half of its post-war gold stocks and the west countries asked further the US authorities to convert dollars into gold, the United States didn't accepted it and the Bretton Woods system failed.

The second reason is the difference between the inflation objectives of the United States and Europe. The United States, in order to finance the war in Vietnam, imposed on the rest of the world a higher rate of inflation than was optimal for Europe. Consequently, western European countries chose the flexible exchange rate system, sacrificing the valuable convergence with one another, which their economies had achieved around the fixed dollar after the Second World War. Europe was trying to create a rival to the dollar in the form of a new European currency that would be easy to deal with the fixed exchange system.

Friedman agreed with Mundell (Mundell and Friedman 2001, 21-23) in many aspects regarding the benefits of fixed exchange rates but he wanted to add that fixed exchange rate system had a great defect: a country that expands its monetary supply (for example the United States) can benefit by imposing costs on other members of the system until these countries must accept its currency at an unchanged rate. When the exchange rate is changed, and the inflation is not more sustainable, so the rules are broken, the system naturally cannot have any reason to survive. Friedman, differently from Mundell, argues that a major advantage of a flexible rate is that a country will bear the benefits and the costs of its own monetary policy fully. If a country during the flexible rates system expands its monetary policy, will not directly affect all the system and its trading partners but rather indirectly by reducing investment and trade flow. This process is very important not only economically but also politically because it reduces the occasions for international conflicts. Flexible exchange rates offered a way of adjusting monetary and fiscal policies through the market without political conflicts. So Friedman's "verdict", is that the *Bretton Woods* system failed because the fixed exchange rates system was not able to avoid economic and political conflicts in the long run.

The elimination of the gold backing from the US dollar was quickly followed by the ending of fixed currency relationships and the lifting of most of the restrictions on the movement of capital, throughout the 1980s, since several countries were forced to ditch national controls under the rising pressure of international markets. The result has been a series of storms and crises within the international financial system. As a matter of fact, in 1987, differences between the US and German monetary authorities over interest rate policies contributed directly to the October stock market collapse. In order to avoid a global collapse and recession, monetary authorities led by the US Federal Reserve injected large amounts of liquidity into the international financial system. These actions prevented a financial crisis with major consequences for the trade between Europe and North America.

The decade of the 1990s was full of regional financial crisis. It started with the British sterling crisis of 1992, followed two years later by the turmoil in bond markets in 1994 and the Mexican bailout of 1994-95. In 1997, the Asian crisis arrived, followed by the Russian default of 1998 and subsequent danger to the US financial system in the wake of the collapse of long-term capital management in September 1998. The 2008 financial crisis and the global recession that followed put more pressure on the global financial system worldwide.

The implications of the growing size and the speculative nature of financial movements in the times of globalisation called for a "new system of *Bretton Woods*". In 1996, Michel Camdessus, the Managing Director of the IMF, stated that despite the monetary system had changed since 1944 the goals of *Bretton Woods* were as valid today as they had been in the past. He highlighted that international cooperation would be required to create a new *Bretton Woods* system, which in his view means that countries must make a greater effort to understand the economic policies of other countries and they must listen to the judgement of others about their own national policies (Camdessus, M. 1996).

The main objective of this book is to focus on the longstanding monetary debate on fixed versus flexible exchange rates, and theories related to optimum currency areas and monetary unions. The monetary debate will be introduced in a historical context by taking into consideration a variety of views, opinions, historical facts and theories since the end of WWII to present. The new developments in global currency areas and monetary unions will give more insights into the evolution of the national currencies and exchange rates.

The Structure of the Book

The book is divided into six chapters, each of them containing a considerable number of segments with tables and illustrations. Chapter one discusses the role of exchange rates in the balance of payments theories after the WWII and the convertibility of national currencies to the gold standard. Chapter two will take into account the discussion about the theories of capital mobility, fiscal policy and dynamic adjustment under alternative exchange-rate systems. This chapter will also focus on the credibility of monetary policy and the role of a central banker on optimal contracts. Chapter three investigates in depth the long-lasting monetary debate on fixed versus flexible exchange rates, exchange rate regime classifications and shock absorbers.

Chapter four explores the theories about optimum currency areas and the creation of monetary unions. In addition, chapter four will also deal with costs and benefits of a common currency, the centralized monetary policy in a monetary union and the debate over fiscal federalism. Chapter five, among others, discusses the recent theories on current financial crisis and unconventional monetary policies. It also explores the impact of quantitative easing on interest rates, exchange rates, fiscal policy and considers other unconventional monetary concepts such as balance-sheet recession, etc. Chapter six discusses in depth the new approaches of new exchange rates theories developed in recent years.

Chapter 1

Exchange Rates and Balance of Payments Theories

Introduction

In the late fifties of the last century, the discussion of possible arrangements for international payments and liquidity was reopened. The opinion of economists was that the balance of payments of the United States was in disequilibrium and that the international monetary arrangements in place were showing inadequate structural soundness. Some of them tried to consider the case for flexible exchange rates as a method of dealing with the problems of international liquidity and balance-of-payments equilibrium. The system of flexible exchange rates, different from *Bretton Woods* system, was considered to offer, under ideal circumstances, a solution to problems of both international liquidity and external equilibrium. One of the main objections to the gold standard system was that it served as the mechanism by which a depression originated in one part of the world was transmitted throughout the rest of the world. Under gold standard regime, there was a high degree of positive correlation between the rate of output in one part of the world and output elsewhere (Laursen S. and Metzler A. 1950).

Two well-known economists in early fifties - Laursen and Metzler (1950) - proposed the flexible exchange rates as an alternative of fixed exchange rates to break the link between the output of individual countries and the fluctuations of the world demand. Professor James Meade, instead, deals with the balance of payments, international labor and capital movements between nations maintaining at the same time full employment domestically. Other advocates of flexible exchange rates like Milton Friedman and Egon Sohmen provide greater room for maneuver for monetary policymakers. Policy makers are free to use monetary supply for other macroeconomic policies such as stabilizing employment or inflation. This chapter will discuss some of the issues related to the application of flexible exchange rates to the balance of payments, convertibility to gold standard and demand elasticities after the WW II.

Currency Depreciation and the Balance of Trade

During the interwar period of the 20th century, the international gold standard system was criticized as it served as an instrument for transmitting depressions from one country to another which made it difficult for one country to pursue an independent fiscal and monetary policy. The problem was seen as a conflict between the domestic monetary policy and international equilibrium. Later with the development of the Keynesian theory of employment and its implications to international factors made it harder for economists and policymakers the discussion of monetary policy. The quantity of money, the level of prices, the total demand for goods and services, were all subject to external influences. The level of employment and output in most of the domestic markets were beyond the reach of the traditional monetary and fiscal policies. The gold standard system was not only responsible for the quantity of money in circulation but also for the direct link between the demand for exports and the national income.

The Keynesian theory of employment emphasized the demand for an international monetary system that would free individual countries from the restrictions of the gold standard to follow independent monetary programs of stabilization. During the interwar period experience, the demand for imports in most countries was inelastic, so the system of fluctuating exchange rates was not so efficient in correcting the disequilibrium in the balance of payments. The high degree of instability of exchange rates in the early twenties was a consequence of inconvertible paper money in the very short period as day to day or other short periods such as quarters and semesters.

Bickerdike (1920) took into consideration the discussion of exchange stability and found out that a multiplicity of products of exchange increases the chance that some of them will have comparatively elastic demands, but unstable movements of exchange rates as experienced in the early twenties are not likely to occur in the future as normal conditions have been reached (Bickerdike, 1920, 121-122). So far, if large repayments of loans or payments of interest, have to be made on certain dates, there is always scope for speculation of exchange rates to the great disadvantages of the debtor countries if gold standard was not going to maintain its discipline.

The major point in Bickerdike's view is that the change of general price-level is slow compared with the change produced at the price of ordinary trade items when the quantity offered is increased, which prevents the speculative operations in the short-period market. Individual speculators who want quick advantages by procuring commodities from abroad may cause depression to the exchange rates forcing them to raise the general price of certain supplies.

So, the solution to put a stop to the instability of foreign exchange rates was to check imports by imposing heavy taxes and restrictions (Bickerdike, 1920).

Harberger (1950, 47-60) in early fifties analyzed in a Keynesian-build model the effects of depreciation on the balance of trade. He assumed that the exchange rate is held fixed by means of national and international stabilization funds and subject to changes only through the alternation of these funds. In his model, it is assumed that there are only two countries, each of which produces only one good. Income is defined as the quantity of the national good currently produced. The initial effect of depreciation on the trade by assumption is zero, and the sum of the elasticities of demand for imports of the two countries is greater in absolute value than when production is fixed. Income definitions and equilibrium conditions are given as:

$$y1=z1+x1 \tag{1.1.a}$$

$$v2 = z2 + x2 \tag{1.1.b}$$

The demand for imports for both countries is given as:

$$x1 = a2 + b2k + c2y2 \tag{1.2.a}$$

$$x2 = a1 + b1/k + c1y1 \tag{1.2.b}$$

and the demand for home goods is given as:

$$z1 = d1 + e1k + f1y1 \tag{1.3.a}$$

$$z2 = d2 + e2/k + f2y2 \tag{1.3.b}$$

where y1 and y2 represent production of the national goods of both countries, z1 and z2 represent home demand in each country for its home-made commodities x1 and x2, while $e1$ and $e2$ are the exchange rates of the respective countries. The properties to import are given as c1 and c2, and the marginal properties to consume home-made commodities are given as $f1$ and $f2$. Defining $\eta 1 = b1/x2$ and $\eta 2 = b2/x1$ as the elasticities of demand for imports in both countries and $h1=I - f1\text{-}c1$ and $h2=I - f2\text{-}c2$ as the marginal properties to save ($s=x2/x1$ the initial value of imports to exports in country 1) we have that production in each country is infinitely elastic with respect to price of goods in terms of home currency. The balance of trade of country 1 in terms of the currency of country 2 is given as:

$$B1 = x1p1k\text{-}x2p2 \tag{1.4}$$

where $p1$ and $p2$ are the stabilized price of both countries. The balance of trade of country 1 in terms of demand for imports (using 1.2a and b) from country 2 is obtained as:

$$\frac{dB_1}{dk} = x_1 + b_2 + b_1 + \frac{c_2 dy_2}{dk} - \frac{c_1 dy_1}{dk} \quad (1.5)$$

In this model there are at least two main assumptions: first, the marginal propensity to save, import and consume domestic goods operate on real consumers' income; second, saving is a function of real consumers' income (Harberger 1950, 52-55). So the real consumers' income in term of exchange rate k is given as:

$$\frac{dy_1'}{dk} = \frac{dy_1}{dk} + \frac{\varphi y_1'}{\varphi k}; \quad \frac{dy_2'}{dk} = \frac{dy_2}{dk} + \frac{\varphi y_2'}{\varphi k}; \quad (1.6)$$

where y_1' and y_2' are the real consumers' income (made commensurable with production y). And the trade balances of countries 1 and 2 expressed in terms of domestic currency are given as:

$$\frac{dB_1'}{dk} = \frac{h_1 dy_1'}{dk}; \quad \frac{dB_2'}{dk} = \frac{h_2 dy_2'}{dk}; \quad (1.7)$$

where B_1' and B_2' are the respective trade balances of both countries. By definition, the trade balances B_1' and B_2' are given in terms of exchange rate k as:

$$\frac{dB_2'}{dk} = -\frac{dB_1'}{dk};$$

$$\frac{dB_1'}{dk} = \frac{d}{dk}\left(x_1 p_1 - \frac{x_2 p_2}{k}\right) = \frac{dB_1}{dk} + x_2 - x_1 \quad (1.8)$$

After making some substitutions in equation (1.5) and (1.8), we get the trade balance in the following form:

Harberber following the Keynesian tradition assumed that the change in "real consumers' income" is equal to initial income times the percentage of income initially spent in imports times the change in the exchange rate so that the trade balance could be written in the following form:

$$\frac{dB_1}{dk} = \frac{h_1 + h_2 x_1 (1 + \eta_2 + \eta_1 + c_1 + c_2)}{h_1 h_2 + c_1 h_2 + c_2 h_1} \quad (1.10)$$

where η1 and η2 are the elasticities of demand for imports which contain income and substitution effects as well. So, the sum of the elasticities of demand for imports is the unity plus the sum of the marginal propensities to import. The critical value for elasticities, $|\eta_1' + \eta_2'|$, in the variable-production case, when trade is initially balanced, is equal to the unity. In the case of the fixed-production case the critical value for elasticities, $|\eta_1' + \eta_2'|$, is less than the normal acknowledged unity. It is also possible that for the fixed values of marginal propensities, there might be some initial deficit for which the critical value is the same for the fixed and variable production cases. The output may decline, and the balance of trade may improve as a result of depreciation.

On the other side an increase in output together with the deterioration of commercial balance is also possible since when trade is initially balanced, it can be negative even when *dB1/dk* is positive. If the balanced trade is expressed in terms of domestic currency, it is possible for the commercial balance to improve while production increases, or to deteriorate as the production either increases or decreases as a result of depreciation by country one. But it is impossible for both countries to get improvement in the balance of trade in terms of domestic currency and a decrease in production as a result of currency depreciation. The balance of trade is affected by the initial deficit due to the depreciation which is opposite in sign depending on whether the balance of trade is expressed in terms of domestic or foreign currency (B*1= -B2).

From the Harberger's Keynesian model we realize that countries incurring depreciation as a way to eliminate the balance of payments deficits will have percussions on prices and employment, and the amount of depreciation necessary to restore equilibrium will be greater than estimated. In the case of fixed prices, the sum of elasticities of demand for imports is lower when incomes are controlled by government policy than when they are allowed to fluctuate. In this case, depreciation helps to improve the balance of payments. But in other cases depreciation may lead to a deterioration of trade deficit if the marginal propensities to import are high making, as a consequence, the sum of elasticities of demand for imports high.

A few years later, another economist, Svend Laursen (1955, 180-188) took into consideration the "Dollar Shortage School" argument that international productivity differentials contribute to the balance of payments difficulties. He analysed different norms for monetary and wage policies under conditions of divergent rates of productivity growth in advanced and less developed countries and found that it's not true that growth differentials between countries have brought instability to the balance of payments as result of dollar shortage.

If two countries are initially in an underemployment equilibrium and if the level of expenditure arises in one of them, this will result in a higher level of income in both countries. But the country that originates the expansion is more likely to have a deficit. Despite the originating causes are different the resulting successions of events are similar but not completely identical, due to the fact that relative price and cost changes in the case of productivity growth are likely to have a higher impact compared to that of a general rise in the level of economic activity. So, for example, if productivity in western industrialized countries has grown more rapidly than in less developed countries there is no proof that the less developed countries must endure balance of payments deficits and cut on current expenditures. This condition is more likely a result of market imperfections at home or in third countries or other special situations not directly related to national differences in productivity growth.

Flexible Exchange Rates as an Alternative to Gold Standard System

The gold standard regime was a convenient system for the industrialized economies that needed a stable exchange rate regime for their bilateral and multilateral trade relationships with other countries, and it worked well until there were no recessions and financial crisis. But when the recessions came to threaten the stability of the western economies the gold standard mechanism was not very accommodating as a recession occurring in one part the world would affect other economies in other parts of the world, therefore the implementation of the proposed flexible exchange rate regime after the World War II was considered to break this bond.

In general, the effective demand and output of every country are governed by extension of economic conditions in the rest of the world. It was a shared opinion among economists that during the interwar occurrence the flexible exchange rate alternative to fixed exchange rates was not successful unless capital movements were subject to some type of control from governments. The short-run movements in exchanges rates are likely to be unstable as the demand for imports and exports is quite inelastic, which will not eliminate short-term differences on international payments between countries.

In normal circumstances, the flexible exchange rates will isolate the price movements in case of cyclical fluctuations in one or more countries. Under a system of flexible exchange rates, the monetary demand for a given country with an independent currency and a given output would be unaffected by a tightening abroad. But, in the case, the monetary demand changes and if the nature of the mobility of resources is low a shift in demand from one sector of the economy to another will create a reduction on demand with no chance for prosperity for the country under the flexible monetary regime unless the change brings capital movements.

Two well-known economists in the early fifties, Laursen and Metzler (1950), were attracted by the effects of exchange rates regimes in the economy and started to analyze the properties of the monetary policy in a floating system. According to them, monetary policy in a flexible exchange rate regime would not contribute to the world-wide depressions and inflations that may characterize the gold standard system. In fact, Laursen and Metzler (1950) focused their study on analyzing the effects on prices and output under a flexible exchange rate regime in a dynamic system between two countries. They consider two postulates to analyses their model. The first postulate states that the price of foreign exchange rate tends to arise when the demand for this exchange rate exceeds the supply and drops when the supply exceeds the demand.

Let $y1$ and $y2$ be the net income for Country I and Country II. Let Π represents the price of Country I in terms of Country II's currency. Based on international exchange rates, a rise in Π indicates a depreciation of Country I's currency meanwhile a fall indicates appreciation. The price of Country I will vary in proportion to Π, therefore Π can be used as an index of import prices, while in Country II the index of import prices will be $1/\Pi$. The main foreign-exchange price will be the price of Country II's currency in terms of Country I's currency. Any modifications in this price will be controlled by the balance of payments in Country II (Laursen and Metzler 1950, 291-5). The first dynamic postulate is given as:

$$\frac{d\pi}{dt} = s\left[\left(\frac{1}{\pi}\right)c_1(y_1, \pi) - c_2\left(y_2, \frac{1}{\pi}\right)\right] \tag{1.11}$$

where s is the speed of adjustment in the foreign-exchange market $c1$ and $c2$ represents the domestic-currency expenditure of both countries which can express in the respective import functions, $c1=c1(y1, \Pi)$ and $c2=c2(y2,1/\Pi)$, and $y1$ and $y2$ are the incomes for Country I and II.

The second postulate is a consequence of the first postulate, and it states that in a dynamic system the output in a given country tends to rise when the demand for goods and services exceeds the current rate of output and drops when the demand for a current rate of output falls. Therefore, the demand for a country's output will be equal to the domestic expenditure of all goods and services to which will be added the domestic-currency value of exports and detracted the domestic-currency value of imports. The second postulate can be expressed as a system of three dynamic equations: two-income dynamic equations for the income of Country I and II and the third one for the adjustment of the foreign-exchange rates. This dynamic system represents the demand function of both countries and is given by three equations,

$$\frac{dy_1}{dt}=s_1\left[\mu_1(y_1,\pi)+\pi c_2(y_2,\frac{1}{\pi})-c_1(y_1,\pi)-y_1\right] \tag{1.12}$$

$$\frac{dy_2}{dt} = s_2\left[\mu_2(y_2, \frac{1}{\pi}) + \left(\frac{1}{\pi}\right)c_1(y_1, \pi) - c_2\left(y_2, \frac{1}{\pi}\right) - y_2\right] \tag{1.13}$$

$$\frac{d\pi}{dt} = s_3\left[\left(\frac{1}{\pi}\right)c_1(y_1, \pi) - c_2\left(y_2, \frac{1}{\pi}\right)\right] \tag{1.14}$$

where *s1, s2* and *s3* as, in expressions (1.12), (1.13) and 1.14), are positive quantities and represent three speeds of adjustment. Laursen and Metzler on their analyses are more interested in the stability of the system rather than the solution. This can be achieved by using the Taylor series for the equilibrium values of *yº1, yº2* and *Πº*, thus the linear form of equations (1.12), (1.13) and (1.14) appears as,

$$\frac{dy_1}{dt} = s_1(\mu_1 - p_1 - 1)(y_1 - y_1^0) + s_1 p_2 \tag{1.15}$$

$$(y_2 - y_2^0) + s_1[k_1 + c_1(\eta_1 + \eta_2 - 1)](\pi - \pi^0)$$

$$\frac{dy_2}{dt} = s_2 p_1(y_1 - y_1^0) + s_2(\mu_2 - p_2 - 1) \tag{1.16}$$

$$(y_2 - y_2^0) - s_2[k_2 + c_1(\eta_1 - \eta_2 - 1)](\pi - \pi^0)$$

$$\frac{d\pi}{dt} = s_3 p_1(y_1 - y_1^0) - s_3 p_2(y_2 - y_2^0) \tag{1.17}$$

$$- s_3 c_1(\eta_1 - \eta_2 - 1)(\pi - \pi^0)$$

where *μ1* and *μ2* represent the total expenditures for Country I and II expressed as *μ1=μ1(y1,Π)* and *μ2=μ2(y2,Π), k1* and *k2* are the price effects, p1 and p2 are the marginal propensities to import expressed respectively as 0<p1=δc1/δy1<1 and 0<p2=δc2/δy2<1 and η1, η2 are the elasticities of the demand for imports in countries I and II. The solution of the linear forms (1.15), (1.16) and (1.17) of the dynamic system represented by three equations (1.12), (1.13) and (1.14) can further be expressed in terms of determinants *Aij* (matrices):

$$\begin{aligned} y_1 &= y_1^0 + A_{11}e^{\gamma_1 t} + A_{12}e^{\gamma_2 t} + A_{13}e^{\gamma_3 t} \\ y_2 &= y_2^0 + A_{21}e^{\gamma_1 t} + A_{22}e^{\gamma_2 t} + A_{23}e^{\gamma_3 t} \\ \pi &= \pi^0 + A_{31}e^{\gamma_1 t} + A_{32}e^{\gamma_2 t} + A_{33}e^{\gamma_3 t} \end{aligned} \tag{1.18}$$

where the constant *Aij* which is part of the determinant (1.18) depends upon condition at the time t=0 and γ1, γ2, and γ3 are the roots of the next determinant of the matrices obtained from (1.18) written as

$$\Delta = \begin{vmatrix} s_1(\mu_1 - p_1 - 1) - \gamma \ldots\ldots s_1 p_2 \ldots\ldots s_1 k_1 + s_1 c_1(\eta_1 + \eta_2 - 1) \\ s_2 p_2 \ldots\ldots s_2(\mu_2 - p_2 - 1) - \gamma \ldots\ldots - s_2 k_2 - s_2 c_1(\eta_1 + \eta_2 - 1) = 0 \\ s_3 p_1 \ldots\ldots - s_3 p_2 \ldots\ldots s_3 c_1(\eta_1 + \eta_2 - 1) - \gamma \end{vmatrix} \tag{1.19}$$

Given that the values of income equations (1.15), (1.16) and (1.17) *y1, y2* and *Π* will not be stable and reach the equilibrium levels of *y°1, y°2* and *Π°* unless the γ1, γ2, and γ3 in (1.18) and the roots of (1.19) are all negative. By expanding the complex determinant (1.19) and rearranging all terms like the powers of γ we have:

$$\gamma^3 + a_1\gamma^2 + a_2\gamma + a_3 = 0 \tag{1.20}$$

In equation (1.20) by putting γ *=0,* we have that *a1* is the sum of all principal first-order minors of determinant derived from (1.19) without change of sign. In the same way, a2 and a3 are the combinations of *s1,s2,s3Δ*. Given that the roots of (1.20) must be negative the necessary and sufficient conditions that must be met are given as

a1 > 0; (a1 a2 - a3)>0; a3>0. (1.21)

Given that the a3 = *s1,s2,s3Δ* we have,

$$\begin{aligned} a_3 &= s_1 s_2 s_3[(1 - \mu_1)(1 - \mu_2)c_1(\eta_1 + \eta_2 - 1) \\ &- k_1 p_1(1 - \mu_2) - k_2 p_2(1 - \mu_1)] > 0 \end{aligned} \tag{1.22}$$

where *μ1, μ2, p1, p2, k1* and *k2* have positive values less than unity. Under these conditions in expression (1.22) we have that the determinant Δ is not positive, except in the case when the sum of the two import demand elasticities, *η1, η2,* will exceed the unity.

The prevalent view among economists after the WWII was that under a fixed set of demand as a point of departure when the commodities are produced and sold at constant cost there is a dividing line between stability and instability in international trade at the point the elasticities are equal to one, ($\eta 1+ \eta 2 =1$). Laursen and Metzler (1950, 297), instead, by allowing changes on income adopted a different approach. According to them, induced movements of income[1] bring the rise of imports in the depreciating country and a decrease in the volume of exports. By studying the effects of this change, we have that the depreciation leaves at first the balance of payments unchanged, but the ultimate effect will be a deficit for the depreciating country. Therefore, the effects of income movements have converted an apparent neutral situation into an unstable one. And the dividing line between stable and unstable systems, as suggested by Laursen and Metzler (1950, 297-98), occurs first at a point when the demand of elasticity is higher than unity, ($\eta 1+ \eta 2 >1$), and second when the marginal propensity to spend is less than unity in each country.

Laursen and Metzler (1950), found that the shock absorption performed by flexible exchange rates is not perfect. Both the composition of a country's output and the level of its output will be affected under this regime by economic fluctuations. Even with favorable elasticities, exchange flexibility does not entirely possess the power often attributed to it of hurting stable economies' output and employment from the movements of unstable economies. Under this regime output and employment may rise in some parts of the world and decrease in others, while the real income is affected mostly by a country's terms of trade. In a floating exchange system, a country's output tends to fall when its terms of trade improve and to rise when its terms of trade deteriorate. As a conclusion, we have that the flexible exchange rates regime is not perfect but acts better than a fixed exchange rates or a gold standard system.

---

[1] Income and employment tend to rise in the depreciating country, and the demand for imports tends to increase. Meanwhile in the second country, where the import prices have fallen, the proportion of income spent on goods and services decreases and the level of output gets reduced, originating a decline on the demand for imports and a decline on employment.

The Balance of Payments Difficulties

The Western European countries in the postwar period were suffering from a huge dollar shortage and a balance of payments disequilibria[2]. The postwar recovery for European economies was slow, and the need for loans and financial aid from the United States was much greater than their ability to pay. Meanwhile, the United States was running enormous balance of trade surpluses, and its economy was growing fast as a result of the big orders for industries to support the Korean War. The U.S. reserves in gold and dollar were vast and increased very fast. It was necessary a monetary policy to help the Federal Reserve reduce the immense accumulation of dollars. In few words, the dollars had to leave the Federal Reserve and the United States and become available for international use especially for the Western European countries which were struggling to meet their payments. Consequently, the United States had to stop the dollar accumulation process and run a balance of payments deficit to help other countries in difficulties. Generally speaking, international productivity differentials among countries contribute to the balance of payments disequilibria. Considering the substantial progress of the American economy after the WW II, it was difficult for the rest of the world to eliminate the imbalance of payments.

The easiest and fastest way to help the Western European countries after the war – instead of going through the Wall Street banking market where it was in place a ruling conservative lending policy by granting loans only when repayment was assured – was to create an international fund where the countries could dip in on large financial amount of money on good terms compared to traditional banking system. In fact, in 1947 the United States created the European Recovery Program (ERP) called the Marshall Plan (the initiative was named after the U.S. Secretary of State George Marshall who was one of the promoters of the plan) which the main ambition was to offer large-scale financial and economic aid to rebuild Europe mainly through

---

[2] Broadly speaking, the balance of payments accounts can be defined as a sum of accounting records of all monetary transactions, during a specific period, between the economy of a country and the rest of the world which include payments for the country's exports and imports of goods, services, financial capital, and financial transfers. The balance of payments identity can be expressed as:

current account + financial account + capital account + balancing item = 0

where the "current account" is composed of 3 sub-divisions: the goods and services account (the overall trade balance), the primary income account (income from loans and investments) and the secondary income account (transfer payments). By equilibrium in the balance of payments we mean an equality between all current payments and current receipts and current capital payments and receipts.

grants from U.S. aid programs rather than loans from the big U.S. banks. Starting from the year 1950, the United States by deliberately encouraging an outflow of dollars, ran a balance of payments deficit with the objective of providing liquidity mostly to the western industrialized countries and later eventually to the rest of the world especially to various pro-U.S. regimes in the developing countries. From 1948 to 1954 the United States through the Marshall Plan provided to 16 Western European countries $17 billion in grants. The Marshall Plan or the ERP was an extraordinary help for most of the Western European nations to adjust their balance of payments.

Regarding this subject, Professor James Meade in early fifties (1951) published his notorious work on "The Balance of Payments". His book deals mostly with the financial payments, international labor and capital movements between nations maintaining a level of almost full employment. Meade took into consideration the policies on achieving an internal and external balance of payments in the face of certain assumed disturbances to equilibrium. The Meade's analysis runs in terms of comparative statics rather than the dynamic process of changes and follows the elasticity approach.

In his study, Prof. Meade makes a distinction between direct and indirect measures for achieving an internal and external balance of payments and places the conditions under which these measures work. The indirect measures consist of general tools on attaining the internal and external balance, while the direct measures consist of more specific instruments to reach the targets on the balance of payments. Meade supports indirect as opposed to direct controls because of their effects on the real income of the world economy. He, in fact, utilizes financial policies for internal balances and international policies for adjusting exchange rates to receive external balance by eventually limiting direct controls for protecting particular industries. For these policies to work, it is necessary that the system has enough elasticity of demand for imports to allow the price adjustment mechanism to work. Meade distinguishes between autonomous and accommodating transactions in order to better explain the principle of surplus or deficit in a country's balance of payments. Autonomous transactions are simply created for the motives of profit like interest incomes and have no connections with the balance of payments. Meanwhile, the accommodation transactions or differently called the "balancing transactions" have real effects on the balance of payments and include capital items, visible and invisible exports and imports.

The balance of payments is the net balance of autonomous trade and transfer items. The deficit or surplus in the balance of payments corresponds to the deficit or surplus in the balance of foreign accommodations with the balance of autonomous and accommodating transactions essentially in balance all the times. Meade (1951, 6-17) defines the balance of payments deficit as the potential deficit that is the amount of accommodating finance in any period of time, so it can avoid the depreciation of exchange rate without putting in place government controls to restrict the movements of exchange rates or limit the volumes of imported goods in order to limit the demand for foreign currencies. A country, developing an adverse balance of payments and facing a worsening of its terms of trade (as the only means of correcting it), will face a drastic fall in real incomes which will make the core working force works longer hours or increases the productivity level.

A country aiming at internal balance will compensate the secondary effects on employment of primary changes in demand whether these changes are spontaneous and whether they are initiated at home or abroad. Meanwhile, a country aiming at external balance will similarly offset secondary effects on the balance of payments of any changes in demand however and wherever the changes are initiated. The two objectives might be aimed simultaneously, but there may be conflicts of policy that make it difficult to be achieved in either or both the countries. So, if the rigidities exist in the domestic economy, flexible exchange rates may be a matter of indifference (or independence) if domestic policy instruments are plentiful in quantity or quality to keep the foreign exchange market in balance and also achieve other economic goals. But when the available policy instruments are very few or enable to reach all preferred objectives, the alternative goes in favor of employing a flexible exchange rate to free these tools from direct concern with the balance of payments.

Meade does not reject commercial policy as an instrument of the balance of payments adjustments. In his opinion, a deficit country or a less developed country that runs continuously in the deficit would most likely use restrictive commercial policy rather than an expansive one as it cannot afford unfavourable movement in real terms of trade that would occur if the external balance was going to be attained by traditional means. He asserts that

> "… it is, of course, possible that the movement away from the modified free-trade position is so extensive and that the movement of the terms of trade against the deficit country which is avoided by the use of restrictions on imports or on capital movements is so slight, that residents in deficit country would be absolutely better off if the method of exchange depreciation had been used. What would be gained through there being a large world cake to divide would be greater what would be lost through having a rather smaller proportionate share of the cake…" [Meade J. E., 1951, 329]

To restore the international balances of payments, it is necessary that all the countries adopt the exchange rates variations (free exchange rates) which will reinforce the external balance without worsening the internal balance. Meade states that:

> "...the method of variations in exchange rates is adopted as a means of restoring equilibrium to internationals balances of payments, then it is important that all the countries taking part in this system should consciously adopt domestic financial policies for internal balance. For the adoption of such policies will not only avoid any unfortunate internal results from those exchange-rate variations which are required to give external balances, but it will positively reinforce the desired affects of the exchange-rate adjustment upon external balance..." [Meade J. E., 1951., 169-70]

The suggestion is to create: first, financial policies for internal balance, as an effective mechanism against domestic inflations and deflations; second, an international system of free exchanges or adjustable peg, as an efficient tool against overvaluation of deficit-country exchange rates; and third, a proficient shield in forms such as *ad valorem* import duties, that allow the adjustment of trade to price changes.

In addition, the effects of control (through control of capital movements and current transactions) should be not only on the balance of payments but also upon the real income and the distribution of real income among different countries to reach a modified free-trade-position that will allow countries to obtain the balance of payments. The balance of payments adjustment can be achieved by price mechanism like variable exchange rates, flexible wage rates etc. without departing from the position of modified free-trade position. Any departure from this position affecting the distribution of real income between countries and putting at risk the balance of payments has to be avoided, and in case it happens the richest countries, responsible for the distribution of world income, has to intervene to adjust the imbalance.

Meade (1957), a few years later, takes into consideration the case of the balance-of-payments of the newly created European Free-Trade area. His view is that the basic of balance-of-payments rule for the free-trade area must be adjusted in a way that each government must be responsible for maintaining the overall equilibrium in the balance of payments of the whole monetary area.

This can be reached by two ways: using the national and supranational approach. By using the national approach, the balance of payments equilibrium can be achieved if each individual member of the free-trade area puts in place commercial policies to restrict imports from outside countries into its national market in order to safeguard the balance of payment equilibrium. By using the supranational approach the countries of the free-trade area should create a joint authority which would determine the total amount of outside goods which could be imported into a free-trade area to protect the balance of payments of the free-trade area with the rest of the world (Meade 1957, 389).

The free movement of capitals between member countries with their national currencies fully convertible is supposed to be another feature of the free-trade area. The member's control over exports of capital to countries outside the European free-trade area is efficient if the free movement of capitals within the free-trade area is maintained through harmonized exchange control regulations between the country members. There are also 3 stabilization policies that can be put in place by the European countries of the free-trade market: first, the surplus European countries must set up measures to avoid the deflation, and deficit countries must take action to avoid the rising of inflation; second, the foreign-exchange values of the currencies of the members having a surplus on the balance of payments must be appreciated, and those experiencing a continues balance of payments deficit must be depreciated; third, the foreign-exchange reserves must be moved to deficit countries to readjust their balance of payments (Meade 1957, 394).

Meade's proposal goes even further, and it's very innovative at that time. He suggests the creation of an independent European Monetary Fund which will be able to harmonize and centralize the monetary policies of each country into one supranational monetary policy. The European Monetary Fund is nothing more than the embryo of the European Central Bank, the highest monetary authority of the European Monetary Union half-century later.

Another renowned economist, John H. Williams in 1953 had developed an argument along the lines of the balance of payment difficulties. According to Williams, the adjustment between two countries having problems with the balance of payments will not come through money flow and its effects on comparative price levels but rather through changes in real income. In fact, if there are different rates of growth of productivity between countries, the commercial trade will be less favorable to countries having slower growth in productivity. For the countries lagging behind the industrialized countries, first, the adjustment requires a decline in their real income and second the benefits of their foreign trade are reduced by a swift increase in productivity abroad (Williams J. H., 1953, pp. 13-14).

The study of another economist, Laursen (1955, 180-188), suggests that the conclusions of Prof. Williams are not completely correct because the historical experience has demonstrated that less advanced countries have not seen a decrease in their trade benefits as a result of productivity growth in other countries. On the contrary, this category of countries has seen a rapid increase in their foreign trade benefits coming from productivity increase in other advanced nations. For example, by taking into consideration two countries that initially have a high rate of unemployment, if the level of expenditure rises in one country, in the first moment, it will result in a higher level of income in both countries. In a second moment, the more rapidly advanced country which has originated the expansion is more likely to have a deficit. Instead, the less rapidly advanced country despite has less productivity gain may well benefit from the expansion through comparative advantage on export industries as a result of improving terms in foreign trade.

The expectations are that the balance of payments will improve even for the country with smaller productivity gain because of the positive effects on the terms of foreign trade and because of the real income increase at differential rates. Relative movements of productivity and real income changes in the two countries will determine changes in the balance of trade which may improve or deteriorate the balance of payments, resulting in surplus or deficit. The existence of national disparities in productivity growth and real income changes do not bring in a consistent balance of payments bias in favour of more advanced nations.

Another prominent economist in monetary issues, Harry Johnson (1976), has at least classified three main approaches to the balance of payments: the elasticity/absorption approach, the Keynesian multiplier approach and the monetary approach. Johnson introduces two different notions - the expenditure-switching and expenditure-reducing - to distinguish the elasticity and absorption approaches. The expenditure-switching effects of the devaluation occur when there is a perfectly elastic supply of imports and exports, with the import prices fixed in domestic currency and export prices fixed in foreign currency.[3] The expenditure-reducing aspect of the devaluation takes place when the domestic absorption and the aggregate demand function get reduced as they move away from the full-employment level of output. According to Johnson, using the elasticity/absorption approach under the conditions of full employment, it will highlight the fact that the devaluation depends entirely on the reduction in the level of real domestic spending. The reduction in spending can be obtained by using policy alternatives to reduce domestic spending rather than using the inflation policy and the impact of inflation on spending.

---

[3] If the expenditure-switching effects meet the Marshall-Lerner condition, then the sum of the price elasticities of demand for imports and exports exceeds the unity.

The second approach, the Keynesian multiplier approach, according to Johnson (1976) describes the implications of changes in expenditure on output, on income and output for balance-of-payments equilibrium. In fact, the net balance-of-payments outcome of a devaluation is based on increased import effects of the multiplied increase in expenditure set against the expenditure-switching effects of devaluation which allow to increase exports and decrease the level of imports that are considered as a fraction of expenditure. The Keynesian multiplier approach puts together the elements of the absorption and elasticity approach. Part of the Keynesian approach is also the Keynesian policy approach which can use two policy instruments, such as monetary and fiscal policies to accomplish both internal and external balance. In this approach, the domestic money supply component is adjusted in conjunction with the desired stock of foreign exchange in order to achieve the external balance.

The third approach, the monetary approach, assumes that monetary inflows and outflows associated with surpluses or deficits are not sterilized, but simply influence the domestic money supply. The deficits and surpluses in the money market are an only stock adjustment and not equilibrium flows, therefore they should not be treated with the same tools that treat them as equilibrium phenomena. The monetary approach, different from the Keynesian approach, does not consider the insulating of the domestic money supply from the effects of balance-of-payments surpluses and deficits. The key device of monetary approach is the price flow mechanism because the money supply adjusts automatically to reinstate equilibrium in the balance of payments. The price level adjustment and the equilibrium of balance of payments guarantee the equilibrium of money supply and demand. The pre-existing condition of full employment is not taken into consideration in the monetary approach, however, it allows changes in domestic absorption and aggregate demand with no equivalent changes in net imports as there is no need to use the sterilization mechanism because the monetary supply will adjust endogenously until the balance of payments returns to equilibrium.

The Case for Flexible Exchange Rates in Friedman

Milton Friedman was one of the most distinguished monetary economists who favored the system of flexible exchange rates and other liberal ideas in economics in the early fifties of the twentieth century. In his work published in 1953, "Essays on Positive Economics" which includes his famous essay "The Case for Flexible Exchange Rates", he advocates for a return on flexible exchange rates. Friedman, who was one of the most renowned economists of the Chicago school position on the monetary debate, was very unmistakable regarding the application of the flexible exchange rates. He was a strong advocate of free markets in foreign exchanges as the most realistic alternative of the world economy after the WWII dominated by rigid internal prices, wages and internal quantitative restrictions.

A free exchange rate regime gives stability to the balance of payments if there is an unrestricted multilateral trade with no controls over imports/exports and reasonable tariffs on the goods and commodities crossing the border. An unstable system of exchange rates, instead, gives instability to the economic structure which cannot be cured by freezing the exchange rates or by restoring controls and tariffs on imports/exports.

He asserted that in a free open market under flexible exchange rates, the first impact of any tendency toward surplus or deficit in the balance of payments will be in the exchange rate. So if a country has a surplus in the balance of payment the exchange rate will tend to rise and if it has a deficit in the balance of payment the exchange rate will tend to fall. If the conditions responsible for the rise or the fall in the exchange rates are regarded as temporary, the holders of the country's currency will tend to change their assets in such a way as to reasonably moderate the movement in the exchange rate (Friedman 1953, 161). The holder's final position of the country's currency, technically speaking, depends on the effect that movements in exchange rates have on the demand and supply of a country's currency. The effects of a rise in the exchange rate, which produce a surplus in the balance of payments, make commodities cheaper in terms of domestic currency by increasing imports and reducing exports. On the other hand, a reduction in the exchange rate, producing a deficit on the balance of payments, makes imports more expensive in terms of domestic currency and exports less expensive to other countries.

Under flexible exchange rates, changes made quickly and constantly tend to produce corrective movements before tension and stress can accumulate and eventually cause a crisis. In general, the change of an exchange-rate has no reason otherwise to become a crisis because the system practically ensures average stabilizing speculation, rather than frequent changes and abnormal speculations. The justification of this is that the exchange rates are changed infrequently and only when they are consistent difficulties and accumulated pressure on it. The flexible exchange rate is nothing more than a non-frequent regulator of existing accumulated pressure on exchange rate.

Gold has a big part in the system of flexible exchange rates. Its role is to be a counterpart of flexible exchange rates and, as a commodity-reserve currency, it could be, changed in the open market to promote stability. Gold is a "backing" card for a national currency, and it promotes confidence to investors and market operators if it is not sold or bought at a fixed price. Rather than the United States buying gold in exchange for dollars from other countries at a fixed price, as it was common practice during the gold standard regime, would've been better to have a free gold market where common people can hold gold without restrictions as well as other currencies. This transformation would make gold lose ground as a special-reserve commodity in the monetary system and obtain the status of a common commodity-currency which value would have been determined by the ups and downs of the stock exchange market.

The exchange rate is somehow related to internal price changes as well. Changes in internal prices or income would have same effects on exchange rates as on speculative transactions if movements of internal prices were flexible as exchange rates. For example, a temporary decrease in domestic prices would encourage speculative purchases of goods to avoid future higher prices, and at the same time, a momentary increase on prices would stimulate less purchase of commodities until the prices get back to normality, thus moderating the price movements.

Therefore, if the domestic prices were as flexible as exchange rates, it would make no difference if the adjustments will come from changes in exchange rates or internal price movements. But unfortunately, the domestic prices in the real economic world tell a different story. They are highly inflexible. Internal prices are more flexible moving upward than downward. This creates a distortion of adjustments in some sectors in response to changes in external conditions. The adjustment is even harder if there are taken into considerations the wage rates which are less flexible than prices. Despite this, there are situations when the domestic price changes are desirable. In fact, there is a case when internal price changes come as a result of changes in the real underlying conditions of trade, in particular, goods and services which move in a smaller order of magnitude than the general level of domestic prices.

The 'average' speculation in a foreign-exchange market under a flexible exchange rate system is not a destabilizing but stabilizing factor. Friedman's opinion is that speculation is stabilizing rather than destabilizing as there is no evidence to support this conclusion (Friedman 1953: 175). If during any time any speculative movements, which threatened to depreciate or appreciate a currency is regarded as destabilizing, will establish after all that the speculators were right. They, in fact, were anticipating the depreciation or appreciation of that currency relative to another strong currency independently of the speculative activity. The speculative movements were doing nothing wrong than predicting the change, and they should be calling stabilizing rather than destabilizing.

The variations in a flexible exchange rate respond to disturbances in the underlying national economies. Thus, the best technique of adjustment affecting international payments and external trade is the flexible exchange rate. It is best suited to some disturbing conditions involving international payments: in fact, the use of reserves is not by itself a good plan on restoring international balance; direct controls on imports, exports and capital movements are ineffective in a free society, as suggested by Friedman (1953), because they bring the same effects on trade and balance of payments as changes in exchange rates or internal prices and incomes; changes in internal prices and incomes are strongly undesirable due to rigidities in internal prices and wages. Maintaining the status of full employment was another goal of internal policy, in addition to the stabilization of internal prices. According to Friedman, a floating exchange rate system is supposed to be better than a fixed rate system when the dominant shocks are real, because it can adjust better a real shock, rather requiring changes in price level and income. The flexible exchange system is compared with the "daylight saving time". Milton states that:

> "...the argument for flexible exchange rates is, strange to say, very nearly identical with the argument for daylight saving time. Isn't it absurd to change the clock in summer when exactly the same result could be achieved by having each individual change his habits? All that is required is that everyone decides to come to his office an hour earlier, have lunch an hour earlier, etc. But obviously it is much simpler to change the clock that guides all than to have each individual separately, change his pattern of reaction to the clock, even though all want to do. The situation is exactly the same in the exchange market. It is far simpler to allow one price to change, namely, the price of foreign exchange, than to rely upon changes in the multitude of prices that together constitute the internal price structure..."
>
> [Friedman, M. 1953: p.173]

These arguments in favor of flexible exchange rates raised many eyebrows among economists at that time because they believed in fixed exchange rates particularly in the post-war period where many industrialized countries were having difficulties with the balance of payments. Hahn's criticism asserts that:

> "...It is recommended that we adopt flexible exchange rates on the basis of the unproven assertion that "there will always be some set or sets of (exchange) rates that will clear the market" (p.160) and the equally unproven (and indeed almost completely unanalysed) assumption that this equilibrium at the desired level of domestic income can be reached if countries are not in the vicinity of such long-run equilibrium already..... Of course, if (a) multilateral free table and stable incomes are absolute desiderata, and (b) domestic prices are

> assumed fixed, flexible exchange rates necessarily follow. But then we should have the case made out for multilateral trade and not for flexible exchange rates...."
>
> [Hahn, F. H.: 1954, 400]

The main aim of the monetary policy was to develop an efficient system of free and unrestricted multilateral trade in order to eliminate or trim down the extensive restrictions on international trade that grew exponentially during and after the World War II hurting hard the free trade. Reducing the rigid exchange rates would achieve two major goals on international trade system: first, unlimited multilateral trade and second, freedom of each country to attain internal monetary stability by using without restrictions its own monetary tools and by establishing with other countries separately or jointly a flexible exchange rate system determined freely by the open market forces. The unpegged exchange rate system advocated by Friedman would not be a real threat to international monetary market and balance of payments but a stabilizing power that will drive up the international trade.

Gold Standard and the International Monetary System: A Historical View

Gold was established as a gold standard for most of the modern western nations during the industrial revolution in late 18th and early 19th century. Under a gold standard system, the monetary authority defines the weight of gold coins or fixes the price of gold in terms of national currency. The fixed price is sustained by the authority to buy and sell gold at mint price. As far as the price is fixed, there are no restrictions on the ownership and use of gold.

Generally speaking, the gold standard has evolved from earlier commodity money systems.

The previous commodity money systems were bimetallic, where gold was used for high-value transactions, meanwhile, silver or copper coins were used for low-valued ones. The ratio of the mint price of gold relative to the mint price of silver (the bimetallic ratio) was set close to the market ratio to guarantee the circulation of both metals. This ratio was not based on the Gresham's Law[4].

---

[4] Gresham's law, in economics, is a monetary principle stating that "bad money drives out good money". For example, if we consider two forms of commodity money in circulation which have a similar value, issued by monetary authorities, the more valuable commodity will disappear from circulation.

The world was able to switch from bimetallism to gold monometallism in the 1870s. There is still an ongoing debate, the reasons for this shift. It is believed that the shift was merely political, as the advanced nations of that time, such as the United Kingdom, wanted to stimulate the commercial and industrial power, while Germany used the Franco-Prussian War indemnity to finance the creation of gold standard regime. On the other side, the debate was focused on the massive silver discoveries in the 1860s and 1870s as well as technical advances in coinage that increased the supply of this metal. Despite the cause of the switch from bimetallism to gold monometallism the research done in the 1990s by Oppers (1996) and Flandreau (1996) suggested that the shift was unnecessary and undesirable since France, the principal bimetallic nation, had enough reserves of both metals to continue the standard. However, the move to the bimetallic standard, through the production and substitution effects would have provided much more price stability than did gold monometallism.

The gold standard regime on its simple variant was a pure gold coin standard. This type of monetary regime involved high resources of gold, and subsequently, in most countries, substitutes for gold coin emerged. In fact, in the private sector, commercial banks issued notes and deposits convertible into gold coins, which in turn were held as reserves to meet the conversion demands from the public. During the war period, the convertibility was suspended temporary, on the expectation of renewal upon termination of hostilities. The gold standard regimes developed into a mixed coin and fiduciary system following the principle that any substitute can easily convert into gold. The problem with convertible system emerged when there were risks of conversion attacks of internal and external drains. The internal drain was supposed to happen when there is a distrustful public attempt to convert commercial bank liabilities into gold, and the external drain was when foreign demands on central bank's gold reserves threatened its ability to maintain convertibility. Because of this mounting tension between substitution of fiduciary money for gold and the stability of the system, central banks became the lender of last resort and were forced to use the tools of monetary policy to protect their reserves in gold.

The international monetary system under the classical gold standard regime had the monetary gold stock distributed based on the member nations' demand for money and use of substitute gold. In case there were disturbances to the balance of payments, they were automatically equilibrated by the Humean price-species-flow mechanism. Based on the Hume's mechanism, gold would flow from countries with balance of payments deficits (cause by higher price levels) to those with surpluses (caused by lower price levels), keeping, in turn, their domestic money supplies and price levels in line.

However, under the gold standard regime, the exchange rates were supposed to be perfectly rigid, in practice, the rate of exchange was bounded by upper and lower limits – the gold points – within which the exchange rate could float. The research on this topic has demonstrated that although in the gold standard regime exchange rates frequently departed from par, violations of gold points were rare as were devaluations, and the adjustment to the balance of payments disturbances was enabled by short-term capital flows (Eichengreen, 1985). Capital would flow between countries and reduce the interest rate differences. Generally speaking, by the end of 19th century the world capital market was very efficient, and capital flows mostly replaced gold flows in effecting adjustment.

The role of central banks in western countries was pivotal in stabilizing the international gold standard. The central banks used discount rates and other tools of monetary policy to adjust the balance of payment disequilibria. Sometimes the central banks violated the rules by not raising their discount rates which artificially altered the price of gold in the face of a payment deficits, but were never sufficient to jeopardize the whole convertibility system. Because of the credibility of commitment to gold convertibility, the violations were tolerated by market participants as they view them as transitory attempts by central banks to reduce interest rates without having much effect in economic activities.

Given that London was the center of the world's principal gold, commodities and capital markets in the nineteenth century, outstanding sterling dominated assets were vast, and sterling served as an international reserve currency. Therefore, if the Bank of England would manipulate the discount rate other central banks in Europe will adjust their rates to hers. But it is also true that the other big countries, such as Germany and France had control over discount rates within their respective economic spheres of influence.

The gold standard regime was a self-regulated system that was able to ensure long-run monetary and price stability, as explained by Fisher I. (1922), through the commodity theory of money. The purchasing power of gold was determined by the commodity market, meanwhile, the price level was determined by the demand and supply of monetary gold. The demand for monetary gold was determined from the demand for money while the monetary gold stock was the residual between the total world gold stock and the non-monetary demand (Barro, 1979). Any changes in the monetary gold stock were the result of gold production supply and changes of use between monetary and non-monetary gold.

Gold standard itself was a self-regulating and a stable monetary system as changes in the price level would reflect the real price of gold, leading to offsetting changes in gold production and shifts between monetary and non-monetary uses of gold. However, in the short-run, the shocks to the gold market and changes in real activity generated price level volatility. The gold standard as a regime embodied a monetary rule or commitment mechanism that controlled the actions of monetary authorities and prevented governments from setting policies successively in a time unreliable manner. In few words, based on this approach the commitment to the fixed price of gold will prevent governments from creating unexpected fiduciary money issues in order to capture seigniorage revenue or defaulting on outstanding public debt.

The gold standard regime during the 1880-1914 period was considered as a contingent rule that allowed many countries to avoid the problems of high inflation and stagflation that disturbed the last three decades of the twentieth century. The contingent rule was also called the rule of escape clauses that allowed the monetary authorities to preserve the price of the currency in terms of gold fixed except in the case of emergencies such as wars, natural disasters, etc. (Bordo and Kydland 1996). During war times the gold convertibility was suspended as it was considered the option of issuing paper money to finance war expenditures or using public debt by issuing government bonds in nominal value that will eventually be paid off in gold or depreciated paper money.

The gold standard contingent rule was able to work efficaciously for a number of core countries such as United Kingdom, France, Germany and the United States because the monetary authorities of these countries adhered devotedly to the fixed price of gold except during the war periods. In a different way from the core countries, a number of peripheral countries during the 1878-1914 period had difficulties in following the rule of the gold standard, and their experience was characterized by frequent suspensions of convertibility and devaluations. The incentive of the peripheral countries to enforce the gold standard was the access to capital obtainable from the core countries, therefore, they were required to adhere to the gold standard because they could also get loans with low-interest rates contracted in London and other major capital markets (as a result of 'good behavior').

Despite the benefits of the gold standard to provide a relatively stable nominal anchor and commitment mechanism it collapsed in 1914 at the dawn of the WWI. It was reinstated as gold exchange standard after the WWI between 1925 and 1931 and as a gold dollar standard after the WWII from 1959 to 1971. The gold standard regime also had high costs of maintaining a full-bodied gold standard. It was estimated that the cost for the U.S. in 1950 was about 1.5 percent of real GDP (Friedman, 1953). The volatility of the demand and supply to produce gold and the growing concern to base the gold standard on a durable exhaustible resource, posed the prospect of deflation.

The break of the WWI in August 1914 brought massive worldwide financial crisis that led the investors across the world to liquidate the core currencies like sterling, dollar and franc in exchange for gold, which led to the breakdown of the gold standard regime. After the WWI the western countries expressed the desire to return to gold parity at the original parity. Four years after the war in 1922 at the Genoa Conference, the Financial Commission headed by British government urged the world powers to return to gold standard, but restricting the use of gold as currency, thus establishing a gold bullion standard and a more cooperative policy on discount rates to prevent competition for gold. The most important event after the war was the return in April 1925 by the United Kingdom to the pre-war convertibility at $ 4.86. Other countries with high inflation such as France and Italy returned to standard gold at a devalued parity.

Despite the return to parity, there were still flaws in the standard gold convertibility. The first problem was the adjustment problem. The main supporter of the standard gold, United Kingdom, continues the balance of payment deficits and gold outflows because of the overvalued currency, which generated deflationary pressure, low growth and high unemployment and the Bank of England had to adopt a tight monetary policy to keep the convertibility. On the other side, France had payment surpluses and gold inflows because of the undervalued currency and the Bank of France did not allow the gold inflows to expand the monetary supply and raise the price level, instead, it sterilized the inflows by absorbing monetary gold from the rest of the world.

The second problem was the liquidity problem of the gold standard that was insufficient to finance the growth of world trade and output. Due to high inflation, a perceived shortage of gold, following the strict rule of Genoa Committee central banks in western world started substituting foreign exchange for gold which created a confidence problem. This, in turn, increased the reserves of pounds and dollars relative to the gold reserves in London and New York. The increase of political complexion and labor unions in Western European countries after the WWI make it more difficult to defend convertibility. Speculative attacks made on short-term capital flows and the lack of cooperation between central banks make the system collapse at the break of Great Depression in 1931.

After the WWII the planning of Bretton Woods aimed to avoid the chaos of the interwar period. As mentioned in the introduction section, the articles of Agreement signed at Bretton Woods, New Hampshire in July 1944, symbolized a historical compromise between American and British plans to combine flexibility and freedom for policymakers of a floating rate system that British team wanted with the nominal stability of the gold standard regime underlined by the United States. The Bretton Woods system was established as a pegged exchange rate, but countries could alter their parties in terms of gold and dollar if major disequilibrium persisted. This time the center of the convertibility was the U.S. and not the United Kingdom. Bretton Woods was different from the classical gold standard from at least three points of view.

First, it was an arrangement authorized by an international agreement between governments, meanwhile, the gold standard evolved informally. Second, domestic policy autonomy was encouraged even at the expense of convertibility, whereas for the gold standard the convertibility was the key part of the system. Third, the capital movements between countries were suppressed by controls.

Although the Bretton Woods system was better than Standard Gold regime, it collapsed between 1968 and 1971 in the face of U.S. monetary expansion that aggravated the worldwide inflation. The United States was not able to keep the dollar standard as they were not able to maintain price stability and control inflation. The dollar standard became impractical as the adjustable peg system became volatile at the increasing capital mobility. The open market speculations against the fixed parity could not be stopped by either traditional monetary policies or international rescue packages. The downfall of the Bretton Woods system ended the U.S financial predominance in the international monetary system and opened the road for a new center of international monetary management based on a multipolar system.

National Currencies and Convertibility to Gold Standard

Robert Triffin, a well-known Belgian American economist at Yale University, on the early sixties studied the process of convertibility to the gold standard which seems to show the first converting problems. In his studies published between 1960 and 1966, he considered convertibility as the right to convert one currency into other currencies often at fluctuating rather than fixed exchange rates.

The development of international monetary management and the return to convertibility of the main European currencies at the end of 1958 changed the nature of convertibility. After the abandon of the automatic gold standard, the introduction of convertibility facilitated the expansion of international financial transactions among countries, and the role of national reserves was no longer principally to maintain the convertibility of a nation's currency into gold but to meet the balance of payments and the external deficits. Therefore, the central banks have to adjust their reserves based not on the liquidity but the expected fluctuations in the balance of payments.

The increase of liquidity in the Western countries from 1957-58 to the mid of the sixties has been accompanied by a growth of dollar balances and a sharp decrease of the United States gold reserves which threaten to harm the reputation of the dollar as a worldwide reserve currency. The Triffin dilemma stated that if the United States were the only supplier of the world's reserve currency, and if the countries had a high demand for liquidity there was no other choice for the U.S. but to run persistent current account deficits. As the world economy was expanding demand for reserve assets was climbing. The United States was the only reserve supplier that could supply other countries by running a current account deficit and issuing dollar-dominated obligations to finance it. If the United States for some reasons decided to stop running balance of payments deficits, and if the US Federal Reserve stopped printing money to finance reserves for countries caught up in expansive monetary policies, the resulting shortage of liquidity would bring the global economy into a vicious circle. But incurring such payment deficits also meant that, over time, the excess global liquidity risked creating an inflation spiral that would erode confidence in the dollar as the reserve currency. This might have caused other countries to doubt whether the United States could maintain the promised gold convertibility or might be forced to devaluate the almighty dollar.

There were a number of Western European Countries like West Germany that were showing an appetite for the accumulation of reserves despite the excess cash balances following the pace of trade and payments growth, while other countries were striving for an increase of reserves more rapid than the growth of world trade. The estimation of the IMF (International Monetary Fund) at that time was that as a result of global trade expansion the reserves must increase by 3% annually where the gold supplies would cover some 70% of the additional reserves. By the end of 1958, the U.S. gold holdings exceeded short-term liabilities to other countries by $ 5 billion. But the rising of foreign claims against the U.S. gold reserves make the short-term liabilities disappear quickly and threaten the liquidity of the dollar and as a result of a large part of others' countries international reserves were at risk (Ellsworth P.T. 1961: 211).

The solution, based on Triffin's study (1960), was not the revaluation of gold because it would create big problems to the balance of payments in the world economy, nor do the fluctuating exchange rates offer a good explanation. Despite the accommodating of monetary and fiscal policies and rate variations would help hit some important targets it would not resolve the problem of adequate reserve levels. It was evident that countries experiencing balance-payments difficulties without adequate reserves would be forced somehow to adopt exchange rates depreciation or in the worst of the cases quantitative restrictions which could damage the fragile international payments mechanism. Triffin's way out, taking into consideration the earlier Keynesian plan at *Bretton Woods* Conference, was to convert the IMF into a sort of world central bank with deposits providing international exchange that would relocate the growing and the destabilizing national currency component of international reserves. These IMF deposits, made equivalent to gold and fully acceptable in world payments, will stabilize the exchange rates and the international payments mechanism. As in the case of a central bank, the Fund (IMF) would have the capability to lend the unused reserves of surplus countries to those in deficit and to be involved in open-market lending operations in order to support the expansion of the world trade.

Triffin's work of more than 50 years ago provides a wonderful trace of thinking about the 2008-2009 crisis. In the 1950s, where the dominant monetary policy was based on fixed exchange rates, the panic among industrialized countries was the convertibility of dollars into gold. In the recent crisis, the situations may be different, but the case scenario seems to be the same. The fear of dollar and euro devaluation, inflationary default on Treasury bonds in the U.S. and European Union countries or capital losses on securitized products linked to widespread insolvencies and a fragile banking system may help revive the picture of dollar inconvertibility in the late sixties of the 20th century.

The refuge to gold seems to be the optimal alternative for many investors around the globe unless the Federal Reserve in the U.S. and central banks in Europe and other countries were able to find a better way to deal with the crisis. Triffin's research was also actual in the late 1990s and early 2000s where the Federal Reserve officials chose to accommodate the initial demand for liquidity and reserve accumulation by lowering interest rates. Low-interest rates helped meet the demand for the huge amount of liquidity to the rest of the world. This move, by Federal Reserve, deteriorated the credit standards and increased the vulnerability of the banking system. On the other side, the low-interest rates and the large quantity of liquidity injected into the economy helped the rapid growth worldwide, but with the cost of building up a massive indebtedness concentrated mainly in the United States as the issuer of the world's main reserve currency. The young and prominent Eurozone as the issuer of the second world's reserve currency was the second victim of the 2008-2009 crisis.

For the United States, despite being the largest world economy, was not an easy task being the issuer of the world's main reserve currency. The United Kingdom, as well experienced chronic instability between the interwar period during 1918-1939 due to the outstanding “sterling balances” overseas which threatened to destabilize the financial system of that time and to deplete the limited gold reserves if the holders tried to convert sterlings into gold. The era of direct convertibility into gold at the dawn of 21st century is gone but the age of large U.S. Treasury bond holders by other countries, such as China, is more present and risky than ever.

Flexible Exchange Rates and Demand Elasticities

The effects of exchange rates on export and import demand, in the short run, tend to be low caused by low price elasticity of demand. Therefore, the elasticity of the exchange rate on the short term depends on whether the sudden movement of prices, measured by the indirect effects on money demand, are able to meet the effects of shifting demand.

Egon Sohmen was a sturdy advocate and strong believer in the usefulness of flexible exchange rates. In his work, published in 1961 he considered some of the controversies in exchange rates. For Sohmen, the greater effectiveness of monetary policy under flexible rates, which will make the fiscal policy a powerful tool for price-level stabilization and employment, may well be seen as a rational explanation to abandon the fixed exchange rates (Sohmen 1961, 83-90). In fact, based on his analysis, the system of flexible exchange rates is superior to the pegging of rates, and he disagrees with those economists who fear that the low demand elasticities in the short run might make foreign exchange markets highly unstable (Sohmen 1961, ch.7). According to Sohmen, this view tends to imply that in a flexible exchange rates regime a system might exist only if there is an unstable equilibrium which will eventually create unemployment and destabilization. This is not true because at least one exchange rate that guarantees a statically stable equilibrium in the foreign exchange market must exist at every instance (Sohmen, 1961, p.7).

He disagrees with the thesis of Laursen and Metzler (1950) that floating rates necessarily require tight controls on capital movements and prohibition of speculation where the speculative activity does accentuate the instability of the rates if they are not pegged. He advances the thesis that speculative activity tends to aggravate the disequilibrium whenever the pegged rate is even slightly out of the line, although this would not happen under flexible exchange rates, because in the real world there is no excessive fluctuation of national currencies, at least in industrialized countries. By taking into consideration the case of Canada, he demonstrates the validity of his argument by indicating that the maximum fluctuates of Canadian dollar from 1952 to 1960 has never been above 5 cents. Sohmen states that:

"... the disturbances caused by the discrete changes characteristic of the 'adjustable peg' are considerably more serious than those provoked by the smooth, day-to-day fluctuations in a system of fluctuating rates..." [Sohmen E., 1961, p.119]

Perhaps, one of the most contentious subjects involving flexible exchange rates is whether or not they contribute to inflation. It was a widespread idea that any devaluation of the currency would automatically cause inflation and worsen the balance of payments. Therefore, fixed exchange rates could impose a better anti-inflationary discipline on monetary authorities than a floating regime. Furthermore, even the direct controls on movements of capital or the tightening of import controls as a substitute for devaluation would not help resolve the problem of inflation, because the degree of inflation is independent of exchange rate regime. All is needed is virtuous monetary policy. The welfare costs of exchange rates controls and occasional rates exchanges incurred by countries experiencing inflation far prevail over the cost of any additional inflation that might result in flexible rates. Therefore, there is no basis to fear the deflation of the currencies in different countries inflexible exchange rates regime because: "the devaluation is an inflationary factor that would defeat its own purpose before too long" (Sohmen 1961, p.109).

An interesting point analyzed by Sohmen (1957) is the elasticity of demand in international trade and foreign-exchange market. If an appreciation of a country's currency improves its balance of payments and if a depreciation deteriorates the balance of payments there is no need for a controlled exchange rates as spontaneous fluctuations will tend to move away from an unstable position in the foreign-exchange market to a more stable position.

The relation of the elasticity of demand and the foreign-exchange market can be expressed by a simple geometric demonstration of the supply and demand schedules in terms of units of foreign currency. It is assumed that each country produces only one export commodity that has a linear import demand schedule of negative slope in foreign currency (country) and that there are infinite supply elasticities followed by equipro-proportional price changes and constant internal prices of each country's exports. In figure 1.1 the exchange rate, *r*, is defined as units of domestic currency per unit of foreign currency, and the demand schedules of imports are given as a function of the exchange rate only.

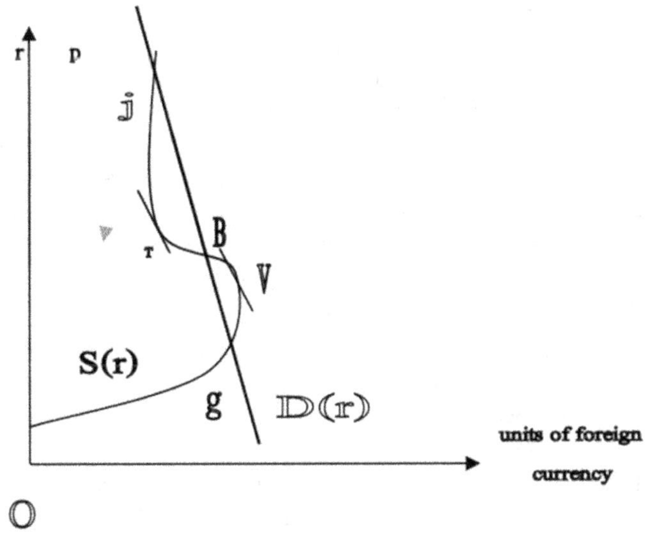

Figure 1.1: Elasticity of demand and the foreign exchange market

In Figure 1.1 the demand schedule of foreign exchange *D(r)* is a linear function of the foreign price *1/r*, and the supply schedule *S (r)* has a twisted form as it bends backward up to B (stable point) and then forward.[5] The configuration of Figure 1.1 shows that the demand schedule for foreign exchange is inelastic. In fact, the range from V to T is an unstable region, as a depreciation will either increase the deficit in the balance of payments

---

[5] If the demand function for import, given as a function of the exchange rate *r*, is written by $M = f(r)$ then the total figure of domestic currency spent on imports would be *Mr* and the demand for foreign exchange will simply be $D=M=F(r)$. By assuming that the demand schedule for exports has the linear form

$$E = c - \frac{d}{r} \qquad 1.a.$$

where *1/r* is the domestic price of exports in terms of foreign currency. The supply of foreign exchange, *S*, therefore the total revenue of exports expressed in terms of foreign currency is given by the expression

$$S = \frac{E}{r} = \frac{c}{r} - \frac{d}{r^2} \qquad 1.b.$$

where *S* has the following properties:

$S \to 0$ as $r \to \infty$ and $S \to -\infty$ as $r \to 0$,

The *S* curve reaches the maximum point at r= 2d/c where the elasticity of underlying commodity demand is -1 (Sohmen 1957, 433).

between B and T or reduce the surplus between V and B. Point B which is the intersection of *S (r)* and *D(r)* is the only point where the balance of payments is zero and where the Marshall-Lerner condition is applied.[6] Besides point B, stable points can exists also below and above the unstable region VT, if for the import demand curves the quantity demanded becomes zero at the upper end of the demand schedule by assuming that the demand curve *D(r)* approaches the price axis asymptotically without reaching it (Sohmen 1957, 434). If an economy finds itself in the proximity to an unstable equilibrium, an appreciation or a free fluctuating exchange rate would improve the country's balance of payments by helping to create a surplus.

The authorities, through substantial sales of foreign exchange using the reserve funds, can push the exchange rate to the lower rather than upper stable equilibrium level. This can help the exchange rate to stay on the lower equilibrium level located at the intersection of *S(r)* and *D(r)* at g point in Figure 1.1. At the lower equilibrium point, the central bank can repurchase the foreign currency at a lower price and resell it at a higher price creating a great advantage for a deficit country. For the trading partner country, the exchange authorities would have enough reasons to move the exchange rate to the opposite direction or the upper equilibrium level (j point). Therefore, there must be a point of stable equilibrium above the region of the instability of the deficit country that has symmetry with the trading partner. The upper stable equilibrium level for one country is the lower one from the point of view of the trading partner country (Sohmen 1957, 436). In a flexible exchange system, independently of the short or long demand elasticities, the trade of commodities in the market will bring the fluctuations of the exchange rate to a limited range of interval at stable levels of equilibrium for partner countries.

The flexible exchange rate is not a destabilizing system. If the low demand elasticities for imports lead to an unstable equilibrium in the foreign exchange market, there is always a stable equilibrium point close to the unstable range of flexible exchange rate values that will not create unemployment and destabilization but will improve the trade balance and reach a certain level of growth between trading countries.

Business was able, especially starting from the late sixties and early seventies, to respond better to the challenge of the high exchange rate. A lot of businesses were capable of finding their stable internal equilibrium even with

---

[6] The definition of the Marshall–Lerner condition states that a positive impact on trade balance can be reached after currency devaluation, if the sum of price elasticity of exports and imports (in absolute value) are greater than 1.

higher exchange rate by making some adjustments like cutting their export prices and hence accepting lower profit margins to preserve competitiveness or targeting their investments in new product lines where demand is price inelastic and less sensitive to exchange rate fluctuations. These adjustments also involve outsourcing components from overseas in less developed countries in order to keep production costs and unit labor cost down or producing products with a higher income elasticity of demand, where factors such as design, product quality, marketing and customer satisfaction are important in securing orders.

Some Conclusions about the Exchange Rates and Balance of Payments Theories

In general, scholars of classic free-trade inspiration like Milton Friedman and Egon Sohmen tend to be in favor of a fluctuation system of currencies as it does not oblige the monetary authorities to intervene, it does not expose them to the risk of depleting reserves and leaves the task of determining the rates of exchange compatible with the equilibrium of the balance of payments to the free open market. Economists in favor of the regulation of the international system like Harberger and Laursen put the instability of the currency market to the fore, finding the remedy in fixing exchange agreements, but at the same time arranging for support for the countries that have to overcome phases of the deficit in their balance of payments. In late fifties and early sixties when the *Bretton Woods* system was in crisis the economists, monetary theorists and policymakers were looking to find the best choice between fixed and flexible exchange rates. In the framework, the best regime seems to be the one that stabilizes macroeconomic performance, that is, minimizes fluctuations in output, raise consumption, keep stable the domestic price level, lowers employment and support a steady rate of growth.

The choice between floating and fixed rates is not as simple as it may seem at first. Countries using fixed exchange rates can change the value of their currency if the cost of maintaining a certain exchange rate is too high and eventually conflicts with other goals. During periods of flexible exchange rates, the governments find much easier to use formal or informal targets for the exchange rate when it comes to monetary authorities to decide whether to expand or contract the money supply. Another argument in favor of a floating exchange rate is that it allows monetary policy to be used for other purposes. For example, a floating regime leaves the authorities free to allow inflation to rise which is an indirect approach, in a certain sense, to increase tax revenue. This is smart monetary policy, but at the same time, it bears here the danger for investors and the stock markets to believe in a credible policy to control inflation. Nevertheless, in an even more flexible regime, the costs of an unsustainable policy may be revealed at an earlier stage than in a pegged one –through the observation of extensive movements in exchange rates and prices.

In general, in the real world, we rarely observe exchange rates that are completely fixed or completely floating. In both monetary systems, the stability of the exchange rate is usually one among many of the monetary authorities' objectives. Often, the controversy between fixed and flexible exchange rates reflects a lack of agreement about the impacts of uncertainty in the exchange market.

Chapter 2

Dynamic Adjustments under Alternative Exchange-Rates Systems

Introduction

Markets can put different pressure on the movements of exchange rates which may result in the increase or decrease of private capital inflows. A monetary system may work well if capital is internationally mobile but poorly if capital is immobile.

According to Robert Mundell (1968, 152-156), a flexible exchange rates system may not work well for an economy in which capital flows are highly sensitive to interest rates but may work better than a system of fixed exchange rates if capital flows are immobile. Under fixed exchange rates, when capital is mobile the interest rate corrects the balance of payments; if capital is immobile, the interest rate affects the balance of payments only to such an extent to create inflationary or deflationary pressure in the goods-and-services market (Mundell, 1968, 157-166). Under flexible exchange rates, when capital is immobile the interest rate has a direct effect on the goods-and-services market, whereas the exchange rate has a direct effect on the balance of payments.

It's interesting the behaviour of authorities when capital inflows increase in one country. In this case, the authorities' desire is in one hand to contain inflation and on the other to maintain a stable exchange rate. Many countries, to avoid uncontrolled consequences of large capital inflows in open market operations, have adopted a large range of monetary policies and measures such as the increase of monetary reserves that banks can maintain against the deposits, the widening of exchange rate bands in order to allow the currencies to appreciate or depreciate, or simply placing some limits on the banking sector's foreign exchange exposure to stay on the safe side.

Meanwhile, such instruments "adjust" the pressure on currency and ease inflationary pressure, none can be done to prevent an appreciation of real exchange rates completely. If monetary policy is locked by an exchange rate anchor, the burden, according to Mundell-Fleming model, falls on fiscal policy. But this is not always possible because the policymakers who try to adjust fiscal policy in the short run would not be able to adopt a rigidly fixed exchange rate regime. A gradual exchange appreciation to absorb the pressure of capital inflows in the country would appear as a much better way of maintaining long-run economic stability. Moreover, a rightful influence on the market by the central bank and monetary authorities would allow the exchange rate to adjust in response to capital inflows and by far accommodate upward pressure. This chapter will shortly take into consideration some theories and models regarding capital mobility, employment policy, fiscal and monetary policies under alternative exchange-rate systems and dynamic adjustments of exchange rates.

Fiscal and Monetary Policies under Different Exchange Rate Regimes

Generally speaking, the effects of fiscal policy for a single country should have more impact under fixed exchange rates than under a flexible exchange rate system. This implies that any single fiscal policy adopted by the government in any given country should play an important role in local economic fluctuations. Monetary policy, instead, has the great benefit of flexibility and rapidity of adjustment to different situations and conditions involving the macroeconomic structure of an economy. It doesn't need a complex legislative action that is required for fiscal policy, but it does give the possibility of choice to consumers and investors that if correctly done will influence positively the investment/consumption ratio stimulating growth and stability, otherwise will bring the economy in recession and collapse. Monetary and fiscal policies can be used to achieve internal stability and external objective like the balance-of-payments equilibrium in a country with perfect capital mobility.

Technically speaking, monetary policy normally aims at external objectives meanwhile the fiscal policy at internal objectives. According to Robert Mundell (1968, 233-239), the monetary and fiscal policy are more effective under flexible than under fixed exchange rates when there is no perfect capital mobility. However, in a system with perfect capital mobility, monetary policy is completely useless under fixed exchange rates, and the same thing can be said about fiscal policy under flexible exchange rates.

In addition, the fiscal policy takes into consideration changes in government expenditures at a certain tax structure meanwhile monetary policy is the optimal government choice to meet the demand for money at a chosen interest rate. The exchange rate policy is the cushion or the intermediary policy that allows the right choice between setting the exchange rate and the country's balance-of-payments position counterbalanced by changes in foreign exchange holdings. A simple macroeconomic model that defines the national product of an open economy is given as follows:

$$Y = C{+}I + G{+}X{-}M \qquad (2.1)$$

where C is the consumption of constant prices, I is the investment, G is the government expenditure, and X and M are respectively the domestic values of exports and imports at constant prices. The real national income in equation 2.1 can also be expressed in terms of interest rate, i, and exchange rate r.

$$Y = A\ (Y, i, r) + G + X(r) - M\ (Y, r) \qquad (2.2)$$

where A is the domestic absorption that depends on real national income given by Y, the domestic interest rate, i, and exchange rate, r. The demand for money expressed as a function of national income and interest rate is given as:

$$L\ (Y, i) = \lambda + R \qquad (2.3)$$

where λ is an independent parameter and R is the domestic value of foreign reserves (the sum $\lambda + R$ is also called,"reserve bank credit" which is the basis for the monetary supply expansion). The country's balance-of-payments constraint in terms of domestic currency is expressed as

$$X{-}M + K = Re \qquad (2.4)$$

where K is the net capital inflow in domestic prices, and Re is the value of foreign-exchange reserves given as $R{-}R0$. The balance-of-payments equation (2.4) can as well be expressed in terms of national income Y, exchange rate r and interest rate, i.

$$\left[X(r) - \frac{1}{r} M(Y, r)\right] + K(i) = R - R_0 \qquad (2.5)$$

It is assumed that foreign interest rates are constant and capital movements are independent of the rate of exchange, therefore there is no possibility for speculative capital flows (Sohmen, 1967, 517). In a modern industrial world, the appreciation/depreciation of exchange rates determine the level of domestic demand. An improvement of the terms of trade following appreciation would increase the domestic demand, and as a consequence, the domestic absorption given by real national income has an effect which is proportional to the level of imports given as:

$$\frac{\partial A}{\partial r} = \frac{\partial A}{\partial Y} M = (1-s)M \tag{2.6}$$

where s is the marginal propensity to spend. Differentiating the trade balance, T, in terms of domestic currency with respect to exchange rate, r, we have

$$Tr = Xr\text{-}Mr\text{+}M \tag{2.7}$$

By differentiating equations (2.2), (2.3) and (2.5), we obtain the following matrix

$$\begin{bmatrix} (s+M_Y)....-A......(sM-T_r)........0 \\ L_Y.................L_i.............0............-1 \\ -M_Y...........K_i...........T_r...........-1 \end{bmatrix} \begin{bmatrix} dY \\ di \\ dr \\ dR \end{bmatrix} = \begin{bmatrix} dG \\ d\lambda \\ 0 \end{bmatrix} \tag{2.8}$$

where the fiscal policy is expressed by $dG>0$ and monetary expansion by $d\lambda>0$. By reading matrix equation (2.8) in technical terms, we have that a system of fixed exchange rates is when $dr=0$ at all times. This condition will make the third column of coefficients in the matrix disappear. While in the case of flexible exchange rates we have that $dR=0$, and the fourth column of the matrix would vanish.

In the case of fixed exchange rates we have that the determinant of the system has the following positive form,

$$\Delta c = (s+MY)(Ki-Li) - Ai\ (MY+LY) \tag{2.9}$$

Differentiating the determinant 2.9 with respect to G and λ we have that the effects of fiscal and monetary policies on effective demand are given respectively by these two positive expressions

$$\frac{dY}{dG} = \frac{K_i - L_i}{\Delta_c} \tag{2.10}$$

$$\frac{dY}{d\lambda} = -\frac{A_i}{\Delta_c} \tag{2.11}$$

In the case of fixed exchange rates, once the fixed exchange rate is determined by authorities, the interest rate and government deficit are the main two policy variables meanwhile national income and reserve position are the targets to meet by using a monetary-fiscal policy combination.

The achievement of a real income level for the government is not an easy task under fixed exchange rates. In fact, there is a burden that a country should bear with some consequences.

The first part of this burden is the interest forgone on the foreign debt in the case of induced capital inflow. The government can afford to pay high-interest rates at short-term held-debts but not in the long run where the burden is insupportable.

The second part of the burden is when the combination of the consumption-investment mix would tend to increase the level of output as a result of heavy investment decided by the government to keep a certain level of income. But this increase could be offset by the higher interest rate policy which would make the demand for new capital inelastic, and hence reduce the overall investments.

And the third part of the burden is the high rate of government expenditures required to accomplish a given level of real income with the balance-of-payments constraint (Krueger 1965, 201-202). The government cannot afford a deficit in the balance-of-payments, therefore it must bear the burden of keeping up with fixed exchange rates by having a lower level of government expenditures and a lower level of real income than in the case of flexible exchange rates.

Returning to the case of flexible exchange rates we have that the basic determinant of the system is written as

$$\Delta_t = \begin{bmatrix} (s + M_Y)\ldots\ldots & - A\ldots\ldots\ldots(sM & - T_r) \\ L_Y\ldots\ldots\ldots\ldots\ldots\ldots\ldots\ldots & L_i\ldots\ldots\ldots\ldots\ldots\ldots\ldots & 0 \\ - M_Y\ldots\ldots\ldots\ldots & K_i\ \ldots\ldots\ldots\ldots\ldots & T_r \end{bmatrix} = \tag{2.12}$$

$$sL_i(T_r + M_YM) + L_Y(T_rA_i + sMK_i - T_rK_i)$$

The determinant of the flexible exchange rates (2.12), in order to sustain positive employment effects of fiscal and monetary policies, needs to have a positive sign if the system is dynamically stable. The system is dynamically stable if in the main three sectors there are linearized systems that guarantee determinant (2.12) has a positive sign expressed by linear system equations as follows,

$$\frac{dY}{dt} = -v_1[(s + M_Y)(Y - Y_0) - A_i(i - i_0) + (sM - T_r)(r - r_0)]$$

$$\frac{di}{dt} = v_2\left[L_Y(Y - Y_0) + L_i(i - i_0)\right] \tag{2.13}$$

$$\frac{dr}{dt} = v_3[-M_Y(Y - Y_0) + K_i(i - i_0) + T_r(r - r_0)]$$

where *v1, v2* and *v3* are the speeds of adjustment in each sector (Sohmen, 1967, 519). The linear system equations (2.13) have in common the determinant Δf multiplied by the factor - *v1, v2 v3*. Furthermore, given that Δf is positive based on Routh-Hurwitz criterion (Samuelson P.A. 1947, 431-435) we have the main expression of the aggregate demand for fiscal policy in the system of flexible exchange rates given as,

$$\frac{dY}{dG} = \frac{L_i T_r}{\Delta_t} \tag{2.14}$$

Excluding the case when the elastic supply of internationally mobile capital is perfect we have that, when *dY/dG= 0,* the fiscal policy does not have any influence on the level of employment. An increase in government spending, G, through the combining effects of trade balance and capital movement leads to the appreciation of the domestic currency under the system of flexible exchange rates. The effect of monetary policy on the main aggregate demand is expressed as

$$\frac{dY}{d\lambda} = \frac{A_i T_r + K_i(sM - T_r)}{\Delta_t} \tag{2.15}$$

This expression is always positive (except in the case of the Keynesian "liquidity trap" when *Li*= -∞), and *dY/dλ* holds because the trade balance normally improves when interest rates fall, and exchange rates are under a flexible system. The condition for the fiscal policy to be more effective under fixed exchange rates is when there is full convertibility of capital movements and is given by the inequality,

$$\frac{K_i}{-L_i} > \frac{M_Y}{L_Y} \tag{2.16}$$

Equation (2.16) has been used for the first time in this form by Rhomberg (1964, 11) and it states that if capital flows are perfectly elastic with respect to interest rate changes and if government through central bank did not issue any new money when the level of income is rising, the fiscal policy is very effective and generates a balance-of-payments improvement attributable to the rising interest rate rather than fiscal budget. Rhomberg's analysis tends to prove that this kind of fiscal policy may have been responsible for the Canadian Government success (in the 1960s) to reduce employment rate under flexible exchange rates (Rhomberg 1964, 27-28).

Rhomberg's study in the early sixties made us think that under a regime of flexible exchange rates a country can use its monetary policy effectively by increasing monetary supply in order to obtain a higher level of employment. The policymakers, by using the monetary policy in a regime of exchange rate fluctuations due to capital flows, may be able to export recession to other countries which may maintain the same level of income and avoid recession only if they lower their own interest rates or increase government deficits with an additional fiscal budget. In addition, under a floating exchange rate system, the transmission of inflationary or deflationary pressures through expansive or tight monetary policy would result in decreased or increased inflationary stress in the rest of the world due to the free mobility of capital flows internationally.

If the authorities of a country wish not to lower the equilibrium of income and employment when the rest of the world lowers it, the interest rate structure has to be chosen between lowering its own interest rate in order to match the international interest structure or to put extra burden by increasing the government expenditure and fiscal deficit (under a flexible exchange rates). Thus, the combination of monetary and fiscal policies is much more effective under flexible exchange rates than under fixed exchange rates in adjusting the level of income and employment.

Capital Flows and Effects on Employment under Fixed and Flexible Exchange Rates

The effects of capital mobility on the level of output, real income, and employment under different exchange-rate systems had been an interesting object of study among economists in the 1960s and 1970s of the last century. The idea of this process consists of the fact that if capital is highly mobile, the interest-rate effect upon capital imports overwhelms the interest-rate effect upon the goods-and-services market, so it seems that internal stability is achieved more by the indirect effect of altered interest rates in capital inflows, appreciating or depreciating the exchange rate rather than by the direct effect upon the goods-and-services market itself.

The well-known Fleming-Mundell model on perfect capital mobility introduced by Marcus Fleming (1962) and Robert Mundell (1963) has been extensively used to demonstrate that fiscal policy would be ineffective in raising output and employment under flexible exchange rates. According to this model, in the short-run, the money supply and the fixed domestic price level establish the fraction of real income that public wish to hold in the form of real balances and savings.

If there is an expansionary fiscal policy, the exchange rates will appreciate which will result in reduced exports but will leave the aggregate demand unaffected simply because the domestic price level and real output are determined jointly by the aggregate supply function and monetary equilibrium. But if the fiscal policy cannot influence the output and employment it will be able to affect something else. In fact, it has an influence on the composition of the aggregate demand and the current account deficit or surplus in the balance of payments through the movements of exchange rates. In Fleming-Mundell model, the capital movements (outflow) can affect income and employment through the influence on the trade balance under a flexible exchange rates system.

The analysis of long-term capital inflows for some economists has shown more interest than the short-term capital movements. The study of Penner (1962) and Melvin (1968), named as Melvin-Penner model, had the purpose to show how long-term capital inflows are spent by investors and businessmen. Their model takes into consideration three kinds of long-term capital inflows based on the way they are spent or used by businessmen and investors.

The first type of capital inflow is the foreign loans which are used by investors to finance capital goods and services domestically. The second type is the borrowing of foreign funds to finance imports of foreign goods. And the third type of capital inflow is used mainly to purchase real and financial domestic assets. All these capital movements occur because foreign investors wish to invest in a country seeking for better investment opportunities or because investors from that country prefer to borrow abroad with lower interest rates and invest the money domestically where they think they can get a better return. These capital flows are assumed to be independent or autonomous of the merchandise trade sector because they have an effect on changes in the national income.

The model of **Melvin-Penner** assumes that there are only two countries where prices are equal to unity, and any differences in the price level will take place only if there is any appreciation/depreciation in the exchange rate. The price of a domestic currency is denoted by r, which is expressed in units of foreign currency per unit of domestic currency. Denoting by $p12$, exports of country 1 and $p21$ exports of country 2, and Y1 the demand by country 1 as a function of the output of country 2, we have:

$$p12 = p12\,(Y2, 1/r) \qquad (2.17)$$

$$p21 = p21\ (Y1,r) \tag{2.18}$$

In the same way, the variables that represent the demand for each country's domestically produced goods and services are given as:

$$p11 = p11\ (Y1,r) \tag{2.19}$$

$$p22 = p22\ (Y2,1/r) \tag{2.20}$$

where *p11* and *p22* is the real domestic absorption of produced goods including consumption, investment and government spending. And the real output of each country is written respectively as

$$Y1 = p11\ (Y1,r)\ +\ p12\ (Y2,1/r)+ma \tag{2.21}$$

$$Y2 = p21\ (Y1,r)+\ p22\ (Y2,1/r)+na \tag{2.22}$$

and consists of two parts, the real exports given by equations (2.17) and (2.18) and real absorption given by equations (2.19) and (2.20). The *m* and *n* are constants meanwhile *a* is a parameter that characterizes independent changes in the components of Y. Equations (2.21) and (2.22) can be expressed in terms of one currency *r*, as

$$0 = p21\ (Y1,r)r- p12\ (Y2,1/r)-ka \tag{2.23}$$

where *k* is an another constant. To analyse the changes in equations (2.21), (2.22) and (2.23) we go through a differentiating process. Differentiating first equation (2.21) with respect to *a* and writing *1/r=r** we get the following expression in terms of constant *m*,

$$m = \frac{dY_1}{da} - \frac{\partial p_{11}}{\partial Y_1}\frac{dY_1}{da} - \frac{\partial p_{12}}{\partial Y_2}\frac{dY_2}{da} - \frac{\partial p_{11}}{\partial r}\frac{dr}{da} - \frac{\partial p_{12}}{\partial r*}\frac{dr*}{da} \tag{2.24}$$

where $\partial p_{11} / \partial Y_1$ is the marginal propensity to spend in country 1, and $\partial p_{12} / \partial Y_2$ is the marginal propensity to import of country 2 (Melvin 1968, 322). Given that *dr*/da=-(1/r²)(dr/da)* the expression (2.24) gets another form

$$m = \left(1 - \frac{\partial p_{11}}{\partial Y_1}\right)\frac{dY_1}{da} - \frac{\partial p_{11}}{\partial Y_2}\frac{dY_2}{da} - \frac{dr}{da}\left[\frac{\partial p_{11}}{\partial r} - \frac{1}{r^2}\frac{\partial p_{12}}{\partial r\ *}\right] \tag{2.25}$$

By using the elasticity of demand for imports equation (2.25) will get another form if both numerator and denominator of the first term of the expression in bracket is multiplied by *p11* and the second term by *p12* and assuming that *r=1*, we have

$$m = \left(1 - \frac{\partial p_{11}}{\partial Y_1}\right)\frac{dY_1}{da} - \frac{\partial p_{12}}{\partial Y}\frac{dY_2}{da} - \frac{dr}{da}\left[\frac{\partial p_{11}}{\partial r}\frac{r}{p_{11}}p_{11} - \frac{\partial p_{12}}{\partial r*}\frac{r*}{p_{12}}p_{12}\right] \tag{2.26}$$

where $(\partial p_{12} / pr*)(r* / p_{12}) = d_{12}$ is the elasticity of demand for imports of the second country, meanwhile $(\partial p_{11} / \partial r)(r / p_{11}) = d_{11}$ is the cross-elasticity of demand for domestic output when there is a change in the exchange rate. Substituting *d12* and *d11* to (2.20) we have the new expression

$$m = \left(1 - \frac{\partial p_{11}}{\partial Y}\right)\frac{dY_1}{da} - \frac{\partial p_{12}}{\partial y}\frac{dY_2}{da} - [d_{11}p_{11} - d_{12}p_{12}]\frac{dr}{da} \tag{2.27}$$

By substituting $\partial p_{11} / \partial Y_1 = p'_{11}, \partial p_{12} / \partial Y_2 = p'_{12}$ and $A_1 = (d_{11}p_{11} - d_{12}p_{12})$ equation (2.27) can be simplified as,

$$m=(1-p'_{11})\frac{dY_1}{da}-p'_{12}\frac{dY_2}{da}-A_1\frac{dr}{da} \tag{2.28}$$

which is the final form of equation differentiation (2.21) (Melvin 1968, 323). In the same way, by differentiating equation (2.22) and defining the marginal propensities as we have done with (2.21), we get a final form in terms of constant *n*,

$$n = (1 - p'_{22})\frac{dY_2}{da} - p'_{21}\frac{dY_1}{da} - r^*\frac{dr}{da}\left[\frac{\partial p'_{21}}{\partial r} - r^*\frac{\partial p_{22}}{\partial r^*}\right] \tag{2.29}$$

As before, by substituting $A_2 = (d_{21} p_{21} - d_{22} p_{22})$ where *d21* is the elasticity of demand for imports of the first country and *d22* is the cross-elasticity of demand for products produced domestically with respect to exchange rate for the second country we have

$$n = (1 - p_{22}^{'})\frac{dY_2}{da} - p_{21}^{'}\frac{dY_1}{da} - A_2\frac{dr}{da} \qquad (2.30)$$

In the same way for expression (2.23) we get a final form

$$\begin{aligned} -k &= -rp_{21}^{'}\frac{dY_1}{da} + p_{12}^{'}\frac{dY_2}{da} \\ &- r^{*}\frac{dr}{da}\begin{bmatrix} \frac{\partial p_{21}}{\partial r} r^2 \\ + p_{21}r + r^{*}\frac{\partial p_{22}}{\partial r^{*}} \end{bmatrix} \end{aligned} \qquad (2.31)$$

By using $A_3 = (p_{21} + d_{21}m_{21} + d_{12}m_{12})$ equation (2.31) gets the simple form as

$$-k = -p_{21}^{'}\frac{dY_1}{da} + p_{12}^{'}\frac{dY_2}{da} - A_3\frac{dr}{da} \qquad (2.32)$$

From equations (2.28), (2.30) and (2.32) we can reach the general form of the model by putting them in matrix expression

$$\begin{bmatrix} (1-p_{11}^{'}) \ldots\ldots - p_{12}^{'} \ldots\ldots - A_1 \\ -p_{21}^{'} \ldots\ldots (1-p_{12}^{'}) \ldots\ldots - A_2 \\ -p_{21}^{'} \ldots\ldots p_{12}^{'} \ldots\ldots - A_3 \end{bmatrix} \begin{bmatrix} \frac{dY_1}{da} \\ \frac{dY_2}{da} \\ \frac{dr}{da} \end{bmatrix} = \begin{bmatrix} m \\ n \\ -k \end{bmatrix} \qquad (2.33)$$

This matrix determines the values of the vector *[m, n, -k]* when there is a change in the demand of each country. For example, a demand increase in the second country for imports from country 1 will result in a situation where the vector *[m, n, -k]* assumes values as *m=1, n=0 and k=1.* The matrix can be solved for *dY1, dY2* and *dr*. Solving the matrix above (2.33) by *dY1* we have

$$dY_1 = \frac{da}{D}\{m[A_2 p'_{12} - A_3(1 - p'_{22})] - np'_{12}[A_1 + A_3] - k[A_2 p'_{12} + A_1(1 - p'_{22})]\}$$

(2.34)

where D is the determinant of the coefficient matrix which can be written as

$$D = A_1[p'_{12}p'_{21} - p'_{21}(1 - p'_{22})] - A_2[p'_{12}p'_{21} - p'_{12}(1 - p'_{11})] - A_3[(1 - p'_{22})(1 - p'_{11}) - p'_{21}p'_{12}] \quad (2.35)$$

In the same way, solving the matrix (2.33) for *dY2,* we have

$$dY_2 = \left(\frac{da}{D}\right)\{mp'_{21}[A_2 - A_3] - n[A_1 p'_{21} + A_3(1 - p'_{11}) - k[A_1 p'_{21} - A_2(1 - p'_{11})]]\}$$

(2.36)

And again solving the matrix (2.33) for *dr* we get

$$dr = \frac{da}{D}\left\{\begin{matrix} m[p'_{21}(1 - p'_{22}) - p'_{12}p'_{21}] + n[p'_{12}p'_{21} - p'_{12}(1 - p'_{11})] \\ + k[p'_{12}p'_{21} - (1 - p'_{22})(1 - p'_{11})] \end{matrix}\right\}$$

(2.37)

Given that expressions for *dY1, dY2* and *dr* contain the determinant *D,* the system is stable only if *D>0.* It is assumed that the marginal propensities to save for both countries are the same. Re-considering (2.35) and after using *e21, e12, f2* and *f1* (see the box below 2.a, 2.3b) and re-arranging the terms we obtain the new expression for determinant *D,*

$$D = [(1 - p'_{11} - p'_{12})(p'_{12})(p'_{21})]\left\{\begin{matrix} \left[\dfrac{1 - p'_{12} - p'_{22}}{p'_{12}}\right] \\ (e_{21} + e_{12} - 1) + e_{21}(1 - f_1) + e_{12}(1 - f_2) - 2 \end{matrix}\right\}$$

(2.38)

where e21, e12, *f2* and *f1* are expressed in absolute values. The determinant of the coefficient matrix, *D,* will be positive if the following condition is met

$$\left(\frac{1 - p'_{12} - p'_{22}}{p'_{12}}\right)[e_{12} + e_{21} - 1] + e_{21}(1 - f_1) + e_{12}(1 - f_2) > 2$$

(2.39)

which is a general Marshall-Lerner condition as it contains the elasticity of demand for imports *(e12+e21 +1).* Assuming that *f2=f1=0,* equation (2.39) can be transformed as

$$\left(\frac{1-p'_{12}-p'_{22}}{p'_{12}}\right)[e_{12}+e_{21}-1]>2 \tag{2.40}$$

where $(1 - p'_{12} - p'_{22})$ is the marginal propensity to save which is larger than the marginal propensity to import *p'12*, if the first term of equation (2.40) is larger than 1 (Melvin 1968,328-330).

This will assure the stability of the model. But a value *e12+e21 =2* is even sufficient to ensure stability, as (1+p'22)/p'12>1 must be more than satisfactory for the system to be in equilibrium. This proposal, as seen in chapter 1, has been suggested by Harberger (1950) and Laursen and Metzler (1950). Another monetary economist, Tsiang (1961), suggested that the stability condition in Melvin-Penner model may be undermined if the model was extended to include a monetary system where the interest rate is allowed to change which will make the stability condition less rigid.

Three types of capital inflows

As mentioned earlier, Penner's first type of capital inflow was foreign loans used by investors to finance capital goods and services domestically. According to Penner (1962, 529), if there is an increase in imports, it will be a reduction in the government expenditures on import-competing products. Therefore, the relationship between the first's country elasticity of demand for imports *e21* and the cross-elasticity of demand for country 1 for its domestic production, *e11,* is given as

$$e_{21}=\frac{\partial p_{21}}{\partial r}\frac{r}{p_{21}} \tag{2.a}$$

$$e_{11}=\frac{\partial p_{11}}{\partial r}\frac{r}{p_{11}} \tag{2.b}$$

Both expressions can be simplified by eliminating *r*, so they take the following form

$$e_{11}=f_1\frac{p_{21}}{p_{11}}e_{21} \tag{2.c}$$

$$e_{22}=f_2\frac{p_{12}}{p_{22}}e_{12} \tag{2.d}$$

where $f_1 = \dfrac{\partial p_{11}}{\partial r} \Big/ \dfrac{\partial p_{21}}{\partial r}$ and $f_2 = \dfrac{\partial p_{22}}{\partial r^*} \Big/ \dfrac{\partial p_{12}}{\partial r^*}$, *f1* and *f2* represent the degree of substitution between imports and domestic production for each country. Under Penner's conditions, any changes in national output based on the first type of capital inflow will be zero. From equation (2.34) assuming dY1= 0, and given that m=1, n=1 and k=0 we get

$$(1-p'_{22})[-A_3 - A_1] = 0 \tag{2.e}$$

Substituting A3 and A1, we have equation (2.e) in terms of *p* rewritten as,

$$-(1-p'_{22})\left[p_{21} + p_{11}e_{11} + p_{21}e_{21}\right] = 0 \tag{2.f}$$

Given that $e_{11} = f_1\left(\dfrac{p_{21}}{p_{11}}\right)e_{21}$ we write

$$-(1-p'_{22})p_{21}e_{21}\left[\frac{1}{e_{21}} + f_1 + 1\right] = 0 \tag{2.g}$$

Reorganizing *e11* and *f1* we obtain a different form of (2.g)

$$-(1-p'_{22})p_{21}e_{21}\left\{\left[1-\frac{1}{e_{21}}\right] - f_1\right\} = 0 \tag{2.h}$$

where it proves that dY1=0 only when (assumed marginal propensity to save less than 1)

$$\left[1-\left(\frac{1}{e_{21}}\right)\right] = f_1 \tag{2.i}$$

Assuming that *n=-1* from equation (2.37) we have that dY1=0 if the following condition is fulfilled

$$(1-p'_{22})[-A_3 - A_1] = 0 \tag{2.j}$$

Substituting (1-p'22) with (1-p'12 - p'22) and reorganizing (2.h) we write

$$(1-p'_{12}-p'_{22})p_{21}e_{21}\left\{\left[1-\frac{1}{e_{21}}\right] - f_1\right\} = 0 \tag{2.k}$$

where as in (2.h) $dY_1 = \dfrac{da}{D}[-p_{12}'(A_1 + A_3)] = 0$ only when $[1-(1/e_{21})] = f_1$. This condition explains that the income of receiving country depends on the price elasticity of demand for imports in country 1, given by *f1* and *e21*.

Penner's second type of capital inflow is used to finance the purchase of foreign goods which does not increase the internal demand for output and does not make any modifications on exchange rates. In this case from equation (2.37), we have that parameters *m* and *k* will be equal to zero and *n* will change based on the spending of the output in country 2 as a result of the capital flows. In this scenario, we have that if capital inflows were financed from the savings of the second country (when n=1), then from equation (2.37) the output of country 1, denoted by *dY1*, is given as

$$dY_1 = \frac{da}{D}[-p_{12}'(A_1 + A_3)] \tag{2.l}$$

Setting dY1= 0, we get

p'12[-A1-A3]=0 (2.m)

which is similar to (2.e), therefore it takes the form as

$$p_{12}' \; p_{21}e_{21}\left\{\left[1 - \frac{1}{e_{21}}\right] - f_1\right\} = 0 \tag{2.n}$$

This expression proves that if the second type of capital inflow has no effect on country 2, then the effect on country 1 will be zero as well. But if the effect of capital inflow has a positive outcome on country 2, then the national income of country 1 would depend on the value of *e21* and *f1* which means it could decrease, increase or remain the same.

The third type of capital inflow, according to Penner (Penner 1962, 532), is used mainly to purchase real and financial domestic assets and is more likely to be deflationary compared to other types of capital inflows, as it appreciates the exchange rate without increasing the demand for domestic goods and services. If *n=0* from equation (2.37)we can write

$$dY_1 = \frac{da}{D}[-p_{12}'A_2 - (1 - p_{22}')A_1] \tag{2.o}$$

Setting *n=-1* then equation (2.37) becomes

$$dY_1 = \frac{da}{D}\left[p_{12}'(A_1 + A_3) - p_{12}'A_2 - (1 - p_{22}')A_1\right] \tag{2.p}$$

Setting *dY1= 0*, substituting *(1- p'22)= p'12 +S* and converting to absolute values we obtain

$$- p_{12}e_{12}\left[\left(1 - \frac{1}{e_{12}}\right) - f_2\right] - S(e_{12} + f_1e_{21}) = 0 \tag{2.q}$$

where *S* is the marginal propensity to save. Assuming that *f2=f1=1*, expression (2.q) turns into

$$p_{12}' - S(e_{12} + e_{21}) = 0 \quad (2.r)$$

which can hold for apposite values of the parameters, and therefore *dY1* assumes positive or negative values. On the other hand, if *f2=f1=0*, expression (2.q) becomes

$$- p_{12}(e_{12} - 1) - S(e_{12}) = 0 \quad (2.s)$$

where the left –hand of the above equation (2.s) is negative, and thus for the third type of capital inflows *dY1* will have negative values (Melvin 1968, 325-330).

Concluding, if the Penner's first type of capital inflow is used to buy goods and services manufactured domestically or internationally it is necessary to know the domestic elasticity of demand for imports and the existing degree of substitution between imports and domestic products. If the Penner's third type of capital inflow is used to acquire mainly real and financial domestic securities, then the values of elasticities and substitution parameters for both countries and the marginal propensities to save and import must be known. Thus, it's hard to say that capital inflows are to be considered as contractionary or expansionary (Melvin 1968, 333).

But if the monetary policy is successful on increasing the money supply under the assumption of infinity elasticity of supply of output, national income will rise allowing people to hold large amounts of money which can be invested in a certain type of capital flows. This will keep employment and the balance of payments at satisfactory levels.

Intermediate Imports under Flexible Exchange Rates

The analysis of the consequences of an increase in the price of the imported intermediate goods is another important topic that was taken into consideration by economists in the 1970s during the 1973 oil crisis. Two well-known articles that by and large summarize the thought of monetary theorists during the oil crisis in the 1970s were written by Findlay and Rodriguez (1977) and Obstfeld (1980). These two studies are of particular interest as they give some insights regarding the effect of "oil shock" on finished goods, on the exchange rates and the balance of payments. These studies among others came across the finding that an intermediate import price increase is likely to affect the current-account surplus and the deficit on the balance of payments.

The effect of an intermediate import price rise on the economy's balance of payments will affect the exchange rate which may appreciate or depreciate in the short-run. On the other side, a disturbance on the exchange rates will revise the price of imported intermediate goods which can affect the domestic output and employment from the supply side.

We start analyzing more in details a model of this kind (Findlay-Rodriguez model, 1977) by assuming that input/output ratio between intermediate goods and gross output is constant. The intermediate good could be oil which is used up in the process of production to deliver a final good. The neoclassical production function of the gross output of an economy is given as

$$Y = \text{Min}\,[F\,(K, L), \lambda T] \qquad (2.41)$$

where Y is the gross output, K the capital stock, L employment, T the quantity of the intermediate input used in production and λ is a choice of units of the intermediate inputs. Profit maximization in a production function is when net marginal product of labor is equal to the wage,

$$(p\text{-}pi)\ F'(L) = w \qquad (2.42)$$

where p, pi and w are the nominal prices of Y, T and L. Expression (2.42) can be re-written as

$$p(1\text{-}ep^*)\ F'(L) = w \qquad (2.43)$$

where $pi = E\,p^*$ and $e = E/p$. E indicates the nominal exchange rate, p^* is the price of imported intermediate goods input in foreign currency, and e is the real exchange rate (Findlay and Rodriguez 1977, 209). The net output of the economy can easily be expressed as the gross output minus the real cost of the imported intermediate input,

$$y = Y\text{-}ep^*T = (1\text{-}\ ep^*)Y \qquad (2.44)$$

where Y can be eliminated as it depends on p and ep^*, therefore expression (2.44) can be written as:

$$y = y\ (p, ep^*) \qquad (2.45)$$

and dividing both sides of (2.44) by y we get the three conditions of diminishing returns to labor

$$\frac{\partial y}{\partial p} = (1 - ep^*)\frac{\partial Y}{\partial p} > 0$$

$$\frac{\partial y}{\partial p^*} = (1-ep^*)\frac{\partial Y}{\partial p} - eY < 0$$
$$\frac{\partial y}{\partial e} = (1-ep^*)\frac{\partial Y}{\partial e} - p^*Y < 0 \qquad (2.46)$$

The aggregate demand, *y*, can be expressed in terms of real national income and other aggregate components

$$y(p, ep^*) = C(y)+I(r)+X(e)-MC(y,e)-MT(y, ep^*) \qquad (2.47)$$

where *C* is the national consumption, *I* is the domestic investment, *r* is the real domestic rate of interest, *X* is the total exports, *MC* is the import of consumer goods, and *MT* is the imported intermediate input that meets the conditions $\frac{\partial C}{\partial y} > 0, \frac{\partial X}{\partial e} > 0, \frac{\partial MC}{\partial y} > 0, \frac{\partial MC}{\partial e} < 0.$[1] From (2.44) we have that the imported intermediate input MT can be written as

$$MT = Y - y = \frac{ep^*}{(1 - ep^*)} y \qquad (2.48)$$

with $\frac{\partial MT}{\partial y} > 0, \frac{\partial MT}{\partial e} > 0, \frac{\partial MT}{\partial p^*} > 0$. And the balance of trade expressed in terms of *X*, *MC*, and *MT* is given as

$$B = X(e) - MC(y, e) - MT(y, ep^*) \qquad (2.49)$$

where $\frac{\partial B}{\partial y} < 0, \frac{\partial B}{\partial p^*} < 0, \frac{\partial B}{\partial e} > 0$. The money market is in equilibrium in the short-run if the nominal supply of money (determined exogenously by the central bank) is equal to the portion of the national income money given as,

$$M' = kpy(p,ep^*) \qquad (2.50)$$

where *k* is the fraction of the national income money assumed that $r=r^*$. Expressions (2.47) and (2.50) indicate the conditions for equilibrium in the goods and money markets, and after going through total differentiation, they can be transformed as

---

[1] International interest rate, r^*, and domestic interest rate, *r*, are assumed to be equal under assumption of perfect capital mobility $r=r^*$.

$$\frac{dp}{de}\Big|SS = \left[\left[\frac{\partial B}{\partial e} - \left(1 - \frac{\partial C}{\partial y} - \frac{\partial B}{\partial y}\right)\frac{\partial y}{\partial e}\right] \Big/ \left[\left(1 - \frac{\partial C}{\partial y} - \frac{\partial B}{\partial y}\right)\frac{\partial y}{\partial p}\right]\right] \tag{2.51}$$

$$\frac{dp}{de}\Big|MM = -\frac{\partial y}{\partial e} \Big/ \left(\frac{\partial y}{\partial p} - \frac{y}{p}\right) \tag{2.52}$$

These two equations give the slopes of SS and MM depicted in Figure 2.1. The SS and MM slope show respectively the combinations of *p* and *e*, at the home goods market and domestic money market (Findlay and Rodriguez 1977, 211).

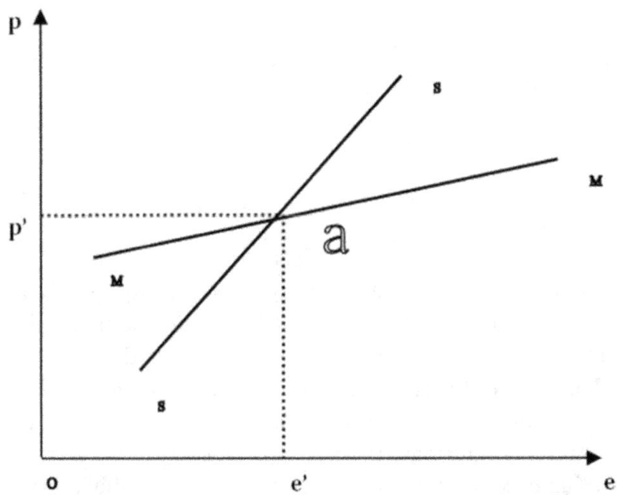

Figure 2.1: The equilibrium of the domestic goods and money market

The intersection of slopes SS and MM in fig. 2.1 establishes the equilibrium values *p* and *e* of the domestic price level and exchange rate. From equations (2.51) and (2.52) derive that both SS and MM have positive slopes, but SS is steeper than MM which brings us to the new expression

$$\frac{dp}{de}\Big|SS > -\frac{\partial y}{\partial e} \Big/ \frac{\partial y}{\partial p} > \frac{dp}{de}\Big|MM \tag{2.53}$$

The intersection of *SS* and *MM* at point *a*, in fig. 2.1, guarantees the money market equilibrium and the stability of the system in the short-run but not in a longer period. In fact, in the long-run an increase in *p* will increase *e* and the system does not assure the monetary equilibrium. The monetary equilibrium will be restored if there is a fall in the output of the economy, *y*, which will require an increase in *e*. This will push *MM* to the right of point *a*, which will improve the balance of payments. In the same way, it will be an equilibrium in the goods market if *e* is reduced which will increase income and deteriorate the balance of payments. In this case, *SS* must pass to the left of *a* and be steeper than *MM*.

When the price of imported intermediate inputs rise on the domestic economy, it will be interesting to look the effects of *p* and *e*. The differentiation of equations (2.47) and (2.50) with respect to p^* (price of imported intermediate goods input in foreign currency) where *p* and *e* are held constant gives us two new equations of the type

$$\frac{\partial L_Y}{\partial p^*} = \left[1 - \frac{\partial C}{\partial y} + \frac{\partial MC}{\partial y}\right]\frac{\partial y}{\partial p} + \frac{\partial MT}{\partial p^*} + \frac{\partial MT}{\partial y}\frac{\partial y}{\partial p^*} \geq 0 \tag{2.54}$$

$$\frac{\partial L_M}{\partial p_*} = -k\frac{\partial y}{\partial p^*} > 0 \tag{2.55}$$

where *LY* and *LM* are the excess supply in domestic goods and money markets. The rise of p^* reduces *y* which in turn reduces the value of intermediate imports. In equation (2.54) the imported intermediate input, MT, will be higher after the rise in the $p^*$and downward adjustment of *y* if the total elasticity of demand for the intermediate input is less than the unity, one. In equation (2.55) instead, the rise of p^* when *p* and *e* are held constant which creates an excess supply on the money market as *y* falls in real value. In terms of Figure, 2.1 MM schedule must shift to the left as *p* rises or *e* falls in order to restore the equilibrium in monetary market, meanwhile, the *SS* schedule can move in either direction as there is uncertainty regarding the sign of (2.54). Considering the differentiation of (2.47) and (2.50) again and solving for dp/dp^* and de/dp^* we get two equations that show effects on *p* and *e* on a new equilibrium position.

$$\frac{dp}{dp^*} = -k\left(\left[\frac{\partial MT}{\partial p*}\frac{\partial y}{\partial e} + \frac{\partial y}{\partial p^*}\frac{\partial B}{\partial e}\right]\Big/\Delta\right) > 0 \tag{2.56}$$

$$\frac{de}{dp^*} = k\left(\left[\left(1 - \frac{\partial C}{\partial y} - \frac{\partial B}{\partial y}\right)\frac{\partial y}{\partial p^*}\frac{y}{p} + \frac{\partial MT}{\partial p^*}\left(\frac{\partial y}{\partial p} + \frac{y}{p}\right)\right]\bigg/\Delta\right) \geq 0 \quad (2.57)$$

$$\text{where } \Delta = k\left\{\frac{\partial B}{\partial e}\left[\frac{y}{p} + \frac{\partial y}{\partial p}\right] - \frac{y}{p}\frac{\partial p}{\partial e}\left[1 - \frac{\partial C}{\partial y} - \frac{\partial B}{\partial y}\right]\right\} > 0.$$

Both equations (2.56) and (2.57) have a positive sign which means that when the domestic price level rises, the nominal money supply remains unaffected. In addition, to keep the system in equilibrium the gross output, y, must fall as a result of the rise of imported intermediate goods, p^*. The exchange rate, e, in order to accommodate the new equilibrium position may either rise or fall (Findlay and Rodriguez 1977, 214).

Regarding the effects of fiscal and monetary policy on price level, real exchange rate and output when nominal wage and the price of intermediate input are given we have that an increase in the nominal money supply will require not only an increase on the p but also a fall in e to restore equilibrium in the money market. An expansionary monetary policy put in place by monetary authorities will increase the price level and exchange rate but will have positive effects on real output (by increasing it) since the increase of imported intermediate input will make the domestic labor force cheaper compared to the international competitive labor market.

On the other front, an expansionary fiscal policy through an increase in government expenditure will somehow lower the domestic price level which will have a positive effect on the real output and real wage, but the contrary effect will be to appreciate the real exchange rate and reduce the price of the intermediate imported goods.

Increased output and high real wages will reduce the rate of unemployment despite this may not be sufficient, since there is a contractionary impact on employment as a result of the burden of higher salaries imposed by a domestic labor market that employers have to pay to hire new employees. The employers rather prefer to keep the same level of employment and try to increase productivity through restructuring their organization. In few words, when nominal wage and the price of intermediate input are given, the expansionary monetary policy will improve the trade of balance while the expansionary fiscal policy will worsen it.

In the case when the price of intermediate goods is fixed in real terms monetary and fiscal policy will be unable to affect the real output and employment. Expansionary monetary policy will have little impact on the real economy as the domestic prices, and nominal wages will be increased in the same proportion. Expansionary fiscal policy will worsen the trade of balance quickly as a result of an increase of the price level of exported consumer goods compared to imported consumers goods reducing, therefore, the volume of exports and rising level of imports for inputs.

In the case when the real wage is fixed but the real price of the intermediate imported goods change the real output would depend only on the real exchange rate and not on the domestic price level because its effect on varying the real wage will be easily offset by a change on nominal wages. Expansionary nominal money supply will raise the domestic price level but will leave the real exchange rate and real output unaffected. An expansionary fiscal policy through an increase in government expenditures will reduce the domestic price level and appreciate the real exchange rate increasing in this way the domestic output and eventually at some degree the level of employment as a result of cheaper imported intermediate goods.

The effects of "oil shocks" on finished goods in the short-run and long-run have also been studied by another economist, Paul Krugman in a brilliant research paper published in 1983. This study discusses the problem of oil price increase from the point of view of transfer theory in a three-country (U.S., Germany, and OPEC) partial equilibrium balance of payment model. The model consists of oil importers countries that share equivalent share of oil demand and OPEC countries which share similar share of spending.

A rise in the oil price would leave unchanged the exchange rates among oil importing countries, and it will apparently worsen their balance of payments. But, indirectly it will improve their balance of payment as OPEC countries spend their income from selling oil on the purchase of goods and assets from the oil importers countries. And the reason why the OPEC countries invest in big oil importers such as western countries is that they want them to import more oil in the future which means that the balance of payment deficits between various oil importing countries should correspond to the future surpluses once they are able to satisfy the demand for goods and assets for OPEC countries. When there is an oil price increase or oil shock the propensity to save of OPEC countries is not greater than that of western countries which consume a large quantity of oil. Therefore, the marginal propensity to save in OPEC and western countries is the same despite the oil price increase because of a permanent transfer between oil consuming countries and OPEC which reduces saving in western countries and increase it in the OPEC, but the total saving among all countries remains the same (Krugman 1983, 280).

It is well known the fact that large surpluses earned by oil shocks and continued oil price increases in the seventies, eighties and nineties from the OPEC countries like United Arab Emirates, Saudi Arabia, Kuwait, Qatar, Iraq, Iran etc., were used to buy luxury goods and assets and without doubt very expensive military equipment and installations from western countries. This transfer process of excess savings from OPEC to western world has guaranteed that western oil consumer countries in exchange of their goods and assets continue to buy oil in large quantities despite price increases from oil producer countries.

It's important to emphasise that the OPEC surpluses from the early seventies to the crisis of 2008 have had no major effect on international interest rates as there were just transfers.

If the oil price increases have no effect on international terms of trade and international interest rates, the income effects based on Krugman's model may be sufficient to provoke appropriate adjustment on the level of spending in different regions (including the main two western countries in the model, U.S. and Germany) in order to enable OPEC countries to consume and save more at unchanged international relative prices.

Trade Policy under Fixed and Flexible Exchange Rates

It might be interesting to have a quick look on some of the effects of trade or commercial policies when full employment and balance of payments are in equilibrium as a result of exchange rate adjustment combined with a stabilization policy. Generally speaking, a restraining trade policy under alternative exchange rate regimes can be seen as corresponding to a border tax at the appropriate rate which can cause the internal relative price of the traded good to rise and improve the balance of payments in the short run, increasing in this way the nominal income not only in the short but also in the long run. Mundell instead considers,

> "......commercial policy to be any policy that restricts imports or promotes exports without directly affecting the level of saving or investment. Such a policy affects both internal and external balance schedules." [Mundell 1961, 514]

The effects of commercial policy on internal balance schedule are comparable to that of fiscal policy since at the fixed exchange rate the level of income has to be higher and at the same level of income, the exchange rates have to be lower to prevail over the deficit in the balance of payments. Mundell, among others, agrees that commercial policy under fixed exchange rates has the capability to improve the balance of payments causing some inflation, meanwhile, under flexible rates, it creates a deficit as there is an appreciation of the domestic currency and is deflationary.

Another subject of study regarding commercial policies is the inflationary and deflationary effects of tariff application under fixed and flexible exchange rates. Egon Sohmen (1958) considered the case when domestic currency is under flexible exchange regime, and the economy is fully employed, with perfect flexible wages and prices and constant money supply. Based on his analysis, if the protection is above the optimum level, tariff reduction will cause the domestic output to rise based on the exchange rates system. Devaluation along with tariff reduction would be inflationary or deflationary depending on the level of tariffs, below or above the optimum level.

The Edward Tower's (1973) model on commercial policies under fixed and flexible exchange rates gives some hints on the optimal tariff and trade policy under alternative exchange rates systems. By and large, governments are usually committed to maintaining steady prices and low inflation rates. Therefore, the exploration of tariff reduction policies to preserve a high level of employment and equilibrated balance of payments, and eventually help ignite a trail of growth are always welcomed by businesses and communities. Considering a small country producing one main good with demand for its product depending on the exchange rate, we have that its balance of payments is simply given as

$$B=rX-M=0 \quad (2.58)$$

where B is the balance of payments, X represents exports, M stands for imports and r is the foreign currency unit expressed in domestic currency unit . The gross output including the tariff-inclusive price is expressed as

$$dY=dA+dX-d(Mp) \quad (2.59)$$

where A is the nominal absorption, p is the tariff-inclusive price of imports given as $p=(1+t)/r$ and $T=tM/r$ is the tariff revenue in terms of import M and the variable r. Imports depend on the price of domestic price of imports and the level of absorption and can be expressed as

$$dM = \frac{\gamma M dp}{p} + \frac{md}{A} \quad (2.60)$$

where m is the marginal propensity to import and γ is the elasticity of demand for imports. A is the nominal absorption but the real absorption A' is expressed as the difference between nominal absorption and the level of imports converted to the price of domestic produced goods

$$dA'= dA-Mdp \quad (2.61)$$

Differentiating p, T, r and A' and combining the equations from (2.58) to (2.61) we get four new expressions

$$dp = \frac{(x - 1 + mp - xmt)dt}{e} \qquad (2.62)$$

$$dT = \frac{[(x + \gamma - 1)p - x\gamma t]}{pe} \qquad (2.63)$$

$$dr = \frac{(\gamma - mp)dt}{pe} \qquad (2.64)$$

$$\frac{dA'}{M} = \frac{[\gamma - mp][1 + t(1 - x)]dt}{pe} \qquad (2.65)$$

where exchange rate, e, is given as $e=x+\gamma-1-tmx$ and $x>0$ is the elasticity of demand for exports given as $dX/X=-xdr/r$. Equation (2.62) shows that any increased protection causes the tariff-inclusive price of imports to rise or fall depending on the elasticity of demand for the country's exports (if greater or less than 1-m). Equation (2.63) gives the maximum revenue tariff, whereas equation (2.64) and (2.65) define the case when there is an increased protection that improves the terms of trade and may eventually at some degree raises each country's welfare (when the elasticity of import supply is assumed to be infinite). From equation (2.62) it derives that the impact of exchange rates depreciation with repercussions on the price of imports will be inflationary depending on the elasticity of demand for exports that is less than $t<(1-mp)$ and it will be deflationary if $t>1/(x-1)$ (Tower 1973, 441).

When we talk about commercial policy under fixed exchange rates, it means that authorities can interfere in the foreign exchange market. Under fixed exchange rates the introduction of a protective tariff is deflationary only if the elasticity of demand for imports is greater than 1. An increase of the protective tariff will raise the price that the private sector must pay for imports, causing an involuntary augment on spending, and as a result, the terms-of-trade effects being more inflationary than before and eventually worsening the balance of payments.

If elasticities of demand for imports and exports in the short-run are close to unity, the commercial policy under fixed exchange rates may be difficult to determine as it may involve output in a different direction and the effects on the balance of payments restriction on foreign exporters may be very uncertain. In few words, the commercial policy under fixed exchange rates is not the optimum solution for policymakers because of the difficulty of foreseeing its effect on output and the possibility of foreign retaliation for countries experiencing duties and tariffs such as import surcharges, etc. It is more plausible to use domestic fiscal policies that do not affect the international trade between partners and the outcome of output in respective countries directly.

Things change largely when the commercial policy is used under flexible exchange rates as the authorities do not intervene in the foreign exchange market. Therefore, setting the balance of payments $dB=0$ and taking into consideration the tariff-inclusive price increase of imports given as $p=(1+t)/r$, we have four cases given by four respective expressions using differentials (Tower 1973, 449): The first case and the first expression is when the revenue is spent at home

$$\frac{Rdp}{p} = \frac{(x - 1)(1 - a)dt}{1 + t} \tag{2.66}$$

where R is the revenue and a is the marginal propensity to absorb out of disposable income. The second case is when the revenue is acquired by foreigners,

$$\frac{Rdp}{p} = x(1 - a)dt \tag{2.67}$$

The third case is when the revenue is retained by government or distributed to the private sector,

$$\frac{Rdp}{p} = \frac{[(x - 1)[1 - a - amt] - ma]dt}{1 + t} \tag{2.68}$$

And the fourth case and expression is when the revenue is given to domestics,

$$\frac{Rdp}{p} = \frac{(x - 1)(1 - a)dt}{1 + t} \tag{2.69}$$

Expression (2.66) shows that when the revenue from increased protection is spent at home, it has an uncertain effect on the price of imports as it may rise only if the elasticity of demand for exports is greater than one. In the second case, (expression 2.67) when the revenue from protection is acquired by foreigners or non-residents, and the exchange rate is fixed, increased protection will be inflationary as it causes the price of import to rise, but it will be deflationary if the elasticity of demand is less than one. Assuming that the exchange rate is flexible the increased protection would have no impact on output. The third and the forth expressions (2.68 and 2.69) considers the case when the revenue is retained or distributed to the private sector (with trade-effects ignored), therefore when there is an increase in commercial protection it will be deflationary if the initial protection level is normally lower than the maximum revenue tariff (under flexible exchange rates). But if the trade effects on output and the possibility of foreign retaliation are considered, increased protection will be deflationary if the initial tariff is below the optimum revenue level (under flexible exchange rates).

Mundell (1961) analyses the effects on output when all tariff revenues are distributed as a neutral income subsidy, hence the real absorption depends on real disposable income. Mundell's increased protection improves the terms of trade, but it is deflationary if the initial level of protection is below the optimum tariff which is calculated based on the elasticity of reciprocal demand. Thus, commercial policy depends on the function that is fixed in real terms and is deflationary.

Many countries since WWII have opted for stable commercial policies able to improve economic welfare and preserve the multilateral trading system. Despite this, some economists and policymakers believe that the liberalization measures adopted by a range of countries, especially by some transition economies, remain dubious and very fragile. For example, during the nineties the Balance of Payments Committee of the World Trade Organization (WTO) reviewed 39 requests from member countries to temporarily suspend their international obligations regarding commercial policies as they were looking to increase protection for short periods on temporary bases. This was not good news for the process of globalization in developing countries, but at least it has a point. The process of globalization and liberalization is not so easy for some countries. It takes time, dedication and huge sacrifices for the economies of these countries, but at the end, if they can get to a competitive international market it pays back.

The new liberalization era that started at the beginning of the nineties in the transition economies of Eastern Europe made the domestic industry lose the competition and not perform well as a result of flexible exchange rates, high rates of inflation and insufficient growth in productivity. The incapability to put down inflation at an acceptable level or at least at the level of West Europe countries and the failure to lower the level of interest rates to boost domestic investments increased inflationary pressures in quite few transition economies of Eastern Europe. Consequently, there was extra stress added on governments to increase trade barriers, and each country was remedying somehow different alternatives of restricting the level of imports. But the delay in implementing higher protection for the domestic industry resulted in slow growth and slow recovery.

What happened to the Eastern European countries during the early nineties was that the initial high boom was accompanied by high inflation which followed e severe recession and the exchange-rates stabilization policies were not very successful as they were meant to be. Instead, in other transition economies where the starting point was a recession and a much lower inflation rate the recovery and growth were much faster. In both cases, where the exchange-rate-based stabilization was applied the transition countries were affected by the recession and thus there were calls from the private sector and domestic industries for more protection from the international competition.

The protection of the domestic industries in countries like Czech Republic, Slovakia, Bulgaria and Romania which started the liberalization process in the early 1990s declined considerably because of the introduction of the flexible exchange rate. Based on the study of Drabek and Brada (1998) it is not quite sure what caused the worsening of the trade performance. Was the decline of domestic industries and loss of competition or the attempt of these countries to offset the effect of their exchange rate policies with some consistent changes in commercial policies?

As emphasized by the research of Drabek and Brada (1998) the deterioration of the trade balance of the transition countries taken into consideration during the period 1992-1997 came mostly because of the appreciation of real effective exchange rate (REER). Just to mention few of them; the Czech Republic and Poland experienced a worsening in their trade of balance in 1994 which continued until the end of 1996. Slovakia's trade balance deteriorated between 1995 and 1997. Romania's trade deficit grew rapidly in the course of 1996 and by mid-1997. Bulgaria's trade deficit deteriorated sharply by the second half of 1996 and by the first quarter of 1997, it reached the highest level of deficit in a decade. Hungary instead, was the country that maintained a stable trade deficit for the whole period. The instability in their exchange rate policies was followed by instability in commercial policy. Therefore, import restriction policies were introduced to improve the balance of payments and protect the domestic industries from the international competition.

The Czech Republic in April 1997 introduced an import restriction policy in the form of foreign exchange deposits amounting to 20 percent. Later, under the pressure of the European Union and WTO and after relieving the competitive pressure on Czech industry, this deposit was eliminated. Bulgaria introduced an import surcharge in June 1996, and Romania had the import surcharge since May 1992. In the same way, Slovakia introduced an import surcharge in March 1994 which was eliminated by June 1996, but it was re-introduced in July 1997. Hungary and Poland introduced an import surcharge respectively in March 1995 and December 1992, and later it was eliminated by the end of 1997 in both countries.

Regarding the protection of specific core domestic industries, the transition economies of Eastern Europe introduced even more drastic measures. Slovakia introduced the quality certificates and import deposits, while Poland adopted measures to protect its car industry that was heavenly threaten by western automotive industries. Hungary and later Poland put in place some global quota on consumer goods imports like certain electronic products etc. Romania, instead, introduced a system of reference prices for six products in 1994 which was later changed to a new tariff for a larger range of products in 1995.

Summarizing, the increasing pressures to change commercial policies and the move to an increase in import restrictions for transition economies facing a competitive international market came mostly as a result of deteriorating trade imbalance related to appreciating real effective exchange rates, high inflation, and loss of international competitiveness.

Dynamic Adjustments of Exchange Rates

In the long-run, the movement of a flexible exchange rate usually follows the course of relative price levels. So, any increase in price levels of intermediate and finished goods in 3-8 years will make the floating exchange rate adjust to these prices. In the short-run, the demand and supply in the market of domestic and foreign financial assets along with the interest rates determine the rate of flexible exchange rates

The adoption of a system of flexible exchange rates by western economies in the 1970s spread a wide range of exchange rates volatility that was more than expected by the community of economists who strongly backed up such a system. The volatility of flexible exchange rates raised some questions regarding the stability of the system especially when there were exogenous domestic disturbances and in the case of allocation of domestic resources altering the relative prices. The instability of flexible exchange rates responds quickly to a domestic monetary disturbance in the very short-run where the prices of commodities don't have enough time to move to a new level of equilibrium by reflecting the new exchange rate.

Rudi Dornbusch (1976) – the German-born economist who spent most of his career working in the United States – was one of the first economists to have worked on this process called "overshooting" which is related to the exchange rate volatility in the short term. His work published in 1976 in the

Journal of Political Economy shows that in a regime of perfect flexible exchange rate a domestic monetary disturbance will heavily influence the exchange rate in the short-run when the price of all goods and services is still at their initial value rather than the long-run when the prices adjust to their new equilibrium values. As prices are sticky in the short run, they adjust slowly towards the long run equilibrium, but the financial markets adjust instantaneously.

Dornbusch model starts with a disturbance on the monetary market, like for example an increase on monetary supply which will decrease the interest rates in order to accommodate the excess supply of money because of the sticky prices. The fall in domestic interest rate is compatible with the new equilibrium in the nominal exchange change, but the households are expecting the nominal exchange rate to appreciate along the path that follows the long-run equilibrium. The expectation of appreciation helps the nominal exchange rate to over-depreciate (overshooting) as the domestic currency - which is undervalued because of the monetary disturbance - is expecting to appreciate in the future. These effects give to the process of overshooting an interesting sensitivity related to the demand for money and market sensitivity related to the expectations of deviations of the nominal exchange rate from equilibrium value.

In the long-run, there will be an adjustment as the excess of demand for commodities will push the prices up in the domestic market reducing in this way the real money balances and raising interest rates to its pre-disturbance level. Therefore, the Dornbusch model tries to explain the variance of the exchange rate exceeding the underlying fundamentals (like money supply) linking negatively correlated domestic price and exchange rate changes, in contrast to the expectations that the movements of these variables (domestic price and exchange rate changes) will be correlated positively.

The exchange rate dynamics on Dornbusch model rely on the rigidity of nominal prices. Sequent models following Dornbusch path are built on the more flexible environment and try to focus on dynamic adjustment obtained eventually by the reallocation of capital in response to change in investment returns. The dynamic system created in this way gives rise to the interrelation between resource allocation and exchange rate adjustments.

Another study done by Neary and Purvis (1983) describes the implications of the dynamics of the real and nominal exchange rates in the short and long-run supply responses in the face of exogenous shock. The contribution of Neary and Purvis (1983) emphasizes the many ways through which real disturbances rather than monetary disturbances influence the equilibrium of exchange rates. Neary and Purvis take into consideration a simply monetary model based on the nominal exchange rate (exogenously determined) in order to observe the effects of resource boom on the nominal exchange rate. The dynamics of the model consist of how the capital stock can be adjusted if there is a response on recognizing eventual changes in returns. Given that domestic and foreign nominal interest rates are related to the interest rate parity (IRP) condition we have that

$$i=if+e' \tag{2.70}$$

where, *i* and *if* are the domestic and foreign nominal interest rates and *e'* is the nominal exchange rate. Following the model of Neary and Purvis (1983, 299) we have that there are three goods, two traded goods (commodities, like raw materials oil or finished goods like vehicles) and one non-traded goods (services) and the demand for money requested by the public in real terms in equilibrium depends on real income and nominal interest rate.

$$m - p = \alpha\lambda - \frac{i}{\eta} \tag{2.71}$$

where m is the monetary demand, p is the domestic price index ,α is a parameter and λ is the elasticity of demand for capital. The domestic price index, p, can also be expressed as,

$$p=\beta ps+(1-\beta)e \tag{2.72}$$

where β is the spending of non-traded goods, and ps is the price index for non-traded goods. The money market equilibrium by using the real exchange rate and real income becomes,

$$m - e = \alpha\theta_v v - \frac{i}{\eta} - \beta\pi \tag{2.73}$$

where π is the real exchange rate, p is the price index written as $p=e-\beta\pi$ and y is the real income defined as $y=\theta\gamma\gamma$. The monetary equilibrium, as described above, determines the nominal price of traded goods, e, and of non-traded goods $ps=e-\pi$. The monetary equilibrium is depicted in Figure 2.2. For given values of π, m, v, the monetary demand is given by the upward slope line MM, which shows that an increase on e. creates an extra demand for money by simply reducing the supply of real balances, and an increase on i has the opposite effect to create an excess supply by reducing the demand for money.

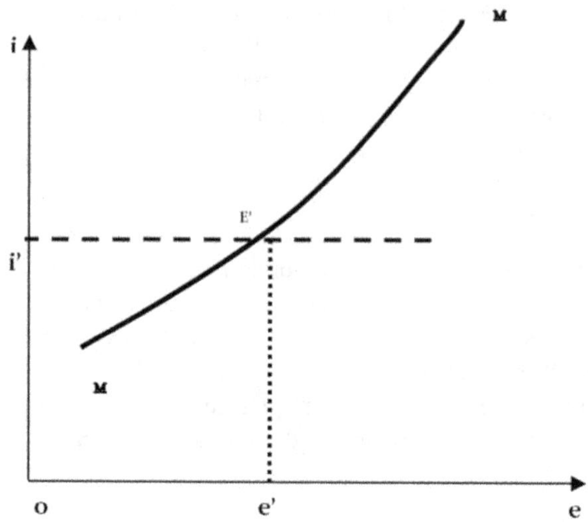

Figure 2.2: The monetary equilibrium and nominal exchange rate

The excess on the supply of money balances is located on the left and above of MM and, below and on the right of MM is the excess demand for money. Combining equations (2.70) and (2.74), putting $e'=0$ and indicating with e^* the nominal exchange rate we get the equilibrium on the long-run nominal exchange rates expressed,

$$e^* = m + \frac{i}{\eta} + \beta^* \pi - \alpha\theta_v v \tag{2.74}$$

where the coefficient m guarantees the neutrality of money.

The real shocks like resource booms have a strong relationship with monetary dynamics. A resource boom, as in the case of a rapid increase in the availability of the natural resources, can lead to increased demand for services and therefore to an increased demand for labor in the services sector. The resource boom can also lead to a boost of the national income but also can cause a proportionate increase in the demand for capital in the resource sector affected by this boom.

The resource boom can also cause a long-run appreciation and contributes to exchange rate variability. If a real shock happens, for example, a resource boom increase, it will have a direct effect on the exchange rates. Therefore, combining equation (2.73) with equation (2.70), we have that the exchange rate following a real shock evolves as

$$e' = \eta(e + \alpha\theta_v v - m - \beta\pi) - i_f \qquad (2.75)$$

The nominal exchange rate in the long-run solution can be expressed as

$$e' = \eta(e - e^*) + \eta\beta(\pi^* - \pi) \qquad (2.76)$$

The above equation, by using $\pi^* = -(b_1 / b_2)k_{M^*}$, can be written in a more suitable form as,

$$e' = \eta(e - e*) + \left(\frac{\eta\beta\varphi_L}{\psi}\right)(k_M - k_{M^*}) \qquad (2.77)$$

where φ is the fraction of capital stock, ψ is the aggregate level of wage elasticity of demand for labor, φL measures the labor intensity of manufacturing relative to services, and *kM** is the capital stock dynamically responding to a resource boom as *kM** = *-(b1/a)v.* A matrix form of equation (2.6.8) (2.77) can be written as,

$$\begin{bmatrix} -\phi_1 \ldots\ldots\ldots\ldots\ldots 0 \\ \eta\beta\varphi_L / \psi \ldots\ldots\ldots \eta \end{bmatrix} \begin{bmatrix} k_M - k_{M^*} \\ e - e^* \end{bmatrix} = \begin{bmatrix} k'_M \\ e' \end{bmatrix} \qquad (2.78)$$

where *Φ1* is the distributive factor share in the manufacturing sector, and the dynamic adjustment is given by a simple equation such as *k'M* = *Φ1(kM*-kM)*. The matrix (2.78) has two characteristic roots: μ1=- *Φ1<0* and μ2=- *Φ2>0* and shows generalized saddle-path stability as pictured in Figure 2.3. (Neary and Purvis 1983, 299-302)

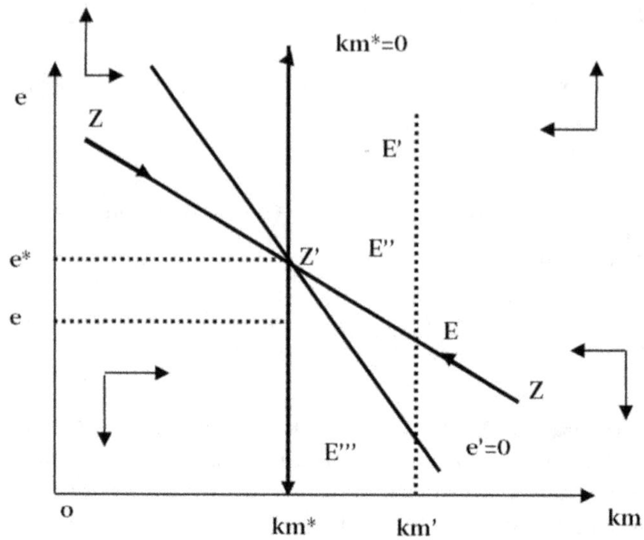

Figure 2.3: Nominal exchange rate and dynamic adjustment of manufacturing capital stock

The nominal exchange rate deviation, *e*, and the deviation of manufacturing capital stock, kM, from their initial equilibrium are linked as follows,

$$(e\text{-}e^*)= s(kM - kM^*) \tag{2.79}$$

where *s* comes from solving the matrix equation (2.78) and takes the form as

$$[s\text{-}1][-A+\eta I]=[0\ 0] \tag{2.80}$$

where A is the connotation of the transition matrix (2.78). Combining (2.77), (2.78) and (2.80), we have that, *s* can be written as

$$s = -\left(\frac{\eta\beta\varphi_L}{\psi}\right)(\eta + \phi_1) < 0 \tag{2.81}$$

Expression (2.81) shows us that the stable path *zz* is negatively sloped and any possible initial equilibrium position in *E', E'', E''* will move to point *E* from which will converge monotonically to Z.

Following a disturbance, which normally gives changes to the long-run equilibrium (kM, e^*), we can find the initial value of the nominal exchange in the short-run, e, by substituting s, kM^*, and e^* in expression (2.79);

$$e1 = e0 + \sigma v \tag{2.82}$$

where $e0$ is the initial value of the exchange rate, and σ is the short-run elasticity of the nominal exchange rate with respect to resource boom (Neary and Purvis 1983, 303). σ meets the condition;

$$\sigma = \frac{1}{a}(sb_1 + \beta b_2) - \alpha\theta_v <> 0 \tag{2.83}$$

where $b1$, $b2$ and a are parameters showing long-response of exchange rates and the sign of σ depends on the rise and fall of the exchange rate, e. A positive short-run elasticity σ, will make the exchange rate rise on impact while a negative σ will make the exchange rate decreases on impact reaching initial equilibrium in either E' or E" on Figure 2.3. The long-run reaction of the nominal rate is written as

$$e^* = e0 + \sigma' v \tag{2.84}$$

where σ' is the long-run elasticity given in a similar form as (2.83),

$$\sigma' = \frac{\beta b_2}{a} - \alpha\theta_v <> 0 \tag{2.85}$$

The long-run elasticity can also be expressed in terms of short-run elasticity on condition that the exchange rate on impact is below its long-run value, as shown by the negative slope of the saddle path zz in Figure (2.3) and is written as

$$\sigma' = \sigma - \frac{sb_1}{a} > \sigma \tag{2.86}$$

Following the Neary and Purvis (1983) model for the short and long-run elasticity, there are three possible cases. The first case consists when $\beta b2 < a\alpha\theta v$, then σ and σ' are both negative. In this case, there is a short-run overshooting as the short-run elasticity of the exchange rate is larger than the long-run elasticity of absolute value and the initial equilibrium would have been on E' in Figure 2.3. The second case is based on the condition that if $a\alpha\theta v, < \beta b2 < a\alpha\theta v - sb1$ then σ is negative and σ' is positive, which means that exchange rate on impact falls and then rises as it would appear from the initial equilibrium E'' on Figure 2.3. The third case is when both σ and σ' are positive when $\beta b2 > a\alpha\theta v - sb1$, which means that the exchange rate on impact rises and keeps rising during the whole dynamic adjustment as it would appear on initial equilibrium *E'''*.

Combining expressions (2.75) and (2.81) we have that the nominal exchange rate can be written in a dynamic form,

$$e' = \Phi 1(e^* - e) \tag{2.87}$$

which shows that the speed of adjustment of capital stock toward its steady equilibrium is determined by the speed of adjustment of the exchange rate toward its equilibrium value. Equation (2.87) illustrates the exchange rate adjustment that happens only under the rational expectations which by using expression (2.70) it can be transformed into arbitrage condition given as,

$$i + e\Phi 1 = if + e^*\Phi 1 \tag{2.88}$$

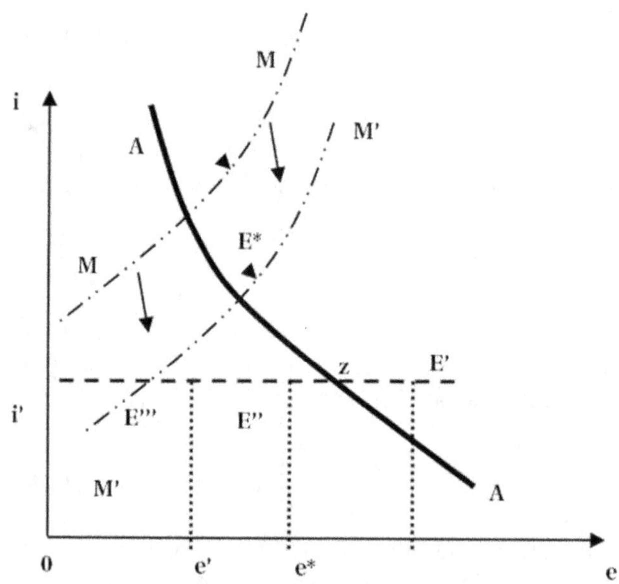

Figure 2.4: Monetary dynamics and the resource boom

Arbitrage condition is represented by the sloped curve AA in Figure 2.4. A resource boom can swing to the right or the left depending on the long-run effect on the nominal exchange rate. The domestic interest rate *i'* – when resource boom happens – will cause the nominal exchange rate to move to, *e'*, and the monetary demand *MM* will move to slope *M'M'*. The initial exchange rate equilibrium could be one of the points E', E" or E"' on Figure 2.4. The first initial equilibrium, *E"'*, corresponds with the overshooting of the nominal exchange rate. The second initial equilibrium happens in E", when the real exchange rate rises enough to offset the liquidity effect. And the third initial equilibrium *E"*, is the middle possibility as it takes place when the real exchange rate rise a little but not enough to offset the liquidity effect, where falls on impact and then rises in the long run (Neary and Purvis 1983, 304). The dynamic behavior of the nominal exchange rate proves strong dependence on the real exchange rate. Any influence of the market on the nominal exchange rate will put in place identical movements to adjust the prices toward their new equilibrium.

In Neary and Purvis model (1983) presented here as also explored in Neary and Purvis (1982), the real disturbances have implications on the exchange rate dynamics while the nominal disturbances which have a considerable effect on the nominal exchange rate would not influence the resource allocation and other variables. Both models of Neary and Purvis published in the distance of one year from the each-other show the implications and effects related to the dynamics of the real and nominal exchange rates in the short and long-period during boom resources considered as exogenous disturbances. The exchange rate overshooting results in Neary and Purvis (1983) is based on the real rather than monetary shocks, meanwhile in Dornbusch model (1976) overshooting process is based on monetary and not the real shocks.

Another characteristic of these two models is that in Neary and Purvis (1983) there is a slow adjustment of real variables like the intersectoral allocation of capital stock, whereas in Dornbusch (1976) there is a slow dynamic adjustment of nominal variables such as the money price goods, etc. It has also been noted that the dynamics of the nominal exchange rates in response to real shocks, in both Neary and Purvis models (1982 and 1983), have very similarities and are qualitatively equivalent to the Dornbusch's model (1976) which was based on domestic price rigidity and monetary shocks.

Credibility and Optimization in Monetary Policy

The monetary debate about the choice between fixed and flexible exchange rate in recent literature has assumed that monetary authorities can optimized a policy reaction function which can lead to a commitment perceived by the public as fully credible. Credibility, in the opinion of monetary authorities, is a fundamental issue that needs to be kept under control for a better design of monetary policy. This observation represents policymaker's attempt to optimize an objective that reflects the public preferences on both inflation and unemployment rate.

Monetary expansion policies designed to raise output and employment have as a countercyclical response the public dislike on inflation increase which threatens purchase power and monetary wealth. In fact, a rational policy maker in a given country might try to implement a monetary policy that will bring undesirable effects by leaving unemployment rate unchanged instead or reducing it and inflation being excessive. This result reveals the incapability of policymaker in charge of monetary policy to entrust the course of future actions in monetary matters.

This monetary aspect called 'monetary policy credibility', has been first described by a group of monetary economists such as Kydland and Prescott (1977) and Barro and Gordon (1983), and shows the reasons why during the 1970s and early 1980s the industrialized countries experienced stagflation. Kydland and Prescott (1977), in their pioneering study, believe that a credible monetary needs a commitment through legal measures or other procedures to limit the countercyclical and undesirable effects of monetary policy. This credibility model in making monetary policy is often called as the Kydland-Prescott, Barro-Gordon model. The objective of this model is to explain the timing and the extent of the effects of policymakers' actions given the current conditions and a correct evaluation of the end-period position. Once people form their expectations about economic conditions of the domestic market the policymakers' prediction is then conditioned by the expectation function of private agents.

Private agents normally are committed to nominal contracts in a given period before contracts come into effect. Employee representations and unions are focused on real wage, so they form the forecast of next period's inflation on nominal wages to be committed today. If forecasts are wrong, the real wages will deviate from their expectations. The unemployment rate, based on Keynesian standards, depends on the rate of inflation. Therefore, higher inflation than expected will increase the rate of employment, and on the opposite side, lower inflation than predicted will raise unemployment. Unemployment rate equals the natural rate of unemployment plus a negative inversely unexpected proportional inflation given,

$$U_t = U_t^n - \beta(\pi_t - \pi_t^n) \qquad (2.89)$$

where Ut is the unemployment rate of real activity and U_t^n is the natural unemployment rate, πt and π_t^e are the normal and unexpected inflation rates respectively (Barro and Gordon 1983, 592-96). The constant parameter β is the Phillips curve slope which depends on relative variances for general and specific shocks. Normally, a real disturbance zt, will affect the future natural unemployment rates, but here it is assumed that will disperse gradually over time, therefore will have no effect on the long run. The society sustains a cost of unemployment, *Ct*, that depends on period's value for unemployment rate and inflation, and takes the form as follows,

$$C_t = a(U_t - kU_t^n)^2 + b(\pi_t)^2 \quad \text{where a, b>0, } 0 < k < 1 \tag{2.90}$$

The first term of cost of unemployment equation denotes the departure of the unemployment rate from a target unemployment value, kU_t^n, which depends definitely on the natural rate (where k is the external effect and reaches efficiency when k=1). Government decisions on unemployment compensations and tax credits will influence the value of external effect, *k*. The efficiency level captured by government's optimization on the fiscal side consists in a value of *k*, that satisfies condition 0 < k <1, which helps choose the monetary policy as well (Barro and Gordon 1983, 594-96). Given the rate of monetary growth in the economy, the policymakers chose the normal inflation rate, *πt*, at each period to please society's preferences and minimize the expected present value of costs *Ct*. Expected present value of costs is characterized as,

$$E\left[\sum_{t=1}^{\infty} \frac{C_t}{(1 + r)^t}\right] I_0 \tag{2.91}$$

where *r* is the exogenous discount rate, and *I0* is the information available at the time of present value expectations. Policymakers and private-sector agents have high expectations regarding inflation and unemployment rate.

Each agent formulates its inflation expectation, π_t^e, for which he must take into consideration the policymaker's optimization dilemma based on the cost minimization problem (specified by equation 2.91) to determine the choice of the normal inflation rate, *πt*. It is assumed that future expectations of inflation, π_{t+1}^e, are independent of the current normal inflation rate *πt*. . Private agents will view the monetary authorities setting an inflation rate *πt*., based on the past information I_{t-1}, which is available at the beginning of period *t*. Therefore, inflationary expectations of policymakers is formed in accordance with a reaction function based on the past information given as,

$$\pi_t^e = p_e(I_{t-1}) \tag{2.92}$$

where $p_e(I_{t-1})$ is a reaction function of the private agents (Barro and Gordon 1983, 596). The reaction function above can be used to determine the rate of unemployment *Ut*. In fact, by using equation 2.89 and then 2.92, we have that the rate of unemployment is given as,

$$U_t = \gamma U_{t-1}^n + (1 - \gamma)U^n + \mu_t - \alpha(\pi_t - p^e(I_{t-1}) \quad 0 < \gamma < 1 \tag{2.93}$$

where μt is the real shock distributed with zero mean and influences the future natural employment rate. By substituting *Ut* and π_t^e in equation (2.90) the cost of unemployment *Ct* for period t is written as,

$$C_t = b\{(1 - k)[\gamma U_{t-1}^n + (1 - \gamma)U_n + \mu_t] - \alpha[\pi_t - p^e(I_{t-1})]\}^2 + c(\pi_t)^2 \tag{2.94}$$

Given the inflationary expectations in equation 2.92, the monetary authorities will select an inflation rate *πt* that will minimize the unemployment cost *Ct* given by equation 2.94. The first-order condition for the authorities who want to minimize *Ct* in the following period would be given by differentiating equation 2.94 with respect to *πt,* as

$$\pi_t' = \frac{d\theta}{d\pi_t} = \frac{b\alpha}{c}\{-\alpha[\pi_t - p^e(I_{t-1})] + (1 - k)[\gamma U_{t-1}^n + (1 - \gamma)U_n\} \tag{2.95}$$

which implies that $E(\mu_t | I_{t-1}) = 0$. The public is aware that policymaker cannot follow the inflation expectation given by reaction function in equation 2.92, but rather the inflation rate that satisfies equation 2.95. The unexpected inflation rate, π_t^e, using equation 2.95, leads to another form for the expectations function,

$$\pi_t^e = p^e(I_{t-1}) = \frac{\alpha b}{c}(1 - k)[\gamma U_{t-1}^n + (1 - \gamma)U^n] = \frac{\alpha b}{c}(1 - k)E_{t-1}U_t^n \tag{2.96}$$

The equilibrium policy can be reached if the monetary authorities, given the expectations on equation 2.96, chose an inflation rate, *π't,* from equation 2.95 that corresponds with π_t^e. The equilibrium equation is given as,

$$\pi_t^{'} = \frac{\alpha b}{c}(1 - k)E_{t-1}U_t^n = \pi_t^e \quad (2.97)$$

The equilibrium is based on the idea that private agents' perceptions regarding expected inflation are to minimize the expected cost of unemployment (*Et-1Ct),* which will make them choose $\pi_t^{'} = p^e(\bullet)$ in every period (Barro and Gordon 1983, 597). The choice of reaction function that minimize *ECt* for all periods is known as a particular inflation rate that takes into consideration the constant growth rate rule and is shown as,

$$\pi_t^* = p(I_{t-1}) = 0 \quad (2.98)$$

where unemployment rate at period t, *Ut,* depends on the term $\pi_t - \pi_t^e = \pi_t - p^e(I_{t-1})$. The government, through its own monetary authority, can easily deceive private agents and the public in general simply by reducing unemployment temporarily using an inflation rate that satisfies,

$\pi_t > \pi_t^e = p^e(I_{t-1})$ in a certain period. However, the monetary authorities may not choose to select a choice of inflation rate that equals the given expected inflation rate, or if they choose the inflation rate that equals the expected inflation rate, this does not happen or get adjusted automatically. There is a trade-off that exists between reduced costs of unemployment and increased costs from inflation.

The monetary authorities will retain satisfactory to choose the option regarding inflation as $\pi_t > \pi_t^e$ or $\pi_t < \pi_t^e$, so it can achieve a trade-off between the lower unemployment rate and higher inflation (and vice versa). But, if the level of excepted inflation π_t^e is high then the marginal cost of inflation will be offset by the marginal gain from tumbling unemployment. This equilibrium condition is given by equation 2.97. The type of equilibrium given in equation 2.98 is frequently referred as optimal but time-inconsistent, and the discretionary equilibrium in equation 2.97 is normally called suboptimal, but time-consistent (Kydland and Prescott 1977, 480).

The term "time-inconsistent" is normally related to policymaker's incentives to break away from the rule when private agents base their expectations that the rule will be followed. In some cases, the rules can be enforceable for policymakers, especially if they are committed to following a certain monetary policy, and in other cases, the commitments are not binding, so the optimization policy takes place period by period. In the "time-consistent" equilibrium the marginal benefit of having higher inflation is counterbalanced by the marginal cost when $\pi_t = \pi_t^e$.

The policymakers could fool around the private agents' expectations but is not in their interest to do so as the equilibrium is not optimal from anyone's perspective because it requires costly inflationary monetary policy with not much gain in output and employment. Even if monetary authorities commit their monetary policy to low inflation rate or close to zero, it is not optimal as it prevents policymakers from using monetary policy to stabilize the economy against supply shocks. But monetary authorities can commit its policy ex-ante to an optimal policy rule which is given as,

$$\pi_t = \frac{v_t}{1 + \chi} \tag{2.99}$$

where vt is an output supply shock and χ is a constant that weighs the cost of inflation relative that is suboptimal to output. This is called the second-best monetary policy since it does not eliminate the original distortion between the target and natural output levels.

Reputational equilibria are other forms of equilibrium that materializes when governments through monetary authorities relinquish on short-term gains for the sake of maintaining long term credibility in conducting monetary policy. Reputational models normally admit a multiplicity of equilibria and considerable coordination is required to achieve the most reputational equilibrium. Based on the behavior of private agents there are 2 options: the cooperative solution which generates $U_t = U_t^n$ and $\pi_t = 0$, meanwhile the non-cooperative alternative generates a period-by-period solution that produces a lower outcome as $U_t = U_t^n$ and $\pi_t = \pi_t' > 0$.

The first option can be chosen from period one and generates a favorable trade-off between low employment and high inflation. By selecting the cooperative solution for period one, where inflation is given as $\pi_t = \pi_t' > 0$, we have the best possible reaction given the expectations (Barro and Gordon 1983, 605). The second option for monetary authorities is when $\pi_t = 0$ in each period which leads to $U_t = U_t^n$ and $\pi_t^e = 0$. There is a short-term gain with the intention of achieving future cooperative outcomes. The main point of the credible monetary policy is the relation between current policy choices and consequent inflationary expectations.

The reputational equilibrium is reflected in the weighting of benefits from two types of behavior. There will be no reputational equilibrium if the theoretical one-period benefit from low unemployment prevails over the present value of the losses from higher inflation in future periods. The reputational equilibrium can be broken down by at least few causes.

First, the cooperative solution game rule cannot be sustained continuously until it reaches the final period because the breakdown can easily be transmitted to all earlier periods.

However, the reputational equilibrium can be persistent if there is a higher probability of termination that raises the discount rate to apply to results of future periods. A higher rate of discount reduces the benefits of low inflation in the long-term reputation compared to the gains of low unemployment in the short run. Therefore, a cooperative solution with a finite horizon makes the reputational equilibrium very difficult to sustain.

Second, the cooperative solution is not reached if option one of the cooperative solution becomes preferable to option two of the non-cooperative solution. An increase in the natural unemployment rate might reduce the short-run benefit of reduced unemployment as a result of present losses when the higher future inflation rate is taken into consideration.

Third, there is no direct relation between current actions, πt, and future expectations, π^{e}_{t+i}, unless there exists an enforced rule that links actual and anticipated values together. Monetary authorities would have the incentive to claim that inflation, unemployment rate and monetary growth were caused by previous administrations and would wish to announce the end of previous unbalances and restore trust on private agents regarding inflation and monetary growth as quickly as possible starting in the current/first period. Despite the difficulties, the reputational equilibrium must be sustained by formal rules which can generate acceptable outcomes in few fields.

Monetary growth and inflation are reflections of credibility and optimization in monetary policy within a given institutional regime. The intention of the pioneering research led by Kydland and Prescott 1977 and Barro and Gordon 1983 was to model the regular behavior of a monetary authority such as a central bank that determines the underlying rules of the game. The rules or equivalent commitments managed by monetary authorities are crucial in determining the behavior of inflation which can have implication on influencing other public policies by the government to stimulate stability and growth in the economy. The prediction of optimal monetary policy is based on the selection of a rule or its equivalent and the establishment of a strong national monetary institution that would guarantee stable inflation rates, which will have positive effects on the economy.

There is also a dissimilarity between monetary authorities' choice and efficient day-to-day operations within a given policy regime which is in a certain way related to economists' role as monetary policy advisers. It looks that national monetary authorities, especially in industrialized countries, are more concerned on day-to-day operations without changing the rules of the game within a policy regime, rather than on taking the proposals of monetary economists for eventually altering the underlying rules of the game and policy institutions. Therefore, the most general rule of policy advice from a central bank's perspective is to identify improvements in different monetary areas without changing policy institutions.

The Role of Central Bankers and Optimal Contracts

It has been a long tradition for the national government of developed countries to delegate the monetary policy to independent central bankers. The independent central bank will choose a central banker who has relative preference weight on inflation control and economic stability. In western countries and democratic societies, the government is elected by citizens, and the governor of the central bank is chosen by the government for a term of 3-5 years.

The government focus is based on finding a central bank governor from a pool of private and public banks that meets the criteria of such preferences by conducting a monetary policy that maximizes the government expectations (or the government function utility) on inflations and output fluctuations. In this context, the monetary policy of a sovereign country is related to a multilevel principal-agent problem. A study published by Rogoff in 1985 recommended the entrustment of monetary policy to an independent conservative central bank, called "weight-conservative" by putting more weight on inflation stabilization than the society as a whole does.

The objective of this section is how to determine the central bank monetary policy in order to induce a socially optimal policy. The research done by Walsh (1995) and Persson and Tabellini (1993), in the nineties, use the delegation of monetary policy from government to central bank as a principal-agent problem and recommends a contract for the governor of central bank whereby the control of inflation and price stability is the priority of the monetary policy. The Walsh's study (1995) was the first to consider the contracting approach to examine the central banker's incentive problem. Walsh's model demonstrated that an optimal contract for a central banker is achieved when there is a linear incentive contract in place that eliminates the inflation bias of discretionary policy.

The government will simply penalize the governor of the central bank by an amount that is proportional to the realized socially optimal monetary policy of inflation. In a similar way, Persson and Tabellini (1993) demonstrated that the credibility problem might be resolved by using a performance contract that enacts penalties by exceeding the pre-determined level of inflation on the central banker. Based on Walsh's model (1995) we consider an economy characterized by an aggregate supply function that gives the relationship between output and unexpected inflation as below,

$$y_t = y_c + a(\pi_t - \pi_e) + \eta_t \qquad (2.100)$$

where *yt* is aggregate output at time t, *yc* is the equilibrium level of output in the absence of supply shocks or when there is no anticipated inflation, *πt* is the nominal inflation rate, *πe* is the public's inflationary expectations, ***a*** is a positive constant that represents the effects of money surprise on output, and *ηt* is the rate of growth of nominal wage that meets public's expectation of inflation.

Assuming that government and central bank share same relative preferences over inflation and output shocks at each period and focusing on the nature of incentives offered to central banker, we have a quadratic central banker's loss function given as (Walsh 1995, 155,

$$L_t = \frac{1}{2}\left[\pi_t^2 + \varepsilon(y_t - y_e - k)^2\right] \qquad (2.101)$$

where *k* is a constant that represents the amount of output that excess the equilibrium output, and *ε* is a positive constant that gives the forecast and is considered as the weight of central bank with respect to output expansion relative to inflation management. The value of *k* must be positive because only in this way it will be provided with an incentive for a policymaker to attempt to create inflation surprises. It is assumed that the central bank has a zero target inflation rate. Substituting equation (2.100) to (2.101) the loss function assumes the form as,

$$L(\pi_t, \pi_{te}) = \frac{1}{2}\left\{\pi_t^2 + \varepsilon\left[a(\pi_t - \pi_e\right] + \eta - k^2\right\} \qquad (2.102)$$

The forecast of *ε* is proportional to the optimal response of the money supply. A positive aggregate supply shock increases output which in return causes the money supply to decrease in order to stabilize output. All 3 agents in this model, the government, the central bank and the public have a certain degree of knowledge regarding the distribution of the output shocks, but only the central banker knows exactly the magnitude of current shock. Given that objective function is quadratic in inflation rate and output an optimal inflation policy is a linear function in *ηt* that assumes a linear form, $\pi_t = \pi' + a_1\eta_t$, where the central banker knows the extent of the shock *ηt*. Therefore, to determine an optimal inflation policy the central banker needs only to govern the optimal inflation rate *π'* and the parameter *at*. Based on Barro and Gordon (1983) research, there are at least three kinds of monetary policies that can be chosen from the monetary authorities.

In the first case, the central banker is committed ex-ante to a policy rule of linear contingent inflation that meet the condition *πt* = *πte*. The role of the central bank is to choose inflation *π'* and the parameter *a1* to minimize expectations that are given as E [L(πt, π)] . By substituting *πt* and *πe* in the loss function 2.102, the optimal contingent inflation rule represented by *πr*, which minimizes the value of social loss conditional on the realization of *η* and the constraint that meets the condition $\pi_e = E(\pi_t) = 0$ is given as,

$$\pi_r = -\frac{a\varepsilon}{1 + a^2\varepsilon}\eta \tag{2.103}$$

In order to reduce the supply shock's effect on output and obtain the optimal outcome of output and inflation, inflation has to decrease with the supply shock. The expected social loss where the society reaches its desired socially optimal rule, *πr*, is given by the expression below (Tian G. and Huang K. 2011, 446-9),

$$E[L(\pi_{tr}, E\pi_{tr})] = \frac{1}{2}\left(\varepsilon k^2 + \frac{\varepsilon}{1 + a^2\varepsilon}\vartheta_x^2\right) \tag{2.104}$$

The value of *πtr* is optimal and gives the lowest social loss by carrying out this socially optimal monetary policy.

In the second case, it is assumed that the monetary policy rule is not credible if it is managed directly by the government or by the central banker whose objective function is given by 2.102. In this case, general public expects that the monetary authority will use the conditional rule *πr* so the expected inflation rate by private agents is $\pi_e = E(\pi_t) = 0$. An optimal inflation policy *πtc* chosen by central bank to minimize the value of the loss function 2.102 is given as,

$$\pi_{tc} = -\frac{a\varepsilon}{1 + a^2\varepsilon}(k - \eta) \tag{2.105}$$

And the expected social loss function has the following form,

$$E[L(\pi_{tc}, E\pi_{tr})] = \frac{1}{2}\frac{\varepsilon}{1 + a^2\varepsilon}(k^2 - \vartheta_x^2) \tag{2.106}$$

Equation (2.106) is lower in value compared to equation (2.104), therefore the central banker is motivated to be not credible by adopting a monetary policy rule with a surprise inflation rate given as,

$$\pi_c = E(\pi_{tc}) = \frac{a\varepsilon}{1 + a^2\varepsilon}k \tag{2.107}$$

In the third case, the government preserves direct control of the monetary authorities but cannot commit itself to a state-contingent rule. The public, under the assumption of rational expectations, does not believe that the central bank will use the contingent rule πtr. For given inflation expectations πte, the government choose πt for each period t to minimize the period loss function L. If the expected inflation is given by $\pi_{td} = E(\pi_{td}) = a\varepsilon k > 0$ which has an inflation bias on average, then the discretion rule is given as,

$$\pi_{td} = a\varepsilon k - \frac{a\varepsilon}{1 + a^2\varepsilon}\eta_t \tag{2.108}$$

And the expected social loss using the discretion rule is given by,

$$E[L(\pi_{td}, E\pi_{td})] = \frac{1}{2}\left[\varepsilon(1 + a^2\varepsilon)k^2 + \frac{\varepsilon}{1 + a^2\varepsilon}\vartheta_x^2\right] \tag{2.109}$$

which exceeds the expected social loss given by target equation (2.104) (Tian G. and Huang K. 2011, 448-50). With a target that exceeds the natural output level, discretion results reach the second-best equilibrium where there is an optimal state-contingent rule. If the ranking of expected social loss is given as,

$$E[L(\pi_{tc}, E\pi_{td})] < E[L(\pi_{tr}, E\pi_{tr})] < E[L(\pi_{td}, E\pi_{td})] \tag{2.110}$$

then, the central banker may be keen to deviate from the optimal policy if the time discount factor is not large enough and no additional pressure or cost is imposed on a central banker. This means that the economy would suffer from higher inflation with an even higher expected social loss. Therefore, a time-inconsistency problem will lead to a non-optimal socially monetary policy.

The central banker needs to be given additional incentives to apply the desired socially optimal monetary policy, otherwise, its monetary policy is not credible. Any additional incentive contract might be costly to use for a central banker. As in Walsh's model (1995), where the socially optimal monetary policy rule πtr satisfies the first order condition, and the contract is contingent on πtr and production shocks, the central banker, however, will be penalized even it has no reason to use non-reliable monetary policy. A large production shock ηt may require big contract cost and tax money to implement a socially optimal monetary policy. In this method, a contract penalty will be enacted when the reputation force alone is not big enough to prevent the central banker from not being honest by using the inflation bias of monetary policy, which will comport the loss of reputation.

If a contract can be used together with reputation enforcement from the public, it will be able to implement a socially optimal policy rule. A hybrid approach that put together the reputation approach and contracting approach is studied by Tian G. and Huang K. (2011). The result of this study recommends that if the reputation enforcement alone cannot explain the time inconstancy problem, then the contract cost of implementing a socially optimal inflation policy can be reduced by joining the reputational approach with the contracting approach.

Political economy problems and time inconsistency are the main approaches to designing the institution of a central bank. If the central banker and government try to use inflationary bias of discretionary monetary policy they must challenge a trade-off between inflation prevention and stabilization policy. If the contracting approach is used, the inflation bias will vanish without disturbing the stabilization policy. The Walsh contract (1995) is not optimal, as demonstrated by Candel-Sanchez F. and Campoy-Minarro C. J. (2004), because by changing one of the assumptions in the contracting approach, it disrupts the participation restriction of the central banker, and proves that the contracting approach does not eliminate the inflation bias totally.

The outcome is based on the supposition that government can enforce the contract on the central banker who violates the participation constriction assuming that the central banker keeps the expected inflation results, despite the reason that the central bank does not want to participate. Even in the case when the government has enough power to enforce the contract on the central banker who violates the participation constraint, this will not affect the central banker's incentives.

Special Drawing Rights and the Global Reserve Currency

The Special Drawing Rights (SDR) is an international reserve asset created by the IMF in 1969, during the dollar standard crisis, to supplement the existing official reserves of member countries and support the Bretton Woods fixed exchange rate system. The international supply of two key reserve assets - gold and US dollar – proved to be inadequate to support the expansion of world trade and satisfy the demand of capital markets. Hence, the major world economies decided to create a new international reserve asset under the direction of IMF. The SDRs are normally allocated to member countries in the proportion of their IMF quotas and serve as the unit of account of the IMF and other international organizations, and its value is based on a basket of core international currencies.

At the beginning, the SDR was designed as the equivalent of 0.888671 grams of fine gold that was equal to one dollar. In 1974, the SDR was redefined as a basket of currencies of 16 IMF members with at least 1 percent of world trade, which unfortunately proved to be inadequate as some of the currencies were not widely traded. In 1981, the valuation criteria were changed to include the currencies of the five members with the largest exports of goods and services in the previous years. The five currencies that formed the SDR basket were: the US dollar, the Japanese yen, the Deutsche mark, the French franc and the pound sterling.

In 1999 with the introduction of euro, the Deutsche mark and the French franc in the SDR basket were replaced with the equivalent amount of euro without changing the weight of replaced European currencies in the basket. Later in 2000, another criterion has been introduced to guarantee that currencies included in the SDR valuation basket are most widely used to make payments for international transactions and extensively traded in the principal foreign exchange markets. The SDR interest rate recently is set weekly on the basis of the weighted average of interest rates on the short-term instruments in the markets of the currencies included in the SDR valuation basket.

The SDR also has its limitations. Despite the initial intentions, until now the SDR has been used only as a reserve asset and its main function has been to serve as a unit of account of the IMF and some other international organizations. The SDR has not fulfilled its initial intended scope to become a major component of global reserves. The SDR is not a currency, nor a claim on the IMF, but rather a potential claim on freely usable currencies of IMF members. In fact, the holders of SDR can obtain the currencies that form the basket of the SDR in exchange for their SDRs mainly in two ways: first, through prearrangement of voluntary exchange plan between members in a regulated market; and second, by the IMF designated members with strong external positions to purchase SDRs from members with weak external positions. The SDRs cannot be used to intervene in foreign-exchange markets or in other transactions with participants which means that the SDR itself is not an attractive monetary unit for official reserves of central banks worldwide.

Despite the SDRs represents only a minimum portion of the world reserves, there have been a lot of efforts to promote its use in the private markets, but unfortunately with no results. The SDR is not a market-based asset issued by national entities, as it has always been administered and controlled by the IMF in every aspect, from its valuation and yield to whom may hold it and what it may be used for. Therefore, the value of the SDR and its yield is not determined by the market and does not respond to an excess of supply and demand pressures but simply reflects the changes on its underlined component currencies that form the SDR basket.

In 2009, during the 2008-9 financial crisis, the Governor of the People's Bank of China, Zhou Xiaochuan, made a proposal to promote the use of SDR as a sopra-sovereign reserve currency and to enlarge the SDR basket of currencies. He also suggested that the IMF member countries' reserve be part of the centralized management of the IMF over the formation of an open-ended SDR denominated Fund which would consent the subscription and the redemption on the existing reserve currencies by various investors. This proposal was backed by other countries, such as Brazil, India and Russia, that also supported the idea for a reform of the international monetary and financial system to increase global financial stability and eliminate economic disproportions. China has debated that since the global financial crisis of 2008-9 the US dollar-dominated international financial system has exposed investors to US risk, and there is a need to create a super-sovereign currency whose value does not depend on any particular country's economic performance (Bergsten F. and Subramanian A.,2009).

Although the Chinese proposal has not been accepted by the U.S. and the European Union, it has had possible actions for the use of the SDR as a reserve currency. The debate about this proposal has put in place a number of proposed actions:

- Reform of the IMF, regarding governance in terms of governing bodies, and majorities required for its activities to be carried out and the quotas of representation.
- Change the way the SDRs are allocated: by making the SDR issued automatically on regular bases; adjust total SDR issues on a counter-cycle way; and allocate the SDRs based on the need and not merely quotas; make IMF function like an international bank by providing liquidity to nations in case of shortage (Eichengreen B., 2009).

- Review the basket of the component currencies.
- Promotion of the use of the SDR in international trade, investment, corporate debts and the issue of SDR denominated securities.
- The establishment of a settlement system between the SDR and other currencies, allowing the SDR to become an accepted mean of payment in international financial transactions world-wide.

It is believed that IMF will be able to raise more funds if the U.S. open the market for the SDR-dominated securities. The issuance of the notes denominated in SDR would allow members to invest in IMF paper and offer a direct supplement to IMF resources for financial assistance to its members that could occur at the time of loan disbursement to a member. In September 2009, between China and the IMF was signed a note purchase agreement, for 32 SDR billion, which is the equivalent of US $ 50 billion.

There is another proposal, for the IMF, not only to be the issuer of the SDR denominated notes but also to support and act as a market maker in the initial phase of the SDR notes (Eichengreen B., 2009). If the SDR becomes an attractive unit in the market, the central banks around the globe will hold it as a reserve to ease their countries' international transactions and intervene in foreign exchange markets using the SDR units rather than core currencies.

A deep and liquid market in SDRs necessitates a critical mass of SDR issuance and a critical mass of trading, and also requires return rates comparable to those of the US dollar debt securities in order to make them attractive. The IMF should be ready to buy and sell SDR claims to all interested entities private or public at narrow bid/ask spreads competitive with those of the US dollar, subsidizing if necessary the market at the initial phase, until private market-makers would be able to provide those services at comparable costs. This is a similar process done by Fed of the United States in the 1920s when it started to buy and sell US dollar acceptances, backstopping the market. For the IMF, this monetary process requires a cost that all members should agree to support in order to establish a more balanced international monetary architecture.

If the IMF decides to create a market for SDRs and if the SDR becomes a global currency, it should also pay interest at a rate attractive enough to encourage its use as an investment for central banks' reserves. In addition, in order for the demand for SDRs denominated securities to grow it should be expected to have a positive difference between the market rates and theoretical rates. In theory, the different SDR denominated securities issued by different governments would show different spreads related to the associated ratings of the countries and/or corporate issuers, and we could expect a convergence of these interest rates once the market for SDR denominated securities is well established.

IMF decided on November 30th, 2015, after its Executive Board meeting to include the Chinese renminbi (RMB) in the SDR basket valuation formula. The effective date to join the SDR was set as October 1st, 2016 on the ground that Chinese currency is determined to be freely usable currency. The idea of including RMB as the fifth currency in SDR basket has been rumored for some time since 2010 when the previous review of SDR concluded that China, was qualified to be part of the SDR under two criteria: first, the Chinese currency was a major global exporter of goods and services; second, Chinese renminbi was deemed to be freely usable in the global market.

The Chinese renminbi inclusion on SDR is considered to be a natural consequence of China's economic progress and country's increased importance in global trade and capital flows. The IMF recognizes the new international economic environment where renminbi (yuan) plays an important role and where there is a growing global demand for yuan-denominated assets.

China has been pushing its exchange rate regime towards marketization since 2005, and it has fast-tracked the reforms since 2008 during the financial crisis, evolving a more liberalized offshore yuan market for all exchange rate related activities increasing also the number of agreements with international financial centers. For this purpose, the Chinese government has created yuan bond markets in Hong Kong, London and Singapore in order to contribute to the internationalization of renminbi (yuan) beyond the conventional trade and settlement value of the currency and towards the formation of a real reserve currency capacity. Furthermore, the Chinese government in 2014 created the Shanghai-Hong Kong Stock Connect in order to bring together the onshore and offshore markets.

The SDR basket weights before the SDR reform of 2016 were as following: U.S. dollar, 41,9%; Euro 37.4%; Pound sterling 11.3%; and Japanese Yen, 9.4%. The SDR basket weights after the SDR reform of 2016 were as follows: U.S. dollar, 41.73%; Euro 30.93%; Pound sterling 8.09%; Japanese Yen, 8.33% and Chinese Yuan, 10.92%. The figures 2.5 and 2.6 below show the SDR basket weights in pie percentages.

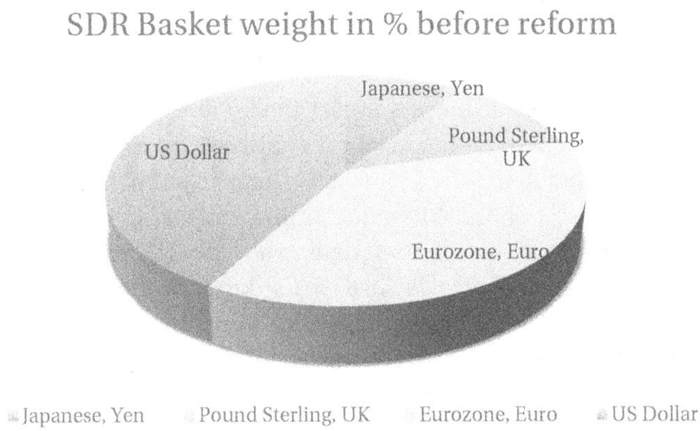

Figure 2.5: SDR Basket chart before the 2016 reform

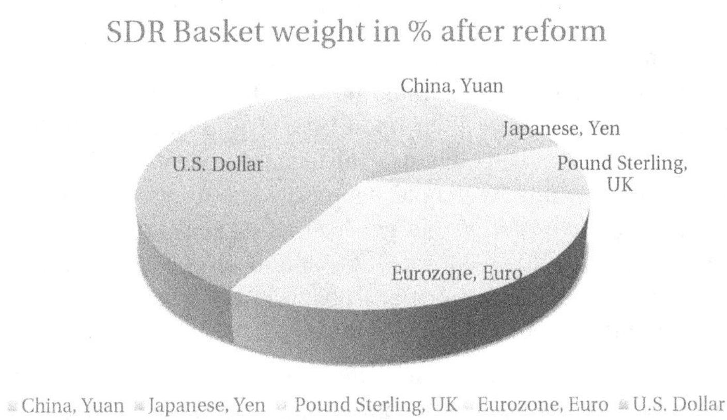

Figure 2.6: SDR basket chart after the 2016 reform including Chinese national currency.

The inclusion of the Chinese renminbi in the SDR basket with coming at the expense of euro, Yen and Pound sterling, keeping almost unchanged the U.S. dollar weight. The 2008-2009 financial crisis has further emphasized the urgency and the importance of the IMF reform to prevent issues such as the U.S. dollar inflation, large US deficits and the widespread worries about the risk of losses in the value of the reserve currency (Triffin Dilemma).

IMF reform includes the issue of SDR denominated bonds by IMF and Governments to be placed in the international market, with an interest rate attractive enough to encourage their use as an investment for central bank reserves. There is also the need for a supra-sovereign reserve currency to help reduce global imbalances and provide an adequate level of liquidity and the IMF to act as a market maker, at least at the initial phase.

The new global economic powers, such China, Brazil, Russia and India, have put more pressure since the financial crisis of 2008 for a new architecture of the international monetary and financial system, given that they have already acquired an increasing share of its value. China, for example, holds more than 1 trillion US dollars in its central bank and the US might not be in a comfortable position to have the use of its currency as the global reserve currency, and at the same time as the world's consumer and importer of last resort. The US position can be compromised if it depends on foreign investors to bail out its financial sector and finance large external deficits. Therefore, the proposal for a new global reserve based on the new international monetary system and SDR is still open.

Some Conclusions about Dynamic Adjustments under Alternative Exchange Rates

Mundell's idea in the late sixties of the last century was that with fixed exchange rates the authorities would have to abandon the efforts to expand the money supply because their open market purchases would be exactly offset by the sale of foreign exchange (currencies) in defence of the fixed rate, but with a flexible rate they could depreciate the exchange rate instead of depleting the reserves and would produce an export surplus. So, Mundell's approach (Mundell 1961, 1963, 1968) is that in a small country a coordinated combination of fiscal and monetary policy is the key to macroeconomic stabilization under fixed exchange rates.

Otherwise, a fiscal policy is not effective under flexible exchange rates because it will tend to expand income, which will increase the demand for money, raise the interest rate, bring capital inflow, appreciate the exchange rate, and replace the original expansion of income. Differently, from Mundell's view (Mundell R. A., 1963, 475-85), Johnson (1966), Jones (1968, 921-43), and Holmes (1972, 215-226) take into account the case of two countries (not more small countries as in Mundell's case, but two big countries such as US, Great Britain or Germany), and demonstrate that monetary policy had certain effects on all macroeconomic variables, but this is not true for fiscal policy changes. Without such knowledge, Holmes (1972) argued that the effects upon the direction of change in the exchange rate, if one country would expand its fiscal policy will be unknown. The same conclusion was obtained from the effects of fiscal policy on international gold flows under fixed exchange rates (Holmes 1972).

When capital inflows accelerate, the real exchange rate is under inflationary pressure and will appreciate through higher domestic inflation; therefore the central banks to avoid such consequences, especially during the 1990s, used the process of sterilization consisting on neutralizing the inflows by using offsetting open market operations. Such operations work well only in the short term, but not in the long term, for three reasons. First, sterilization would prevent domestic interest rates to decrease in response to capital inflows, attracting even greater capital in the short run. Second, sterilization tends to become less effective over time because the domestic financial markets are really small compared to international capital flows. Third, fiscal losses from intervention, arising from the difference between the interest earned on foreign reserves and interest paid on debt which is mostly denominated in domestic currency, will increase, so sterilization has a cost that sometimes can be considerable.

As capital inflows between countries increase, thanks to the growth of international trade, there is always a tension between monetary authorities' desire to contain inflation and a stable exchange rate. Given that the operations of the open market can do little to help monetary authorities to reach exchange rate stability, as they have only a limited impact in offsetting the monetary consequences of large capital inflows, different countries have adopted a variety of additional measures. In some countries, the authorities have raised the number of reserves that banks are required to maintain against deposits, or have widened the exchange rate bands for their currencies and allow a certain degree of appreciation.

A number of countries have put in place some protective regulations by limiting the banking sector's foreign exchange exposure. Meanwhile, such instruments have the capability to "adjust" the pressure on currency and ease inflationary pressure, none can be done to prevent an appreciation of real exchange rate completely. If monetary policy is locked by an exchange rate anchor, the burden, according to Mundell-Fleming model, falls on fiscal policy. But this is not always possible as policymakers who adjust fiscal policy in the short run should not be able to adopt a rigidly fixed exchange rate regime. A gradual and steady exchange rate appreciation by accommodating upward pressure would emerge as a better way and risk-free of maintaining long-run economic stability. In addition, policymakers, when they perceive necessary, can use their authority to influence market expectations by allowing the exchange rate to adjust in response to capital inflows.

Chapter 3

Determination of Exchange Rates Regimes

Introduction

The advocates of fixed exchange rates believe that exchange rates uncertainty makes international trade more difficult. After the world abandoned the *Bretton Woods* system of fixed exchange rates in the early 1970s, both real and nominal exchange rates became more volatile than anyone had expected. The volatility of flexible exchange rates has been attributed mostly to irrational and destabilizing speculation by international investors. Business operators often claim that this volatility is harmful because it increases the uncertainty linked to business operations. Nonetheless, the volatility can be helpful if there is a continued presence of authorities in the market to calm the expectations of private participants independently of the volume of official transactions. The supporters of fixed rates argue that a pegged rate is the last barrier to inflation since the need to maintain the peg constrains excessively expansionary fiscal policies.

The advocates of flexible exchange rates respond that the private speculators have the superior ability to predict the future; therefore the success of these speculators will enable them to accumulate enough financial resources so they can continue the stabilizing intervention in the market. They also argue that political factors may constrain the central bankers from changing the peg when they wish, so, a continually moving market-determined rate may conduct to allocate efficiency than a fixed over-valued or under-valued exchange rate.

Flexible rates are preferable to pegged rates in terms of utilization as they are sometimes more convenient for investors and policymakers but pegged rates may be preferable in terms of efficiency. According to Aliber (1972, 432-441), this argument involves the comparison of the long-term yield differential under the two exchange rate systems. In fact, if the long-term yield differential is no greater under floating rates than under the pegged rates, floating rates are preferable because of their utilization advantage. For monetary authorities there is not such a simple thing to decide which is the best choice; a purely fixed exchange rates, a purely floating exchange rates, or a range of choices with varying degrees of flexibility that can help internal and external stability.

There is also an intermediate regime between pegging and floating called "managed to float" [1] and countries that use it have, let say "fear of floating". This intermediate regime included the adjustable peg under which a country would normally have fixed exchange rates but reserved the right to change the system in extreme circumstances (as in case of fundamental disequilibrium). In the sixties and seventies, this monetary regime was vulnerable to speculative crises although the system was designed to have enough flexibility to avoid the misalignment assuring the authorities about exchange rate stability (Williamson J., 1965).

The choice of the fluctuation of national currency was prevalent in Latin America in the 1970s but, in the long term, this was not able to defeat currency crises associated with very high price increases. Since the 1980s, the IMF has encouraged countries in Latin America and the Far East to use currency systems based on limited exchange agreements (*pegging*) with the continents' key currency, respectively the dollar and yen. However, no preventive measures were envisioned to protect the currencies. The system of pegging to the key currencies also underwent a crisis in the mid-1990s: the most serious episodes were in Mexico, Argentina, Brazil and, later, in the major countries of South-East Asia, Taiwan, Malaysia, Indonesia and Singapore. This chapter will be focused mainly on the monetary debate among economists on fixed versus flexible exchange rates that have gone on for decades without having a "winner".

Monetary Policy Coordination and Exchange Rates

At the end of the 1960s, when the *Bretton Woods* system was in crisis, the popular opinion moved in favor of flexible exchange rates. Milton Friedman, from the Chicago School, was one of the first economists to assert that the only motivation behind variations of exchange rates was the differential of inflation and that flexibility was necessary in order to maintain the Purchasing Parity Power (PPP). According to Mundell,

> " ...Frank Graham, Charles Whittlesey, James Meade and Milton Friedman, writing independently in the 1940s and 1950s, brought the case for flexible exchange rates into modern literature, but for very

---

[1] The intermediate system or "managed floating" is called also the system of BBC regime where BBC stands for Basket, Band and Crawl. For more see (Williamson 1996) and (Dornbusch and Park 1999).

> different reasons: Graham and Whittlesey wanted to decouple the dollar from gold to prevent what they called the "Golden Avalanche". In the post-war world, Friedman argued for flexible exchange rates as a preferable alternative to exchange controls, and Meade argued for flexible exchange rates as a means by which a socialist government could better manage Britain's economy."
>
> [Mundell 2001, 14]

For the most part, the economists who advocate for flexible exchange rates agree at least on two main points: First, a flexible exchange rate carries out the regular variations of the exchange rate, which is not always connected to *overshooting* and does not create problems for the real economy.

Second, a variation of exchange rates is simple and more practical than a variation of a million consumption prices (sometimes the rigidity of prices need long and heavy adjustments from the supply side).

The switch to flexible exchange rates, which happened in 1973, involved a degree of unforeseen instability. If the assumption of Purchasing Parity Power (PPP) was verified and the variations of exchange rates compensated for the differential of inflation, we would have a relatively constant real exchange rate or at least exchange rates characterized by a regular course. But in reality things were different; the cause of exchange rate variation is often connected to competitive structural changes in the economy. From an economic standpoint, the real exchange rate in equilibrium changes, but these changes are not very frequent and sometimes continue for a long time. In practice, the real exchange rate oscillates, so there are periods of appreciation followed by a return to the initial position of PPP. This indicates that the real exchange rate does not always correspond to fundamental structural changes. These oscillations can also be presented as the product of monetary forces or *overshooting*. The flexible exchange rate is very volatile, especially in the medium term.

The thesis against fixed rates proves that we do not really know the exact value of the exchange rate. This implies that those who are called to address the exchange rates of one country do not always have a solid basis for fixing and defending the right parity. The overvaluation or undervaluation of fixed exchange rates often results from political pressures; an argument that in the absence of a clear rule for the fixation of the parties, monetary authorities probably base their decisions on political convenience.

At the beginning of 1970s the United States gold reserves had fallen to the lowest level since the end of World War II, while Europe's western countries held a consistent stock of gold higher than that of U.S. The bulk of this enormous shift of gold from the United States to Europe was done in the late

1950s and early 1960s. In less than 20 years the United States had lost two-thirds of the reserves of gold it held at the end of the war. So, the anchored dollar standard was in crisis, and the US policy government was not able to govern at the same time its reserve ratio and the international monetary system.

Europe somehow managed to control the world rate of inflation by pressure put forth on the composition of the US balance of payments. In fact, as Mundell recalls, in the 1960s the U.S. and Europe were on a collision course with respect to the international monetary system, — what Prime Minister Harold Wilson of U.K. called a "monetary war" (Mundell 1997, p.7). The international monetary system was in difficulties in the late 1960s by the U.S. expansionist financial policy as a consequence of the war in Vietnam and also as the consequence of financing welfare states policies. Correspondingly, the fixed exchange rates system imposed high inflation rates in Europe and also massive speculation.

The slide to flexible exchange rates in 1971, after systemic crisis and the inconvertibility of the dollar, did not come as a result of international conference agreement (as in the case of Bretton Woods) or IMF decision but was a unilateral action of the United States when President Nixon took the dollar off. Then the major western countries took their currencies off the dollar. Although, from a political standpoint the agreement to move to flexible exchange rate was a decision made in 1973 by three men coordinating their countries' respective monetary policies on exchange rates; George Schultz, US Secretary of the Treasury, Giscard d'Estaing, Minister of Finance in France, and Helmut Schmidt, Minister of Finance in Germany. George Schultz was a distinguished labor economist and had been a colleague of Milton Friedman at the University of Chicago in the 1960s, and later become Secretary of Treasury in Nixon's cabinet (Mundell 2001, p. 15).

After the monetary crisis in the 1970s, industrialized countries used to meet every year, beginning in 1975 to coordinate their monetary policies regarding world economy and monetary problems. The first "appointment", was the summit of the Group of the five (G-5) which included the leaders of the United States, Japan, France, Germany and the United Kingdom. Italy and Canada joined one year later, and in 1998 Russia formally joined also the Group which became the Group of Eight (G-8). The Group of Eight G-8 continued until 2014 when it becomes the Group of Seven (G-7) because Russia was suspended due to tensions with Western countries over annexing Crimea in March of that year.

In addition, we saw other groups, like the G-10 group, and then G-24 which included some big third world countries. The G-77 group was made mainly of third world countries. The most important group was obviously G-7, made up of the most industrialized countries of the world. These countries play an important role in the world economy in terms of real GDP and political decision. The industrialized countries of G-7 and big third world countries of the G-24 group are pledged to maintain a tidy course of foreign exchange rates.

Three are the principles of cooperation and coordination arrived at during these summits:

The first one was that there are to be no objective values for exchange rates, the PPP and other values given the difficulty of trying to get the exchange rates under control.

Second, international monetary cooperation is destined to diminish variations in exchange rates, but not to eliminate them. Monetary authorities, in general, would accept whichever exchange rates of the long period that the markets will consider more appropriate, but would prefer to approach it slowly.

The third principle was that the central banks of industrialized countries are pledged to intervene in foreign exchange markets in a coordinated way, if necessary. In the last twenty to thirty years central banks have intervened at various times simultaneously and massively, to put foreign exchange markets under control. In some cases, they have been able to stop or at least slow down strong oscillations of exchange rates, meanwhile in other cases, other attempts have failed.

Furthermore, extensive international economic and monetary cooperation has carried out the creation of monetary areas on a regional scale. In this regard, I can mention the creation of the European Union and the success of the euro (at least before the crisis of 2009-2012) which is the fruit of a long period of cooperation, economic and political integration that began over sixty years ago. Despite all these achievements, there is still much more work to do to affect and improve the coordination of international monetary policies that can help ease the economic and monetary crises around the globe.

It is also reasonably true that there are qualitative benefits of coordination due to the cross-border spillovers, which could reach higher levels in crisis situations as coordinated actions to provide stronger stability than the sum of uncoordinated individual measures. The development of the global economy since the North Atlantic financial crisis in 2008 has emphasized the main role the monetary policy in the reserve-currency countries has on the rest of the global economy. Considering the cross-border spillovers, there is an on-going monetary debate about the benefits of coordination of monetary policy among the major central banks worldwide. The general opinion on this topic is that there is no direct benefit from international coordination of monetary policies, therefore the global economy is better off if central banks focus on their respective domestic inflation and growth objectives.

On this context, the contribution of Obstfeld and Rogoff (2002) indicate that standard open-economy models envisage that under normal conditions gains from coordination relative to self-oriented policies pursuing domestic policy objectives are likely to be minor. Despite the study done by Obstfeld and Rogoff, the conclusion is not contradicted by increasing economic and financial integration. In order to avoid the deteriorating of global economy especially in the aftermath of the Lehman collapse in 2008 in the United States, the G-20 leaders at their Washington Summit on November 15, 2008, agreed to the need for a broader policy response and macroeconomic cooperation to restore growth and stability worldwide avoiding negative spillovers.

The G-20 Leaders' meeting let to a number of initiatives to strengthen financial sector which included the establishment of the *Financial Stability Board* (FSB) on April 2009 (London Summit 2009) to coordinate the work of national financial authorities and international standard setting bodies to develop and promote the implementation of effective financial sector policies. The G-20 summit of 2009 led the world leaders to pledge extra resources available to the IMF to reach the staggering amount of US$ 750 billion and to support the new SDR (Special Drawing Rights) allocations of US$ 250 billion, and another US$ 100 billion of additional lending for the multilateral development banks.

Despite there is an ongoing discussion regarding the international monetary policy coordination, the traditional view of domestically-oriented monetary policies is still seen as the optimal monetary policy although there are calls for a re-assessment. Given that there is no regular coordination among the major central banks on monetary policy, there is a deal of debate that transpires among major central banks at various international forums. The main international forum for such discussions is the Bank of International Settlements (BIS) that promotes international cooperation among financial and monetary officials, by hosting bi-monthly meetings of central bank governors and deputy governors. The BIS bi-monthly meetings are held in Basel, where central banks and deputy governors discuss the current development of monetary policies and the outlook for the global economy and financial markets.

The matter of international monetary policy coordination or the lack of it by the main central banks such as US Fed or ECB has attracted a lot of attention in the economic literature. According to Buiter (2014) and Eichengreen (2014) the most powerful central bank in the world, the US Fed, needs to acknowledge that any change in its monetary policy has substantial spillovers on other economies. The US should negotiate permanent dollar SWAP facilities with major emerging economies in the same way it has done with the advanced economies to avoid negative spillovers.

In the aftermath of the 2008-9 financial crisis, the unconventional monetary policy has been uncoordinated. In fact, with the constraint of the zero bound on policy interest rates, central banks of the advanced countries, guided by US Fed, had turned to unconventional monetary policies to provide more monetary accommodation through the quantitative easing (QE) by using large-scale asset purchase (LSAP) policies to reduce the long-term interest rates in order boost the economic activity. Due to this monetary policy, the balance sheets of the central banks have expanded significantly in an uncoordinated manner led by the US Federal Reserve.

The US Fed, the Bank of England, the Swiss National Bank have triplicated and quadrupled their respective balance sheets between the end of 2007 and the end of 2012. The balance sheets of the European Central Bank and Bank of Japan have expanded rather moderately by around 55 and 87 percent respectively during the same period. The ECB's balance sheet had by the end of 2012 more than doubled compared to the mid-2007, as seen in Figure 3.1. If taken together, the combined balance sheets of the US Federal Reserve, the ECB, the Bank of England, the Bank of Japan, and Swiss National Bank have more than doubled in a period of about 6 years (2007-2013) reaching the consolidated total amount of US$ 10 trillion in August 2013.

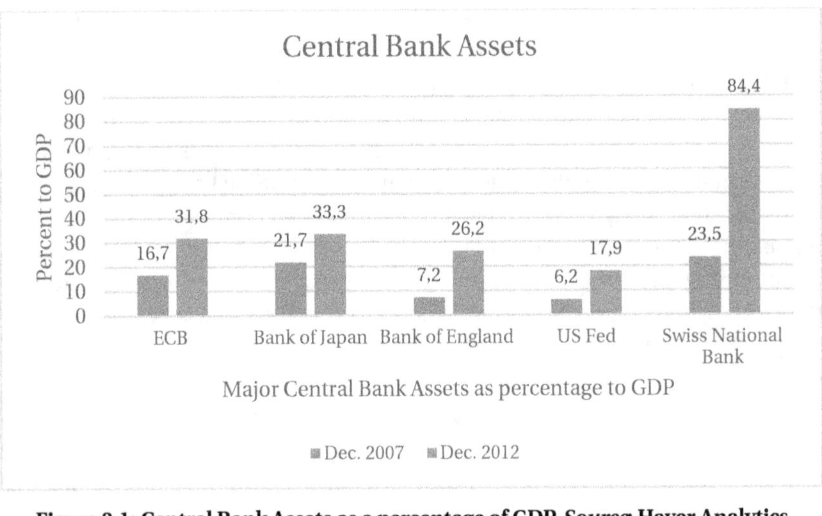

Figure 3.1: Central Bank Assets as a percentage of GDP. *Source*: Haver Analytics Database, 2013.

On the other side, talking about monetary policy coordination, it has been a higher degree of coordination among major central banks regarding the provision of liquidity through swap facilities. In 2008, after the sub-prime crisis, due to concerns about credit risk and to keep the inter-bank funding in US dollars flowing, the Federal Reserve entered into US dollar liquidity lines with ECB and Swiss National Bank. The swap facilities were later extended to other 12 major central banks in a coordinated manner. The US Federal Reserve boosted the available swap line liquidity from US$ 67 billion in December 2007 to the US $ 620 billion in early October 2008.

Similar arrangements have been explored by central banks through the G-20 summits with the assistance of IMF, by using risk mitigation measures to protect the reserve currency in possession of central banks from potential losses that could arise from the extension of swap facilities involving currencies that are not freely convertible. Therefore, increasing coordination among monetary authorities around the globe could do much to actually curb the volatility of the financial markets and exchange rates and stabilize the capital flows in advanced and emerging economies.

Political Choice and Exchange Rates Regimes

Economic theory does not give any unequivocal indication on the best currency system, and probably the best answer is that it depends on the country's external and internal circumstances. There are reasons that support both a currency system based on exchange agreements and a system of free currency fluctuation. Historical experience shows that neither one nor the other can offer absolute guarantees against currency crises. Scholars of classic free-trade inspiration, such as Friedman, tend to be in favor of a fluctuation system of currencies as it does not oblige the monetary authorities to intervene, it does not expose them to the risk of depleting reserves and leaves the task of determining the rates of exchange compatible with the equilibrium of the balance of payments to the currency market. Economists in favor of the regulation of the international system, such as Robert Triffin, Nicholas Kaldor, Susan Strange, put the instability of the currency market to the fore, finding the remedy in fixing exchange agreements, but at the same time arranging for support for countries that have to overcome phases of deficit in their balance of payments.

Historically, most of the economists have favoured a system of floating exchange rates; even Keynes was for flexible exchange rates principally at the western economies like the United Kingdom, United States, France or Germany able to influence the world monetary stability. Other renowned economists who favoured the floating system were James Meade in Britain and Irving Fisher in the United States. Meanwhile, Milton Friedman from the "Chicago School" was one of the first economists to assert that the only motivation behind variations of exchange rates was the differential of inflation and that flexibility was necessary to maintain the Purchasing Parity Power (PPP). The interesting point is that a flexible exchange rate follows more a random walk, rather than a pattern or an equilibrium level, which normally tends gradually toward relative purchasing power with half the adjustment being completed within a medium-term under 5 years (Rogoff 1996). In recent decades, some other prominent economists like Robert Mundell, have advocated a return to fixed exchange rates.

The principal argument in favor of a floating exchange rate is that it allows monetary policy to be used for other non-monetary purposes. Policy makers are free to use monetary supply for other macroeconomic policies such as stabilizing employment, inflation and economic growth.

Instead, under fixed exchange rates regime monetary policy is pegged to the single goal of maintaining its announced exchange rate. Advocates of fixed exchange rates argue that floating exchange rate is vague and uncertain especially if it is taken into consideration during a given period of time and makes the international trade more complicated and subject to limitations by national authorities. The end of Bretton Woods system of fixed exchange rates in the early 1970s, brought quickly big changes to the real and nominal exchange rates as they became more volatile than monetary authorities had predicted.

In part, this volatility was attributed to irrational and destabilizing speculation by international investors and brokers as they were trying to make big earnings given the new opportunity to use flexible exchange rates. On the other side, business operators started arguing that this volatility was dangerous because it tends to increase the uncertainty associated with international business transactions. Despite this exchange rate volatility, the amount of world trade has continued to increase under floating exchange rates.

The thesis against fixed rates asserts that we do not really know the exact value of the exchange rate. This implies that those who are called to address the exchange rates of one country do not always have a solid base for fixing and defending the right parity.

Advocates of fixed exchange rates regimes sometimes argue that a commitment to a fixed exchange rate is one way to discipline the monetary authority and prevent excessive growth in the money supply. There are many other policy rules to which the central bank could be committed. Fixing the exchange rate has the advantage of simplifying the implement for policymakers since the money supply adjust automatically, but this policy leads probably to greater instability in income and employment.

According to Williamson (1999), there are at least four conditions to satisfy when a country decides to introduce a fixed exchange rate. The first condition is that the economy must be small and very open to international trade which will help to be absorbed by a larger currency area. The second condition is that a country must use a fixed exchange rate with his major trading partners which on return plan to peg their currency. The third condition is when the country wishes to follow a macroeconomic policy which consists of an inflation rate consistent with the country to whose the currency plans to peg. The fourth condition is when the country is prepared to take on institutional arrangements that will assure continued credibility of the fixed rate commitment. If these conditions based on Williamson's study are not satisfied, it is much better to choose other monetary flexible systems that allow a certain degree of flexibility on the exchange rates.

The choice between floating and fixed rates regime is not as simple as it may seem at first. Countries using fixed exchange rates can change the value of their currency if maintaining the exchange rate conflicts too severely with other goals. During periods of floating exchange rates, countries often use formal or informal targets for the exchange rate when deciding whether to expand or contract the money supply. Otherwise, we rarely observe exchange rates that are completely fix or completely floating. In both monetary systems, the stability of the exchange rate is usually one among many of the monetary authorities' objectives (for many economists it is also a political choice).

There is also a range of intermediate monetary regimes that are collocated between fixed and flexible exchanges rates. Some of them are the adjustable peg regime, the managed floating system and crawling bands or monitoring bands regime.

The adjustable peg regime is when a monetary system has a fixed exchange rate in the short term, but the government or the monetary authority maintains the right to alter it if the circumstances indicate a change is needed to keep the economy stable.

The "managed floating" system which is intermediate regime between pegging and floating seems to be better than a fixed rate or a freely floating rate, and better than a lightly managed rate. But there are three reasons suggested by Williamson (2000, p.1-13) that such a system is likely to be inferior to a more structured regime. First, the regime is not quite clear as it is complicated for the public to know whether the policy being pursued is indeed one of seeking to limit disarrangements from a sensible estimate of the equilibrium rate. The second inconvenience of managed floating is that it prevents some types of policy cooperation, and may definitely allow monetary policy conflict as competitive targets or competitive depreciation. As Williamson writes,

> "...a clear example of the type of policy cooperation that might make sense but that would be precluded by a managed float is a peg to a common basket, which I have argued would be attractive in East Asia in order to avoid competitive devaluations, given how competitive those economies are with each other. The sort of policy conflict that would not be constrained is competitive devaluation, i.e., each of several closely competitive countries seeking targets for their exchange rate that give them a competitive edge over their rivals..."
>
> [Williamson. J., 2000, p. 6]

The third weakness of a non-structured managed floating is that sometimes there is no declaration of the parameters leading the management of exchange rates by monetary authorities. For example, the expectation of authority intervention at the margin should make operators and speculators act in a stabilizing way although practically not always happened so. It is very probable that speculators act in a destabilizing way and potentially the managed floating system might create series problems to the stability of exchange rates.

A crawling band regime is when the monetary authority of a country (central bank) is committed by the public obligation to keep the country's exchange rate within a wide band around a parity that is regularly adjusted to maintain it in line with a competitive exchange rate. The "crawl" is usually the inflation differential, and the central bank has to ensure the market that inflation does not get out of the width of the band which is something like +/– 10% around parity, and the band is adjusted slowly or in small steps (Williamson J. 1999. p.4). The crawl facilitates the countries to adjust their balance of payments and help the current account adjustments by appreciation or depreciation depending on the positive or negative internal and external shocks. Table 3.2 presents cases of crawling band exchange rate regimes for some countries that mostly have used it from the early 1990s.

Known Cases of a Crawling Band Exchange Rate Regime

	Period	Band Width	Anchor Currency
Chile	1989-present	+ 15%	Basket
Colombia	1991-present	+ 7%	US$
Israel	1991-present	+ 7%	Basket
Indonesia	1997	+ 6%	Basket (de facto US$)
Ecuador	1995-present	+ 5.5%	US$
Russia	1996-present	+ 15%	US$

Table 3.2 Source: Williamson (1999).

The crawling band, like all other exchange rate commitments, are normally defended by the central bank intervention when the exchange rate gets close to the edge of the band. Sterilization and capital controls seem to be some of the main tools used by the central bank to defend the crawling band. The sterilization tool is generally used when the central bank has perceived an undesired inflow and decides to sell government bonds on the open market to keep the money supply constant. Capital control is another instrument used by central banks to keep obligatory reserves against short-term foreign loans.

Another alternative of the crawling band regime is the "monitoring band regime". This regime was studied and initiated for the first time in India in 1997 by a committee of international monetary professionals that generated the so-called the *Tarapore report* in order to establish an appropriate capital account convertibility for a big open economy like India. The monitoring band regime is more relaxing than the crawling band as it does not engross an obligation for the central bank to defend the edge of the band. The central bank has a higher degree of flexibility in deciding when to intervene. It will interfere if the rate gets far away from the band. The flexible intervention policy is often utilized to ensure the market that the central bank can employ policy tools to protect the band regime if the exchange market is driven by herd behaviour.

The intermediate monetary regimes such as the managed floating system or crawling (or monitoring) bands appear for different reasons be more preferred than fixed or flexible exchange rates as they give to monetary authorities extra degrees of freedom in policymaking.

Some Notes on Exchange Rates and Currency Crises in Open Economies

I have found useful and interesting for quite some time to know something more about the link between exchange rates and currency crises. Regarding monetary and financial crises, in the modern literature, there are at least three main types of crises: banking crisis, debt crises and currency crisis. Bank crises are developed if two key conditions are met (according to Reinhart and Rogoff 2011, and Leaven and Valencia 2010): first, the banking system is hit by financial distress as a result of significant bank runs, losses in the banking system and ultimately in some cases bank liquidations. Second, the government assists the banking system in financial distress by intervention measures trying to limit the significant losses in the banking system.

On the subject of the second type of crisis - the debt crisis -, we must distinguish between external and domestic debt crisis. An external debt crisis normally happens when one country failures to meet the principal or interest payments on the due date with the international institutions and the rescheduling of the debt is eventually completed in less favorable terms than the original obligation. The domestic debt crisis is defined in the same way as an external debt crisis with the exception of the debt holders, who are domestic and in addition the domestic debt crisis employs the freezing of bank deposits or the forcible conversion of deposits from US dollar to domestic currency.

The third type of crisis - the currency crisis - refers to a situation where the rapid and deep devaluation of the domestic currency with respect to core currencies such as US dollar brings high inflation, the decline in output, slow economic growth and recession.

The currency market, the trend of exchange rates and their regulation are extremely delicate and complex critical factors for all countries. The choice of economic policies presented to authorities appears controversial, both from the point of view of theory and from the historic experience. In particular, they have to compare the advantages of full integration in the global economic system, and the very high risks and costs connected with the difficulties of regulation of currency markets which can lead to serious currency crises. Choosing between fixed and flexible exchange rate or intermediate regime is extremely important, and a very tough decision for monetary authorities as growth may easily be interrupted if a bad choice is made.

The third type of crisis - a currency crisis- generally occurs when the currency of one country tends to take on market values that are in contrast with the exchange agreements stipulated by the monetary authorities or, in the absence of agreements, when it shows a strong and persistent tendency towards devaluation. In both cases, the immediate cause is a persistent excess of the demand for currency compared to the supply, meanwhile, the basic cause is a fundamental deficit in the balance of payments. A currency crisis often arises at the same time as a financial crisis. The critical point of the currency crisis lays in the fact that devaluation, and above all the expectations of devaluation are self-fuelled stimulating the sale of the national currency and therefore increasing devaluation (*speculative attack*). Monetary authorities are prompted to intervene to stabilize the rate of exchange by selling reserve currency. But the total of the reserves is limited, and therefore the monetary authorities cannot commit themselves to intervening for an unlimited period of time. Hence, the typical symptoms of a currency crisis and the most common recovery interventions used are as follows:

a) the official reserves are quickly depleted.

b) in the case of stipulated exchange agreements, it is often optioned to dissolve the agreements and give passage to fluctuation with the extensive and immediate devaluation of the national currency.

c) in the case of continuous devaluation, adoption of policies to correct the balance of payments

d) recourse to international loans to reconstitute the reserves, generally agreed with the IMF and subordinated to the adoption of the above policies.

If the official foreign reserves are depleted, the government must allow the exchange rate to float, resulting in a devaluation of its currency. This causes domestic goods and services to become cheaper relative to foreign goods and services and more competitive both in the domestic markets against imports and in foreign markets against other exports. On the other hand, devaluation of the domestic currency with respect to anchor international currencies such as US dollar, Euro, and UK Pound exceeding 15% will causes the increase of the price of imported raw materials used in domestic manufacturing sector, increasing the domestic price level and reducing in this way the real value of money supply.

The things get a bit more complicated if the country has taken loans denominated in a foreign core currency as the devaluation will increase the value of the debt in terms of domestic currency which will create problems to serve the debt, especially if the country has limited export income. Moreover, the country will eventually have to contract foreign loans in order to cover current account deficits as a result of devaluation. This has to be done in an environment where the international market confidence has been shaken by a devaluation of the domestic currency breaking possibly the previous commitment on monetary stability, which will require domestic budget cuts and contractionary fiscal policy. Despite there are positive aspects on devaluation, such as the important competitiveness effects in the domestic and international market, the negative effects will kick in immediately, especially if the currency devaluation get worse than predicted and where there are large foreign currency debts.

The currency devaluation-related to a successful speculative attack can cause a decline in output, possible inflation, and a disturbance in both domestic and foreign financial markets. The standard macroeconomic framework such as the Mundell-Fleming model (Fleming, J.M. 1962, Mundell, R.A. 1963) applied to national issues is unable to explain currency crises. In this framework with perfect capital mobility, a fixed exchange rate regime results in capital outflows when the central bank lowers interest rates and results in capital inflows when the central bank raises interest rates. Consequently, the efforts of the monetary authority to change the interest rate are undone by the private sector. In a flexible exchange rate regime, the central bank does not intervene in the foreign exchange market to defend a favorable and competitive exchange rate, instead, all balance of payment surpluses or deficits must be financed by private capital outflows or inflows, respectively.

There are a number of models and theories that can give some explanations on the symptoms and therapies of currency crises. These models are classified into three groups or generations, each of which is supposed to explain particular aspects that lead to currency crises.

The first-generation models of a currency crisis developed by Krugman (1979, 1996) and Flood and Garber (1984) are based on monetary and fiscal imbalance. These models rely on government debt and the incapability of the government to control the budget deficit which is the main cause of currency crises. Krugman's (1979) and (1996) models describe a country using reserves to peg and keep fixed its exchange rate. The fixed exchange rate regime is the focal target of the speculative attack. The government is unable to avoid a budget deficit which is mostly covered by a continued expansion of domestic credit (or by money creation). This will lead to inflation and sudden devaluation of domestic currency which will force government and monetary authorities to use the foreign currency reserves to defend as much as possible the fixed exchange rate regime. As central bank continues to deplete its reserves, the investors and agents convert their portfolios from domestic to foreign currencies to protect their investments from the depleting value of domestic currency.

Once the central bank reserves are depleted, the fixed exchange rate regime is no more sustainable. The identification of distress between domestic fiscal policy and a pegged exchange rate regime and the timing of speculative attack that lead to currency crisis was solved by the study of Flood and Garber (1984). The first generation models explain that the weak country fundamentals are known to be unsustainable with the fixed exchange rate which can cause a currency crisis. Based on this it is established a unique relationship between the fundamentals and the timing of crisis. According to Krugman (1996), the depleting of the reserves determine the timing of the speculative attack that brings the system to the crisis, and this is the moment where investors and brokers believe that the attack has finally succeeded.

The second-generation of currency models was inspired by the Latin American crisis in 1994-95. Unlike the earlier models of the first generation, the second-generation models are most helpful in explaining self-fulfilling contagious currency crises. Obstfeld (1994), Eichengreen, Rose, and Wyplosz (1996) were the first economists to work on these new models that take into consideration the policy adjustment by the authorities in response to speculative attacks. The focal point of these monetary models is the possibility of currency crises to occur even without any weakening of economic fundamentals. There are at least two main equilibria:

First, - when there is no speculative attack - there is no changes in economic fundamentals and the government is in control of a pegged exchange regime maximizing its objective function of macroeconomic stability. Second, - when the attack on fundamentals occurs - will be validated after the exchange rate has changed to a new level and the investors expect to take in full consideration of the new situation. The pure expectations of investors leading to one equilibrium or another facilitate the possibility of self-fulfilling crisis. A relative change in expectations such a steep pessimism among investors will trigger a capital outflow that can eventually lead to devastating results such the collapse of the exchange rate system. The expectations might be self-fulfilling if the credibility and track record of the government to defend the peg regime is not good and if the banking sector is weak. If the market interest rates rise, the central bank may have problems to defend the fixed exchange rate, as the reserves and short-term liabilities denominated in foreign currency will create a lot of difficulties for monetary authorities to manage when a rapid currency devaluation is in course.

The government will try to avoid a costly bailout at public expense and will be hesitant to use higher interest rates to finance the defence of the pegged regime. The expectations of the investors and the credibility of the government how to handle the crisis make the speculative attack self-fulfilling. According to Obstfelds (1996), the fundamentals are not so important in the second-generation theories as they determine only the range of possible equilibria, but there exists a "grey area" in which multiple equilibria and self-fulfilling crisis have high potentialities to occur.

The third-generation models point to another important effect that causes the currency crisis, the contagion. A growing number of monetary economists starting with Krugman (1999) and Aghion, Bacchetta, and Banarjee (2000, 2001, 2004) developed the third-generation of currency crisis models. Stimulated by the facts presented by the East-Asian crisis of 1997-1998, these models place the contagion effect and the behaviour of investors and private sector at the centre stage. For example, a devaluation of currency by one country leads its investors and its trading partners to devalue their respective currencies in order to stay competitive in the international market. The contagion effects will trigger the crisis if investors are not able to pay attention to the host country that has problems with economic fundamentals. And if the currency crisis has already started in the host country, this may be an indicator of a future crisis in the neighbouring countries.

The weakness of the banking system creates difficulties to firms as it reduces the credit available to private sector increasing the probability of a crisis. Firm's access to domestic loans is restricted to the portion of their assets (by requiring collateral assets to issue loans). The constraint on domestic lending creates the bases for interest rates to rise, but not enough to compensate investors for the increase in perceived default. However, the increase on the domestic interest rates does not raise the supply of domestic lending but rather reduces the number of loans and financial capital available to firms, increasing in this way the firms' incentive to default. A high-interest rate will make the lending very difficult, and an increase in the nominal interest rate can be disadvantageous for the economy as it reduces the capacity for investment.

The real drop in output will put further pressure on exchange rate aggravating the crisis. The most common strategy and alternative for monetary authorities when the currency crisis hit is to lower the interest rate in order to inject investment, but the expansionary monetary policy must not be inflationary since it has to create the conditions to ease the liquidity constraints. Therefore, in third-generation models, the combination of large depreciation with credit restraints, high debt, low foreign reserves and domestic borrowing in foreign currency increase the likelihood of a currency crisis.

A widespread assumption used in third-generation crises models is the uncovered interest parity which ensures a relationship between interest rates and currency exchange rates.[2] According to Aghion, Bacchetta, and Banarjee (2001) in a country characterized by private sector credit constraints where the nominal price rigidities are the norm, the restrictive monetary policy is the best response to the threat of a currency crisis if uncovered interest parity holds and the credit multiplier depends on interest rates only. On the other side, the expansionary monetary policy with lower interest rates and is a satisfactory response if interest parity holds and the credit multiplier depends on nominal interest rates as suggested by Aghion, Bacchetta, and Banarjee (2000). In addition, the exchange rate is martingale[3] and the credit multiplier can depend on both types of interests; real and nominal interest rates (Hassan 2006).

After the Second World War (WWII), the historical experience has shown that neither fixed exchange rates nor flexible ones can offer absolute guarantees against currency crises. John Williamson in his paper about fix and flexible exchange states that:

> "...It is indeed true that a number of countries, including Brazil, Chile, Colombia, Indonesia, Korea, Russia, and Thailand, have announced since the Asian crisis that they were going to allow their exchange rates to float. But two recent academic studies question whether these declarations reflect policy realities. The first of these two papers is by Calvo and Reinhart (2002), who analyze the behaviour of exchange rates, reserves, the monetary base, and interest rates in a number of countries that describe their exchange rate regime as one of floating. They take the United States and Japan as providing a calibration of what may be expected in terms of the volatility of these variables under floating rates. ...It can be seen that most of the emerging market

---

[2] It is given that *i* represents the yield of a bond at time *t* maturing at a future date *k*, and *i** is the yield of a foreign bond at time *t* maturing at time *k**, and *d* is the depreciation of the domestic currency between times t and k, relative to the currency of the country where the bond is issued. The uncovered interest parity assumption affirms that the equality, $(i-i^*)= d$, holds if there is risk-neutrality.

[3] Martingale is used in the probability theory and it represents a stochastic process where at a certain time, the expectation of the next value in sequence is equal to the present observation value given the values of other prior observed data at the current time.

> countries with rates described as floating had more volatility than fixed-rate Thailand but less volatility than the United States and Japan. India and Korea are closer to Thailand than to the benchmark floaters, while Malaysia, Peru and Uguanda are intermediate....These results show no obvious relationship between volatility and whether or not a country claims to manage its float."
>
> [Williamson J. 2000, p. 3-4]

The floating exchange rates can probably absorb any currency shocks but cannot prevent speculative attacks from currency speculators. Otherwise, the fixed exchange rates would force monetary authorities to intervene to stabilize the rate of exchange by selling reserve currency with the risk of depleting official reserves.

A quick review of monetary crises in recent years shows that in the 1990s and early 2000s, several countries in Asia, Europe, and Latin America experienced some unprecedented currency crisis. In Europe, in the 1990s we got the so-called the exchange rate mechanism (ERM) crisis during the two-year period 1992-1993. One year later in Central America, the Mexican (Tequila) crisis started in 1994 and ended in 1995. The Turkish crisis occurred in 1994, and the Asian crisis in 1997-1998. The crisis, then widespread in Russia in 1998 and moved again to Latin America (Brazil) in 1998-1999. In the early 2000s, the crisis hit Turkey from 2001 to 2002 and Argentina in 2001-2002.

The Southeast Asian currency crisis in 1997 was caused by large prospective government's deficits related to a banking system in trouble. There were few rapid growth countries involved in the crisis. It was a crisis for Malaysia, Indonesia, Thailand and South Korea, but not for China, Japan, Hong Kong and Taiwan, although indirectly the effect of the crisis influenced the whole South Asia. These countries, according to Mundell (2001, p. 7-39), escaped the crisis because they used specific target monetary policies (similar to target inflation) and had large foreign exchange rate reserves, so they did not accept the IMF policies (the most common IMF policy, in general, led to the rejection of fixed exchange rates as an anchor for domestic currencies without replacing a successful alternative and this was against the principles of Mundell). Some analysts called it an "Asian-IMF Crisis" due to the recovery programs "governed" by IMF in the 1990s in some of these countries that didn't have a good impact on the economy.

The speculative attack is another characteristic that affects the currency crisis especially when the government deficit rises. This is true despite the government's foreign reserve position or the initial level of its debt. Meanwhile, the government has not the capability to prevent a speculative attack it can affect its timing. If the government – using anti-crisis tools – tries to delay the speculative attack, it will hit harder and will come with a substantial cost as the inflation will be higher under flexible exchange rates.

A currency crisis has more chance to occur when there is an abrupt and unexpected change in the nominal exchange rate. According to Licchetta (2009), the vision of a crisis takes place when there are some common determinants of currency crisis that make it inevitable such as the real exchange rate rises faster above its medium and long-run trend, there is a rapid growth in foreign currency relative to the level of international reserves, disequilibrium in the balance of payments and budget balance deficits, slower GDP growth and contagion effect by neighboring countries if they already are "infected" by the crisis.

An empirical study done by Gunsel, Tursoy and Rjoub (2010) in countries affected by crises in the 1990s and at the beginning of 2000s like Argentina, Brazil, Mexico, Malaysia, Philippines, South Korea, Thailand, Russia and Turkey suggested that changes or shocks that go above the trend on economic fundamentals such the rate of inflation, interest rate, growth rate of GDP, real exchange rate and the ratio of reserve adequacy (M2) to foreign exchange reserves are positively related to the probability of the crisis to occur. More specifically, the worsening of some key parameters (variables) such as the budget balance deficit, the real exchange rate and the ratio M2 to foreign exchange reserves – also adding the contagion effect – increase the prospect of a currency crisis in the short-medium term significantly.

There are at least four major factors that can influence the onset and success of a speculative attack (Chiodo and Owyang 2002, 7-17): (i) a fixed exchange rate and a central bank prepared or obligated to defend it with the reserve of foreign currency, (ii) rising fiscal deficits that the government cannot control and therefore is likely to monetize, (iii) central bank control of the interest rate fragile credit market, and (iv) expectations of devaluation and/or rising inflation.

It is exactly what happened in 1998 with the Russian currency crisis. In the 1990s, the currency crises suddenly drew worldwide attention to speculative attacks on government-controlled exchange rates which later became case-study scenarios. To prevent these events from happening in the future, would be better to reach an agreement to lock exchange rates (Mundell 2001) and conduct a common monetary policy that could be worked out among the United States, Europe and Japan plus other major Asian and Latin American countries.

There are some other findings such as that of Stiglitz (2002) showing the probability of crises does not depend on whether a country adopts a fixed or flexible exchange rate regime. A recent empirical study conducted by Combes, Minea and Sow (2012), using a panel of 90 countries over the period 1980-2009, suggests that the choice of the exchange regime does not matter in the prediction of the financial crises as the problem lies in other monetary and financial variables and macroeconomic policies which are more important in determining the likelihood of the crisis. For example, on the currency crisis side, the study proposes how the government can resolve the problem of the deficit. If the government makes use of seigniorage as a way to absorb fiscal imbalances, it will be inappropriate as it undermines the capability of monetary authorities to keep the fixed exchange rates regime which consequently leads to an inevitable collapse of the peg.

The empirical tests prove that pegged regimes are more vulnerable to debt crisis than intermediate regimes, meanwhile flexible exchange rate regimes are less exposed to currency and debt crisis. As a result, there is no direct link between exchange rate regimes and financial crises (Combes, Minea and Sow, 2012), therefore the right medicine to prevent crises is not the choice of the appropriate exchange rate regime but rather the implementation of macroeconomic and financial policies that prevent the economy from using unproductive actions (such as unsustainable fiscal policy, uncontrolled credit growth and debt path) to drag it to recession.

The Never-ending Debate on Fixed vs. Flexible Exchange Rates

After the Second World War, the debate about exchange rates in terms of fixed versus flexible exchange rates emerged in many industrialized countries, regardless of the fact that few countries practiced either of them, but chose instead one of the numerous intermediate regimes. In some of his writings, Keynes recognized the negative effects of a system of flexible exchange rates on effective international demand, because of the *beggar-thy-neighbour* outcome of competitive devaluations. Keynes' view was that if one country were protecting its domestic aggregate demand, a floating exchange rate would become a device through which recession would spread to the rest of the world. Many Post Keynesian economists such as Johnson H. (1963), Harrod (1965), Davidson (1992, 2003) have rejected flexible exchange rates because of the fear of destabilizing internal and external equilibrium that would encourage speculation, requiring greater central bank intervention in the foreign exchange markets than under a fixed exchange rates system.

For Johnson (1963) for example, the advantage of a system of fixed exchange rates lies mainly in its unifying effect, and that this effect presupposes freedom of international competition. In fact, a system of fixed exchange rates is intended to protect the advantages of a unified currency on a world scale. Therefore, such a system has the same sort of advantages to the participating nations as does a unified national currency to the regions of the nation. Johnson's observation is that a single currency would be even more unifying than a system of national currencies with fixed exchange rates. Other advantages of unified international currency consist on that there are no barriers to international trade and payments to achieve equilibrium in the balance of payments and it is accompanied by determined efforts to reduce barriers to international movements of goods and factors.

According to Johnson (1963, 112-119), the trouble with present fixed rates (in the sixties) was that they were not fixed firmly enough. Thus, the allowable deviation of rates from par should be narrowed and not widened as used change frequently. For Johnson, the question of short-term and long-term liquidity problems should be solved by more efficient means than by the arrangements among central bankers. His solution was for the creation of a genuine world central bank, whose the first responsibility was to provide the increase in international reserves at a rate adequate to support the growth of the world trade at a high level of a world economic activity (Johnson H. G. 1963, 114-119). The question of a single international currency and the foundation of a world central bank in Johnson's idea remained, of course, out of the question for the time he wrote the paper (1963). It is out of the question in our times as well where we do have few currency areas such as euro, dollar and yen, and one monetary union (the case of EMU). However, the contribution of Johnson is much appreciated on building up a different monetary regime in a time when the *Bretton Woods* system was receiving his first "attacks".

Despite the case for fixed and pure flexible exchange rates, some authors such as Kemp (1962), Krueger (1969) and Hause (1966), considered another choice for exchange rates which is – occasional exchange rates or gradual adjustment – that perhaps fits better the expectations of monetary authorities. The first argument in favour of gradual adjustment is that it is preferable to the fluctuations brought about by large changes occurring in a crisis atmosphere. As monetary authorities desire to maintain a certain disequilibrium rate, they will opt to partial exchange control and non-optimal domestic economic policies. This will sustain costs that could be avoided if monetary policymakers will allow exchange rates adjustments (Krueger 1969, 17-20).

In addition, they give speculators few margins, since speculators are sure that the exchange rate of a deficit country will not be appreciated. So, speculators can purchase assets in other currencies where their main cost will consist of making the transaction and any interest differential, while their potential gain will be obtained in case of devaluation. In this way, the speculators may force a devaluation, and as a result of a considerable profit at the expense of the rest of the community (Kemp, 1962).

The second argument for gradual adjustment in exchange rates is that frequent changes in exchange rates reduce the community's welfare. This argument is developed by Hause (1966). He assumed full-employment throughout two time periods. During the first period a country would have a deficit, and in the second period, a surplus equal in amount but opposite in sign. Hause then compared the time of the pattern of consumption with that of an equilibrium payments position. He assumed perfect intertemporal substitution in consumption of the domestic good with itself, and derived a consumers' surplus measure of the cost and applied it to Argentine data for the period 1959-62. He found that although a single country might gain by such a policy (using pure flexible exchange rates) - due to a low elasticity of demand for imports – world welfare as a whole is always diminished.

Marcus Fleming (1971) , who contributed with Robert Mundell in studying the role of monetary and fiscal policy under fixed and flexible exchange rates - put the following question to connect balance of payment and exchange rates in case of floating: what would happen if several countries maintained a parity for current transactions, while isolating the market for capital transactions and allowing fluctuations in the capital exchange rate? The answer is based on the analysis reflecting the floating capital exchange rate, and taking into consideration the assumption that if segregation could be forced, countries would sell (buy) their net current surpluses (deficit) in the capital exchange market. Thus, fluctuations in the capital rate would induce the net capital flows to offset current imbalances.

Fleming's view is for substituting the rigid maintenance of fixed exchange rates with fixed parities combined with occasional discrete devaluations. Fleming (1971) focuses his research on capital flows and not on the welfare effects, which might be considerable: exchange control of current transactions would be necessary to ensure market isolation (segregation), but the social and private costs of international borrowing and lending might diverge substantially.

Rudiger Dornbusch and Paul Krugman - after almost three years of experience with flexible exchange rates following the collapse of Bretton Woods system (1971) and the introduction of flexible exchange rates in 1973, and exactly in 1976 - considered the effects of flexible exchange rates in the short-run. They studied the case of mark-dollar which in the mid-seventies was representing the key exchange rate in the world. The exchange rate between mark and dollar in just three years (1973-75) has moved up and down by roughly 10 to 15 percent every six months showing virtually no trend.

They proved that the asset-market approach, which stresses the role of portfolio-balance and stock adjustments in exchange-rate determination, yields the same result as the traditional Keynesian model when the latter incorporates mobility (as in the Mundell-Fleming version) and downplays the role of current-account adjustments in the short run. Their scheme implies that, when some disturbances affect the exchange market in the short-run, asset markets adjust immediately.

The result changes if the exchange rate produces a change in relative prices on the terms of trade. This subsequently causes a change in the current account, which is the reflective image of the change in the capital account, in the medium term. Authors suggest that a flexible exchange worsen the Phillips trade-off; but with the fixed exchange rate, monetary policy does not work at all because an over a valuated dollar of monetary expansion simply escapes to the rest of the world and is undone through exchange-market intervention by the central bank (Dornbusch-Krugman 1976, 537-75). The foremost Dornbusch-Krugman conclusion for macroeconomic policy is that it is necessary a monetary tool, such as an exchange-intervention by monetary authorities, to use as active monetary policy to neutralize any random disturbances from the exchange rate.

The main objections to (pure) flexible exchange rates seem to be at least three: i) the floating rates would remove domestic constraints against inflation; ii) speculation under floating rates must be destabilizing the system, and iii) there is increased uncertainty under a flexible exchange rate regime which might bring traders to reduce the volume of world trade.

To the argument that fixed exchange rates impose an anti-inflationary discipline on monetary authorities, Friedman (1953) and Sohmen (1961) would simply reply that the degree of inflation is independent of exchange rate regime. Friedman thinks that countries with a distaste for inflation can avoid it incurring in virtuous monetary policy. The speculation argument has received the most attention. Friedman (1953) assumed that speculation would be destabilizing only if speculators lost their money (on the net), and there should be no presumption that they would, and if they did, it would represent a net transfer from speculators to the rest of the society. But if speculators will not lose money there will be no transfer of speculation to the rest of the society. Farrell (1966) considered the Friedman (1953) proposition and found it to be valid only if non-speculative demand is independent of prior speculative activity.

Farrell's[4] conclusion is that a theory of speculative behaviour and formation of expectations is needed since the profit test is not as simple as Friedman has suggested. The strange behaviour of speculation and also the uncertainty with which traders might be confronted has stimulated work on the forward exchange market. The forward price of foreign exchange is seen as determined by trade and speculative demand and supply, as well as by interest arbitrage. Some other economists such as Kemp (1962) have argued that the trade and speculative aspects of forward exchange transactions are inextricably entangled.

Friedman's reply to this assumption is that trade and speculative functions can be viewed separately from an analytical viewpoint. Another economist, Stein (1961), identifies banks as professional speculators in his treatment of the forward market. On either view, the question as to how expectations are formed is critical. The speculative behaviour is also used to refute the uncertainty argument against flexible exchange rates.

McKinnon (1971) proposed the optimum flexibility and the system of gliding parities. His argument stated that there is a need to utilize the short-run stabilizing influence of the exchange mechanism on domestically generated fluctuations in income and prices. The system of "gliding" parity or the "crawling peg" system was best suited for resolving the conflicting objectives in exchange rates. The basic idea was to retain a narrow band for movements in spot rates but to permit parity (at the centre of the range) to move steadily upwards or downwards at a speed which can be encompassed within interest-rate differentials.

The parity would be changed sufficiently frequently that the individual movements would be smaller than the cost of exchanging currencies (McKinnon 1971, 340-50). This mechanism would provide "automatic" realignments of currency values rather than relying on negotiations for "automatic" realignments of currency values which are always difficult to obtain. In this sense, the scheme of McKinnon (1971) or the "automatic mechanism of gliding peg" was different from the proposal of John Williamson (1965) who would rely on the official determination to change par values under the "crawling peg" system.

In 1966, a group of renowned economists tried to change the "rigid" rules of *Bretton Woods* system and put forward a proposal to widen the limits within which countries are obliged to keep the gold value of their currencies (Fellner

---

[4] A major problem has been to devise a satisfactory definition of "stabilizing". Farrell and Kemp, in general, define speculation to be stabilizing if the variance of price over time with speculation is less than that which would occur in its absence.

W, Machlup F., and Triffin R., 1966). Their purpose was to increase the flexibility in relative currency values. But widening the "range" of gold points was not the right way of increasing flexibility. Although, in 1968 when major central banks formalized the agreement not to buy or sell gold in the private gold market the system of gold-dollar-standard was at a point of non-return. There were no available therapies to cure it. A few years later the system collapsed. The switch to flexible exchange rates, which happened in 1973, involved a degree of unforeseen instability among industrialized and developing countries. It was the intervention of major central banks, often simultaneously and massively, that have tried to put under control the exchange rate market. Sometimes these interventions have been successful, others times not at all with depressing consequences for the economies of these countries.

In general, after the failure of *Bretton Woods* the case for greater flexibility of exchange rates appears to be wide, although not universally, accepted among academic economists. The fear of fully market-determined exchange rates have put forth a number of proposals for modified "pure" flexible rates. The best proposals in the seventies were that exchange rates would retain a pegged par value, but permissible fluctuations around par rates would be increased. Foreign exchange authorities might or might not intervene within these limits.

Before concluding this section I would like to present the monetary debate briefly with the arguments, pros and cons, about fixed exchange rates between two Nobel economists Robert Mundell and Milton Friedman summarized in few articles published in 2000, which has started approximately six-seven decades ago and still has not been concluded.

Mundell considers a fixed exchange rates system as a monetary rule where the central bank can build a virtues monetary policy while a flexible exchange rates system as something which is governed in the absence of monetary rule. In terms of monetary rules, the real choice is between a fixed exchange rates and an alternative monetary rule such as the target inflation or other monetary goals. When a country is influenced by a monetary instability, like high inflation, it should adopt a monetary rule and carry out a virtues monetary policy to control the growth of monetary supply. And this can be better in the case of fixed exchange rate system (Mundell R and Milton F. 2000).

The application of fixed exchange rates according to Mundell is not appropriate to all the countries. Big and powerful countries like the United States and Japan or monetary unions like the European Union have no alternative to inflation targets. The big economies are independent of the monetary policy concerning exchange rates and an inflation target. Their inflation rate generally tries to reflect their economic rate of growth or at least the global rate of growth. For Mundell, the monetary system choice depends first on the current rate of inflation, second on the position of a country (if the country is close to a monetary currency like the dollar or euro area) and third, on the capacity of sharing the inflation rate with the stable area. Most probably, different from Mundell's view, the position of a country is not always a good condition for the choice of monetary system.[5]

Friedman (Friedman and Mundell, 2000) argues that independent monetary policy and consequently a flexible exchange rate is better than a hard fixed exchange system. A rapid growth generates a balance of payments surplus that is adding to its money supply. This influence the rising of wages in real and nominal terms (real terms more slowly than nominal terms). The rise in nominal wages to offset inflation is a pure noise that can lead to unrealistic expectations in wages recipients and employers. The adjustment to the rapid rise in productivity would be much easier if consumer prices were stable and the currency was appreciating relative to other big currencies (dollar and euro) or the currency members' union.

For example, the membership of Ireland in the euro area, during rapid economic growth, forced the Government of Ireland to use its scarce internal market (the counterpart to its balance of payments surplus) to purchase additional euros for financing the higher consumer price level but did not have any productive function. If Ireland or another country with rapid growth had its independent monetary policy, the capital used to purchase additional euros would be available for internal investments (Friedman and Mundell, 2000).

While Mundell during his academic career has been more "flexible" on using fixed exchange rates, the position of Friedman hasn't changed. Friedman was

---

[5] Most likely the most important condition after the current rate inflation is the stable currency and economic growth. For examples there were the fifteen-member CFA franc zone in Africa (before the introduction of the euro) that have fixed for a long time their currency to France although they were not neighbors, or the use of the U.S. dollar by Panama and recently by El Salvador and Ecuador although they are not neighbors. What they sought was the inflation rate target and the stable currency, to serve as a foundation for the resolution of other economic and political problems. In some empirical studies few economists (Broda Christian, 2001) have argued that countries which operate under flexible exchange rates have performed better than fixed rate countries in their responses to terms-of-trade shocks. Presumably, the better performance results from the extra freedom for monetary policy in the floating rate systems.

one of the most convinced advocates of flexible exchange rates and remained stubborn to his position even after the introduction of Euro and the creation of a monetary union.

From an economic point of view, the strongest argument for independent monetary policy is that if the country operates with a flexible exchange rate, the monetary authority can design a policy that responds optimally to its own economic disturbances. Typically, the desired policy will look countercyclical, or against shocks, and can be expansionary during recessions and contractionary in rapid economic growths. Under the pure floating rate - according to Friedman - the country seems to be immune against foreign exchange crisis. For example, the crisis in Japan was not accompanied by a foreign exchange crisis, and the cause of this was that changes in exchange rates absorb the pressures that in a fixed exchange rate regime lead to crises. The foreign exchange crisis that affected Korea, Thailand, Malaysia, and Indonesia in the 1990s did not spill over to New Zealand or Australia because those countries had floating exchange rates (Friedman, 1998).

Quite different from Friedman's view seems to be the position of Calvo and Reinhart (2002) who argue that many central banks in supposedly flexible exchange rate systems have been unable in practice to carry out policies that look desirable. Monetary authorities have a "fear of floating" and are not willing to allow the exchange rate to move in a way that would consent a countercyclical monetary policy.

In contrast, under a fixed exchange rate, monetary policy has to be subordinated to the maintenance of the exchange rates. The fixed exchange rates regime includes a peg to another large currency which may or may not be permanent, and this is quite enough to guarantee the currency stability. The empirical studies conducted by Reinhart in 36 countries from 1970 to 1999 has demonstrated that the fixed exchange rates have led to less inflation, and what is the most important, the adoption of this system lead to no "fear of floating" (Reinhart, 2000).

Exchange Rate Regime Classification

International monetary organizations like International Monetary Fund (IMF) have started classifying countries using different exchange rate regimes after the end of Bretton Woods system. It's interesting to mention that the IMF, from 1975 through 1998 has classified the exchange rate regimes in three main categories: pegged or fixed against a single currency, limited flexibility on the exchange rate, and more flexible exchange rates including other managed and independently floating. This classification, also known as the "de jure" classification was based on what the IMF members were declaring to IMF board about their exchange rate policies. The main limitation of this classification was that countries were officially claiming to be doing (de jure) a certain exchange rate regime when in reality they were trying actually to pursue (de facto) another one. This behavior would reduce the transparency of the exchange rate policy, making the tracking, observation and analysis of the exchange rate regimes less accurate.

In 1998 the IMF introduced a new classification system based on what countries are doing in reality (de facto) regarding the exchange rate regimes avoiding in this way the (de jure) classification. The new system takes into consideration the exchange rate variability as well as policy actions affecting the exchange rate and classifies the exchange rate regimes based on a different level of arrangement flexibility assessing the choice of the exchange rate regime in relation to the independence of the monetary policy. According to this classification there are at least eight exchange rate regimes: 1) exchange arrangements with no separate legal tender, 2) currency board arrangements, 3) conventional fixed-peg arrangements, 4) pegged exchange rates within horizontal bands, 5) crawling pegs, 6) exchange rates within crawling bands, 7) managed floating with no pre-determined path for the exchange rate, 8) independently floating.

Exchange rate regimes belonging to category 1, 2 and 3 are considered hard pegs, categories 4, 5 and 6 are considered soft pegs and the last two categories, 7 and 8, are considered floating regimes. The requirement for improvement in the classification system was supported by the need to analyze the "de facto" policies such as the variability in the exchange rate, international reserves movements, and the level of foreign exchange rate intervention. The "de facto" classification of exchange rate regimes based on IMF database (2008) is given on Tables 3.3a and 3.3b.

Exchange rate arrangement (Number of countries)	Monetary Policy Framework								
	Exchange rate anchor					Monetary aggregate target	Inflation targeting framework		Other1
	U.S. dollar total (66)		Euro (27)	Composite (15)	Other(7)	Total (22)	Total (44)		Total (11)
Exchange arrangement with no separate legal tender (10)	Ecuador El Salvador Marshall Islands Micronesia, Fed. States of	Palau Panama Timor-Leste	Montenegro San Marino		Kiribati				
Currency board arrangement (13)	Antigua and Barbuda[2] Djibouti Dominica[2] Grenada[2] Hong Kong SAR St. Kitts and Nevis[2]	St. Lucia[2] St. Vincent and the Grenadines[2]	Bosnia and Herzegovina Bulgaria Estonia[3] Lithuania[3]		Brunei Darussalam				
Other conventional fixed peg arrangement (68)	Angola Argentina Aruba Bahamas, The Bahrain Bangladesh Barbados Belarus Belize Eritrea Guyana Honduras Jordan Kazakhstan Lebanon Malawi Maldives Mongolia Netherlands Antilles Oman Qatar Rwanda Saudi Arabia	Seychelles Sierra Leone Solomon Islands Sri Lanka Suriname Tajikistan Trinidad and Tobago Turkmenistan United Arab Emirates Venezuela, Rep. Bolivariana de Vietnam Yemen, Rep. of Zimbabwe	Benin[4] Burkina Faso[4] Cameroon[5] Cape Verde Central African Rep.[5] Chad[5] Comoros Congo, Rep. of[5] Côte d'Ivoire[4] Croatia Denmark[3] Equatorial Guinea[5] Gabon[5] Guinea-Bissau[4] Latvia[3] Macedonia, FYR Mali[4] Niger[4] Senegal[4] Togo[4]	Fiji Kuwait Libya Morocco Russian Federation Samoa Tunisia	Bhutan Lesotho Namibia Nepal Swaziland	Argentina Malawi Rwanda Sierra Leone			
Pegged exchange rate within horizontal bands (3)			Slovak Rep.[3]	Syria. Tonga					

1) Includes countries that have no explicitly stated nominal anchor, but rather monitor various indicators in conducting monetary policy.

2) The member participates in the Eastern Caribbean Currency Union.

3) The member participates in the ERM II.

4) The member participates in the West African Economic and Monetary Union.

5) The member participates in the Central African Economic and Monetary Community.

6/ The central bank has taken preliminary step toward inflation targeting and is preparing for the transition to full-fledged inflation targeting.

7) The member participates in the European Economic and Monetary Union.

8) As of end-December 1989.

Table 3.3a Source: IMF staff reports; IMF, World Economic Outlook Database and IMF staff estimates, April 2008.

Exchange rate arrangement (Number of countries)	Exchange rate anchor					Monetary Policy Framework			
	U.S. dollar 17 (total 66)		Euro (27)	Comp. 6 (tot. 15)	Other(7)	Monetary aggregate target 17 (tot. 22)	Inflation targeting framework (44)		Other (11)
Crawling peg (8)	Bolivia China Ethiopia Iraq Nicaragua Uzbekistan			Botswana Iran, I.R. of.					
Crawling band (2)	Costa Rica			Azerbaijan					
Managed floating with no pre-determined path for the exchange rate (44)	Cambodia Kyrgyz Rep. Lao P.D.R. Liberia Mauritania Mauritius Myanmar Ukraine			Algeria Singapore Vanuatu		Afghanistan, I.R. of Burundi Gambia, The Georgia Guinea Haiti Jamaica Kenya Madagascar Moldova Mozambique Nigeria Papua New Guinea São Tomé and Príncipe Sudan Tanzania Uganda	Armenia[6] Colombia Ghana Guatemala Indonesia Peru Romania Serbia[6] Thailand Uruguay		Dominican Rep. Egypt India Malaysia Pakistan Paraguay
Independently floating (40)							Albania Australia Austria[7] Belgium[7] Brazil Canada Chile Cyprus[7] Czech Rep. Finland[7] France[7] Germany[7] Greece[7] Hungary Iceland Ireland[7] Israel Italy[7] Korea, Rep. of	Luxembourg[7] Malta[7] Mexico Netherlands[7] New Zealand Norway Philippines Poland Portugal[7] Slovenia[7] South Africa Spain[7] Sweden Turkey United Kingdom	Congo, Dem. Rep. of Japan Somalia[8] Switzerland United States

1) Includes countries that have no explicitly stated nominal anchor, but rather monitor various indicators in conducting monetary policy.

2) The member participates in the Eastern Caribbean Currency Union.

3) The member participates in the ERM II.

4) The member participates in the West African Economic and Monetary Union.

5) The member participates in the Central African Economic and Monetary Community.

6/ The central bank has taken preliminary step toward inflation targeting and is preparing for the transition to full-fledged inflation targeting.
7) The member participates in the European Economic and Monetary Union.
8) As of end-December 1989.

Table 3.3b Source: IMF staff reports; IMF, World Economic Outlook Database and IMF staff estimates, April 2008

A de facto classification as this one showing on Tables 3.3a and Table 3.3b reveals the wide range of exchange arrangements within IMF members with no overlap among categories and categorizes countries based on transparency and verifiable rules. The classification system shows one main pattern that exchange rate is determined by the market rather official intervention, a feature reflected in the flexibility of exchange rate. In de facto classification it is important to know if the arrangement is floating or not. The criterion for a float is that the exchange rate is widely determined by the market. The practical behavior of the exchange rate and the foreign exchange policy actions taken by monetary authorities allow giving a better judge whether the exchange rate is determined mainly by market forces by official policy intervention.

Once the arrangement has been identified as floating, it can further be recognized as free-floating if there is no official policy action in the last six months. The exchange rate volatility is normally computed as the average of the absolute monthly percentage changes in the nominal exchange rate during a regular year. Meanwhile, the volatility of exchange rate changes is calculated as the standard deviation of the monthly percentage changes in the exchange rates (Levy-Yeyati E. and Sturzenegger F., 2005, p.1607).

As seen in the classification Tables 3.3a and 3.3b, most of the developed economies use flexible exchange rate regime under "independently floating" category. The monetary authorities of these countries have allowed a certain degree of volatility in the exchange rate, relative to their degree of intervention. Some of these countries in the 1990s, especially EMU countries such as France (which later became part of the European Monetary Union having no independent legal tender currency) intervened actively to keep their parity in line with the DM (Deutsche Mark) after the EMS crisis of 1992, but Italy and Spain, instead, choose to allow a greater exchange rate flexibility. Ireland has its currency fixed to DM in 1992 when suddenly got devaluated, and the massive intervention of the Irish Central Bank to defend its currency did nothing to prevent it from collapsing. Some other countries like Denmark and Croatia which were not part of EMU area have consistently fixed their currencies to DM. Other emerging countries like Chile, Brazil and Mexico were floating since the 1980s but because of the currency crisis hitting these countries in the late 1990s and with the massive intervention of their central banks to avoid the currency collapse some of them such as Brazil were classified as fixed (for then returning to independent floating after the currency crisis and speculative attacks).

Small open economies, such as Bahamas, Belize, and Lesotho, given their limited independence for monetary policy, have fixed their exchange rates to the currencies of their main partners. Broadly speaking, most of the countries since the collapse of Bretton Woods system in the early 1970s have expressed a tendency towards flexible arrangements. Based on IMF classification the number of countries choosing a fixed rate has fallen from 75% in 1974 to 50% in 2000. On the other side, another finding is that the number of countries using a fixed exchange rate regime without openly declaring it, a phenomenon known as "fear of pegging", has increased rather than decreased in the period 1995-2005 (Levy-Yeyati and Sturzenegger, 2005, 1618-19).

According to Calvo and Reinhart (2002), there are a number of countries that proclaim to use exchange rate regimes but actively intervene intensively in exchange market to limit the volatility of the nominal exchange rate. These countries were labeled as having "fear of floating". Based on the study of Calvo and Reinhart (2002) there may be strong motives to behave in this way, such as the high costs of keeping the flexible exchange regime without intervening especially if the country has an emerging economy. In fact, if the floating exchange regime is kept in the way it is without interference, a strong devaluation in a developing country could lead to less access to capital markets, highly disruptive balance sheet effects when key sectors of the economy have built up liabilities in foreign currency, high inflation, disruptive effects on the raw materials market and trade. A strong evaluation of the domestic currency, instead, could cause fewer exports on raw materials and delay growth in the main tradable sectors.

Two well-known economists, Alesina and Wagner (2003), tried to address the "fear of floating" practice as a relationship between exchange rate policies and overall institutional quality. Countries with strong institutions are more likely to support a fixed exchange rate once they have pronounced it, but countries with weaker institutions would be more likely to announce a fixed regime and then eventually be forced to float breaking the promise to keep a stable monetary policy. According to Alesina and Wagner (2003) the fear of floating is nothing more than a "signaling device", where countries through their monetary authority intervene in the exchange market to raise credibility and distinguish themselves from other countries that have poor monetary institutions and are forced to costly depreciation losing their trustworthiness in the international market. The "signaling device" will inform the market about the characteristics and the strong institutions of that country able to support the fixed exchange rate and has no fear of floating.

In many occasions, markets might be keen to prefer floating regimes, because a flexible exchange rate may give the signal to markets that the monetary authority of that country is unlikely to defend an unsustainable peg and this perception would lower the risk of speculative attacks. In addition, markets may have a subjective view against fixed exchange rate in part from the negative experience of the international currency crisis in the 1990s and early 2000s generated mostly in those countries with de facto fixed exchange rates.

Another reason why markets favor floating regimes is that the inflation target strategies used by an increasing number of countries allow them to reach the inflation target. According to Andrew Rose (2007), as of June 2006 inflation targeting countries have steadily increased in the last decades reaching a quarter of world GDP, which means that floating regimes are appreciated and welcomed by the market.

Another study conducted by IMF staff (Barajas, Erickson, and Steiner 2008) suggests that a number of countries are phasing a new phenomenon called "fear of declaring" the exchange rate policy and their actual level of exchange-rate intervention. According to these researchers, the international markets would reward countries that tend to use de facto floating regimes. Barajas, Erickson, and Steiner (2008) in their valuable empirical research use the spread of the *Emerging Market Bond Index Global* (EMBIG), which measures the premium above U.S. Treasury securities in basis points for dollar-denominated sovereign debt, as an evaluation of market perceptions of each country. In addition, by using a cross-referencing approach that utilize time and cross-country variability, the study considers the effect on these spreads of de jure regime choice and the actual degree of exchange rate intervention, also using other variables to manage the underlying fundamentals. Countries claiming to use fixed exchange rates intervene more heavily in the foreign exchange market by buying or selling international reserves will have lower spreads on average than countries having floating regimes.

Table 3.4 shows the results of fixed-effects regressions of country-specific EMBIG spreads over quarterly observations in 1997-2007 period using domestic fundamentals. It also explains that the main fundamentals such as the general government balance, level of international reserves, public debt and the volatility index have much of the impact in sovereign spreads. There are eight columns on table 3.4 each of them corresponding to eight exchange rate regimes according to the new 1998 IMF classification system mentioned at the beginning of this section. In table 3.4, we have that spreads decline with improvements in fiscal balance and level of reserves and increase in market volatility and stock debt. Spreads have the tendency to be lower in countries using a de jure fixed regimes, meanwhile in countries using de jure managed floating regimes spreads are comparable to those countries that claim pure floating.

This phenomenon, as shown in Table 3.4, demonstrates how a coefficient on intervention index always has a negative sign, which confirms the thesis that fixed exchange rate, de jure or de facto brings normally lower spreads. Column 5 on table 3.4 illustrates that exchange rate volatility under intervention index in the last 8 quarters is positively related to spreads, but the intervention on the current quarter has a negative impact even when the real exchange rate volatility is included as shown in column 6. Lower spreads in de jure fixed regime might suggest that countries are exiting the fixed regimes during periods of currency crisis and the regressions would attribute to floating regimes higher spreads arising during the periods of turmoil. Column 7 and 8 in table 3.4 shows that by using CRISIS variable, the negative impact of exchange rate fixity on spreads persists, however it is not coming as a result of the exit strategy from fixed to float regimes used by countries facing monetary difficulties. There is the perception among monetary policymakers that during the currency crisis to different regimes are not given equal treatment by market operators. Some exchange regimes are penalized harder than others by capital markets.

Determinants of EMBIG Spreads, All countries								
	Dependent variable: EMBIG Spread							
	1	2	3	4	5	6	7	8
Inflation	**0.95** **[0.54]**	**1.20** **[0.62]**	**0.44** **[0.23]**	**1.06** **[0.59]**	**-0.87** **[0.53]**	**-0.70** **[0.44]**	**-0.30** **[0.18]**	**-0.38** **[0.25]**
Current Account	**2718.18** **[0.93]**	**3927.55** **[1.24]**	**3484.11** **[1.19]**	**3912.98** **[1.3]**	**1120.41** **[0.54]**	**1295.93** **[0.63]**	**1228.18** **[0.62]**	**1638.98** **[0.8]**
General Government Balance	**-** **7576.78** **[1.86]’**	**-** **6927.93** **[1.88]’**	**-** **7228.15** **[2.01]’**	**-** **6531.38** **[1.91]’**	**-** **6215.77** **[2,28]”**	**-** **5930.04** **[2.17]”**	**-** **5471.81** **[2.19]”**	**-** **4764.67** **[1.99]’**
Reserves minus gold	**-2027.1** **[1.62]**	**-329.34** **[2.7]”**	**-** **2966.62** **[2.63]”**	**-** **3033.03** **[2.6]”**	**-** **2749.39** **[2.66]”**	**-** **2667.33** **[2.62]”**	**-** **1688.89** **[1.85]’**	**-** **1978.41** **[2.01]’**
Public debt (t-3)	**2955.1** **[2.87]”**	**2441.14** **[3.83]’”**	**2128.19** **[3.81]’”**	**2438.56** **[4.11]’”**	**1495.71** **[3.18]’”**	**1598.75** **[3.32]’”**	**2708.9** **[3.47]’”**	**3004.07** **[3.52]’”**
Volatility Index	**14.6** **[4.15]’”**	**10.18** **[3.9]’”**	**10.15** **[3.97]’”**	**10.84** **[4.23]’”**	**10.05** **[4.3]’”**	**10.43** **[4.37]’”**	**8.8** **[4.2]’”**	**9.51** **[4.43]’”**
De jure Fixed		**-668.71** **[2.23]”**	**-487.22** **[1.72]’**	**-476.37** **[1.75]**	**-292.47** **[1.51]**	**-237.22** **[1.19]**	**-448.89** **[1.87]’**	**-465.36** **[1.86]’**
De jure Managed floaters		**3.03** **[0.03]**	**118.0** **[0.87]**	**73.8** **[0.53]**	**416.7** **[1.78]’**	**417.76** **[1.72]’**	**79.02** **[0.75]**	**24.03** **[0.26]**
Intervention Index								
Average over previous 8 quarters			**-** **1161.24** **[3.19]’”**		**-320.0** **[0.76]**		**-** **1362.18** **[2.82]’”**	
Current quarter average				**-618.24** **[2.68]”**		**-362.54** **[2.93]’”**		**-596.74** **[2.63]”**
Real Exchange rate volatility					**7705.74** **[2.08]”**	**7527.84** **[2.22]”**		
CRISIS1 (t-2, t+2)							**1282.22**	**1221.15**

							[2.33]"	[2.23]"
Constant	-930 [1.79]'	-316.95 [0.86]	544.29 [1.2]	42.6 [0.13]	-352 [0.76]	-377.07 [1.11]	539.28 [1.33]	196.0 [0.65]
Joint significance test for year dummies (Ho: γt for all t)								
Test statistic	2.33	2.03	2.49	2.24	2.56	2.35	1.73	1.21
p-value	0.047	0.081	0.036	0.056	0.033	0.047	0.14	0.335
Number of observations	739	705	705	704	680	679	670	669
Number of Countries studied	25	25	25	25	24	24	24	24
R^2	0.38	0.43	0.45	0.44	0.49	0.5	0.53	0.52

Table 3.4 The results of fixed-effects regressions of country-specific EMBIG spreads over quarterly observations in the 1997-2007 period. The numbers in square brackets are the heteroskedasticity-consistent standard errors. The quotation signs, ', ", '" indicate significance respectively at 90%, 95% and 99%. Source: Barajas, Erickson, and Steiner 2008 (IMF staff papers publication).

Table 3.5, instead, shows the results of fixed-effects regressions of country-specific EMBIG spreads for the same period of observation as Table 3.4, but in addition, introduces the interaction terms between the crisis dummies and the de jure regimes. Although spreads are higher for de jure floating regimes during the non-crisis period, there is proof that when crises erupt these regimes are penalized much less by capital markets than other exchange regimes. In table 3.5, as in table 3.4, we have at least 9 categories of explanatory variables which are the country fundamentals such as the average 12-month inflation rate, the external current account, general government balance, the public debt expressed as a ratio to GDP, the volatility index, dummy variables for de jure fixed and de jure managed floating regimes, an exchange intervention index, crisis dummy variables and the standard deviation of the monthly percentage changes in real exchange rates over a period of preceding 8 quarters. Column 1 and column 3 represent respectively a fixed exchange regime and a managed floating regime, column 2 and 4 indicate only managed floating regimes.

Determinants of EMBIG Spreads, All countries				
	Dependent variable: EMBIG Spread			
	(1)	(2)	(3)	(4)
Inflation	-0.34 [0.21]	-0.46 [0.32]	-0.94 [0.72]	-1.0 [0.83]
Current Account	1935.87 [0.99]	730.58 [0.43]	530.37 [0.32]	-647.26 [0.38]
General Government Balance	-4125.01 [2.2]''	-4536.65 [2.04]'	-3662.19 [2.36]''	-3823.93 [2.01]'
Reserves minus gold	-2010.46 [2.06]'	-1261.71 [1.35]	-1813.44 [1.98]'	-1092.21 [1.24]
Public debt (t-3)	2686.84 [2.95]'''	3032.59 [3.63]'''	2289.15 [2.85]'''	2629.42 [3.87]'''
Volatility Index	7.95 [4.05]'''	7.89 [4.33]'''	8.56 [4.62]'''	8.34 [4.65]'''
De jure Fixed	-692.37 [2.71]''	-395.18 [1.9]'	-527.15 [2.96]'''	-239.54 [1.22]
De jure Managed floaters	-166.38 [1.41]	19.44 [0.15]	39.2 [0.26]	208.58 [1.13]
Intervention Index				
Average over previous 8 quarters	-1359.46 [2.86]'''			
Current quarter average			-439.95 [3.11]'''	-448.51 [3.09]'''
Real Exchange rate volatility			5911.18 [2.52]''	5399.62 [2.35]''
CRISIS1 (t-2, t+2)	1952.93 [6.47]'''		1941.13 [6.55]'''	
CRISIS2 (t-2, t+2)		543.12 [0.84]		524.52 [0.83]
Interactions between *de jure* regimes and the respective crisis definition				
De jure managed. Floaters. CRISIS	99.64 [0.18]	1424.26 [2.3]''	-170.41 [0.42]	1203.83 [1.98]'
De jure floaters. CRISIS	-1570.98 [4.8]'''	122.61 [0.23]	-2017.99 [5.66]'''	-587.42 [0.85]
Constant	1071.11 [2.72]''	423.20 [0.99]	-47.53 [0.15]	-430.45 [1.14]
Joint significance test for year dummies (Ho: γt for all t)				
Test statistic	2.68	3.82	2.15	2.12
p-value	0.027	0.005	0.687	0.076
Number of observations	673	670	647	644
Number of Countries studied	24	24	23	23
R^2	0.56	0.56	0.59	0.58

Table 3.5 The results of fixed-effects regressions of country-specific EMBIG spreads over quarterly observations in the 1997-2007 period and the interactions between de jure regimes and the respective crisis. Source: Barajas, Erickson, and Steiner 2008 (IMF staff papers publication).

Table 3.5 illustrates that fixed and managed exchange floating regimes in columns 1 and 3 measured by CRISIS1variables, and the managed floating regimes in columns 2 and 4 measured by CRISIS2 variables, are penalized harder as these variables show higher figures than an independent floating regime during the currency crisis. The government intervention in de jure regimes can be evaluated as an action carried on to maintain the exchange rate commitment the authorities have made with the external world, while in floating regimes the intervention is estimated as a measure to determine the fear of floating. Any intervention under de jure floating regimes is not penalized by markets, and the only country's variable fundamental that has a significant value is the *current account* row which takes a negative sign (-647.26) in column 4 on table 3.5.

Regarding country's fundamentals, the study of Barajas, Erickson, and Steiner (2008) shows that markets tend to penalize countries facing currency crises (in different stages of currency crisis) and the trading markets value the real exchange stability. Another finding is that when we try to connect the crisis variable with the de jure regimes, the free-floating regimes tend to be penalized less in times of currency crisis and economic turbulence. Countries will choose to declare floating regime although it may require higher cost during normal times to keep the benefits of lower spreads in tumultuous times. And, once the flexibility is declared the capital markets seem to be indifferent, and therefore no penalty for fear of floating.

Exchange Rate Regimes and Shock Absorbers

The discussion among supporters of the hard peg and floating regimes about the best regime acting as shock absorber has brought new empirical work on the relationship between exchange rate regimes and the way in which terms of trade shocks affect economic growth. Advocates of fixed exchange rates sustain the thesis that this type of regime is better as it provides credibility by having lower inflation and stable economic growth. On the other hand, supporters of flexible exchange rates have argued that under a floating regime the economy reacts better and has a greater ability to adjust to external shocks. In addition, countries using flexible exchange rates will be more effective to buffer real shocks coming from other countries, as they will be able to avoid costly adjustment processes.

However, some authors, such as Eichengreen and Haussman 1999, believe that a flexible exchange rate regime will be not so effective in countries where the private and public sectors have large liabilities denominated in foreign currencies. The floating regime - based on this study - has the capability to augment the negative effects of terms of trade shocks, because in the presence of "balance sheet" effects, the currency depreciation created as a result of the external shock will increase the value of the debt expressed in domestic currency (already depreciated). High debts and currency depreciation will lead many companies in private sector to insolvency and eventually bankruptcy, resulting in the drop in the rate of growth and recession.

In 2003, Levy Yeyati and Sturzenegger found some evidence to support the argument that countries with more flexible exchange rate regimes and an open economy grow faster than countries with fixed exchange rates. Later, Edwards and Levy Yeyati 2005, tried to analyze whether negative and positive terms of trade shocks have some asymmetric effects on growth and if these asymmetries depend on the type of the exchange rate regime used. Their study consists of finding that terms of trade disturbances affect in different way countries with dissimilar exchange rate regimes. Edwards and Levy Yeyati 2005 start their analysis with two dynamic equations which express the real GDP per capita growth of country *i* in period t.

$$g_i' = \alpha + x_i\beta + d_i\theta + r_i \qquad (3.1)$$

$$\Delta g_{ti} = \lambda(g'_i - g_{t-1,i}) + \varphi s_{ti} + \gamma u_{ti} + \varepsilon_{ti} \qquad (3.2)$$

Equation (3.1) indicates the long growth-run of GDP in country *i*, where *xi* is a vector of policy variables that determine long-term growth, *di* is a vector of regional dummies, α, β, and θ are parameters and *r* is nothing more than an error variable assumed to be heteroskedastic.

Equation (3.2) points out the rate of growth of per capita GDP in country *i* in period *t*, where *sti* represents external terms of trade shock and *uti* indicates other not specified external shocks. Both the variables representing these shocks are assumed to have finite variance, zero mean and are uncorrelated among themselves. εti is an error variable which is assumed to be heteroskedastic and λ, φ, and γ are parameters indicating the characteristics of the growth process in the second equation. Parameter φ is supposed to be positive as it indicates an improvement in the terms of trade increasing the rate of growth. Another characteristic of the parameter φ is that it depends on the exchange rate regimes, which means that a country having a flexible exchange rate is assumed to have a smaller φ, as the floating exchange rates allow countries to absorb external shocks better than countries using fixed exchange rate.

The analysis of Edwards and Levy Yeyati (2005), consists of examining if the coefficients α and φ are different across exchange rate regimes and is done in two stages. The first stage consists of including a variable that interrelates the terms of trade shock with some indicators used for exchange rate regimes, and the second stage compares the estimated coefficients for the terms of trade variable under different exchange rate regimes.

Some results from the first stage estimation regarding the long-run growth equation 3.1 are reported in table 3.6, which includes annual observations of 183 countries for a period of two decades, 1974-2000. Some of the covariate variables included in the growth regression analysis are: the log of GDP per capita (*gdpin*), the investment ratio (*invgdp*), the variable of secondary education or human capital (*sec*), a variable that indicates an index of the degree of openness of the economy (*openness*), the ratio of government consumption (*gov*), the regional dummies for Latin America, Sub Saharan African and economies in transition (*latam, safrica, and trans*), the index for the pegged exchange rate regime expressed as a cross-section version (*pegged_cross*), and the index for a flexible exchange rate regimes expressed as a cross-section version (*regime_cross*) (Edwards and Levy Yeyati 2005, 2087).

Table 3.6 indicates that the coefficients for both fixed and flexible exchange regimes are negative. But the pegged exchange rate regime has a larger negative coefficient value (-0.854) in *pegged_cross* row under column 2 than the flexible exchange rate regime (-0.656) in *regime_cross* row under column 3 which means that countries with a de facto pegged rate regime tend to grow at a slower rate than countries with more flexible exchange rate regimes.

Cross section first-stage growth regression			
Covariate variables	(1)	(2)	(3)
gdpin	-0.55‴ [0.135]	-0.467″ [0.204]	-0.494″ [0.197]
invgdp	6.276 [4.288]	5.171 [4.259]	5.052 [4.427]
sec	2.969‴ [0.908]	2.591″ [1.138]	2.594″ [1.105]
openness	0.479 [0.970]	1.351 [1.048]	1.531 [1.098]
gov	-2.03 [1.46]	-2.52 [1.55]	-2.234 [1.514]
latam	-0.971″ [0.467]	-0.828′ [0.461]	-0.858′ [0.471]
safrica	-1.48‴ [0.547]	-1.191″ [0.566]	-1.28″ [0.554]
trans	-0.865″ [0.412]	-0.557 [0.615]	-0.621 [0.593]
pegged_cross		-0.854‴ [0.318]	
regime_cross			-0.656″ [0.278]
Constant	0.157 [0.95]	0.588 [0.912]	0.923 [1.001]
observations	100	96	96
R^2	0.45	0.45	0.44

Table 3.6 Cross section growth regressions. The numbers in square brackets are the heteroskedasticity-consistent standard errors. The quotation signs, ‘, ‘’, ‘’’, indicate significance respectively at 90%, 95% and 99%.
Source: Edwards and Levy Yeyati 2005.

There is also a difference on the coefficients of the regional countries. Transition countries' coefficients despite being negative have a higher value than those of Latin America and Sub Saharan African countries which means that they had a higher rate of growth when they moved from rigid exchange rate system to a more flexible one during their transition period.

In the second stage, the dynamics of growth in equation 3.2 are estimated using the *Feasible Generalized Least Square* procedure (FGLS) where coefficients for the terms of trade under diverse exchange rate regimes are evaluated. Table 3.7 shows the growth regression results of the estimation using FGLS for the period 1974-2000.

Growth dynamic regressions using FGLS procedure in full sample						
Variables	(1)	(2)	(3)	(4)	(5)	(6)
[gi'-gt-1i]	0.784''' (0.021)	0.748''' (0.023)	0.782''' (0.021)	0.8''' (0.023)	0.781''' (0.021)	0.744''' (0.023)
Δtt	0.038''' (0.008)	0.046''' (0.009)	0.057''' (0.007)	0.060''' (0.007)	0.030''' (0.011)	0.037''' (0.014)
Δtt_1		0.022''' (0.008)		0.036''' (0.007)		0.014 (0.011)
Δtt_pegged	0.045''' (0.011)	0.046''' (0.011)				
Δtt_pegged_1		0.027'' (0.108)				
Δtt_hard			0.038'' (0.019)	0.052''' (0.019)		
Δtt_hard_1				0.019 (0.018)		
Δtt_regime					0.025''' (0.007)	0.026''' (0.007)
Δtt_regime_1						0.017''' (0.007)
Civil unrest, shock	-0.051 (0.040)	-0.034 (0.39)	-0-.053 (0.040)	-0.045 (0.040)	-0.058 (0.040)	-0.046 (0.039)
Constant	-0,216 (0.488)	-0.388 (0.476)	0.893 (0.473)	-0.386'' (0.493)	-0.886 (0.469)	-1.135 (0.456)
Observations	1733	1650	1733	1723	1733	1650
Δtt+Δtt_1		0.068'' [33.74]		0.096''' [104.3]		0.051''' [12.72]
Pegged		0.073''' [25.21]				
Hard				0.072'' [6.58]		
Regime						0.043''' [23.31]

Table 3.7 Growth dynamic regressions in full sample case. The quotations signs, ', '', ''', indicate significance respectively at 90%, 95% and 99%. Source: Edwards and Levy Yeyati 2005.

From equation 3.2 we have that *sti* represents external terms of trade shock given as *Δtt* in Table 3.7 which defines the percentage change of the relative prices of exports to imports and each column indicates a baseline specification is assuming a different value for each coefficient calculated using regressions and the FGLS procedure. Variable coefficients described as *pegged, hard* and *regime* are pointed out as a combination of coefficients respectively as *Δtt_pegged+ Δtt_pegged_1, Δtt_hard+ Δtt_hard_1, Δtt_regime+Δtt_regime_1.* The estimation of coefficient *gi'-gt-1i*, indicating the dynamic growth in country *i* in period *t*, is positive, significant and smaller than one. Table 3.7 also shows that the expected coefficient of the interactive terms between exchange rate regimes indexes and the terms of trade shock, given as, *Δtt_pegged, Δtt_pegged_1, Δtt_hard, Δtt_hard_1, Δtt_regime, Δtt_regime_1,* are most of the times positive. For example, in column (1) the terms of trade coefficient, *Δtt,* has an evaluated point of 0.038 while the calculated interactive term, *Δtt_ pegged,* yields a point estimate of 0.045 (Edwards and Levy Yeyati 2005, 2091).

These outcomes recommend that in fixed exchange countries a 10% decline in the international trade has been associated with a reduction in GDP per capita growth of 0.83 of one percentage point, meanwhile in floating exchange rates regime countries the same 10% decrease in international terms of trade has been related to a drop in GDP per capita growth of 0.38 of one percentage point. This result indicates that under flexible exchange rate regime the effects of external trade shocks on growth are less than one half than under pegged regimes.

Table 3.8 illustrates the dynamic growth regressions using FGLS procedure in a split sample by different exchange rate regimes. There are four groups of countries, each related to one of the four exchange rate regimes which are most common ones used de facto. The four exchange rate regimes given by four columns are: (1) flexible exchange rate, (2) intermediate exchange rate, (3) pegged exchange rate and (4) hard peg exchange rate regime.

Growth dynamic regressions using FGLS procedure in split sample by regime				
Variables	**(1)**	**(2)**	**(3)**	**(4)**
	Flexible	**Intermediate**	**Peg**	**Hard Peg**
[gi'-gt-1i]	0.887’’’ (0.033)	0.939’’’ (0.038)	0.774’’’ (0.029)	0.873’’’ (0.067)
Δtt	0.032’’’ (0.010)	0.042’’’ (0.011)	0.081’’’ (0.008)	0.130’’’ (0.020)
Δtt_1 pegged	0.020’’ (0.010)	0.021’’ (0.010)	0.045’’’ (0.008)	0.051’’’ (0.020)
Civil unrest, shock	0.113’’ (0.054)	-0.105 (0.080)	-0.087’ (0.052)	-0.128 (0.251)
Constant	-1.830’’’ (0.572)	2.193’’ (1.032)	0.179 (0.377)	1.48 (2.114)
Observations	462	416	845	217
Δtt+Δtt_1	0.052’’’ [12.38]	0.063’’’ [16.22]	0.126’’’ [121.56]	0.181’’’ [32.26]

Table 3.8 Growth dynamic regressions in split sample case by the regime. Here as in other tables the quotations signs, ‘, ‘’, ‘’’, indicate significance respectively at 90%, 95% and 99%. Source: Edwards and Levy Yeyati 2005.

The main characteristic of this table is that the estimated coefficients are different across the split samples and increase with the rigidity of the exchange rate regimes. For example, the sum of the lagged terms of trade coefficients *(Δtt+Δtt_1)* in column 4 reaches a higher value for the hard pegged exchange regime, 0.181, and the very low figure for the flexible exchange rate regime, 0.052. Open countries using flexible exchange rates respond better to terms of trade shocks as they have the capacity to absorb them, and this is demonstrated by lower coefficient values, while countries using pegged and hard pegged exchange rate regimes have the coefficients of the term trade shocks reaching higher values giving these countries less able to absorb the external shocks.

From a different perspective, there is also evidence of asymmetric effects to terms of trade shocks and how alternative exchange rate regimes can deal with the positive and negative terms of trade shocks. This evidence is proved by calculating a number of regressions that distinguish the positive and negative terms of trade shocks. Using the FGLS procedure for heteroskedastic panels again and reconsidering equations 3.1 and 3.2 by adding positive and negative terms of trade shock-parameters we have the new system of dynamic equations,

$$g_i' = \alpha + x_i\beta + d_i\theta + r_i \qquad (3.3)$$

$$\Delta g_{ti} = \lambda(g'_i - g_{t-1,i}) + \varphi sp_{ti} + \eta sn_{ti} + \gamma u_{ti} + \varepsilon_{ti} \qquad (3.4)$$

The two new variables added in equation (3.4) are *spti* and *snti* which refer respectively to the positive and negative terms of trade shocks, and φ and η are coefficients to be estimated. The regressions used in equation 3.4 will prove that if flexible exchange rate regimes are able to absorb the external negative real shocks than the coefficient, η, estimating the negative terms of trade shocks, will be larger in countries using *de facto* a pegged exchange rate regimes compared to countries using a more flexible one. Table 3.9 illustrates the regressions of asymmetric effects in two different samples using the FGLS procedure: one, including all countries and the other one including a sample of emerging countries only.

Asymmetry (FGLS) full sample and emerging countries							
Variables	**(1)**	**(2)**	**(3)**	**(4)**	**(5)**	**(6)**	**(7)**
	All			**Emerging**			
	Flexible	**Intermediate**	**Peg**	**Hard**	**Flexible**	**Intermediate**	**Peg**
[gi'-gt-1i]	0.895''' (0.032)	-0.932''' (0.038)	0.774''' (0.029)	0.881''' (0.067)	0.917''' (0.39)	0.993''' (0.041)	0.806''' (0.033)
Δtt_pos	0.021 (0.014)	0.030'' (0.015)	0.066''' (0.013)	0.076'' (0.036)	0.038'' (0.016)	0.037'' (0.018)	0.065''' (0.015)
Δtt_pos_1	0.040''' (0.014)	0.001 (0.015)	0.041''' (0.012)	0.042 (0.032)	0.030' (0.17)	-0.007 (0.018)	0.032'' (0.013)
Δtt_neg	0.052'' (0.025)	0.059'' (0.023)	0.102''' (0.015)	0.178''' (0.031)	0.063'' (0.028)	0.069''' (0.024)	0.115''' (0.016)
Δtt_neg_1	-0.009 (0.017)	0.046'' (0.020)	0.051''' (0.016)	0.053 (0.034)	0.011 (0.019)	0.055''' (0.021)	0.051''' (0.016)
Civil unrest, shock	0.138'' (0.054)	-0.013 (0.087)	-0.049 (0.06)	0.066 (0.249)	0.086 (0.121)	0.088 (0.129)	-0.138' (0.083)
Constant	-1.728 (0.611)	2.208 (1.026)	1.827''' (0.639)	1.168 (3.517)	-2.344 (1.214)	1.178 (2.040)	0.289 (0.724)
Observations	462	416	845	217	301	326	714
pos=(Δtt_pos+ Δtt_pos_1)	0.061''' [11.46]	0.031 [2.06]	0.107''' [41.28]	0.116'' [5.8]	0.068''' [10.07]	0.030 [1.32]	0.097''' [28.58]
neg = (Δtt_neg+ Δtt_neg_1)	0.043 [2.19]	0.105''' [13.78]	0.153''' [54.79]	0.204''' [19.91]	0.074'' [5.21]	0.124''' [17.28]	0.166''' [60.78]
neg-pos	-0.018 [0.24]	0.074' [3.79]	0.046' [2.47]	0.088 [1.73]	0.006 [0.03]	0.094''' [4.98]	0.069'' [5.04]

Table 3.9 Asymmetric regressions in full sample case by different exchange rate regimes in emerging countries. All regressions include year dummies. Here as in other tables the quotations signs, ', '', ''', indicate significance respectively at 90%, 95% and 99%. Source: Edwards and Levy Yeyati 2005.

The asymmetric effects, in table 3.9, can be seen by the value of coefficients assumed for both negative and positive terms of trade shocks. In fact, the coefficients for negative terms of trade shocks expressed by regression variables, *Δtt_neg*, *Δtt_neg_1 and neg=* (*Δtt_neg*+ *Δtt_neg_1),* are considerably much higher than the coefficients for positive shocks expressed respectively by regressions variables, *Δtt_pos*, *Δtt_pos_1and pos=(Δtt_pos+ Δtt_pos_1)* used for intermediate and fixed exchange rate regimes but not so much for flexible ones. In addition, the test shows the sum of the negative terms of trade coefficients is noticeably higher for the rigid regime countries than for countries using the flexible exchange rate regime.

This, further suggests that pegged regimes respond to real shocks with deeper and longer contractions that may lead to slower growth. The study of Edwards and Levy Yeyati (2005) proves the thesis that flexible exchange rates are considered shock absorbers in many aspects are facilitating countries to accommodate real terms of trade shocks if they are hit by negative external shocks.

Staying on the same subject, there is also another approach called the "money shocks" approach that in the presence of sticky prices and international capital mobility is important in determining real variables like the current account. Some earlier studies have brought enough evidence on the issue in question in predicting current account surpluses in response to monetary shocks in occurrence of sticky prices, such as in Mundell (1963) and Obsfeld and Rogoff (1995) and in envisaging current account deficits in reaction to monetary shocks as in Bergin (1995), Kollaman (1996) and Betts and Devereux (1997).

Another economist, Philip Lane (2000), explored the outcome of monetary shocks in U.S. external account fluctuations. According to Lane's study, a surprise monetary expansion will generate a constant external account surplus, although after one year of initial lag, but in the long run there is an indication that there is an initial negative direct impact effect. The short-run is distinguished from the long-run effects of the monetary shocks. In the event of an unexpected monetary shock in the short run, the initial period prices do not respond immediately to the disturbance.

There are at least three cases of short-run monetary shocks effects. In the first case, the monetary shock causes a short-run surplus in a non-traded sector which causes the price of traded goods to rise, but the intertemporal substitution effects of both short and long run are netted out, so there is no spillover effect on the consumption of the traded goods. This means that the current account remains still in balance with no real effects.

In the second case, an unexpected monetary expansion fuels extra demand and therefore extra production of non-traded goods causing a depreciated of the exchange rate. The increased demand for non-tradable goods has stimulated the consumption of tradable goods, and as a result the price of tradable goods rises. Given that the elasticity of substitution between consumption of tradable and non-tradable is relatively low, the current account goes into deficit in the short-run. However, in the long run, the current account is in the balance because a decrease in the consumption of the long-run tradable goods will require a long run depreciation and a trade surplus which will cancel out the negative effects of the deficit.

In case three, the monetary shock generates a short-run current account surplus. In this case, the consumption of tradable and non-tradable goods has a negative spillover, since the intertemporal substitution effect of the short-run real depreciation dominates the intertemporal substitution effect of a temporarily low price level (Lane 2000, 393). The consequence of this process is an increase in the long run level of tradable consumption. In the long run, the system is in equilibrium since the relative price of non-tradable goods in terms of tradable goods would rise, which make the long run exchange rate to appreciate.

Speaking of long-run and monetary shocks, there are also restrictions arising from the underlying intertemporal economic theory. The restriction consists of the condition that in the long-run current account response to a nominal shock is zero, which means that the cumulative trade balance effect of a monetary shock is zero and in equilibrium. This restriction is not surprising as the long run output may be affected by temporary absorption or even nominal shocks, but this effect seems to be minor and relatively not so important, as the study of Blanchard and Quah (1989) suggests. A monetary shock causing a temporary current account imbalance, under the condition of long-run restriction, has the capability to cause a permanent effect on the trade balance, as the accumulation of net external assets generates international investment income flows that helps the current account balance to return to equilibrium (a zero current account balance) but leaves a permanent trade imbalance (Lane 2000, 400).

Despite all this, the different models and schemes using monetary shocks have produced different estimates of the effects of monetary shocks to the current account fluctuations, so that there is still uncertainty in this analysis. One reason for this ambiguity is that monetary shocks within the framework of intertemporal sticky prices alone cannot effectively explain the current account dynamics. As a conclusion, "money shocks" approach is important, but the monetary policy as a whole has a more complex role in determining the current account fluctuations.

Conclusions about the Determination of Exchange Rates

Let me conclude by drawing some short considerations about the questions of exchange rates. First, I would like to emphasize that the debate between fixed and flexible exchange rates is still open, the literature is huge and is not easy to say which of them is a better option. There are many arguments in favor and against of both exchange rates. Although, the application of fixed or flexible exchange rates by many countries seem to be very different and complex, and not exactly as it is written in economists' essays.

There are good reasons concerning many economists for fixing exchange rates, letting them float or choosing an intermediate exchange regime. In this chapter, we have seen that intermediate regime used in a broad range of countries included the adjustable peg under which a country would normally have fixed exchange rates but reserved the right to change the system under certain conditions. However, decisions on circumstances concerning the choice of exchange rate regimes need to be internally and logically consistent.

When fixed exchange rates are preferred, this option inevitably implies giving up monetary autonomy and pegging the domestic currency to an international anchor currency. It is supposed that during pegged exchange rates the financial capital flows can play a stabilizing, non-speculative role in the economies preventing currency crises. A fixed rate system provides fewer roles for competition because central banks fix the relative prices of their products, but it encourages international cooperation in monetary policies.

On the other hand, the benefit of having flexible exchange rates is that the exchange rates can change in response to external shocks although a country would be more vulnerable to external rather than internal shocks. External real shocks theoretically would have not such a big impact on national income by using the flexible exchange rates but would be transmitted onto national income with a fixed rate, where the impact is much greater although the income response is not so certain. Flexible exchange rates are said to be a "shock absorber".

A trade-off exists between fixed and floating regimes. If economic policy is based on the "anchor" of a currency peg, monetary policy must subordinate to the needs of maintaining the peg. As a result, the burdens of adjusting the external shocks fall largely on fiscal policy, which means that fiscal policy must be flexible enough to respond to shocks. However, it happens that under the more flexible arrangement, monetary policy may be more independent, but inflation can be to some extent higher and more variable. Considerations affecting the choice of the regime may change over time. Under a flexible exchange rate regime when inflation is very high and monetary authorities are unable to control it, a pegged exchange rate may be preferable to a successful short-run stabilization program. In the long-run, to contain an external balance and move toward to full capital account convertibility, especially in a world of volatile capital flows, flexibility may become inescapable.

In the 1990s, many developing countries using fixed exchange rates have moved toward flexible exchange rate arrangements as inflation has come down generally across the developing world giving room for more growth. Different studies have demonstrated that the average inflation rate for countries with flexible exchange rates has fallen steadily. The perceived need for greater flexibility has probability resulted from the increasing globalization of financial markets which has integrated developing economies more closely into the global financial system.

Chapter 4

Optimum Currency Areas and Monetary Unions: History and Perspective

Introduction

The theory about optimum currency areas, different from other economic theories, has relatively a short life. This theory was "born" in the second half of the twentieth century as a consequence of increasing economic integration between countries and regions in different parts of the world. The beginning point for the theory of optimum currency areas (OCA) was Mundell with his earlier classic article "The Theory of Optimum Currency Areas" published in 1961. The theory was then elaborated further by other economists such as Mckinnon (1963) and Kenen (1969).

The main idea about an optimum currency area is that the exchange rate adjustment is needed only to pursue different monetary policies in two or more countries which have considerable factor mobility (capital and labor) and a high degree of openness to international trade in a larger area where these countries belong. If the real shocks occur, in response to which the exchange rate policy adopted depress one region within two or more countries, will simultaneously stimulate other regions within the area. In this case, it might be better for these countries to form one currency area. The use of exchange rates as a policy instrument is hence useful only when there are national differences.

These differences are due to asymmetric shifts in demand (shocks), different national policy preferences, different labor market institutions and fiscal systems, and so on. However, a currency area is good medicine for real shocks but cannot prevent unemployment and inflation among its members as the problems are not the type of currency area used but rather the macroeconomic structure of the currency area.

While in the sixties and seventies the case for OCA was concentrated more on theory, in the eighties and nineties and after the 2000s there were more empirical studies than new contributions to the theory. The aim of this chapter is to give more light on history and perspectives of optimum currency areas emphasizing particularly the formation and evolution of European Monetary Union (EMU).

Currency Areas in the Past and Present

History suggests that most politics, and not economics, is what has determined the currency areas in the past and present. Every time that political stability followed by economic expansion has facilitated international trade expansion, has also done many efforts to introduce an international currency to meet the demand of the trade. There have been economic and political reasons for having an international currency although in the past a single monetary standard has normally followed the expansion of political power able to dominate different regions.

Many big political powers from ancient times to the present such as, the Roman Empire, the Chinese Empire, the Ottoman Empire or the British Empire have established a single currency standard for the regions over which they have ruled. The first attempts to create an international currency for Europe was made in XIX century. The German Zollverein or the customs union between Prussia and German states was established in 1834, and the German currencies were integrated into the mark in 1873.

There are also other two successful examples of monetary unions in the nineteenth century: the Latin Monetary Union and the Scandinavian Monetary Union. Both originated at the time when national currencies were still largely based on metallic monetary standards. Each of them was built on standardized monetary units respectively, the franc and the krone, issued by nominally independent central banks (but not an international central bank); and each was considered a distinct currency area despite the frequent difficulties, until the outbreak of World War I.

The first one, the Latin Monetary Union (LMU), formed by France, Belgium, Switzerland and Italy (Greece adhered to the terms of the Union in 1868, though it did not become a formal member until 1876) as charter members, was established in 1865. The purpose of the LMU was to standardize coinages. Belgium, Greece, Italy and Switzerland decided to adopt a currency system modelled on that of France with franc (equivalently, the lira in Italy and the drachma in Greece) as their basic monetary unit. Each country agreed to imprint coins to a single standard that would be accepted as legal tender by government offices in any of the member countries.

LMU members, considered as a group of sovereign states, were distinguished from other European countries not belonging to LMU by the mutual commitment of their central banks to accept one another's currencies at par and without limit. Despite the global depreciation of silver coinage by all partners the union remarkably hold together and it was business as usual until the breakdown of the World War I. In effect, the LMU was transformed from a bimetallic standard at the beginning of the 1860s (silver and gold) into a gold standard (for the rest of its life), or what used to be called a "limping gold standard". The unprecedented success of the Latin Monetary Union in Europe led to the International Monetary Conference of 1867, which had the purpose of creating a single monetary standard for Europe and the United States by minting a common coin equal to 25 French Francs, 5 U.S. dollars and 1 British pound; but unfortunately, the idea fell through.

However, without a central monetary authority or international currency agreement currencies were fixed to gold. The LMU and the relations between LMU members were re-established after the WWI, but not for long. Switzerland withdrew from the union in 1926, and in 1927 the LMU was formally dissolved. Many of the difficulties experienced by LMU during its life and especially in decades before World War I were attributable to a decentralized structure of the system, allowing each country's central bank to continue to pursue its own domestic policy goals without having a common monetary strategy.

When the depreciation of silver began on the 1860s, some members to escape the currency depreciation had the temptation to increase the amount and circulation of their silver coinage, extracting additional seigniorage gains at the expense of their partners. The only way to hold the union together was for the members to restrict the use of silver coinage which was done in the 70', and in 1878 all silver coinages were suspended, and the LMU was transformed into a sort of "limping gold standard". In 1885 the LMU added the liquidation clause requiring any state wishing to leave the union to convert all of its silver held by other member governments in gold or convertible paper.

From today's perspective, it is clear that this union was meant to fail because even before the start of World War I, there was little sense of common interest among the members although there were efforts done by some members to avoid a costly dissolution of the union. In effect, the primary objective of the members from the beginning of LMU was concentrated on the domestic monetary policies despite the minimum efforts and the convenience to imprint coins according to the standard of the union which were accepted as legal tender by other member countries. There was no coordination or a central monetary authority to help countries go beyond the domestic policies.

The second monetary union, the Scandinavian Monetary Union (SMU) in a similar way as LMU was planned to standardize existing coinages, but based only on a monometallic gold standard rather than a bimetallic standard (silver and gold). In 1873, Sweden and Denmark formed the SMU, and two years later Norway joined the Union. The SMU established the krone as its uniform monetary unit, with national currencies permitted full circulation in all free countries.

As in the case of LMU, members of the SMU agreed to accept one another's currencies without limit. In 1885 the three members went further, agreeing to accept one another's bank notes facilitating free inter-circulation of all paper currency and eliminating the exchange rate quotations among the three currencies. At the beginning of twentieth century, the SMU became a single region for all payments purposes, until relations were suddenly interrupted by the suspension of convertibility at the start of World War I. Despite the attempts, as in the LMU, during and after the WWI to re-establish some elements of the union, especially after the return to gold standard in the mid-1920s, the agreement between SMU members, was not renewed, following the financial crisis of 1931.

Over two hundred years ago, the United Kingdom was the dominant country in the world economy. The exchange rates system was mostly fixed, and currencies used to have a fixed exchange value. At that time, there was no ultimate clearing currency between countries, which had led to the choice of the pound sterling as a reserve currency able to clear final settlements between international traders. This was called the "gold-pound standard," where international traders were allowed to clear their accounts in pound sterling, and the U.K. guaranteed to provide pounds for gold. The pound was used as a clearing currency among countries, and each pound was "supposed to be" backed by a certain amount of gold. Between the 1870s and 1914, the economy of world's major countries ran relative stability, and the currency fluctuations among major currencies were eliminated till the World War I forced countries to suspend their currency conversion.

Despite various efforts, there was no success to stabilize the international financial system after World War I as the war changed the relations between countries and with them the monetary agreement was not the same. The U.K. was not more a dominant country in the world economy and, evidently was not able to provide pounds for gold (as a reserve currency) to other major economies, while the United States was not ready to assume the leadership in the world economy.

After the Second World War, the *Bretton Woods* system (or the "gold-dollar standard") replaced the "gold-pound standard," as the U.S. became the dominant economy in the world. The U.S. also guaranteed the total convertibility between the dollar and gold. In the 1960's, many orthodox economists started arguing against the gold standard system because of the constraint of having a fixed reserve system in which reserves cannot expand when there is a run on gold. Central banks used to increase interest rates when there was a run on gold due to the balance of payments deficits, in order to keep their exchange rates fixed. The need for a domestically and internationally elastic reserve system was imminent. The possibility of a run on gold was threatening the U.S. economy, especially in the early 1970's, when the U.S. was running a huge trade deficit. In 1973, Richard Nixon declared that the U.S. would no longer honour its commitment of converting dollars into gold and it was the end of *Bretton Woods* System. Since then, most of the countries used to adopt the floating exchange rates system.

The most common case of monetary unions has been when a small country tied its currency to a larger country's currency. For example, Belgium a country of 10-11 million people and Luxembourg a small country of a half million people, in 1922 created the Belgium-Luxembourg Economic Union (BLEU) which lasted more than seven decades until the creation of EMU. After the World War I, Luxembourg decided to link itself commercially and financially with its bigger neighbour, Belgium, agreeing to a complete economic union including integration of their separate systems. Belgium's currency, franc, under BLEU benefited full status as legal tender in both countries. Belgium has a full central bank compared to the small Luxembourg Monetary Institute. The Luxembourg franc itself issued by the Luxembourgian Monetary Institute was limited in supply and served as a legal tender only inside the borders of Luxembourg. Despite the existence of independent decision-making bodies, Luxembourg given his considerable disparity of size compared to Belgium has been as an adjunct of the Belgian monetary system.

However, after the WWII there have been several efforts to form currency unions around the world. There are various multinational currency unions in developing countries that have worked well since World War II. In this contest must be worth to mention the case of islands of the East Caribbean, which has continued to merger their monetary system since the British Caribbean Currency. In 1965, the East Caribbean Monetary (Currency) Authority was created, and in 1983 the East Caribbean Central Bank issued a common currency called, the East Caribbean Dollar, to serve as a legal tender for all seven member countries.

The East Caribbean states have signed several agreements among the governments such as East Caribbean Common Market and the Organization of Eastern Caribbean States. The East Caribbean Currency Area has functioned well and without difficulties since its foundation in 1965. It was not a surprise to see that the East Caribbean currency union was stable since the beginning because it was based directly on the authentic feeling of solidarity shared by his members. In fact, in the East Caribbean, the regional identity has always been stronger than the national identity. It has been a long tradition of creating a whole network of related economic and political agreements.

The most successful currency union in developing countries has been the *Communaute Financiere Africaine* (CFA) which has continued a successful currency union among its members since the former French colonies gained their independence in the early 1960s. The roots of Franc Zone go back as far as 1945, when the French government decided to merge the diverse currencies of its African colonies into one common currency called, "le franc des Colonies Françaises d'Afrique" (CFA). In the 1960s, after the independence of France's colonies, the old colonial franc was replaced by two new regional currencies, each conveniently named to preserve the CFA franc appellation. For the seven members of the West African Monetary Union established in 1962 (Benin, Burkina Faso, Cote d'Ivoire, Mali, Niger, Senegal, and Togo) the single currency was called "le franc de la Communautè Financière Africaine", issued by the Central Bank of West African States; and for the six members of the Customs and Economic Union of Central Africa established in 1964 (Cameron, Central African Republic, Chad, Congo, Equatorial Guinea and Gabon), the common currency was called "le franc de la Coopèration financière en Afrique centrale", issued by the Bank of Central African States.

Despite the fact that each of the two currencies is legal tender only within its own region, the two common regional currencies are equivalently defined and are jointly managed, in cooperation with the Bank of France, as an integral part of a single monetary union. The importance of local hegemony is demonstrated clearly in the case of CFA. The durability of CFA is mainly attributable to the central role played by the Bank of France in underwriting Francophone Africa's joint currency agreements. The government of France exercises a decisive influence in the union through the operations accounts maintained by CFA's two regional central banks at the French Treasury, into which they are obliged to deposit the bulk (65%) of their foreign exchange reserves. In return, France guarantees the convertibility of the CFA franc at a fixed price and credit access from the Bank of France. The peg of the French franc to the CFA franc has remained at a ratio of 50:1, for more than four decades, giving currency stability to most of the CFA countries.

Another similar case in Africa has been that of Lesotho, Namibia and Swaziland, which have all tied their currencies to their neighbour, the South African currency (Rand), which is also the biggest country in the region. This currency area is currently called the Common Monetary Area (CMA) and goes back to the 1920s where rand, the South Africa currency, became the legal tender of the neighbours, Botswana, Lesotho, Namibia and Swaziland. In the 1960s and 1970s, the South African currency area developed quickly, given that most of the countries in the region won independence. In 1974, the monetary union was formalized, and it was called the Rand Monetary Area, and later in 1986 it got the actual name, the CMA, but without the participation of Botswana, which endorsed its own national currency, *pula*, introduced in 1976. In the recent years, the CMA has lost its original structure, and some of the members have created their own national currency, although today all three countries continue to peg their currencies to the rand at par.

In East Africa has been another case of a single currency union which had a short life. The British's colonies in East Africa, Kenya, Tanganyika (later Tanzania) and Uganda, under the control of Great Britain administration created in 1919 the single currency called the East African Shilling. The three colonies also inherited a customs union dating back in 1923, as well as a variety of other common services for railways, harbours etc. However, things changed quickly once independence arrived in the region in the early 1960s. As a matter of fact, joint institutions which were hereditary of the past colonial heritage including common currency quickly began to break apart. Therefore, in the late 1960s, all three countries were ready to create central banks and their own national currencies to replace the East African Shilling.

There is also another case of common currencies where several countries gave up control over their monetary policy to a supranational central bank. This is the case of European Union. The big push for monetary union in Europe began with the *Delors Report* of 1988[1], which promoted a gradual move toward a unified monetary system and a single currency. This was the basis for the well-known Maastricht Treaty, signed in 1992 by all the members that brought success to the introduction of a new common currency in 1999, called euro. In brief, the monetary history shows us a continuous aspiration to move toward a single currency when changes are economically and politically feasible. The reason is that the benefits of having a common currency and a common monetary policy exceed the costs of having a multitude of currencies and several monetary policies. These changes show that if political trends have moved toward greater pluralism and democracy in the world, finance, technology and economics have moved toward greater integration.

Comparing the currency unions, it is worth to notice that while economic and organizational factors are influential in determining the sustainability of monetary cooperation, interstate politics are more important. The monetary cooperation and integration or a monetary union can be done by a dominant state or by a network of institutional connections sufficient to make satisfactory the loss of monetary sovereignty to each member.

---

[1]European Commission archive of the Delors I Commission, Retrieved 17 March 2007.

Some Criteria for the Optimality of a Currency Area

The benefit of having different exchange rates between countries is a good strategy in helping them adjust to asymmetric economic shocks. However, a single currency eliminates the ability to adjust prices between countries and regions through changes in the exchange rate. Therefore, the use of the exchange rate as a policy instrument is helpful only when there are national differences. These differences are due to asymmetric shifts in demand (shocks), different national policy preferences, different labour market institutions and fiscal systems, and so forth.

In most cases, policy operations affect the union member-countries in a way which depends on their characteristics such as; the size of a country, the responsiveness of trade balance to changes in the exchange rate, the money demand to changes in income and the aggregate supply to changes in the real exchange rate. This fact shifts the analysis to the problem of the optimality of belonging to a single currency area. One of the pioneers in the theory of optimum currency areas was Robert Mundell who published his first article on this topic in 1961. Right after, other economists started working on the optimum currency areas (OCA) theory. There are at least three main criteria used for the optimality of the currency area: the criterion of factor mobility (Mundell, 1961); the criterion of the degree of openness (McKinnon 1963); and the criterion of the diversification in production (Kenen, 1969).

The Criterion of Factor Mobility in Mundell

In his earlier paper, on Optimum Currency Areas, Mundell (1961) suggested that the regions should be defined on the basis of factor mobility and single currency areas should correspond to regions which have internal factor mobility, allowing the use of a single currency within the region, and external factor immobility with corresponding flexible exchange rate regime with the rest of the world. Mundell considers a simple classical model of two regions A and B, initially in full employment and balance of payments equilibrium, and examines what happens if there is a reallocation in demand from the goods in region B to the goods in region A[2]. His model assumes that there is more than one currency area in the world which different and variable exchange rates between regions. If the demand for the products of the region or country B moves to the products of region or country A, it will create a high level of

[2] "...Assume that money wages and prices cannot be reduced in the short run without causing unemployment, and that monetary authorities act to prevent inflation..." Mundell 1961, p. 658.

unemployment in region B followed by a rising level of inflation in region A and a surplus in A's balance of payments.

To restore the equilibrium depreciation by country B or appreciation by country A is incurred to correct the external imbalance and also reduce unemployment in country B and contain inflation in country A. In addition, Mundell considers a continent which is divided into two big countries, such as the U.S. and Canada using floating exchange rate between them. Given the vastness of a continent such as North America that, for the purpose of the OCA analysis, gets further divided into two regions which do not correspond to the countries: the East which produces cars and the West which produces furniture. If the price-wage system were flexible, a shift in demand from cars to furniture would cause unemployment and decline in wages and price level in the East, inflationary payments, wage and price increase in the West and payments imbalances between two regions. The flexible exchange rate system will correct payments disequilibrium between two countries but not between the two regions. In the absence of the wage-price flexibility and labor mobility east and west need to have two separate monetary policies to adjust inflation and payments imbalances.

A currency area consisting of a pool of countries with national currencies, the ratio of employment in deficit countries is tolerated if the surplus countries are willing to allow a rise in inflation. However, in a currency area including many regions and a single currency, inflation is set by the willingness of central authorities to allow unemployment in deficit regions (Mundell 196, 659). A currency area alone will not be able to prevent both unemployment and inflation among its members. Mundell goes further and proposes the creation of an international monetary authority called World Central Bank, with the power to issue international means of payment, and work to reach an agreement among countries that the burden of international adjustment should fall on surplus countries, which would then inflate until unemployment in deficit countries is eliminated.

The optimum currency area itself is the region which comprises different countries, central authority and a single currency. As a consequence, the flexible exchange rate is not necessary within the common currency area as the national currencies are connected by fixed exchange rates, and does not serve to correct the balance of payments between countries in the currency area. If the optimum currency area is the region, the case for a flexible exchange rate regime would be based on regional currencies and not on national currencies that are part of the regional currency area. Therefore the soundness of the argument for flexible exchange rates depends on the affinity where nations with similar features correspond to one or more regions.

From a monetary dynamics perspective, Mundell (1960) advanced the argument that stabilization policy could be more complex under fixed exchange rates in case the short-term capital was highly immobile, and also more difficult under flexible exchange rates if capital was very mobile than if it was immobile. For this reason, he supported the hypothesis that fixed exchange rate system is better used within areas where factors are mobile, and the flexible exchange rate regime is better off for areas between which factors are immobile. Hence, the optimum currency area itself is a factor of integration that helps increase the mobility of the factors of production and reduce the likelihood of asymmetrical shocks.

The earlier Mundell was for an independent national monetary policy with exchange rate flexibility capable of dealing with asymmetric shocks, but differently, from Meade and Friedman, he supported this monetary regime only when factors were immobile. The advocates of flexible exchange rates such as Friedman (1953) and Johnson (1972) presumed that flexible monetary system was a good regime to preserve the stability of the domestic price level, but they do not propose any macroeconomic adjustment as Mundell did. The "Optimum Currency Areas" was a good case study and appealed both to monetarists and keynesians, although for all different reasons. The case for "Optimum Currency Areas" influenced enormously many scholars especially those who believed in Western Europe as a kind of "unique euro policy", although with its diverse national economies and immobile labour force compared to dollar area, and it became the base for analytical studies of more open-economy macroeconomics. Eichengreen, in the 1990s, recognized Mundell's influence in organizing the structure for the further analysis of a monetary area (like the euro-zone). He argued that,

> "...In Mundell's paradigm, policymakers balance the saving in transactions costs from the creation of single money against the consequences of diminished policy autonomy. The diminution of autonomy follows from the loss of the exchange rate and of an independent monetary policy as instruments of adjustment. That loss will be more costly when macroeconomic shocks are more "asymmetric"...when monetary policy is a more powerful instrument for offsetting them, and when other adjustment mechanisms like relative wages and labour mobility are less effective..."
>
> [Eichengreen 1997, 1-2]

The European Monetary Union has been one of the most studied cases of the optimum currency areas. It was the largest monetary unions created in the last two hundred years, and despite the success of having a single currency, it was not immune of some problems created because of the structure of the union. North and Central Europe have been traditionally more economically developed and with a better infrastructure than southern Europe, which means that a macroeconomic shock hitting the entire monetary union cannot have symmetric but rather asymmetric effects on different countries of the union.

Two well-known economists, Eichengreen and Bayoumi (1993, 104), analysed the shocking aspects of European Monetary Unification and found that because of the different macroeconomic structure between north and south Europe and between central and peripheral countries there is a strong distinction emerging among the supply shocks affecting the countries at the centre of the European Community such as Germany, France, the Netherlands, and Denmark and the supply shocks affecting other EC members located in periphery like the United Kingdom, Italy, Spain, Portugal, Ireland and Greece. The asymmetric shocks raise the concern that a monetary policy fitting all countries of the monetary union cannot be optimal for nations located in the centre of the union (central Europe) and for other nations situated in union's periphery, therefore the occurrence of asymmetric shocks should be seen as a criterion for assessing the optimality of an OCA.

Summarising, the main trade-off identified by Mundell is based on the expansion of the area over which a single currency prevails by improving efficiency but at the same time reducing the possibility of monetary responses to shocks that effect varies subregions in a dissimilar way. The wider the area, the higher is the internal factor mobility across countries (within the area) the greater are the efficiency benefits of possessing a single currency. The optimum lies in the kind of currency area.

The Criterion of the Degree of Openness in McKinnon

McKinnon (1963), differently from Mundell, assumes that the relevant criterion is not only the degree of factor mobility between countries but also the "openness" of the economy or inter-sector factor mobility. He acknowledges Mundell's idea of factor mobility as determining an optimum currency area, but he wants to go further by adding the openness criterion. According to McKinnon, "openness", is defined as the ratio of tradable to non-tradable goods. Under a flexible exchange rate regime and a high degree of openness to international trade, a shift of demand from non-tradable to tradable causes a currency devaluation which means that the price of tradable increases and that of non- tradable decreases by the rate of the devaluation.

Since the ratio of tradable to non-tradable goods is high, the prices level increases sharply. The more important non-tradable goods are in consumers' budgets, the domestic money can serve as a store of value with flexible rates. But as most commodities are tradable, exchange rate adjustments can do little to alter relative prices and changes in the rate would serve to undermine the utility of money as a store value.

By taking into consideration, a large currency area the body of non-tradable would be large, and the pegging value of the domestic currency to non-tradable goods would be sufficient enough to give money liquidity value to all operators in the currency area, although, it may be not sufficient for the foreigner investors. Regarding efficiency in the optimum currency area, we have that internal capital accumulation, and full employment are more significant than external capital movements. Whereas in a small currency area the ratio of tradable to non-tradable goods is large, the monetary implications of pegging the domestic currency to non-tradable-goods are less satisfactory. So, pegging a currency of small area to retain its value in term of a representative group of imports goods from a large currency is the same thing as pegging it to an outside currency. In addition, if they are small areas or countries which trade with each other, it will be better for them to fix their currency to each-other. In this case, the small areas can maintain the liquidity value in their currency.

McKinnon (1963) stresses out that under flexible exchange rates regime the disturbances to payments equilibrium cause a change in the exchange rate and a proportionate change in the process of exportable and importable goods. According to Grubel (1970, 318-24) the greater the share of tradable goods in total output, the larger the price fluctuations in the general price-index, therefore if currency area formation lowers the ratio of tradables to non-tradables goods it increases price stability. The enlargement of the currency area makes difficult for speculators to affect the market price, which in turn reduces exchange rate fluctuations and domestic price instability.

As I mentioned above, McKinnon (1963) - different from Mundell (1961) who believes on the geographic factor mobility among regions - take into consideration the factor mobility among industries. According to him, if there is factor immobility among industries, it would be more easily to consider slicing the world into currency areas along industries groupings rather than geographical groupings. For instance, suppose that we have only two regions in the world and that there is a rise in the demand for the products of region A and a decline in the demand for the products of region B. The value of marginal products of the mobile factors of production in region B will fall, and rise in region A. If B can develop A-type industries the factor movement between two countries is not large. The immobility factor between countries can be arranged by permitting each area of pursuing a monetary and fiscal policy to keep internal stability.

However, if the region B for different structural reasons is not able to develop A-type industries, factor mobility to region A may be the only way to avoid a large drop in the unit incomes of mobile factor of production in B. Thus, a policy planed directly at overcoming the immobility factors movements between A and B may be optimal and for the two countries reaching a high degree of openness in trade should be better to peg their currencies and join in a common currency. According to McKinnon (1963, 20-4), the criterion of the size of openness of a single currency economy in facilitating mobility factors between industries has to be balanced with the criterion of merely geographic factor mobility to determine the most favorable extent of a currency area.

There are two implicit assumptions in the McKinnon theory: first, the principal need for payments adjustment arises from microeconomic changes in demand and supply conditions; second, the price stability prevails in the rest the world. If the international economy itself is unstable, McKinnon's conclusion would have to be propagated to the domestic economy through the fixed exchange.

Corden (1972) was the first to show clearly that the McKinnon criterion was not a general one. He argued that the openness criterion pertains only to the situation in which microeconomic demand changes take place in a domestic market, and does not apply to the case in which macroeconomic turmoil occurs abroad. If the shock comes from abroad and causes the balance of payment disequilibrium, then the economy must insulate itself with flexible exchange rates. Even when McKinnon's stability assumption regarding the external environment holds, one cannot say that there is a positive gain in employing fixed exchange rates; it only means that the more open the economy is, the less costly is to maintain fixed exchange rates in terms of the required increase in the unemployment rate to affect the same degree of payment balance improvement in comparison to more closed economies.

The Criterion of Diversification in Production in Kenen

Kenen (1969), in a different way from both Mundell and McKinnon, proposed the criterion of the diversification in production to define an OCA. The process of formation of an Optimum Currency Area is accompanied by an economic integration process of the each-member country. So, regions are not only identified on the basis of the factor mobility but also on the similarities in the goods they produce. Regional integration implies free circulation of goods and specialization in production. The specialization acts as a factor of differentiation among "regions", and, if it coincides with the original countries, sector-specific shocks will also be country specific shocks which may introduce disruptive force within the union. Anyhow, more diversified economies are less vulnerable to external shocks and need the flexible exchange rates regime to maintain external balance.

In Kenen's view, a well-diversified national economy has not to go through changes in its term of trades and is more protected than a single product national economy. So, if national economies are specialized in diversity export production, they are better protected from external shocks. Diversity in exports helps to stabilize capital formation, easing the burden of internal policies and the sufficient occupational mobility to absorb the labor and capital unused by adverse disturbances. Less diversified economies need to be more open in order to import commodities they necessitate and exports commodities they produce, so they can obtain valuable international core currencies to pay for their imports. As a result of this policy, Kenen's diversification criterion will lead to the Mckinnon's openness criterion.

Kenen's main argument regarding fixed versus flexible exchange rates is that fixed rates are most appropriate to well-diversified national economies as in the case of industrialized countries; and that conversely, flexible exchange rates are better suited to the peculiar problems of the less-developed countries. The last ones, being less diversified and less well-equipped with policy instruments, should frequently change the exchange rates to suit better their performance on external shocks.

Kenen himself qualifies his thesis in some important aspects. He points out that production and export diversification cannot guarantee internal stability, even where external shocks tend to average out unless there is sufficient labor mobility to reabsorb labor and capital made redundant by external shocks. He acknowledges that when changes in export demand arise from business-cycle the whole range of exports will be hit, and therefore the export diversification cannot be expected to protect imported instability. The main argument to his conclusion is that the more diversified an economy, the more appropriate fixed exchange rates are.

Another point considered by Kenen is the "optimum policy mix" or the combination of fiscal and monetary policies on achieving internal and external stability. He argued that not necessary fiscal and monetary zones must coincide. In general, a fiscal area should not be larger than a monetary area. On the other hand, a fiscal area can be smaller than a monetary area; this is what is implied by a system of fixed exchange rates between two or more countries within an optimum currency area. Fiscal policy is important in a common currency area. In fact, if asymmetric shocks hit the common currency area, an integrated fiscal policy between regions would ease the impact through the use of fiscal transfers between regions.

The criteria for the definition of the optimum currency area theory have been largely developed in terms of demand. These criteria suggest that the optimum domain of a currency area is intended to secure an optimum condition under which monetary-fiscal policy is used for purposes of stabilization against shocks in demand. Unfortunately, the above criteria failed to offer guidance as to the size of an optimum currency area. Mundell's factor mobility criterion would easily lead to the establishment of micro-currency areas, if not restrained in its application by other criteria. McKinnon economic "openness" and Kenen's economic diversification criteria do not indicate an upper limit to size.

Combining the early criteria of Mundell, McKinnon, and Kenen for the optimality of a currency area we have that two or more countries can join a monetary union if some characteristics are met such as: factor mobility and price and wage flexibility (Mundell), the occurrence of asymmetric shocks (Mundell), the degree of openness and sector integration (McKinnon), the degree of product diversification (Kenen), fiscal integration between regions (Kenen) and similar economic structures between countries (Kenen).

Unfortunately, some of the criteria lead to conflicting and inconsistent effects. For example, the diversification criterion in Kenen leads to a contradiction. It recommends that pegged exchange rates are better suited to well-diversified national industrialized economies and flexible exchange rates are more appropriate for less-industrial countries and less-diversified economies. But, in reality, and from empirical studies things seem to be quite different. Developed economies, such as U.S.A., Canada and Japan, that are highly diversified and industrialized with a consolidated banking system can afford to have flexible exchange rates, while less developed countries that are less industrialized and have less diversified economies cannot effort to sustain frequent exchange-rate fluctuations as it will eventually create a currency crisis and send the economy into recession. Another contradiction is that large-size economies are more appropriate to use pegged exchange rates than are small economies, in contrast to the criterion of openness which suggests that open economies are better suited to be small and more likely to adopt the fixed exchange rate regime.

Another contradiction becomes evident when there is a high degree of openness between two or more countries, which bring a high level of sector specialization, thanks in part to the removal of barriers. If a shock hits the specialized sectors, it might well become country-specific shocks. This phenomenon recommends the utilization of flexible exchange rates to absorb country's shock contrary to the openness criterion which suggests that increased openness requires fixing exchange rates and joining a currency area.

The contradictions and conflicts led by various criteria of the optimum currency area show that the theory of optimum currency area was born, in a world (in the 1960s) still characterized by the Bretton Woods System of fixed but adjustable exchange rates and limited capital mobility among countries.

Mundell, McKinnon and Kenen still had in mind wage and price stickiness and the existence of the trade-off between inflation and unemployment (Phillips curve).

In the seventies, a second wave of contributors started analysing the existing optimum currency criteria, while also introducing new proposals into the theory. The contribution of Corden (1972), Mundell (1973), Ishiyama (1975), and Tower and Willet (1976) consists on a widespread review of the known optimum currency area criteria and focus on the new ideas and suggestions to the theory. Gorden (1972) emphasized the importance of wage, price flexibility and inflation rate criteria in forming a currency area as they can respond faster to asymmetric shock. A country joining a common currency has to give up the control on the exchange rate and monetary policy, which means that if it is hit by a negative shock, the authorities have to use other policies such as fiscal policy, reduction of prices and nominal wages, and control of inflation.

In his later work, Mundell (1973), highlights that if a common currency area is monetarily and economically integrated doesn't have to fear asymmetric shocks as the risk will be shared among regions that are part of the optimum currency area. The effects of the asymmetric shock would not be so severe if the regions have factor mobility of capital and labor and what is more important are capable of moving easily financial capitals. Therefore, financially integrated economies can form a perfect common currency area and will be able to absorb any asymmetric shock.

Ishiyama (1975) in his study recognized that different criteria are not enough to determine the optimum currency area. His idea is that each country should be able to evaluate the costs and benefits of participating in a common currency area. Other macroeconomic measurements were also considered such as differences in inflation rates, wages increases and unemployment rates among countries forming the common currency area.

Two other economists, Tower and Willet (1976) focused on the relative costs and benefits of fixed and flexible exchange rates for each individual country taking part in the common currency. In their view, joining the currency area will help increase the convenience and the various functions of money as a medium of exchange, unit of account, store of value and standard of deferred payments especially if the economy in question is very open to trading. Despite all these benefits, the entrance to a common currency area offers some limits such as constraints in the use of discretionary macroeconomic policy to achieve internal balance.

After a prominent start in the 1960s and 1970s, there was a hold back in research about the theory of optimum currency areas. For a period of about

20 years, academic interest in the theory of OCA was of second-order importance most probably for lack of practical examples of monetary unification in the developed countries. However, in the early 1990s with the creation of the European Monetary Union, the theory of OCA re-emerged as an active area of research that continues to the present. A report called "One Market, One Money", published by a group of authors in 1992 (Emerson, M., Gros D., Italianer A., Pisani-Ferry J. and Reichenbach H.) draw attention by pointing out that there is no theory capable of assessing the cost and benefits of the economic and monetary union. The report embraces a critical view of the "old optimum" currency area theory and at the same time helps to revitalize the interest in the debate about the OCA theory by stimulating a vast amount of new research among the advocates of the OCA and monetary unions.

Based on this report the OCA theory has provided interesting approaches in the past for the optimality of an OCA which has offered no more than a thin analytical framework to define the optimal economic and monetary competences of a given geographic region such as EU. The "One Market, One Money" report (1992) is in favor of going on with complete monetary integration in Europe of the EU members. In fact, according to this report, the European Monetary Union is likely to be more advantageous in terms of economic benefits than what can be assumed if the European countries apply the OCA properties alone. For example, if we apply the OCA theory alone, we can easily find that the labor mobility among the European members is low, but the mobility of capital is rather high and rising which make the European Monetary Union the only alternative to provide an adjustment channel for labor mobility and other issues. Because of the EU creation in the 1990s, several analytical structures behind the OCA theory underwent a deep modification which led to a reassessment of the effective costs and benefits from the monetary integration perspective.

From Optimum Currency Areas to Monetary Unions

Countries are having similar economic structures and factor mobility normally tend to react to economic shocks in the same way. It follows that there is no point in any of them trying to devalue against the others and they should consider forming a common currency area (Mundell, 1961). In this context, a common currency is identified as a region (having the same economic structure) with one or several currencies whose relative values are fixed mostly in a permanent way but whose common external exchange rate is flexible and determined by the market with no interference from monetary authorities (Grubel 1970, 318). So, if two or more nations with flexible exchange rates wishing to form a common currency area, have to give up their monetary sovereignty to an international agency that will guarantee the regional monetary policy. However, they have not to give up the right to determine government spending, taxation, national policy-making and the welfare state.

According to Grubel (Grubel 1970, 320), there are a number of benefits to the countries joining a common currency area. First, the uncertainty in price between countries is eliminated, and producers consider the enlarged currency area as a huge territory where they can improve their marketing and factor purchasing. The growth of companies permits exploitation of internal scale economies and results in increased specialization. Second, the elimination of foreign exchange rate uncertainty between the two or more countries encourages a more efficient allocation of capital within the currency area. Third, the enlargement of the currency area increases price stability between countries. Price stability is a function of both the frequency and magnitude of price fluctuations. Therefore, currency union increases stability only if the random shocks of each country are less than perfect and positively correlated. The joining of an OCA and the pegging of the exchange rates between countries tend to raise the level and stability of income in the long-run which in turn help decrease the national economic autonomy. This also influences the welfare state of the countries joining the OCA. Grubel argues that:

> "Countries A and B represent an optimum currency area in the restricted sense discussed above if the net welfare gain of the area's population from these partly negative and positive influences is greater than zero. In the choice of the world-welfare maximizing network of currency unions the welfare changes of the A and B population have to weight against the welfare changes of the country C's population; ..."
>
> [Grubel H. G., 1970, 323]

The OCA theory has also emerged out during the debate over the relative gains and costs of flexible versus fixed exchange rates. The OCA is an optimal geographical area where there is a common means of payment either as a single common currency or several currencies whose exchange values have been pegged to one another member, but the exchange rates of the OCA oscillate as a single union against the rest of the world.

The term "optimal" is referred to the macroeconomic goal of maintaining internal and external balance. Internal balance is achieved at the optimal trade-off point between unemployment and inflation, and external balance is referring to both inter-area and intra-area balance of payments equilibrium.

As mentioned above, the traditional literature suggests structural criteria - factor mobility (Mundell, 1961), trade integration (McKinnon, 1963), and regional production patterns (Kenen, 1969) - to assess if a region is an optimum currency area. Other literature (Marston, 1984) emphasised the importance of flexible exchange rates between regions experiencing asymmetric shocks or differences in shock-absorbing mechanisms. More recent literature has focused on the structural patterns of the countries participating in a monetary union (Hagen Von and Neumann, 1994; Frankel and Rose, 1997; Mundell, 1998; Feldstein, 2000).

An efficient labour market is crucial for an OCA to succeed. For example, without a stimulation plan to the regional economies of the EMU area affected by the recession, the unemployed have to move to the regions where the jobs are. But the empirical studies have shown that in an important optimum currency area such as the EMU, the labour mobility among the larger countries (and also within them) is limited. Instead, some studies conducted by OECD have found that mobility in U.S. regions is two to three times higher than in EU member states. However, labor mobility may be unhelpful if it causes a region with low productivity to experience a rapid rise in wages because unemployment has caused skilled workers to migrate in areas with higher job opportunities and wages (for example the case of Eastern Germany where skilled labor force moved to West Germany during the first decade of ri-unification). In any case, the labour mobility seems to be not the optimal solution for temporary disturbances in demand for labour because the cost of moving of a not short distance is considerable.

Capital movement is another factor mobility which may help further the financial integration in an OCA. It may also help to adjust imbalances if capital flows from fully-employed to under-employed areas, but with free markets, capital tends to flow from areas with low returns on assets to ones yielding higher returns. In general, industries serving domestic or regional markets tend to agglomerate in areas with favourable externalities or locations closed to customers and skilled work-force, and certainly not in depressed areas.

Inter-regional economic integration and trade openness are factors that help to maximize the participation of members in an OCA. An open economy, with a high degree of interdependence with other regions (or countries), can benefit most from expanding demand in a neighbouring country. However, a country has also to share with its neighbour the fall of the neighbour's demand. If the demand is stable in its trading partner, a country (especially if relatively small) does not need exchange-rate changes to deal with the balance of payments problems, since a small tightening of such a country's fiscal policy yields a big reduction in its external deficit. But if demand in its partner countries slumps, the devaluation is more rapidly dispersed by price increases, since its high portion of imports to its gross national expenditure must involve a larger direct effect of import prices on consumer prices, which will pass through into wage costs raises.

Economic integration is referred to the extent to which the economies of a region are becoming more similar to each other. If the economies of an OCA are converging, there is less need for any exchange rate adjustment between them since economies will be in expansion or contraction together. The convergence can also be viewed in terms of diversification. If most of the members of an OCA have a similar spread of industries, a country generally cannot suffer an economic slowdown in its own due to a particular slump in one particular sector. In a successful OCA, the productivity is expected to converge across the whole area over the long run. The same thing we can say for the common economic cycle. Countries used to move in line with the "virtual" cycle of the country guide. For example in the case of European Currency Area most of countries tries to follow the country guide which is Germany (exemption the period of German unification with the East).

If countries of an OCA increase their trade integration, it will be a specialization effect where the respective country-members will specialise in the production of those goods in which there is a comparative advantage. This argument bring us to the study of Frankel and Rose (1997) which suggests that increased trade in an OCA can cause either increased sector/industrial specialization between countries in commodities in which they have comparative advantage that can lead to industry-specific shocks or increased trade can cause increased correlation between countries' business cycles that may be endogenous. Correlation between business cycles considered as income correlation depends on trade integration. Therefore, if countries have a substantial trade between them and have a positive income correlation, they might find it advantageous to create a monetary union. Endogeneity of an OCA recommends that the criteria of openness and income correlation are not taken as granted as countries may change their integration policies over time because of the exogenous factors. Despite this, when the potential candidates to form a common currency area join the monetary union they may increase further trade integration which in return will enhance income correlation. In this way, according to Frankel and Rose (1997), countries joining the currency area satisfy the OCA criteria ex-post rather than ex-ante when they did not fulfil some of the OCA criteria.

There are two questions arising regarding the OCA:

How can an OCA become a monetary union? What's the difference between an OCA and a monetary union?

A monetary union is the elimination of the monetary fragmentation between countries in the sense of currency differences and fluctuations which impede the completion of a successful single market. Generally speaking, a monetary union is when two or more states anchor their currencies to another member's currency taken as a standard or when they use a common currency within the union and are subject to single monetary policy. A customs union, instead, is a common market or a market without customs barriers and obstacles. Usually, a customs union is the first step in building up a single enlarged market. Broadly speaking, an efficient custom union- assuming that the union is "natural"- does not need to limit fluctuations of exchange rates, and the benefits of trade creation dominate the costs of trade diversion (Krugman, 1991).

There are no strictly economic obstacles to prevent countries from removing trade barriers and restructuring along the lines of comparative advantage. Following the lines of the European Commission (1990) report "One Market, One Money", a market of commodities gets completely integrated if there is elimination of transaction costs and uncertainties associated with separate currencies, although, it is possible to obtain efficiency advantages from a single currency while maintaining separate, sovereign, political jurisdictions. It is however feasible that while a single market for goods, services, capital and labour would need complex common policies and synchronization in several structural, micro and macroeconomic ordination, a well-organised economic union requires much less centralisation of policy competencies than monetary union. In fact, an economic union different from a monetary union doesn't require a central bank and a central regional commission to supervise the macroeconomic policies of the union.

Capital mobility, as listed above, is another point to go for "deeper" integration. But, the liberalization of capital movements makes intermediate exchange rate arrangements more difficult to sustain. If currencies, in an OCA, are free to move against one other, the single market will not be perfect. The risk remains that governments will try to protect domestic companies against rivals in countries which use devaluation. The greater the volatility, the greater the pressure for national protection. The elimination of capital controls, which is a consequence of a single market project, removes governments an important policy tool used to defend pegged-but-adjustable exchange rates. The problems get more complicated when the currencies come under attack: the unemployment aggravates, the cost of serving public debt raises, the mortgage payments are inflated, and banking system is destabilised. In this case, the governments might be encouraged to abandon the exchange-rate peg in the face of speculative attacks.

As it became more difficult to operate governments should have as a first alternative the choice between floating or pegging the fixed rates permanently. The second alternative should be the case of a monetary union. The shift from fixed to float currencies increases the volatility of exchange rates, and Andrew Rose (1994) has demonstrated it. This is the basis for arguing that economic integration requires monetary integration. Hence, an optimum currency area needs an economic integration, and an economic integration needs a monetary union.

Eichengreen (1997) argues that the connection between commercial integration and exchange-rate stability are not as straightforward as supposed by the literature. It was believed that the currency fluctuations and trade restraints were substitutes and not complements to one-other.

In the early 1950s, major European Countries instituted the European Payments Union (EPU) in a way to use exchange and trade restrictions for the maintenance of pegged rates. Some economists at that time highlighted the connection between pegged exchange rates and the trade restrictions. During the fifties, the advocates of flexible exchange like Robert Triffin and Sohmen Egon and in particular Milton Friedman interpreted the pegged rates supported by different countries and especially by EPU as an encouragement to maintain the trade restriction across Europe. On the other hand, the advocates of fixed exchange rates such as Ronald McKinnon (1971) and John Williamson (1965) blamed the exchange rate fluctuations associated with the post-1973 system of floating rates. When exchange rates fluctuate employee demand wage indexation and frequent renegotiation of wage contracts to prevent the real wages from being troubled by exchange monetary shocks. The depreciation of the currency should cause the wages to rise, but it has not any big impact on the international competitiveness. The exports would increase in the market outside the OCA, and the other countries would respond on moderating their monetary policies.

The real effects of exchange-market shocks may create conflicts between exchange rates variability and market integration. A monetary unification is indispensable to maintain political support for market integration. If exchange rates continue to fluctuate, markets will adapt to moderate their impact on competitiveness. On the other side if exchange rates are locked once for all the problem of competitive depreciation should be resolved, although one can expect to see an additional adjustment in the market structure and response. The problems related to the short-term remain because the labour and product markets will adapt gradually to the pegged regime due to the absence of the exchange-rate instrument. A monetary union is more stable in a long-run solution than a natural OCA.

A General View of the Monetary Unions

Mundell in 1961 defined the Optimum Currency Area as a domain where within its boundaries the exchange rates among countries or regions are fixed. Both Keynesians and Monetarists have opposed the idea of monetary union. The Keynesian feared the removal of devaluation as a weapon of monetary policy. The monetarists' objections consist of the fear that a common European currency might bring the dollar in a weak position and eventually the possibility of fiscal problems among different members of European Union (EU).

Mundell launched his "Plan for a European Currency," in 1970 at the Madrid Conference on optimum currency areas. In a dissimilar way from other participants — such as McKinnon and Grubel who focus their discussion in the theory of OCA —he centres his attention on the idea of an advanced stage of OCA which is a monetary union and the introduction of a unique currency in the case of Europe. Grubel, (1973) for example, in that conference introduced the theory of optimum regional associations which was based on a theoretical analysis of welfare effects accompanying the institutional changes — like the creation of custom unions, common markets, currency areas or the formation of new states — necessary to put into effect the various kinds of regional associations.

The theory of optimal regional associations was interpreted in two distinctive ways: first, as a region of the welfare-maximizing network of associations of which each one is optimum, and second, as a region in which the welfare of its residents is maximized in disregard of the effects on the rest of the world. The important point in this theory is to give credibility to the idea that the regional cooperation in all levels is the best way to maximize the welfare of the members joining the regional associations.

Mundell's plan to disengage Europe from dollar dependence begins by creating an alternative currency or by choosing a (pre-existing) common currency. He considered three options: the first option is to choose gold; the second one is to create a synthetic unit of account and the third one to choose an existing European national currency that will be a new numéraire to which the others would fix their exchange rates. Mundell recommended the third option by choosing an existing currency such as the pound sterling as the best option for numéraire because the United Kingdom was the largest financial centre in Europe and the pound was still a well-respected world currency.

Therefore, if pound sterling were going to become a European currency, it would have pegged its exchange rates to the dollar while other countries instead of pegging to the dollar would have pegged to the pound. Based on this logic, Britain would need larger dollar reserves because she would have taken upon herself the deficit of the whole Europe when Europe was in deficit. The other countries should have deposited their dollars in a special account set up by the bank of England and get in return credit in pounds. If the U.S. would have inflated (deficit) or gone in depression, Europe had to change the pound parity of dollar and the parity of Europe as a whole giving monetary independence to Europe (Mundell, 1970). Britain pound would have acted as an alternative currency to the dollar not only formally for European countries but also for the other countries.

The evolution of European Monetary Union showed that pound sterling was not able to become a numéraire currency despite the original idea of Mundell. Instead, the more stable German monetary policy and the performance of the D-mark as dominant currency in European scenario (after WW II) in strong competition with dollar made a choice for European currency. The Deutsche mark became the numéraire currency of all European currencies and the focal point to rebuild the exchange rate stability and monetary unity in Europe. Mundell's (1970) plan for a European Currency became reality with advent of the euro on January 1, 1999, even though pound sterling, the old powerful and dominant currency of the nineteenth century did not join the monetary union.

By having a look at different world currencies, one may see several examples of movement toward multinationals currencies. On January, 1st 2002 the common physical currency, called Euro, replaced the currencies of the eleven countries in Europe creating *de facto* the European Monetary Union (EMU). Other countries are joining the EU lately were going to adopt the same currency creating the biggest and the most powerful monetary union ever existed. Dollarization has been implemented in Ecuador and El Salvador. Other Latin American countries including Mexico, Guatemala and Peru, are going to take into consideration dollarization.

The *Communaute Financiere Africaine* (CFA) region in West Africa currently called *UEMOA*, which before the introduction of Euro used French franc as a pegged currency has been ongoing negotiations with international organizations to create a new currency for the region or adopting euro. In the same way, the members of the Southern African Development Community have been considering for some time whether to adopt the dollar or form an independent monetary union possible pegged to the South African Rand. Six oil-producing countries (Saudi Arabia, United Arab Emirates, Bahrain, Oman, Qatar, and Kuwait) have acknowledged their objective to form a sort of currency union in the future. Several countries have maintained currency boards with either the U.S. dollar or euro as an anchor. Currency boards are a halfway between a system of fixed exchange rates and currency adoption.

Generally speaking, there are two forms of the currency union. The first form, which is also the most common, is often seen in the cases where candidate countries (usually small countries) adopt the currency of a larger anchor country. In the second case, a group of countries (which meet the OCA criteria) generate a new currency and create a supranational central bank. The second case applies to the eurozone. While the Eastern Caribbean Currency Union (ECCU), the Communauté Économique et Monétaire de l'Afrique Centrale (CEMAC) in Central-Africa and CFA zone in West-Africa are intermediate forms of currency unions. In a different way from the two cases mentioned above, a large number of small and developing countries around the world have fixed their currencies to a large anchor country.

The introduction of euro as a common currency in Western Europe in 1999 had a big influence in other OCAs around the world. There have been some attempts to form a monetary union in two well-known optimum currency areas, one in North America between Canada, the U.S. and Mexico, and another one in Australia between Australia and New Zealand, which unfortunately had failed, although recently new efforts have been readdressed on this direction.

Following the development of North American Free Trade Area (NAFTA), the idea of union in North America and the creation of a common currency has become an issue of growing importance for Canada's policy analysts and economists especially after the introduction of euro in Europe. Grubel (1999) considered the case for the Amero (used in NAFTA area) and eventually the foundation of a North American Monetary Union following the traces of EMU. He proposed that Canada, the United States and Mexico should replace their currencies with the "Amero" and their central banks should be substituted by a North American Central Bank with all three countries represented on its board of governors. However, this view was criticized by David Laidler and Finn Poschmann (2000) who pointed out that there was no interest in the United States giving up the US dollar policy. The only common currency arrangement available to Canada is the unilateral adoption of the US dollar, but they fear the loss of monetary sovereignty for Canada —given the structure of Canadian labor market— and of "lender of last resort' facilities".

In the United States there are common asymmetric shocks between different parts and regions which are dealt with by high labor mobility and substantial transfers of federal funds. Unfortunately, by the adoption of US dollar in Canada, neither benefit would be available to this country. Grubel (1999) emphasizes that the adoption of US dollar as Canada's currency means a large loss in seigniorage which is unacceptable for Canada (the annual seigniorage amount for Canada is estimated at $ 2.5 billion or 1.5 percent of Canadian federal tax revenue). Unilateral dollarization of the Canadian economy will leave no choice to Canadian monetary authorities especially in the case of real and monetary shocks. As Laidler (2005) explains,

> "...Simple unilateral dollarization of the Canadian economy along Panamanian or Ecuadorian lines would leave Canadian regulatory and clearing systems as they currently are. To the extent the harmonization of such arrangements with their US counterparts would be required to achieve full integration of the North American monetary system, then gains from unilateral dollarization might turn out to be disappointingly low. There might be losses indeed because unilateral dollarization would deprive the Canadian monetary authorities of the ability to create new liquidity at will for the financial system should circumstances require it. The importance of this last factor was brought home dramatically by the events of 11 September 2001, when the Canadian clearing system was saved from breakdown only by an immediate and large injection of high-powered money by the Bank of Canada...."
>
> [Laidler D. 2005, 57]

Another author, Harris (2000), proposed a different North American Monetary Union (NAMU) on the basis that the Canadians and Mexicans would join the twelve Federal Reserve Banks in the United States. He discussed the dollarization of Canadian currency and expressed a low opinion of the history of exchange rate management and floating rates in Canada. The main difficulty on the creation of a the North Monetary Union is political. None of the North American countries would like to lose its monetary sovereignty, and none of them wants to give up its seigniorage.

Different from Canada, the Federal Reserve has long experience on using seigniorage to finance the U.S. government's spending and has no problem obtaining consensus inside the US or in passing its decisions on to the Congress. A monetary union is often preceded by the creation of supranational organizations as in the case of EMU where the European countries have conceded sovereignty to European institutions such as the European Council, Commission, Court, Parliament and monetary matters to a Central Bank where all the countries are in the same position with respect to the European institutions.

This seems not to be the case for the U.S., Canada and Mexico. Even before getting to a North American Central Bank, it would be beyond our imagination thinking of creating a North American Council or Commission with competencies across the continent. It is believed that the benefits deriving from introducing a common currency would result in greater productivity, lower transaction costs, lower long-term interest rates (because of the elimination of exchange rate risk) and among all a steady and low inflation rate. The economic integration and the use of common currency have also their weak point because any integrated monetary policy in the continent will not be able to absorb asymmetric shocks in the short-run in such a vast market like North America made of several immense regions.

The studies made on Canada-U.S. exchange rate have demonstrated that volatility in real exchange rate reflects in large part real economic shocks. According to the research of Carr and Floyd (2002), the volatility in the exchange rate is not the result of oscillations in macroeconomic policy or speculative attacks on the demand for money but rather on the magnitude of the asymmetric attacks hitting the economy. The evidence on the effects of monetary shocks calculated by Carr and Floyd (2002, 34) is illustrated in table 4.1 obtained by the unanticipated Canadian and U.S. money supply shocks on Canada/U.S. real exchange rate.

Independent Variables	Dependent variables: real exchange rate	
	(1)	(2)
CONSTANT	-88.58***(-3.31)	-83.47*** (-3.07)
PCOMXEN	0.116***(9.83)	0.114*** (9.48)
POIL	0.076***(3.12)	0.083*** (3.37)
TOTCAUS	0.247**(2.47)	0.225*** (2.23)
DIFFNTAB	1.85***(6.52)	1.9*** (6.64)
RGDPRAT	1268.2**(5.06)	1242.8*** (4.84)
Unanticipated Canadian M1 shocks	-14.98 (-0.53)	
Unanticipated U.S. M1 shocks	102.68 (1.69)	
Unanticipated Canadian M2 shocks		-17.8 (-0.24)
Unanticipated U.S. M2 shocks		-40.58 (-0.49)
R^2	0.842	0.838
Standard error	4.67	4.73
DW	0.336	0.304

Table 4.1 OLS (Ordinary Least Squares) analysis of the effects of unanticipated money supply shocks on Canada/U.S. real exchange rate: 1972/Q1 to 1998/Q4 (Source: Carr and Floyd, 2002)

The indexes on Table 4.1 are explained as follows: PCOMXEN is the index of commodity prices net of energy in U.S. dollars deflated by an unweighted U.S. dollar index of U.S. export and import prices; POIL is the index of oil prices in U.S. dollars deflated by the same unweighted U.S. dollar index of U.S. export and import prices. TOTCAUS is the Fisher's index consisting on the bilateral Canada/U.S. terms of trade; DIFFNTAB is the difference between the negative of the Canadian balance of trade in goods and services excluding the services of capital and corresponding U.S. series; RGDPRAT is the ratio of Canadian to

U.S. real GNP; DIFFGOV is the excess of government consumption as a percentage of GDP in Canada over the same variable in the U.S.

Columns (1) and (2) in the table above also show the residuals from the regressions of the logarithm of money supply shocks for each of the two money supply categories M1and M2 lagged from one to eight quarters of the real GDP logarithm which lags 8 periods as well (Carr and Floyd 2002, 34-35).[3] The figures in parentheses are t-ratios and the star symbols **, ***, indicate statistical significance at the 1.5 and 5 percent levels, respectively. The unexpected and unanticipated monetary shocks derive from a regression of the OLS logarithm of the money supply aggregate. Table 4.1 illustrates that unanticipated Canadian and U.S. M2 shocks are both negative (-17.8 and -40.58) while the unanticipated Canadian and U.S. M1 shocks are negative and positive respectively (-14.98 and 102.68). If the real exchange rates were affected exogenously by the Bank of Canada, the coefficient signs in the Canadian money supply could have been all negative, and likewise, the U.S. unanticipated money supply shocks could have had positive coefficients. But even if three out of four signs in M1 and M2 category were correct and one sign was incorrect will still bring to the conclusion that these dependent variables are statistically insignificant. This evidence by Carr and Floyd (2002) emphasizes the proposal that observed movements in Canada/U.S. (or other bilateral) real exchange rates are determined by real asymmetric shocks and not simply monetary shocks.

Real economic forces can create fluctuations in the demand and supply of commodities in the international market affecting the relative price structure. For example, Asian crises in the late 1990s led to the fall in demand for Canadian exports such as raw materials (oil and mineral prices) which resulted in the depreciation of the Canadian dollar. Had Canada adopted the U.S. dollar in the 1990s, when the real shocks were hitting the Canadian economy, a large number of prices and wages would have to adjust, leading to the fall of price level compared to the U.S. In addition, prices and wages are normally not so flexible in the short-run, which means that Canada would experience rise in unemployment and compromise its standard of living compared to the United States. Therefore, the common currency would not

---

[3] Generally speaking, **M1** is classified as a money supply category that includes all cash and assets that can be converted easily in currency. Here are included physical money like coins, currency bills and assets like demand deposits which are chequing accounts and Negotiable Orders Withdrawal (NOW) accounts, etc.

M2 is defined as a wider money supply category that includes M1 category plus all time-related deposits, savings deposits, and non-institutional money-market funds. M2 normally describes the amount of money in circulation.

have defended Canada against the pessimistic effects of the real negative shocks that combined with unemployment effects would have deteriorated the scenario. Based in the study of Bayoumi and Eichengreen (1994), the asymmetric shocks hitting the U.S. and Canadian economies at the same time are responsible for causing a significant magnitude of variation in the real exchange rate.

A flexible exchange rate regime and a distinguished currency from the US would be very helpful for Canada as it will reduce the shocks that would otherwise convey to domestic money wages and prices. Canada's current monetary policy and the flexible exchange rate regime in place have been consistent and working well able to absorb all kind of real and monetary shocks in the past decades and as predicted by many studies will also work well and support the country's growth in the decades to come.

Australia and New Zealand is another case of missing monetary unions. As in the case of Canada, the discussion for a monetary union began in 1999 with the successful advent of euro in Europe. Three economists in 2000, from the Institute of Policy Studies for Australia, Dr. Arthur Grimes, Sir Frank Holmes and Bowden Roger produced a report in which they considered the two alternatives of creating a common currency: the first alternative regards the simple adoption of the Australian dollar; the second one takes into consideration the creation of ANZAC dollar, a new currency common for both countries.

The Grimes-Holmes-Bowden Report (2000) argued that an agreement of New Zealand with Australia would be more politically acceptable than simply "dollarizing" on the Australia unit, and would involve negotiating the creation of a joint central bank where both countries will be represented. This agreement would bring to the adoption of a common currency, the ANZAC dollar, which in one hand would eliminate the asymmetric shocks of both countries and in another hand would bring more benefits in the whole area as a result of capital market integration. The authors of the report completely recognize that a small economy such as New Zealand must essentially choose between a floating exchange rate and a credible fixed rate in the form of a currency board, dollarization, or monetary union. As in the case of North American Union, some objections regarding the Australian Monetary Union rose. Andrew Coleman (2001) argued that a monetary union would in practice mean New Zealand simply "dollarizing" on the Australian dollar (to a bigger country) without having a significant influence on the management of the currency.

Actually, nor in North America, nor in Australia, nor also in South East Asia and Latin America[4] does exist an agreement on the creation of a monetary union. Most of these areas, according to the theory of OCA, meet the conditions for a monetary union but up to date, there has been no political motivation to do this. Despite the existing economic integration within the areas, the central banks of each country won't give up their monetary policy and sovereignty to reach any kind of agreement for laying down the foundations of a common currency. Comparing them to EMU I should say that eurozone has been truly a great success never seen before and the perspective of having another "euro success" (or whatever name we may call them "Amero", "Anzac" or "Asean") in the international monetary panorama is far from being fulfilled, unless politicians would agree to do so.

A summary of modern currency unions and their compositions:

Communauté Économique et Monétaire de l'Afrique Centrale (CEMAC)

Cameroon, Central African Republic, Chad, Congo Republic, Equatorial Guinea (1985-), Gabon, Madagascar (1960-72).

East Caribbean Currency Union (ECCU)

Antigua and Barbados (1965-72), Dominica St. Kitts and Nevis St. Lucia, St. Vincent and Grenadines.

European Monetary Union (EMU), Euro Zone.

Austria (1999-), Belgium (1999-), Cyprus (2008-), Estonia (2011-), France (1999-), Finland (1999), Germany (1999-), Greece (2001-), Ireland (1999-), Italy (1999-), Latvia (2014-), Lithuania (2015), Luxembourg (1999-), Malta (2008-), Netherlands (1999-), Portugal (1999-), Slovak Republic (2009-), Slovenia (2007-), Spain (1999-).

---

[4] The ASEAN (*Association of South-East Asian Nations*) in Asia and Mer.Co.Sur. *(Mercado Común del Sur)* in Latin America are simply trade association or cooperation agreements that has nothing to do with monetary union and a common currency. Actually, in these areas there is no political agreement on achieving a monetary union and on adopting a single currency. The same logic applies to the OUA (Organization of African Union).

West African Economic and Monetary Union (UEMOA) ex-CFA

Benin, Burkina Faso, Côte d'Ivoire, Guinea Bissau (1997-), Mali, Mauritania (1960-73), Niger, Senegal, Togo.

Dollarized Countries using the U.S. dollar exclusively

American Samoa, Bahamans (Bahamas dollar and US dollar), British Virgin Islands, Caribbean Netherlands (from 1 January 2011), Ecuador (uses its own coins in addition to U.S. coins; Ecuador adopted the U.S. dollar as its legal tender in 2000, El Salvador, Marshall Islands, Federated States of Micronesia (Micronesia used the U.S. dollar since 1944), Northern Mariana Islands, Palau (Palau adopted the U.S. dollar since 1944), Panama (uses its own coins in addition to U.S. coins. Panama has adopted the U.S. dollar as legal tender since 1904), Puerto Rico.

Formal Models of an Optimum Currency Area

On the early 1990s of a number renowned monetary economists built different economic models to explain the structure and the benefit of the countries who are part of an Optimum Currency Area or a single currency union compared to countries who do not participate. Bayoumi (1994) was one of the first monetary economists to build a simple general equilibrium model that clarifies most of the welfare implications of the real aspects of an optimum currency area such as real shocks, labor mobility, transactions costs, openness, etc. Based on this model the creation of a monetary union lowers the welfare of the countries outside the union and increase the benefits of the member countries. Ghosh and Wolf (1994) create a new model by taking into consideration a similar model to Bayoumi (1994) and explore how certain areas of the world such as United States, Europe, etc. could be divided up into optimum currency areas.

The model considered by Aizenman and Flood (1993), instead, illustrates the conditions under which adjustment through labor mobility in a currency union is higher to adjustment through flexible exchange rates. The model of Melitz (1996) proposes a meticulous analysis of the trade aspects related to the creation of an optimal currency area. Minford (1995) produces a model that considers the cash in advance micro-foundations for the OCA approach and the advantages of monetary policies as stabilization tools. Alesina, Barro and Tenreyro (2002) built an OCA model based on trade to explore the differentiated intermediate inputs.

The most representative formal models of an Optimum Currency Area (OCA) are developed by Bayoumi (1994) and Ricci (2008), which will be shortly illustrated here. The model consist of two countries specialized in the production of two goods and is complemented by nominal rigidities, exchange rates, trade costs, non-traded goods. The model has no explicit role for government policy, and there is no discussion on monetary and fiscal policy. The production function of each country to produce one traded good (T), at home and abroad (H at home and A abroad), and one non-traded good (NT) is given as combination of four equations,

$$\begin{aligned} H &= \gamma L_h; \\ A &= \delta L_a; \\ T &= \psi L_t; \\ NT &= \varphi L_{nt}. \end{aligned} \qquad (4.1)$$

where, *H, A, T,* and *NT* are the output of the goods in each region/country and γ, δ, ψ, and φ are the input of labor in each region, and *Lh, La, Lt,* and *Lnt* represent the employment of labor in the same region. A representative home consumer *i,* using the Cobb-Douglass preferences, chooses nominal money balances (*mi*) and consumption of three goods (H, A and T) in order to maximize its preferences, given as (Ricci 2008, 8-10);

$$U_i = \left(H_i,\ A_i,\ T_i^{1-\alpha-\beta}\right)^{\lambda} (m_i)^{1-\lambda} \qquad (4.2)$$

subject to:

$$p_h H_i + e p_a \tau A_i + p_t T_i + m_i = y_i + m_i \qquad (4.3)$$

In the same way, a foreign consumer, *j,* choose nominal money balances (*mj*) and the consumption of three goods (H, A and T) to maximize its preferences, given as,

$$U_j = \left(H_j,\ A_j,\ T_j^{1-\alpha-\beta}\right)^{\lambda} (m_j)^{1-\lambda} \qquad (4.4)$$

subject to:

$$\frac{p_h}{e} \tau H_j + p_a A_j + p_t NT_j + m_j = y_j + m'_j \qquad (4.5)$$

where *ph, pa* and *pt* are the local currency prices predominant in sectors *H, A, T,* and *NT* for traded and non-traded goods at home and abroad, and *e* is the exchange rate. The levels of nominal income of the domestic and foreigner consumers are denoted respectively by (yi) and (yj), meanwhile, the transaction costs are indicated by the parameter $\tau>1$ that a consumer must incur when converting domestic currency to an international currency under a flexible rate regime. This transaction is eliminated under a currency union.

The money supplies in a flexible exchange rate and currency union regimes are given correspondingly as follows:

$$M_{Flex} = M_o(1 + \mu_{flex}) \quad (4.6)$$

$$M_{cu} = M_o(1 + \mu_{cu} + \xi_{cu}) \quad (4.7)$$

where $\mu flex$ indicates the inflation bias that affects the money supply in a flexible exchange rate regime in a given country, meanwhile μcu and ζcu show the inflation bias and the redistribution of money in percentage terms that equilibrates the money market in a currency union. The demand for money, by maximizing the consumer's preferences, are given as follows:

$$M_i = (l - \lambda)(Y_i + M_i) \quad (4.8)$$

$$M_j = (l - \lambda')(Y_j + M_j) \quad (4.9)$$

where *Mi* and *Mj* represent the aggregate money endowments for countries of the home consumer, *i*, and foreign consumer, *j*.

The four goods market (traded (T), and non-traded (NT), at home (H) and abroad (A)) reach market equilibrium through adjustment in the nominal income of both countries (Ricci 2008, 11-15). By considering the first order conditions, the equilibrium for traded goods at home market is given as,

$$p_h H + p_t T = Y_i = (1 - \beta)\lambda(Y_i + M_i) + \alpha' \lambda' e(Y_j + M_j) \quad (4.10)$$

and for non-traded goods at abroad market is given as,

$$p_a A + p_t NT = Y_j = \frac{\beta\lambda(Y_i + M_i)}{e} + (1 - \alpha')\lambda(Y_j M_j) \quad (4.11)$$

Meanwhile, the equilibrium on the two money markets (home and foreigner) are given as follows:

$$Y_i = \frac{\lambda}{1-\lambda} M_i \quad \text{and} \quad Y_j = \frac{\lambda'}{1-\lambda'} M_j \tag{4.12}$$

The equilibrium in the money market is adjusted by exchange rate movements under flexible exchange rates, and by monetary redistribution in a typical currency union (e.s., European Union). The trade balance measured in domestic currency is zero when both the goods and money markets are in equilibrium. It is important to understand the magnitude of the consequences during the short-run adjustment process for unemployment and inflation under both regimes, flexible exchange rates and in a currency union.

Under flexible exchange rates regime, money stocks would change mainly because of the inflationary bias, which will increase the demand for domestic currency. The percentage change in the exchange rate given by, *e'*, and in-country *k*'s nominal income which equilibrates the goods and money market can be derived from equilibrium equations 4.10, 4.11 and 4.12. Therefore, we have,

$$\begin{aligned} M_k &= \mu_k > 0 \\ Y_k &= \mu_k + 2P_{\lambda k} \end{aligned} \tag{4.13}$$

$$e' = \mu - \mu' + P_\beta - P_\alpha + 2P_\lambda - 2P_{\lambda'} \tag{4.14}$$

where µ represents the inflation bias, *Yk* is the nominal income in domestic currency, and *P* is the percentage changes of the preference parameters, between domestically and abroad produced tradables and non-tradables which are adjusted by sectorial labor mobility. The exchange rate flexibility given by equation 4.14 neutralizes any effect on nominal income of foreign monetary shocks or any demand shock to tradables. Under exchange rate flexibility there is a decrease in benefits as the variability of domestic monetary shocks is transmitted abroad creating a difference between the inflationary bias in excess internally and inflation bias in other countries. The higher the monetary shock, the longer it takes the instrument of the exchange rate to adjust inflation, nominal income, employment and other variables to long-term trend.

Under currency union regime, when two countries form a currency union, they adopt the same currency, and all the transaction costs disappear, and all the wages and prices are denominated in the same currency unit. Any change in the nominal income that has the capability to equilibrate the goods markets both home and abroad is derived from equations 4.10 and 4.11, and is given by two new equations:

$$Y_i' = \mu_u + \frac{2\alpha P_\lambda + \beta(P_\alpha - P_\beta + 2P_\lambda)}{\alpha + \beta} \quad \text{and}$$

$$Y_j' = \mu_u + \frac{2\beta P_\lambda + \alpha(P_\beta - P_\alpha + 2P_\lambda)}{\alpha + \beta} \qquad (4.15)$$

where μu is the inflationary bias of the union. (Ricci 2008, 13-14). The money supply can also be derived from equations 4.19, 4.11 and 4.12 and is given as,

$$M_i' = \mu_u + \frac{\beta(P_\alpha - P_\beta + 2P_{\lambda'} - 2P_\lambda)}{\alpha + \beta} \quad \text{and}$$

$$M_j' = \mu_u + \frac{\alpha(P_\beta - P_\alpha + 2P_\lambda - 2P_{\lambda'})}{\alpha + \beta} \qquad (4.16)$$

In a currency union, differently from flexible rates regime, demand shocks to tradables ($P\beta$), and non-tradables ($P\alpha$) and foreign monetary shocks ($P\lambda$ and $P\lambda'$) for home and foreign country affect domestic nominal income with repercussions on unemployment and inflation. However, domestic monetary shocks in the currency monetary union are transmitted abroad and do not affect the stability of the internal monetary system and domestic economy.

There are two ways of adjustment in a currency union that focused on real shocks: labor mobility and federal fiscal system. Labor mobility is normally considered as a form of adjustment for real shocks. Assuming that wages are equal across countries in a currency union, and reminding that $Y'=w\,L$, where w is the wage across countries, from equations 4.11 and 4.12 we can derive the migration flow that will adjust the real demand shocks given as,

$$dL = \frac{\beta L}{\alpha + \beta}(P_\alpha - P_\beta) = -\frac{\alpha L}{\alpha + \beta}(P_\alpha - P_\beta) = -dL \qquad (4.17)$$

where d is the differential operator. More specifically, we assume that there is partial labor mobility which means that only a portion of the trade shock is adjusted, where f represents the degree of labor mobility. Therefore, the nominal income equations (4.15) becomes:

$$Y_i' = \mu_u + \frac{2\alpha P_\lambda + 2\beta P_\lambda + \beta(1 - f)(P_\alpha - P_\beta)}{\alpha - \beta} \text{ and}$$

$$Y_J' = \mu_u + \frac{2\alpha P_\lambda + 2\beta P_\lambda + \alpha(1 - f)(P_\lambda - P_\lambda)}{\alpha + \beta} \tag{4.18}$$

A fiscal tool represents a way of financing temporary shocks and smoothes the effect of real shocks. Assuming that there is currency union tax-transfer that is enacted proportionally to any increase or decrease in nominal income as a result of real shocks. The tax raised from the country experiencing a boom is offset by the transfer which the country is undergoing a recession is entitled to. If a tax-transfer rate *t*, is applied we can have a share ε, of the change in income due to real shocks that are absorbed by the tax-transfer rule, which is given as,

$$t = \frac{\varepsilon}{1 - \varepsilon}\left(\frac{\alpha' + \beta}{1 - \alpha' - \beta}\right) \tag{4.19}$$

From equations 4.11 and 4.12 and taking into account the fiscal rule, and also considering equation 4.18 it is possible to derive the percentage changes in national income in the goods and money market equilibrium when the adjustment carried over by labor mobility and fiscal federalism has been accounted for as follows:

$$Y_i' = \mu_u + \frac{2\alpha P_\lambda + 2\beta P_\lambda + \beta n(P_\alpha - P_\beta)}{\alpha + \beta} = \mu_u + x \text{ and}$$

$$Y_j' = \mu_u + \frac{2\alpha P_\lambda + 2\beta P_\lambda + \alpha n(P_\beta - P_\alpha)}{\alpha + \beta} = \mu_u + x' \tag{4.20}$$

where $n = 1 - \varepsilon - f$ is the part of real shock that is not adjusted by labor mobility (*f*) or fiscal federalism (ε). If $n=0$, labor mobility and federal fiscal transfers fully adjust the demand shocks, and on contrary if $n = 1$ it means that labor and fiscal rule do not contribute to the adjustment at all.

Regarding the expected inflation and unemployment in different exchange rate regimes, we have that because of the rigid wages, changes in nominal income can give rise to inflation and eventually unemployment. Given the wages, wd=w(1+μ), for domestic country and foreign country, wa=w(1+μ), we have that

$Y' = \pi' > \mu$ if $Y' > \mu$ and (4.21)

$Y^* - \mu = -ut < 0$ where $\pi^* = \mu^*$ if $Y^* < \mu$ (4.22)

where also π' and π^* are the domestic and foreign inflation, and *ut* is the rate of unemployment of country *t* as a percentage of its labor force. Combining equation (4.15) with (4.21) we have that expected inflation and unemployment rates that authorities can anticipate under flexible exchange rates are given as,

$$E(\pi) = \mu + \left(\int_{\mu}^{Ys} (Y - \mu) f(Y / Y' > \mu) dY \right) \Pr(Y > \mu) \approx \mu + 2D_e \sigma_\lambda \tag{4.23}$$

$$E(u) = -\left(\int_{Yi}^{\mu} (Y - \mu) f(Y / Y' < \mu) dY \right) \Pr(Y < \eta) \approx D_e \sigma_\lambda \tag{4.24}$$

where *Pr* indicates the probability of the event described in parenthesis, *f(.)* gives the conditional probability density function of *Y*, and *De* points out the value of the normal density function. Meanwhile combining equations (4.21), (4.22), (4.23) and (4.24), we can derive the level of expected inflation and unemployment when countries decide to join a currency union, which is given as,

$$E(\pi) \approx \mu_u + D_e \sigma_\lambda \quad \text{and} \quad E(u) \approx D_e \sigma_\lambda \tag{4.25}$$

where σ is the standard deviation of λ. The different values of equations (4.23), (4.24) and (4.25) demonstrated that expected unemployment and inflation differ under both regimes.

To assess the cost-benefit analysis of a currency union, it is beneficial to define a loss function in inflation and unemployment as suggested by Barro-Gordon (1983) onwards,

$$L_c = E(u_c + \theta_c \pi_c + TD_e) \tag{4.26}$$

where *c* indicates the country, *Ec* is the expectation operator, *uc* is the unemployment rate, πc is the inflation rate, and θc is the relative weight the authority allocates to inflation versus unemployment. The loss function is estimated as a percentage of the labor force in terms of inflation and unemployment. The cost-benefit analysis is measured by evaluating through loss function the difference between the expected adjustment costs in terms of inflation and unemployment when the shock hit the country under the two monetary regimes. By taking into consideration equations (4.23), (4.24) and (4.26), we have that the expected losses for the domestic country under a flexible exchange rate regime is given as,

$$L_{flex} = (1 - \theta)2D_e\sigma_\lambda + \theta\mu + \beta\nu \quad (4.27)$$

where ν is the transaction cost per unit of expenditure on goods produced in the other country. In the same way, the expected losses for the domestic country in a currency union can be expressed by the following equation,

$$L_{cu} = (1 - \theta)D_e\sigma_x + \theta\mu_{cu} \quad (4.28)$$

The combination of two equations, (4.27) and (4.28), imply that the expression of net benefits from participating in a currency union is given as,

$$Bef = (1 + \theta)D_e(2\sigma_\lambda - \sigma_x) + \theta(\mu - \mu_{cu}) + \beta\nu \quad (4.29)$$

The equation may vary for the two countries, specifying that the two countries may not agree on cost-benefits about the adoption of a common currency. The two countries will create an optimum currency area and adopt a common currency only if either country (or more) evaluate the positive net gains from the creation of a currency union.

The net benefits of any country participating in a currency union rise if there is a real positive correlation between countries because the exchange rates are less useful as an instrument of adjustment and international labor mobility and distribution of monetary union's fund (fiscal tools) are substitutes for exchange rate as well. A positive correlation between monetary shocks and demand shocks are transmitted to other countries within the currency union (dissimilarly under flexible exchange rate) which reduces the adjustment cost of a currency union, therefore increasing the net benefit of the country participating in the monetary union. The gap between the inflationary bias of the country participating in the monetary union and the inflationary bias of the currency union is reduced if the country adopts the single currency, which also helps reduce efficiency losses and transaction costs due to the common currency.

However, there are cases when a country is joining a monetary union may have a smaller variance of monetary shocks than the currency area they consider to join in. Similarly, the net benefit for a country joining the optimum currency area, may not be realized if the country inherits substantial real shocks so that the need for adjustment is not necessarily lower in a currency union than under flexible exchange rate regime.

Some Shocking aspects of an OCA

Another aspect of the OCA is if some countries with different market structures are exposed to asymmetric shocks. External economic events may affect them in different ways. In these circumstances, the loss of the ability to alter their exchange rates could impose serious costs in the short and medium term. If the exchange rate cannot be devaluated, the whole burden of adjustment to an external shock will fall on labour markets in the form of reductions in real wages or higher unemployment.

The matter regarding the similarity shocks is that, if the occurrence of supply and demand shocks and the speed of economic adjustment after the shock are similar across countries forming the OCA, then the need for policy independence comes less and the benefit of adopting a single currency is a better choice. The studies in this field became more interesting in the late 1980s and early 1990s thanks to the implementation of some new econometric techniques that allowed to specify aggregate supply and demand shocks and distinguish them from policy responses to these shocks. This approach permits to identify and compare asymmetric shocks across countries.

The research initiated by Bayoumi and Eichengreen (1994, 1996) identified bivariate auto-regressions for output and prices limiting the effect of demand shocks to only prices in the long run while tolerating the effects of supply shocks to the long-run on both prices and output. Bayoumi and Eichengreen (1996) were able to come across positive correlation between the main shocks of the core countries in the EU (Denmark, Germany, Austria, France, Holland and Belgium) which was much higher compared to southern countries of the Eurozone (Greece, Spain, Italy, Portugal), but still below the average of the eight Bureau of Economic Analysis regions of the US.

The positive correlation is stronger among the core group countries that form the EU (such as Germany, Austria, France, Belgium, Holland and Denmark) and periphery group countries (including Italy, Greece, Spain, Portugal, Finland, Sweden, United Kingdom and Ireland). An interesting study about EMU conducted by three authors, Demertzis, Hughes and Rummel (2000), confirmed the view that few policy interventions have been aimed at the supply side where the monetary shocks are more unpredictable rather than on the demand side where there is more symmetry and consistency. The symmetry on the demand side is more likely as a result of demand policies rather than the underlying economic structure. In this contest, according to these three authors, the EMU is held together mostly by policymakers which try to integrate and harmonize the economic performance of the core and periphery countries. If the EMU was to include only core countries then the role of policymakers would have come less. A remarkable point about the European core countries is that when two economists, Forni and Reichlin (1997), searched for a group of European countries called "core" where at least 70-80% of output variance derives from EU factors, and found that all European countries have regions outside the core. In fact, even two EU members, Spain and Italy, which are considered peripheral countries, have instead significant regions that are in the European core. The occurring of shocks in the Europe Union does not make the inter-regional migration between countries effective in the short-run. Labor mobility and migration in the 1950s and 1960s was higher than in the 1990s and 2000s. During the past years has increased the integration between some bordering regions of different European countries. Some of the most industrialized border areas of Belgium, France, Germany and Italy have enjoyed in the last decades a high degree of market integration and a high level of trade in goods and services.

Bayomi and Eichengreen (1996) demonstrated that the response of labour and product market to shocks was faster under the gold standard than under a flexible exchange regime. Given that the capital and labour markets do not respond directly to region-specific shocks, some authors have analysed market mechanisms. Atkeson and Bayoumi (1993) explored the extent to which financial capital mobility can be an alternative to physical capital mobility and found that the agents are predisposed to diversify the risk of region-specific shocks by holding financial assets whose do not belong to region-specific sources of labour and capital income.

There are substantial differences between Europe and the United States in response to the employment rate as a result of employment shock. In the US, a fall in demand for goods and services produced in one particular region creates an unemployment shock which is not persistent due to the high level of interregional migration. In Europe, instead, a fall in demand causes an employment shock and the changes in the unemployment rate are persistent because of the low mobility of the labor force across countries.

Free movement of labor between countries in a common currency area is a crucial force for maintaining economic stability and absorbing the asymmetric shocks between regions. If one region faces difficult economic conditions and goes into recession, labor force can move from the depressed region to the thriving one assumed that there are no restrictions on movements. An efficient interregional labor market can ease the effects of asymmetric shocks through the mechanism of wages adjustment. The wages in a depressed region will fall which will cause prices to fall as well, meanwhile, in the blooming region it will happen the opposite, wages will rise, and prices will increase. Given lower price in depressed regions, it will trigger the demand for depressed region's product in the health region. The blooming region will need less demand due to their higher prices. This process will act as a stabilizer between two regions of the common currency area, boosting the economy of the depressed region and restraining the growth of the booming region. Unluckily, the reality of the EU is that it does not have efficient labor market mobility as in US or Canada.

There are considerable regulations and restrictions between countries of the EU which contribute to the reduction of market labor flexibility. Due to language barriers and other administrative restrictions, it is not common to see workers moving from one country to another that has greater job opportunities within the Eurozone. There are particularly social, cultural, and administrative factors behind the low geographic mobility in Europe compared to the US and Canada. The low mobility is affected by considerable barriers in the housing market across the EU, restricted cross-border portability of social protection and supplementary pension rights, high costs of gaining legal resident status, lack of comparability and mutual recognition of professional qualifications and certainly a number of restrictions on public sector employment.

In the United States instead, where there is no language barrier and restrictions workers are more willing to move from one state to another in the period of prolonged recession. The same thing we can say for Canada where workers can move between provinces during depression time or industry downturn, despite the fact that they are separated by larger geographic distances, even larger than across Europe.

Regional labor force participation and migration play an important role in absorbing shocks in the Eurozone and the US. The immigration in the US is a substantial portion of the labor force, and it accounts for 52% on the increase in regional employment for the first year onward compared to Europe where only after the third year the immigration accounts for the same portion of the increase in employment. The labor force participation in Europe accounts for 78% of the augment in employment in the first year and 50% in the second, meanwhile, in the US the respective figures are 18% and 17%. This confirms the idea that there is more heterogeneity among European regions than US states (Blanchard and Katz, 1992).

Mundell (1973) considered the idea of asymmetric shocks in a relationship with the case for a common currency. He demonstrated how a common currency across countries could lessen the impact of such shocks by using reserve pooling and portfolio diversification. In fact, countries that have a common currency need less monetary reserves to face the external shocks than those who act separately. A country hit by an asymmetric shock can better share the loss with its neighbour and trading partner because both countries may technically contain claims on each other's output in a common currency. While, under a flexible exchange rate without a portfolio diversification, a country struck by an asymmetric shock finds that the domestic-currency assets are devaluated on the international market.

Asymmetric disturbances in the short-term can be coped with price and wage flexibility. A high level of financial integration among OCA members has a crucial role in the adjustment of both short-term and long-term shocks especially if they are asymmetric. Members can diversify their investments and income to protect themselves from regional fluctuations. Fiscal discipline tool plays an important role for OCA members as it allows automatic stabilisation and if it is necessary permits the national government to carry out some expenditure absorption policies. Adequate labor mobility can relieve the adjustment to long-term shocks, and despite this, EMU will not be able to benefit from this factor as the labor mobility is low within most of the European countries.

More recent literature has pointed out the importance of flexible nominal exchange rates in the presence of strongly asymmetric shocks. In the mid-seventies, Vaubel (1978), proposed the Real Exchange Rate (RER) adjustment between regions as a condition for the determination of OCA. He indicated that the base for the study of OCA should be an empirical variance of RER rather than the magnitude of potential sources of RER variance. Afterwards, Mussa (1986) and Metzler (1986) used real Exchange Rate Variance (REV) for empirical studies of the exchange rate regimes. If the RER between two currency areas is stable, the shocks demanding RER adjustment would be small, and as a result, the cost of giving up nominal exchange rate flexibility would be small. Otherwise, a large RER instability should fit better the flexible nominal exchange rates.

In theory, the prices of equities might reflect the present value of current and expected future profits. If shocks are symmetric, what will happen is that, profits will rise in one market and decrease to the other. If real share prices in two regions, having a common currency or fixed exchange rates currencies move together, this may point out that the two regions experience the same shocks or there is a capital movement from the region where the rate of return has fallen to the one where it has risen. Eichengreen writes that,

> "... Real shares prices in Toronto and Montreal were found to move closely together than real shares prices in Dusseldorf and Paris. There was evidence of convergence between Paris and Dusseldorf over time, but even in the 1980s the ratio of real share prices between Paris and Dusseldorf was five times as variable as the ratio for Toronto and Montreal..."
>
> [Eichengreen 1997, 77]

In an analogous way, if the relative prices of the product of two regions show variability, it may reflect that product markets experience the same demand and supply disturbances or that factors of production are flowing to the region where the prices have begun to fall. Cohen and Wyplosz (1989) in their empirical study conducted for France and Germany found out that symmetric shocks are much larger than asymmetric shocks. Their study suggests that symmetric shocks are largely permanent, while asymmetric shocks are mostly temporary.

During the ERM (Exchange Rate Mechanism) of the Europe Monetary System, Bayomi and Taylor (1995), demonstrated that while the ERM system has a little impact on the nature of the shocks striking the economies of member countries, it has a significant outcome on the response of member countries to these shocks making these responses both more similar and more extended. Their results confirm the thesis that the ERM, by limiting the degree of real exchange rates rate variation with other members, has acted as a method for policy coordination between members.

Two other economists, Sach and Sala-i-Martin (1992), have suggested that the regional problems of an OCA can be improved by transferring the purchasing power from booming to depressed regions carried out by the federal fiscal system. According to them a currency area or a monetary union should coincide with fiscal jurisdiction as in the case of the U.S. A federal fiscal system plays an important role on the distribution of incomes to depressed and less advantageous regions. This means that member countries of an OCA or a monetary union like EMU should give up their national fiscal sovereign policy over a regional or union fiscal authority whose primary objective is to oversee and re-distribute the entire fiscal revenue of the union among members. However, a regional fiscal authority for an OCA might not be an easy task, as national governments have to give up their government spending and borrowing which call in cause complicated political implications with some unpredictable results.

Another interesting point of shocking aspects of OCA is the speed of adjustment. The usefulness of the OCA theory relies on the estimation of the extent of the asymmetric shocks and calculating the size of the adjustment cost. One empirical method is to compute the size of the asymmetric shocks in the European region by the variability of real exchange rates between European currencies and compare it with that of the benchmark region such as the U.S. Most of the studies seems to confirm that the variability of real exchange rate in Europe was greater than if compared in relative terms with the U.S. regions.

For instance, Eichengreen (1990) estimated the real exchange rate variability of four US regions and ten European Community countries, and found that the real exchange rates within the EC had more variability than the U.S. Another method to measure the cost of the shocks is to examine the behaviour of output, because increased output fluctuations can mean the cost for giving up the exchange rate adjustment in smoothening output fluctuation. Krugman (1993), in his empirical research, found that the spread of overall growth rates was much larger among US states than among European countries. Thus, according to him, European Union is not yet well prepared for the union.

Further empirical studies conducted by Eichengreen (1997) in two OCA, the Europe Community (EC) and the U.S., had demonstrated that the speed shock adjustment is different. Supply shocks tend to be larger and less correlated across states in Europe than in the United States. According to Eichengreen (1997), EC countries are characterized by relatively low factor mobility, but adjustable exchange rates (before the introduction of Euro) compared to the speed of adjustment to the US regions which are characterized by high factor mobility but fixed exchange rates. Shocks to the US core and periphery regions showed significantly more consistency than shocks to the equivalent European regions. However, the difference is less significant if core EC countries are compared to the United States, suggesting that the rejection of the OCA condition in the EC is essentially due to the heterogeneity produced by peripheral countries. The result which holds both for aggregate demand and aggregate supply shocks reasonably reflects greater factor mobility in the United States than in Europe.

The empirical study of Bayoumi and Eichengreen in 1993 demonstrates that a large supply shock needs a longer adjustment than a demand shock. Table 4.2 shows the standard deviations measured in logarithms of the aggregate demand and supply variances for eleven European Community (EC) countries for the period 1963-88 and eight U.S. regions for the period 1966-86. The extent of the supply shocks for EC countries indicates the existence of two groups of countries. The core of countries such as Germany, France and Belgium have lower standard deviations in the range of 0.01-0.02 (1-2% per year) compared to peripheral countries such as Spain, Portugal and Greece that have higher standard deviations in the range of 0.02-0.04 (2-4% on annual bases). This means that peripheral countries are hit by supply shocks twice as large as the core countries.

Countries/Regions	**Standard Deviations for Supply shocks**	**Standard Deviations for Demand shocks**
EC Countries (1963-88)		
Germany	0.017	0.014
France	0.012	0.012
Belgium	0.015	0.016
Netherlands	0.017	0.015
Denmark	0.017	0.021
United Kingdom	0.026	0.017
Italy	0.022	0.020
Spain	0.022	0.015
Ireland	0.021	0.034
Portugal	0.029	0.028
Greece	0.030	0.016
U.S. Regions (1966-86)		
Mid-East	0.012	0.019
New-England	0.014	0.025
Great Lakes	0.013	0.033
Plains	0.016	0.022
South East	0.011	0.018
South West	0.019	0.018
Rocky Mountains	0.018	0.015
Far West	0.013	0.017

Table 4.2 Standard deviations of the aggregate supply and aggregate demand shocks. (Source: Bayoumi and Eichengreen, 1993)

Negative supply disturbances, in the case of EC, are manifested in two crucial periods respectively in 1973-75 and 1979-80 corresponding to two oil shocks and another one in 1968. In the case of U.S., the supply shocks associated with oil crisis are evident in the same period as in the EC, but differently, from Europe, there is a quick recovery in the 1980s related to some positive supply shocks such as corporate tax cuts and other tax relieves. The demand shocks exemplify the responses of the EC to the two oil shock crisis. In fact, there was a large positive demand shock in 1976 while starting from 1980 frontwards demand shocks were negative. Instead, in the U.S. there was a negative demand shock in 1982 as a result of policy disinflation made by the Federal Reserve System to adjust to the supply shocks.

Going back to Table 4.2, we have that the supply shocks of the U.S. regions are closer to those experienced by the EC core countries but lower than those occurred in the EC periphery. The U.S. region of South West has a standard deviation supply shock of 0.019 which is pretty large for the U.S., but still lower than for any country of the EC. The U.S. core regions such as Mid-East, New England, and Great Lakes have lower standard deviations which mean smaller supply shocks than EC core countries. On the other side, the demand shocks results are quite different from supply shocks. The U.S. regions have larger standard deviations than EC members. The higher standard deviations in the U.S. in demand shocks reflect, the greater specialization of industrial production and the shift in demand from the products of one region to those of another region. The large demand disturbances in Table 4.2 are those corresponding to high standard deviations in the core members of the U.S. with great industrial specialization such as Great Lakes, (0.033), New England (0.025), Plains (0.022) and Mid-East (0.019), while the South East and Far West have lower standard deviations in demand shocks, which means that they are more sectorally diversified.

In the EC the effects of demand disturbances are not the same as in the U.S. as the internal market in the 1980s was not as integrated as in the U.S. market. Regarding the speed of shock adjustment, based on the study of Bayoumi and Eichengreen (1993), we have that the speed of adjustment of the U.S. regions supply shocks occurs within three years compared to the EC countries where it normally takes much longer. Supply shocks are larger and less correlated across countries in Europe than across regions in the U.S. This phenomenon makes the European Community (later EMU) more costly and more difficult to operate as a monetary union in the United States style. Many empirical studies in the 1990s and 2000s have spoken about the two-speed European Monetary Union. The core of EC (or EMU) member countries during the last 3-4 decades have experienced a lower highly-correlated aggregate supply disturbances in comparison to peripheral EC countries in which supply disturbances were larger and more unusual.

The first speed countries in the EC are those associated with Germany and its neighbours such as France, Belgium, Holland and Denmark, which come much closer than other peripheral countries of the EC to representing a feasible monetary union along the United States lines (Bayoumi and Eichengreen 1993, 224).

The market structure of the EC during the transition phase to EMU was supposed to have a balanced and steady growth among European countries in order to make the correlation of supply disturbances become more similar. The process of growth in an integrated European market also had the effect to allow demand disturbances to be less correlated among EC members as a result of increased regional specialization. Changes in demand and supply sides were believed to have occurred on demand and supply shocks across

Europe and converge more closely to those experienced by the regions in the United States. On the other front, a rise in factor mobility among EC countries would have easily increased the speed of adjustment to shocks to approach the U.S. levels.

Two decades later, especially during the recession of 2008-2010, EMU as a whole was not able to absorb the demand and supply shocks as it was suggested in empirical studies in the early 1990s. The European Monetary Union was still running on two-speed adjustment process with core countries such as Germany and France, being relatively specialized, absorbing a good dose of the devastating effects of the crisis and peripheral members such as Greece, Portugal, Spain and Italy, being sectorial diversified, getting the hardest hit because of the large magnitude of supply and demand shock disturbances which caused a terrible slump that almost made some of these countries go bankrupt.

Europe, in general, is not as integrated as the US or Canada. The OCA criteria provide one theoretical rationale for so-called variable geometry or multi-track approach for EMU. The main criticism against EMU intervenes at this point. According to the critics (Feldstein, 1997), the European Union taken as a whole is definitely not an OCA. The reason is the endogeneity of the OCA criteria. Based on the endogeneity criterion the OCA is not a precondition for a monetary union, but rather a monetary union that can make different countries more homogenous and symmetric. The European Monetary Union is seen more as a powerful political jurisdiction capable of ensuring peace and economic stability in a large area compressed between North America, Middle East and Asia rather than a currency union. Feldstein states that,

> "In the end, the desirability of a European monetary union will be judged not by its impact on inflation and unemployment but by its effect on peace and conflict within Europe and with the rest of the world. A united Europe of more than 300 million people with a single foreign and military policy would be a formidable participant in a global balance of power of the twenty-first century, capable of projecting force and forming important strategic alliances...."
>
> (Feldstein 1997, 42)

Costs and Benefits of an OCA and a Common Currency

Costs of a monetary union are the loss of the ability to operate separate monetary and exchange rate policies. Instead, benefits mainly consist of the reduction in transactions costs that resulted from currency exchange. Obstfeld and Rogoff (1996) discuss two of the benefits from currency unions relating to real exchange-rate stability. First, a good portion of accounting costs is reduced, and the better preventability of relative prices stability reduces uncertainty for firms doing business in the countries of a currency union. Second, the currency union countries are not subject to the fluctuations in nominal exchange rates caused by monetary turbulence and speculative attacks that lead to unnecessary short-term fluctuations in real exchange rates. Many economists, since the early sixties of the 20th century, such as Mundell (1961b), McKinnon (1963), Kenen (1969) and Ingram (1962) tried to identify the special characteristics of an OCA, as well as the benefits and costs of the participation in it.

Ingram (1962) noticed that financial market integration is a very important characteristic of an OCA. Referring to the case of the U.S. and Puerto Rico, Ingram emphasised that the high degree of internal financial integration could finance inter-regional payments imbalances. This suggests, according to Kawai (1987), that a successful optimum currency area must be completely integrated into financial trading.

One of the most important characteristics of an OCA is the political integration. It requires close coordination of national monetary authorities and eventually the creation of a supranational central bank, such as the European Central Bank, which implies the concession of the national sovereignty over the control of monetary policy.

When deciding either or not to join a currency area, each country will estimate the benefits and costs of its participation from a purely nationalistic point of view. Of course, this might lead to a nationally and not globally OCA (Kawai, 1987). The main benefit that could be derived from participation in a currency area is the enhancement of the usefulness of money. Using the same currency or different currencies rigidly pegged to one another with full convertibility is synonymous with eliminating the risk of future exchange rate fluctuation. The elimination of exchange rate uncertainty results in saved hedging costs for companies that previously has hedged exchange rate risks.

Reduced transaction costs and elimination of currency risk will promote cross-border investment and trade. The *Commission of European Communities report* (1990, 63), which published a study conducted in the late 80s estimated the efficiency gains of the single currency which eliminates the transition costs and exchange rate uncertainty. In fact, based on this study the savings arising from the elimination of currency conversion were estimated at ECU 14 billion or 0.4 percent of Community GDP. For large economies transaction cost savings were between 0.1 and 0.2 percent of the GDP and for the small economies, the savings were about 1 percent of the GDP.

The elimination of transaction costs incurred by firms was estimated at 15 percent of their profit. Meanwhile, the reduction risk premium of real exchange rate variability by 0.5 percent point could be translated on income increase for the European Community, at about 5.1 percent. All these efficiencies were supposed to lead the European Monetary Union to a significant reduction of transaction costs among its members and a new growth path. Regarding, instead, the external dimension of the single European currency based on the Commission's report (1990, 178) it is estimated that a single currency for all its members will reduce the transaction costs on the exchange market for the trade with non-EC countries by 0.05 percent of the European Community GDP. Furthermore, savings on exchange reserves of EC members was estimated reach a staggering amount of 200 billion USD. The seigniorage is occurring as a result of holdings a single European currency was supposed to be about 0.045 percent of Community GDP, translated in about 35 billion USD.

Another benefit of a common currency is the bond domination in a single common currency instead of a multitude of currencies each bringing its own risk. For example, the European government bonds after the introduction of euro in 1999 were dominated only in euros, instead of single national currencies, eliminating in this way the currency risk premium and higher interest rates related to each country. Nationals governments and corporations of Eurozone have strengthened the long-term structure of their debts by issuing euro-denominated bonds at longer terms and lower interest rates thanks to the elimination of national-related currency risk. This made intra Eurozone portfolio diversification more attractive for investors inside and outside EU and has increased capital mobility among euro members several times as never seen before.

The euro bond market soon became a sturdy rival of the dollar bond market; euro banknotes began circulating the world. It looks like the tremendous growth in private Eurobond issues helped Western European economies get immune from the currency crisis that swept through East Asia, Latin America and Russia in the late 1990s and early 2000s.

A less financially stable country can get great advantage from joining a more financially prudent currency area and enjoy a high liquidity value of money. All countries of the currency area will also have great gains from the risk-sharing domain, the reduction in the official reserves, and the complete eradication of speculative capital flows. However, there are some major costs implied by joining a currency area. First, it is the loss of national monetary policy, as the domestic monetary policy is controlled by a currency area monetary authority. Second, the loss of exchange rate policy independence, as a country can no longer influence through devaluation the exchange rate.

The loss of these two important domestic policy tools may create some problems if a country faces economic conditions that are different from its currency partners. In this case, only one policy instrument will remain available, the fiscal policy, which may not be enough to address all the economic issues, in particular as in the case of European Monetary Union where each country member should stick to the rule of not going beyond 3 percent on annual deficit spending.

Many orthodox economists have written extensively on the OCA theory and on the benefits and costs of participating in an OCA. However, they did not agree upon what could be the best international exchange rates system; fixed or flexible. Charles Goodhart (1998) presented the implications for the analysis of the OCA theory from two different perspectives, the Chartalist approach and the Metalist approach.

The dominant approach in the economic literature seems to be the Metalist one. They claim that money was created to facilitate trade in the market, eliminate barter inconvenience and reduce transactions costs. Money, as a medium of exchange, has an intrinsic value because it was represented by a precious metal. Since it was not safe to carry gold, the goldsmith system developed, which provided notes against gold deposits. This was, in a sense, a primitive banking system where the number of notes issued by the goldsmiths exceeded the amount of gold on reserve, moreover, the goldsmith system developed a fractional reserve system based on the money multiplier. Then, governments took over the system and issued notes backed by a fractional amount of gold, but governments were not honourable because they issued a lot more notes relative to the amount of gold that they actually had in reserves. So, governments frequently went out of the gold standard and substituted fiat money for notes backed by gold.

The Chartalist approach, instead, highlights the role of deficit spending or fiscal stimulus used by a government as the main policy instrument to fight the rising unemployment during a recession period or liquidity trap. The deficit spending creates money which gives a government the capability to command resources and run the economy even during the crisis. The combination of monetary and fiscal policy provide to a government fiscal and political sovereignty and enough means to escape the economic depression. But if a country decides to join an OCA or a monetary union and adapts a common currency with a limited fiscal policy it will lose the "monetary and fiscal sovereignty". This approach criticizes the transactional benefits of using a common currency compared to some other benefits of having a domestic currency and place less importance on the transaction function of money and greater emphasis on its use as a unit of account.

Other orthodox economists, in general, advocate the adoption of an inflation target rather than a monetary rule, and the necessity of having an independent central bank that controls monetary policy, and does not finance government spending. In other words, this approach assumes that the government should not have to do anything with monetary policy. The Euro finds its theoretical justification in this approach, in that, it is meant to take away monetary policy from the eleven governments participating in the initial stage of the monetary union, and give it to a completely independent European Central Bank. However, fiscal policy remains a national issue, even though these nations cannot run a fiscal deficit since they will no longer have the ability to create money because no European Treasury exists. The only way for them to finance their fiscal deficit is to borrow from private markets.

The cost related to the loss of national monetary policy and the national currency is normally considered under conditions where there will be a need for monetary policy under a single common currency because of particular economic situations of single monetary union members due to external shocks, response to external stimuli and the consistency of fiscal policies. It was found that particular situations of different European countries were not so problematic because there was interdependence among members who facilitated integration and growth rendering inoperative the single national monetary policies. In fact, the cost associated with giving up the possibility of the independent monetary policy was not as big as it was previously thought for most European countries.

The elimination of all barriers to international capital flows has limited the difference in the cost of borrowing for EU countries as long as the exchange rates between European currencies were kept stable in the first stage of the EU and then represented by a common currency during the second stage of the monetary union. Given that the European interest rate was determined by the large and powerful European countries (primarily Germany and France), small countries prior to EU did not have the capacity to lower interest rates during recessions unless they were prepared to use the depreciation of their currencies. European financial and exchange rate treaties left small members without the possibility of conducting independent monetary policy, but gave them the representation in monetary policy decisions under the monetary union and opened them the euro bond market so they could issue euro-denominated bonds at lower interest rates.

One of the main observed costs from monetary integration is the loss of direct control over domestic monetary policy, which will prevent the governments to use the monetary policy as a stabilization tool in case of asymmetric shocks. Monetary authorities can do little to alleviate the cost of cyclical fluctuations and soften the rising rate of unemployment. Monetary policy can basically be used to control the rate of inflation rather than the level of desired unemployment and economic activity. Therefore, from this point of view, the cost of losing direct control over domestic monetary policy is considered low.

If a government don't use the monetary policy as stabilisation tool or in stimulus programs to counterbalance asymmetric shocks the loss of monetary independence is not a considerable cost. It is not a surprise that a category of countries showing considerable volumes in trade activities with their partners and price fluctuations will be able to have less impact when they decide to abandon monetary independence. For Calvo and Reinhart (2002) if the monetary policy is not used as stabilization instrument the loss of monetary sovereignty does not come with a heavy loss in terms of costs. This does not mean that there are no arguments supporting the effectiveness of the monetary policy or money non-neutrality.

The study of Mèlitz (1996) support the idea that countries hit by similar shocks require different policy responses because of the early economic positions, price changes, wage flexibility, tax system, and trade volumes, etc. Many developed countries that have the capability to maintain inflation low can evaluate the cost of monetary integration. Some governments instead, choose to break the low inflation commitment by starting the economic stimulus programs in order to reduce the rate of unemployment. After an increase in inflation, the public expects the inflation to rise and more and more agents and firms will adjust the setting of wages and prices to the expected inflation rate which may trap the country in a high inflation equilibrium at the natural rate of unemployment (NRU). The cost of a country to get back to the previous inflation rate and restore credibility among agents and investors might be stretched and costly and the only way to gain low-inflation reliability is to give up gradually the national monetary policy and establish a monetary union with an anchor country that traditionally has kept the inflation and the rate of unemployment at acceptable levels.

Another argument regarding the costs and benefits of OCA is if the changes in nominal exchange rate and the cost of losing direct control over the nominal exchange rate tool are really important. The first observation based on the study of Canzoneri, Vallés and Viñals (1996) is that the cost from not having nominal exchange rate adjustment for countries joining EMU has low significance as any movement in exchange rates is counterbalanced by monetary and financial shocks preventing the exchange rate from achieving the macroeconomic stabilisation function. The second observation is that in some cases and certain circumstances the nominal exchange rate adjustments could be effective to correct the macroeconomic imbalances. In fact, the Italian devaluation of Lira in 1992 helped the country exit from the

ERM, which contributed in the short term to stabilize the macroeconomic parameters. In the same way, the devaluation of Belgium currency in 1982 helped to re-establish the balance of payments and trade account equilibrium at a lower cost than if had not used the exchange rate mechanism.

Despite these cases, the nominal exchange rate instrument cannot be used methodically to support macroeconomic equilibrium results as very often exchange rate can be affected by irrational trend and herd behaviours. But at least, based on the second observation, there could be some consistent costs from losing direct control over the exchange rate mechanism especially in the situations where it is more needed. If this cost brought more severe deflation than expected following the shock, the solution would be to adopt a higher degree of exchange rate flexibility by raising the price and using wage flexibility.

The European Monetary Union and its Centralized Monetary Policy

The movement towards greater economic interdependence has been a constant aspect in the reshaping of Western Europe since 1945. Trade in goods and services and financial flows between Western European Countries have been developed steadily throughout the period. The need of a right monetary regime for Western Europe became a matter of prime political importance, affecting the level of cross-border integration in trade and investment and the capacity of governments to pursue the economic policies of their choice.

A regional policy regime has long been an option for European Countries. Jean Monnet, a French statesman, endorsed the idea of progressively uniting the democratic European nations both economically and politically. As a result, in 1951, Belgium, France, Italy, Luxembourg, the Netherlands, and West Germany signed the Treaty of Paris, which established the European Coal and Steel Community (ECSC). The ECSC unified its six member nations in a single common market for the production and trade of coal, steel, iron ore, and scrap metal thus abolishing all trade barriers between the members for these products. The success of the ECSC led its six members to sign the Treaties of Rome in 1957. These agreements broadened the countries' cooperation by establishing the European Atomic Energy Community (Euratom) and the European Economic Community (EEC). In 1967, the three organizations merged their executive agencies together (ECSC, Euratom, and EEC) and became known as the European Community (EC). The elimination of tariffs on trade within the EC, by mid-1968, allowed member countries to increase the trade in goods and services and without doubts the economic efficiency.

In the early 1970s, the EC began managing the exchange rates of the currencies of some of its members, notably West Germany and France. EC efforts to stabilize exchange rates were strengthened in 1979 when its members formed the European Monetary System (EMS). The EMS required that the value of member countries' currencies not move above or below set limits in relation to each other. Over the years, the European Community admitted six new members[5]. In 1987, the EC completed ratification of the Single European Act. This act called for ending all customs controls and most other obstacles to the free movement of goods, services, workers, and capital within EC members. The year after, in June 1988, during the European Council meeting in Hanover, Germany, a Committee for the Study of Economic and Monetary Union was created, led by then the President of the Commission, Jacques Delors, and included all EC central bank governors.

The committee submitted a report (called later the Delors Report) in April 1989, defining the future structure of the European Monetary Union. The Delors Report considered a three-stage transition to EMU. Following the Madrid European Council of June 1989, stage one was deemed to have begun on July 1st, 1990. It involved the completion of the single market, economic convergence and closer cooperation on economic and monetary policy between the member states. Stage two commenced on January 1st, 1994. It involved the establishment of the European Monetary Institute (EMI) with responsibility for the technical preparations of stage three, especially the development of the procedures and instruments of economic policy needed for a single monetary policy such as: the reinforcement of cooperation between the central banks of the member states; the coordination of monetary policies of member states with intend of ensuring price stability; the monitoring of the European Monetary System, etc. Stage three began on January 1st, 1999 and was supposed to complete the economic and monetary union. This stage included the irrevocable locking of exchange rates amongst the participating countries, the establishment of a European Central Bank (ECB) and a European System of Central Banks (ESCB), to be followed by the rapid introduction of a single currency and close coordination and mutual surveillance of economic and fiscal policies.

Before the stage two, in 1992, representatives of the 12 EC members signed the Treaty of the European Union in Maastricht. This pact, also known as the Maastricht Treaty, took effect in November 1993 and provided for the creation of the European Union. It also called for establishing the European Central

---

[5] Denmark, Ireland, and the United Kingdom were admitted in 1973 meanwhile Greece joined the EC in 1981, and Portugal and Spain became members of the organization in 1986.

Bank and for adopting a single currency, which later was named euro. The central bank began operations in 1998, and eleven EU countries began to phase in use of the euro in 1999. Upon its creation, the euro was the second most important currency in the world after the American dollar.

By January 2002 the physical currency replaced the currencies of the eleven countries and made up the area of euro countries with a total GDP of 75% of the dollar area. Other countries entered the eurozone in 2004, without mentioning thirteen CIA franc countries of West Africa that have already tied to euro through the French franc. In less than 2-3 years Eurozone, with a population of more than 400 million and with a GDP 20-30% larger than the USA, became the largest currency area in the world. Mundell's dream for an alternative of dollar currency became a reality at the beginning of the twenty-one century.

Right from its birth Euro seems to be a strong and competitive currency to threatening the world dollar domination. Whereas the EU and the United States account for 31 percent and 27 per of global GDP respectively, euro currency only accounts for more than 25-30 percent of foreign reserves in third countries as opposed to less than 60 percent held in the dollar. Three years after euro's introduction it appears to have been a gradual shift in the composition of the reserves of large economies such as Russia and China in favor of euro.

The global demand for euros is increasing at a higher rate than similar demands for a dollar. Most likely the change in reserves between the dollar and euro is also influencing the current accounts and capital movements. Actually, it seems that this influence is involving downward long-run pressure on the dollar and upward long-run on the euro's strength. Dollar devaluation can advantage American traded goods, growth and the rate of employment, but can do little to improve the dollar performance. The European Union and the European Central Bank seem more concerned about monetary stability and target inflation rather than macroeconomic policies aimed at growth and elimination of internal market rigidities.

Mundell (2000) considers the fact that the euro is having an important demonstrative effect in altering the way people and authorities think about the flexible areas and currency areas. IMF and the United States have been preaching to countries throughout the world for more than two decades, since the end of Bretton Woods system in 1971, about the efficiency of floating their exchange rates. But, the currency crisis in Southeast Asia in the 1990s demonstrated that destabilizing exchange rates did not always have positive effects on monetary systems.

The introduction of euro[6] has also reached a long-term gain in price competition. The temporary rise in prices of certain goods and services in conjunction with the introduction of euro should be pondered against the long-term gains from price transparency, the effect of easier price comparisons when prices in the entire euro area are expressed in the same currency. Euro is gradually increasing its role as a dominant international currency. The most immediate gain from this role is an increase of the seigniorage income to the extent that euro is more widely held outside the eurozone than the sum of the currencies that preceded it. Taken as a whole, the euro area is the world's largest exporter and importer, accounting for about one-fifth of international trade. Despite this, the US dollar is still the most common counterparty in foreign exchange trading. Although euro is relatively a young currency, it is likely to grow in importance and may in future have the potential to catch up with the dollar's share in the foreign exchange markets.

Furthermore, by replacing twelve currencies, in particular the German mark and the French franc, the euro became immediately a reserve currency by central banks and became part of a currency basket used in other countries (for example in Morocco and other Mediterranean countries) or a solitary anchor for the exchange rate policy of some other countries such as Estonia, Bosnia and Bulgaria. Euro has increased the efficiency of the European financial markets. The use of euro in the international debt market has increased compared with the joint share of its preceding currencies. The share of international bonds denominated in euros and issued by non-euro area residents has increased to about 30%, compared to 20% of currencies that preceded euro. The unified European money market is now more liquid and efficient than markets in the individual countries before the introduction of the euro.

Centralized monetary policy is the core of a monetary union. The adoption of a single currency throughout the member countries precludes any need for individually determined interest rates. The integrated monetary policy in the European Monetary Union is therefore developed by the European Central

---

[6] In the debate over the euro, the contraction in growth was largely attributed to the limitations imposed on EU countries' economic policies, as they did not have a national monetary policy (as it was done by ECB), and to the fiscal policy constraints of the Stability and Growth Pact. It is well known the fact that the budget deficits of both Germany and France have in 2002 and 2003 exceeded the indication value of 3 per cent of GDP, which was established in the EU's Stability and Growth Pact. At the same time, attention in the debate was drawn to the temporary rise in prices of certain goods that occurred when prices were rounded after the introduction of the euro.

Bank (ECB). As specified in the Maastricht Treaty, the primary objective of the ECB is "to maintain the price stability". The ECB is also expected to support the general economic policies of the European Commission. The ECB alone is responsible for controlling the supply of euros and the short-term euro interest rate. The advocates of the monetary union have argued that this shift of authority to ECB would help Europe to achieve and maintain the price stability.

According to Feldstein (1997), the ECB would be more likely to lead to a higher rate of inflation than the continuation of the current arrangements. Feldstein believes that while the "convergence"[7] requirements for entry in the EMU have no doubt helped several countries to accept the discipline required to lower inflation to German levels, there is also the possibility that the overall inflation rate of the EMU area may rise once the ECB is responsible for monetary policy of the whole eurozone and Bundesbank anchor is gone. But over a decade after the introduction of euro, the Bundesbank anchor system is still there, "overseeing" the European Central Bank and the five convergence criteria are still in place for all members participating in the EMU, and no exception was allowed even during the recession and financial crisis of the 2008-2012. Euro countries having trouble meeting the convergence criteria such as Greece and Cyprus are given a strict deadline to comply with the convergence rules in exchange for a bailout (by using heavy budget cuts and spending review).

In the view of the concerns of traditionally low-inflation countries, was essential that the ECB should be able to borrow the credibility of the Bundesbank. For this reason, the mandate at the policy view of the ECB, which was given the authority of safeguarding the currency, is similar to that of the Bundesbank. In practice, safeguarding the currency was mainly interpreted as price stability, and it was stated in the treaty of ECSB. Thus, at the start of stage three of Monetary Union, a European System of Central Banks (ESCB) was created, composed of European Central Bank (ECB) and national central banks (Article 106). Article 105 specifies that "the primary

---

[7] Each EU country must meet the five convergence criteria in order to go to the third stage of the European Union which is the adoption of Euro as a common currency. They are: a) **price stability**: the rate of inflation may not exceed the average rates of inflation of the three member states with the lowest inflation by more than 1.5 %; b) **inflation**: long-term interest rates may not vary by more than 2 % in relation to the average interest rates of the three member states with the lowest inflation; c) **deficits**: national budget deficits must be below 3 % of GDP; d) **public debt:** this may not exceed 60 % of GDP; e) **exchange rate stability**: exchange rates must have remained within the authorized margin of fluctuation for the previous two years.

objectives of the ESCB shall be to maintain price stability". Regarding the behavior of inflation, Europe has had a remarkable record of declining inflation during the last twenty years. Average inflation in the EU has come down from more than 10 percent in 1976 to less than 4 percent in 1986 and less than 3 percent in 1996.

The interest rate is another factor affecting the European Monetary Union. The interest rate may affect the members of the Monetary Union in different ways depending on the cost of capital, asset prices and the level of the indebted private sector. An economy with a private sector highly indebted (depending if it is at short-term, long-term, fixed or variable interest rates) will be very vulnerable to changes on interest rates, and the transmission mechanism of interest rates varies from country to country and region to region. The core EMU countries such as Austria, Belgium, Germany and Netherlands with lower indebted private sector were able to contain for a longer period the decrease in economic activities (from 11 to 12 quarters) as a result of changes in interest rates and monetary contraction compared to peripheral EMU countries with higher indebted private sector such as Greece, Italy, Portugal and Spain where the fall-off in output was much faster and higher (from 5 to 6 quarters).

The ECB's ability to run successful monetary policy is determined mainly by two factors: first, its operational framework and second, the extent to which a change in monetary conditions produces a uniform effect in the participating countries. The Treaty of Maastricht stressed out the need for a politically independent central bank following the tradition of the Bundesbank. Although the ECB's independence is guaranteed by the treaty, it is required to submit an annual report to the European Parliament, European Council, ECOFIN and Commission.

Even though the ultimate goal of Euroland monetary policy is clearly specified as price stability, the Governing Council of the ECB has also adopted a target for money growth. While monetary policy decisions are centered in Frankfurt (the ECB location), the operational aspects of monetary policy implementation are undertaken in a decentralized fashion at the nineteen national central banks. The main features of the Eurosystem's operating procedures have many characteristics similar to those employed by the Bundesbank and other national central banks in the euro area before the introduction of the single currency. In most parts of the cases, the Bundesbank view is reflected the management of ECB.

In order to achieve its primary goal in inflation and its secondary objectives in growth and employment, the ECB needs specific indicators to use them as a financial barometer in order to give early warning of when a change in monetary conditions is necessary. There are two different schools of thought about what the best indicator is for this purpose: the first favors targeting money supply growth; and the second the inflation. In the early 1980s, great importance was placed on the relationship between growth in the money supply and the inflation rate and many central banks set a money supply target that then became the rule in deciding when a change in interest rates was necessary.

In the 1990s, the relationship between money supply and inflation seemed to break down. The reason for this appeared to be the deregulation and structural changes that have occurred in the financial marketplace in recent years. One effect of structural changes has been to alter the speed at which money circulates economy (velocity circulation). If the velocity of circulation remains steady the relationship between money supply and inflation holds good. As a result of the different behavior of money supply growth, many central banks, before the creation of ECB switched to targeting the inflation rate itself.

A target inflation rate is based on a Harmonized Index of Consumer Prices (HICP). In the first year of operation, the ECB council set this at 2 percent. After the creation of ECB and the introduction of euro, the relationship between money supply growth and inflation seems to be not so strong. The inflation gives the impression of moving on its own path and seems to be related specifically to the price competition for trade goods and services or to people's pattern of price behavior for non-tradable goods and services (as in the case of rents, fee services etc.). Although the efforts of ECB to focus on target inflation, the inflation seems to show little or no response to EBC's orders. A restraint monetary policy shows non-influential effects on the stability of inflation. Euro has been performing well, and the currency stability in the European Union is guaranteed by its own members.

Monetary Unions and the Debate over Fiscal Federalism

The theory of OCA does not give any specific feature regarding the fiscal policy. In the sense of OCA if a monetary union requires a fiscal policy to work it is not an optimum currency area anymore but rather a monetary and fiscal union. Economic theory agrees that in currency areas in which labor is mobile, the active fiscal policy is required to reallocate demand from one region to another. In such cases, according to Kenen (1969), the fiscal policy ought to be centralized so that this is carried out smoothly and efficiently.

The problem of fiscal policy in European Community came to light at the end of the seventies with MacDougall Report (1977). The report stated that moves towards the stabilization of exchange rates, or monetary union should involve a major centralization of European fiscal policies to the commission in order to eliminate the regional disturbances (European Commission, MacDougall Report 1977). The Delors Report (European Commission) in 1989 reconsidered the case for fiscal policy within the EMU. Contrary to MacDougall Report, the Delors Report (1989) acknowledged that regional fiscal policy would remain relatively small for the future and that fiscal powers would still be the responsibility of individual governments once the EMU had taken place. However, the report perceived the need to provide some coordination of fiscal policies ahead of EMU, and this led to the Maastricht guidelines on budget deficits and public debt such as the restriction on the size of the budget deficit and total public debt allowed in individual countries.

The effects of fiscal or monetary policy under alternative exchange rate regime for an individual country are referred to the Mundell-Fleming model (Fleming, J.M. 1962, Mundell, R.A. 1963). According to this model, the power of fiscal policy for a single country should be greater under fixed exchange rates and smaller under a flexible exchange rate system. This implies that in an OCA as in the case of EMU single fiscal policies should have an important role to play with local economic oscillations. The EMU countries have acknowledged that in practice, fiscal policy is much less effective than the theory suggests. For example, fiscal expansion in EMU cannot simply be financed by money creation through ECB which is an independent organization and public debt of a single member cannot be monetized by ECB because of Art. 21 of the Protocol on European System of Central Banks clearly indicates that the European Central Bank cannot acquire any public debt directly from the issuer.

As in the case of the US and Canada, a fiscal policy is more effective when is centralized. A centralized fiscal policy operates long-term fiscal transfers as well as short-term stabilization transfers from richer to the poorer regions within the whole union. Therefore, the scope of income distribution among states or regions in a federal fiscal system is to help reach two main objectives. The first one is to reduce income differences among states or regions and to stimulate growth in the poorest regions. The second objective is to stabilize temporary shocks hitting regions by redistributing income from states with higher income to states with low-income conditions.

The importance of this for a monetary union is that it provides investment in poor areas and stimulates productivity and economic efficiency across the union. Such convergence saves the costs of integration of the union. Instead of setting up a centralized and costly fiscal system the EMU from the beginning put in the act the "stability pact". The "Stability Pact" was agreed at Amsterdam in 1996 and stipulated that budget deficit under EMU regime should remain in general 3 percent or below and the national debt (gross public debt) should be no higher than 60 percent of the GDP. The intention of "Stability Pact" was to put major restrictions on each country's fiscal policy.

The rigid fiscal restrictions put most of EMU members in continues difficulties especially after the creation of European Central Bank which limited the possibility of a combined monetary and fiscal policy. The 3 percent deficit limit can be waived if any EMU member experiences a 1 percent drop in GDP, normally in a period of one calendar year, which seems unlikely to take place. Even during the EMU financial and debt crisis in 2008-2009, the 1-2 percent fall in GDP didn't happen within a 12 months period, but over a more extended period (in many cases the yearly forecast data for different EMU members was not accurate). Despite the crisis and the recession of 2008-09, all the EMU countries were required to keep the faith of the stability pact and do their best to discipline their finances by not exceeding the budget deficit limit of 3 percent. These parameters were some of the main conditions for countries hit by the deep financial crisis and economic recession such as Greece, Cyprus and Portugal to receive a bailout from EMU.

It seemed that the stability pact in practice was not as restrictive as it appeared at the beginning when the pact was established in the late 1990s. This means that it continuously runs the risk of implementing fiscal policy without imposing any effective control over it. In fact, the stability pact was open to some misuses in several ways: for example some countries of EMU, once fulfilling the Maastricht criteria for entry, may lower the guard and lured to misrepresent the fiscal budget forecasts; countries may endorse only light measures when obliged to take corrective actions, convinced that the deficit problems will be resolved by itself until the following year's figures become available; countries may breach the stability pact constantly given that the budget deficit will eventually go down before a fine from European Commission has to be issued; given that several EMU members are in proximity to the 3 per cent deficit limit, they might not take it seriously when the deficit limit is surpassed which will undermine the reliability of EMU as a serious monetary union.

The incentive to maintain fiscal-policy discipline was undermined by the fact that frequent contraventions of the Stability pact did not result in sanctions. In reality, even the countries that were initially the main advocates of the Stability Pact, Germany and France, fall short to meet the requirements and also avoided sanctions. This was not a good example for the other EMU countries with less virtuous fiscal discipline than Germany and France.

Differently, in the United States and Canada, regional economic stabilization is carried out primarily at the Federal level. It has been estimated that a third of cyclical GDP downturns in the US regions are cushioned by

Federal taxes and transfers (Bayoumi and Masson, 1995). It is true also that the strength of the US as a monetary union is based mainly on its centralized fiscal policy and of course, political union. In the U.S. all state governments are subject to fiscal restrictions in order to ensure fiscal discipline. The fiscal restrictions are of two types: first, statutory Balanced Budget Requirements (BBR) which limit the government's ability to run a deficit in its current budget. Second, constitutional debt restrictions or constitutional BBR that limit the size of government outstanding but not necessarily the current budget deficit. Constitutional debt restrictions are more restrictive than statuary BBRs.

In the U.S. according to the ACIR (Advisory Council for Intergovernmental Relations) study published in 1989, 25 states have constitutional BBR, 10 states have statuary BBRs, and 14 states have both constitutional and statuary provision, and 1 state (Vermont) did not have balance budget restrictions. Following an alphabetical order there are at least six main types of budget restrictions listed in the order of stringency: A) The governor of the state has to submit a balanced budget to the legislator. B) The legislature has to pass a balanced budget. C) The governor must sign a balanced budget in order to pass. D) A deficit may be carried over but must be fixed in the next fiscal year. E) The state cannot carry over a deficit into next biennium. F) The state cannot carry over a deficit into the next fiscal year.

Most of the US states use a combination of different types of restrictions. A considerable number of states restrict the amount of debt the state government can raise by imposing a debt-limit or by explicating maximum portions of states revenues such as taxable property, state property and other borrowings or revenues that cannot exceed total debt. A debt limit can be surpassed if the government of a state passes a constitutional amendment by a qualified majority in the legislature or by calling a public referendum to authorize the debt.

Governments can choose a simpler way to bypass a debt limit, by issuing other types of debt, such as off-budget activities. This type of debt consists of creating special authorities to administrate projects and give them the power to raise debt. Another way to get around the debt limit is to delegate the state functions to the local government like municipality which can issue municipal instead of state debt. The problem here is that the municipality is not allowed to go bankrupt; therefore the debt despite being issued by a local government is ultimately a liability of state government to pay the debt. The big dilemma has been if fiscal restraints in monetary unions are enough to promote fiscal discipline in order to keep deficit and debt at reasonable levels.

The research, published by Jürgen von Hagen in 1992 regarding the fiscal arrangements of the states in the US between fiscal years 1976 and 1985, demonstrates that the average state debt per capita is much lower in states with very rigorous Balanced Budget Requirements (BBRs) compared to states with less strictness. Debt-income ratios and debt-growth are not so different on average based on the strict BBR. State governments in the US that use high BBR rules are more likely to choose low per capita debt and debt-income ratios. On the other hand, state debt growth is not affected by fiscal restraints. States normally are more willing to comply with fiscal discipline in the presence of fiscal restraints than where there is none. This does not change the case scenario of extreme fiscal behavior such as high deficit and debt which has the same probability to happen in the states with and without fiscal restraints. Therefore, fiscal restraints do not help to hold back the risk of the bail-out of bankrupt state governments. The US evidence (Hagen von, 1992) on fiscal restrictions on government debt/deficit recommends that states, even when they shift to off-budget activities to lower level of debt and deficit, cannot effectively reduce the exposure of insolvency and the possibility of being bailed out by central monetary authority is always present.

The fact that US Federal Reserve has never found itself in a situation to bail out single states does not mean that the fiscal system in the US is perfect. It only means that states, so far have been able to get away with the fiscal crisis using a pool of fiscal tools and policies that have helped them stay financially floating and escape as much as possible insolvency. On the other hand, Federal Reserve cannot use the monetary policy to respond to different state economic situations. Therefore, state governments have a good comprehension of the fact that monetary policy from Federal Reserve is not available to resolve their problems.

Different is the story in Europe. Unfortunately, EU is also burdened with considerably less flexible labor markets than the US or Canada, which according to the theory of OCA should require a more efficient fiscal centralization to counterbalance this phenomenon, rather than the existing less optimal situation. There is a suggestion by Sala-i-Martin and Sachs (1992) that a smooth operation of a monetary union requires a system of fiscal federalism to provide interregional transfers in response to shocks. The restrictions on borrowing by regional governments will increase the pressure on central government to provide this kind of service. In the case of EMU, this pressure may incite the creation of a system of fiscal federalism in which Brussels collects taxes and provide transfers to member states in trouble with the level of unemployment.

According to Eichengreen, if the member states would give up their tax revenues they will begin demanding additional services from the EU, which may deteriorate the financial position of the EMU (Eichengreen, 1997). Even though the observation of Eichengreen has not been proved yet, a more centralized fiscal organization for EMU members is required to lighten the burden of individual fiscal policies and move toward a stronger economic and political integration. This comes with a substantial political and economic cost. EU members must give up their fiscal and a portion of their political sovereignty to European Commission and other European organizations, which is not an effortless task.

Eurozone during Financial Crisis

In 1993, the European Community transformed into the European Union and later in Eurozone introducing a single currency for all of its members. After centuries of conflicts, the European countries established a political union that many believed would proclaim a future federal state.

The critical imperfection of the European Union was that the European community members produced a common currency without a central bank controlled by a supranational finance ministry. The result of this European project was sustained growth for some EU members and debt for others. As we know the terms of Maastricht Treaty that procreated the Eurozone were to limit national debt to 60 percent of GDP, to limit inflation to 1.5 percentage points higher than the average of the three best performing EU states and to keep the annual deficit no greater than 3 percent of GDP. These conditions were certainly very ambitious and motivated but unfortunately, as underscored by the recent crisis, unrealistic and not sustainable in long-term. Few EU members could achieve the Maastricht parameters, so they resorted to manipulating the books. Basically, the non-virtuous EU states sold their debt to third-party investors. In fact, countries like Greece, Portugal, Spain and Italy masked their debts to keep the impression of solvency until the 2008 financial crisis eventually exposed their economic misrepresenting.

Greece was the first country in the Eurozone to fail in 2009 and the first fiasco of the EU experiment. The measures to save Greece started in 2010 when the IMF, the European Central Bank and other European Governments lent € 252 billion to this country, where only €232.9 billion alone has been spent on debt payment and national bank-debt restructuring. But only 10 percent of the money has gone to Greek economy skyrocketing the Greek debt from 133 percent in 2010 to 174 percent of GDP in 2015. Based on IMF estimation, the Greek economy needs a substantial infusion of at least €50 billion each year from 2016 to 2018 to stabilize its economy.

Despite the Greek debt in the Eurozone was so overwhelming during the 2008-2010 financial crisis, it was not new in European history. As a matter of fact, in 1953 the former Second World War allies led by the U.S., at the London conference (the so-called London Debt Agreement) wrote-off 50 percent of

West Germany's $30 billion debt from the First and Second World Wars. The allies permitted Germany to make payments for the outstanding debt over a period of 30 years using only the trade surpluses despite Germany's debt was only 25 percent of GDP in 1953 compared to Greek where the debt was 174 percent of GDP or even Portugal, Spain and Italy where the GDP/debt ratio was over 100 percent in 2015 as shown in table 4.3.

During the period 2014-15 the European Central Bank and the European Commission have refused to consider debt restructuring of Greece without substantial austerity measures, mostly because under German pressure which was fearing a backlash from German voters creating debt management difficulties in the whole Eurozone area.

During the financial crisis of 2008, most of the central banks around the globe quickly lowered interest rates at their minimum level, close to zero, to make money cheaper to borrow so it could revive the troubled economies from falling into deep recession. After 2008, many European Union countries were able to borrow at historically low rates. In addition to low-interest rates, few countries such as Denmark and Switzerland have negative interest rates, which means investors had to pay for the privilege of handing money to their treasuries. The question that may arise is why these countries are not borrowing cheap money to invest in their economies so they can start a virtuous growth process? The answer is: they are afraid of big deficit spending.

Instead of beginning a spending spree, from highways, bridges, roads, schools and hospitals to scientific research and development, most of the European Union countries were preoccupied to with reducing their budget deficits to shrink debt. The approach of German-inspired austerity, an inheritance from the 'debt crisis' that was triggered by Greece in 2009 and other countries that went close to default, obsessed the whole European Monetary Union until at least 2015-2016. The austerity measures across Europe have jeopardized the health of the European economy and its capability to create jobs in short and medium-term.

The sovereign debt of single European Countries used to be costly in the early to mid-1990s, before the takeoff of the European Monetary Union that supplanted the national currencies with the euro. During this period even the bond spreads, which measures the yield gap over benchmark German bonds was often enormous and inconvenient. The bonds of historically weak countries in the EU such as Greece, Portugal, Italy and Spain in the 1990s were required by investors to have yields of five to ten percentage points higher than those of equivalent German bonds. After the foundation of monetary union and the introduction of a single currency for all members of the EU, the bond spreads between European countries got eliminated. In fact, at the beginning of the 2000s, most of the sovereign bond yields among EU members had converged. And what is more interesting, even countries with troubled economies in the EU such as Greece, Spain, Italy and Portugal were able to borrow at practically the same rate as EU core countries notably Germany, England and France.

It was the bond-yield-convergence in EU countries that placed the groundwork for the crisis to come. Countries with weak economies such as Greece borrowed plentifully and invested imprudently (Greece and some other countries use the borrowing funds to pay the civil servant payrolls excessively). Because of the growth programs and increased deficit spending the national debts soared. The subprime mortgage crisis in the US and the Lehman Brothers' Bank collapse in 2008 (with nearly 9 million jobs lost in 2008 in the US alone) started the financial collapse and the consequent deep recession which exposed the fragility of the overleveraged economies. Bond yields in 2008 quickly climbed up as investors precipitously started demanding high premiums in exchange for default risk everywhere including the EU members. Due to the financial crisis, the spreads over German bonds in Greece, Portugal, Spain, Ireland and Italy soared by five to fifteen points more so Greece, Ireland and Portugal found themselves shut out of the debt markets and Spain and Italy came too close.

In the mid-2012, when Greece almost went bankrupt putting at high risk the whole Eurozone, the European Central Bank (ECB) promised to buy bonds of any country in the EU that was having serious financial difficulties. The ECB's guarantee over bonds make bond yields to reverse course, and they started falling slowly as the Eurozone began moving out of recession. The spreads in the Eurozone plunged further at the beginning of 2015 as the ECB revealed the plan to start a €1.1 trillion Quantitative Easing program to purchase mainly public and private bonds which will further improve economic activities in the old continent. The objective of this stimulus program was to spur faster economic growth in the Eurozone since 2007, so it will help return the inflation rate and unemployment to the ECB's goals within three years.

It was also proven that during the second quarter of 2015 many EU countries were paying less money for 10-year bonds than the United States and Canada. For example, during the second quarter of 2015, Germany's 10 year bond yield was at 0.6 percent low, Italy's was 1.8 percent down from a crisis peak of 7 percent, and Portugal's was 2.4 percent. This was really considered cheap money, even when the falling inflation was factored into the equation, but most of the Eurozone governments have been reluctant to consider it as manna from heaven. Unlikely, most of the EU countries have still opted for austerity measures after the deep crisis of 2008, even though the combination of spending cuts and tax increases is proven to be a dangerous idea or an economic growth killer (Blyth M. 2013, ch.3).

Under certain conditions for some countries with weak economy austerity may require more austerity. If government spending is diminished, the gross domestic product will feel it and will get close to zero growth or eventually reduced, and the debt-to-GDP ratio can stall, engorging the relative debt load as a percentage of GDP. Given that the real and relative debt (as a percentage of GPD) rises, there is always the desire to bring it reasonably down which in turn demands more austerity measures. The debt-to-GDP ratio of no growth countries such Italy and Portugal has kept rising, despite slowly than predicted, even if they had continuously reduced the budget deficit in the 2008 post-crisis years. The Greek economy in the recent years has been suffocated by no-ending austerity measures and aggressive reforms demanded by EU and International Monetary Fund in return for bailout packages.

There is also another reason why the EU countries are not using the cheap money to open the spending faucet, even though they need it desperately. The reason is that large budget deficits under the Growth and Stability pact are considered prohibited because the EU Maastricht Treaty limits budget deficit to 3 percent of GDP and government can reach a debt-to-GDP ratio of 60 percent. The Maastricht Treaty was signed in 1992 by the EU members when the money was not cheap, however almost 25 years later in the middle of ECB Quantitative Easing when the money was cheap it was irrational to have such a tight deficit rules. The EU needed to deliver a blow to the economy in the form of productive government spending, to reduce an unemployment rate that was stuck to 11 percent, rather than tightening it up.

Table 4.3 below shows the European Union Debt as a percentage of GDP in 2014 divided by debt classes. Almost half of the EU countries belong to the 81-110% and 110%+ classes with only three countries sitting in the high-end debt class, respectively Greece, Italy and Portugal. Sixteen countries or more than half of EU countries have debt over 60%, beyond the limit allowed by Maastricht Treaty limit. Even the biggest three EU core economies, such as Germany, France and U.K., have had for some time debt to GDP ratio over 60%, breaking the Maastricht Treaty that they themselves created, but were able to manage their economies without going into painful recession.

Debt as % of GDP by EU country in 2014	10-40%	41-60%	61-80%	81-110%	110%+
Austria				84.5%	
Belgium				106.5%	
Bulgaria	27.6%				
The Czech Republic		42.6%			
Croatia				85%	
Cyprus				107.5%	
Denmark		45.2%			
Estonia	10.6%				
Finland		59.3%			
France				95%	
Greece					177.1%
Germany			74.7%		
Hungary			76.9%		
Ireland				109.7%	
Italy					132.1%
Latvia	40%				
Lithuania	40.9%				
Luxembourg	23.6%				
Malta			68%		
Netherland			68.8%		
Poland		50.1%			
Portugal					130.2%
Romania		39.8%			
Slovakia		53.6%			
Slovenia				80.9%	
Spain				97.7%	
Sweden		43.9%			
U.K.				89.4%	

Table 4.3. European Union debt as a percentage of GDP in 2014 divided in debt classes. (*Source*: Eurostat 2014).

Table 4.4 shows the movement of government debt (as % of GDP) for 28 EU countries from the second quarter of 2014 to the first and second quarter of 2015. The data in table 4.4 does not show big variances for most of the EU members from Q2-2014 to Q2-2015. Even the EU-28 average has not changed very much. It has a slight increase from 87.3% to 87.8%. The GDP average growth for the same period is around 0.5% to 1%, which means the EU-members in general, with few exceptions, continue to have a slow but steady recovery from the 2008 recession despite the reduced government spending (austerity measures) and the substantial government debt.

EU-28 countries	Q2-2014	Q1-2015	Q2-2015
Belgium	109.5	110.9	109.3
Bulgaria	20.2	28.9	28.3
Czech Republic	43.7	42.4	41.7
Denmark	45.2	44.3	42.7
Germany	75.9	74.3	72.5
Estonia	10.3	10.0	9.9
Ireland	114.5	104.7	102.0
Greece	177.4	168.6	167.8
Spain	96.4	98.2	97.8
France	95.5	97.5	97.7
Croatia	81.7	87.7	85.7
Italy	134.5	135.3	136.0
Cyprus	109.8	106.8	109.7
Latvia	41.8	35.7	36.0
Lithuania	38.3	38.0	37.6
Luxembourg	23.2	22.3	21.9
Hungary	82.7	77.6	79.6
Malta	74.8	70.0	68.9
Netherlands	68.9	69.2	67.1
Austria	82.2	85.0	86.4
Poland	48.7	50.9	51.0
Portugal	130.4	130.4	128.7
Romania	38.4	38.4	38.0
Slovenia	78.5	81.8	80.8
Slovakia	55.8	54.2	54.5
Finland	58.5	60.3	62.4
Sweden	41.3	44.6	44.4
United Kingdom	87.4	87.5	89.0
Average EU-28	87.3	88.1	87.8

Table 4.4 Government debt (as a percentage of GDP) in 2014 and 2015. *Source:* Eurostat 2015, 3.

European Monetary Union and the Greek Debt Crisis

As we mentioned in the previous segment (The Eurozone during the Financial Crisis), it was well known the fact that countries with historically weak and not very diversified economies in the EU such as Greece, Spain, Italy and Portugal were able to borrow at practically the same rate as EU core countries remarkably Germany and France.

The bond-yield-convergence of the EU countries in the early 2000s was among others one of the conditions that set the foundation for the crisis to come. Greece was one the EU countries with a non-diversified economy mostly based on tourism and as such borrowed abundantly and invested irresponsibly. Greece in some cases used the low yield government-bond-funds to pay for current expenses such as increased civil servant payrolls and early retirement pensions without considering a new fiscal reform to increase the incoming current cash flow to pay for current expenses.

For example, civil servants in Greece employed before 1992 could retire after 35 years of service if they have reached 58, and retire on 80% of their final basic salary compared to civil servants in Germany that could retire after 40 years of service on 70% of final basic salaries. In addition, there were interest groups in Greece such as Olympic Airlines staff, certain categories of farmers and their wives, employees at the National Bank of Greece, etc., obtaining exorbitant pensions from successive governments as a result of unreasonable and unaffordable electoral promises.

In October 2008, the collapse of Lehman Brothers Holdings Inc. in the United States sent shockwaves through the global markets and ignited the Eurozone debt crisis as well. In October 2009 the New Greek government was elected with George Papandreou as Prime Minister, and in January 2010 the Greek Ministry of Finance published the *Stability and Growth Program 2010* report which indicated the main causes for the outbreak of the current government-debt crisis. Finally, in February 2010, Greece declared that it has been understating its deficit figures for years, which raised serious questions about the reliability of Greek finances. It revised the 2009 budget deficit from 6-8% to 12.7% of GDP, and only two months later in April 2010, the Greek government restated the 2009 deficit to 13.6%, meanwhile by using the Eurostat methods the deficit raised further to 15.7% of GDP, making it the highest in the Eurozone. In the meantime, the Greek government debt for 2009 increased from its first estimate of €269.3 billion (113% of GDP) to a staggering €299.7 billion (130% of GDP).

Regardless of the crisis, the Greek government announced a bond auction in January 2010 for 8 billion euros (subscribed 5-year bonds) and in March 2010 sold again 10 billion euros, 10-year bonds. But all this came at a high cost, as the yields increased which caused the deteriorating of the Greek public deficit. In late April 2010, the international rating agencies caught by raising concerns of growing risk of sovereign default downgraded the Greek economy to junk status (not worth on investing) which led immediately to the freeze of the private capital market, with eventually facing sovereign default if there was no intervention done by international financial players.

On May 2nd 2010 to avoid the first Eurozone sovereign default country since the introduction of single currency in 1999, three international organizations, European Commission, ECB and International Monetary Fund (IMF), which later were called Troika, helped Greek economy with a €110 billion bailout consisting on a package of emergency loans to cover the Greek financial needs throughout May 2010 until June 2013, under strict conditions of fulfilling austerity measures. Part of the austerity measures were the in-depth structural reforms, privatization of government assets, cutting government spending and reducing pensions.

Unfortunately, the recession in 2011 worsen for the Greek economy despite the efforts of the Government to implement some reforms, but they were not enough to restart the Greek economy. It was an urgent need for a second bailout to avoid the worse. The second bailout, signed by all parties in February 2012 worth €130 billion reached the total amount of €240 billion from the beginning of bailout program in 2010 which would have been spread in regular tranches until the end of 2014. The last bailout among others included a bank recapitalization package and private creditors holding Greek government bonds were asked to agree to take prolonged maturities, reduced interest rates and a 53.5% face value loss. By the end of 2012, due to the continued delays on fulfilling the bailout conditions, Troika, accepted to offer Greece the last round of debt relief measures and IMF granted another €8.2 billion of loans to be transferred after December 2014 until March 2016.

Greece, in 2014, after accomplishing some government structural surplus and the reduced unemployment rate was able to get access to the private lending market so it could issue government bonds again. In fact, most of the government financing needs in 2014 were covered by the sale of government bonds to private creditors.

The premature parliamentary election in December 2014 followed the formation of left-wing government called Syriza, which repudiated to respect the terms of the bailout and heavy austerity measures. The political ambiguity of the New Leftist government caused another liquidity crisis at the beginning of 2015 hitting hard the Greek financial system and plunging all the stock prices at the Athens Stock Exchange. This caused the rapid increase of government bond interest rates at the private lending market, and again the

Greek government was shut off of the private lending market causing the enormous problem to finance the current expenses.

Greek government tried again to reach a renegotiated bailout with Eurogroup in June 2015 to avoid another sovereign default and the total collapse of the banking sector. It was a possibility for Greece to exit from the European Union due to continues liquidity crisis which made difficult for the government the payment of public salaries and pensions in the single Eurozone currency, Euro. There were suggestions to go back to the old currency to avoid debt and liquidity crisis in euros, but it did not happen. In an unexpected way the new Greek Prime Minister, Alexis Tsipras, announced on June 27th, 2015 that it would hold a referendum to approve or reject the negotiation conditions for another bailout. Eurozone members got frustrated with Greek referendum on bailout conditions but decided to wait for the referendum's results to have more clarity on Greece's future.

The referendum was held on July 5th, 2015 and the majority of Greek citizens voted to reject the bailout terms imposed by Troika. After the referendum, many were expecting Greece to break off from the Eurozone, but it did not happen. The negotiations between Greece and Eurozone members restarted in July, and few days after the referendum on July 13th, 2015 after 17 hours of negotiations EU member leaders reached an interim agreement on a third bailout program with more reasonable terms which was later ratified by several national EU parliaments. It was a politician willingness to keep Greece in the Eurozone despite the unprecedented debt crisis and sovereign default, to avoid the embarrassment of breaking off the first big monetary union after the WWII.

To ensure debt sustainability in the long term, Greece needed at least to grow the real GDP at more than 2 percent per year. But the real GDP growth since Greece joined the EU in 1981 until 2014 averaged 0.9 percent per year. It could achieve 2 percent real GDP growth per year only if labor force participation increases to high levels and unemployment falls, which is not easy to happen given the austerity measures still in place (Blusten P. 2015). IMF had assumed that when things get better for Greece, the private sector would be willing to lend to Greece at market rates. If the current official lending in 2015 were at the high concessionary rate of about 2.2 percent, based on the IMF forecast, the private lenders would refinance Greece at a nominal interest rate of 6.25 percent for the next several decades (Blusten P. 2015, 12-19). Using this rate, and if Greece could generate a primary surplus of 2.5 percent of GDP, it could practicably pay down the debt to sustainable levels in the long-run.

The primary surplus of any national economy as we know tells us how much money is available to pay interest expense after collecting taxes and paying for current government expenditures. If Greece passes the proposed reforms from Troika, such as raising taxes in some sectors and cutting pensions, it will lead to primary surpluses of 4 percent, which would be more than enough to put aside some monetary resources to start paying down the large debt. But the Greek leftist government elected at the beginning of 2015 and the mandate confirmed by the July referendum against austerity plans does not give enough room for maneuver to increase the primary surpluses.

Another solution for Greece could be the write-down of the Greece debt, but this option needs a strong political will of the Eurozone members and international lenders. At the end of 2014 the Greek debt was estimated at about €230 billion own by a pool of creditors such as; privately held debt (T-bonds) €63 billion, Germany €57 billion, France €43billion, Italy €38 billion, Spain €25 billion, other institutional lenders (IMF. ECB, etc.) € 62 billion and others €32 billion. Despite all this debt crisis and the possibility of default which was unprecedented for a developed country, most of the Euro actors are against the idea that Greece should leave the European Union.

If Greece was about to exit the Euro area, as assumed, it could have hurt Euro considered the most successful union currency. The consequences of a Greek exit from Eurozone could be excruciating including:

- The quick depreciation of the euro relative to the US dollar and the risk of losing confidence in markets reading euro and the whole the European monetary union.
- The devaluation of the euro would make cheap the Eurozone exports but will make the imports more expensive raising the cost of the raw materials making the Euro final commodities less attractive for export.
- Membership in the European Union would no longer be considered as irrevocable which means other members might be lured to exit or demand additional debt relief to stay in. As a matter of fact, the Greece departure from the Eurozone could have set off a chain reaction among more important troubled members such as Italy, Portugal and Spain.
- The exit of Greece from Eurozone would make other EU countries to raise interest rates on their bonds, making debt service even more difficult.
- Substantial financial losses for the other EU members and the IMF which hold the Greek sovereign debt of more than 320 billion euro, as Greek will eventually not be able to repay them.

- Negative impact on Troika (European Commission, IMF and ECB) and the credibility of the austerity programs, which have contributed to the Greek prolonged recession.
- Incapability of Greece to access private lending capital markets and the downfall of its banking system for an unspecified period of time with repercussions on the standard living of the middle class.

Since its introduction in 1999, the euro has climbed to highest levels ever reached at about 1.6038 USD in mid-2008 and fallen as low as 0.823 USD in the late 2000s. The euro has endured all the ups and downs in the open market. It dropped almost 10 percent against the dollar in October 2008, in the wake of the Lehman Brother Holding Inc. collapse which sent shockwaves in the global market, only to recover most of the loss by the end of 2008. The single currency of the EU has proved to be extraordinarily resilient too, amid the flow of the Greek bailout talks in 2015 climbing 2.6 percent against the group of top 10 world currencies by the end of March in 2015. Economists give a variety of reasons for Euro strength in the mid of turmoil going from money managers cancelling euro hedges as they dumb bonds and stocks to Greece optimism that this country will make it through.

Four more countries in the EU – Ireland, Portugal, Spain and Cyprus - were somehow in a dangerous debt crisis but not as bad as Greece, which will be illustrated below.

Ireland. Irish main banks lost an estimated 100 billion euros which were associated with defaulted loans to property developers and homeowners during the property bubble in 2008. It spread quickly in other sectors of the economy which almost collapsed by the end of 2008. The unemployment rate rises steeply from 4% in 2006 to 14% by 2010, and the government budget went from an excellent surplus in 2007 to a staggering deficit of 32% GDP in 2010, one of the highest in monetary union area. International rating agencies cut the Ireland credit rating, and Ireland needed assistance desperately from EU and IMF. EU and IMF signed an agreement on November 2010 to give Ireland €67.5 billion in the bailout and in July 2011 EU leaders cut Ireland's interest rate that was paying from 6% to 3.5% and increased the load time from 7.5 years to 15 years.

During the period 2011-2012 Ireland was able to improve the economic outlook significantly and on July 26th, 2012 Ireland was able to return to the financial markets for the first since September 2010 and sold over €5 billion 5-year bonds with an interest rate of 5.9% and 8-year bonds with interest rate of 6.1%. By the end of 2013 Ireland was out of the bailout program and needed no further financial assistance.

Portugal. Portugal was able to resist the first two years of the financial crisis from 2008 to 2010, but in the summer of 2010 international ratings agencies cut the Portugal's sovereign bond rating which led to increased stress on Portuguese government bonds and the economy of this country started to go into financial distress for the rest of 2010. In the second quarter of 2011 Portugal government finally requested €78 billion bailout package from EU and IMF upon conditions to put in place measures to improve the public finances. After a serious of successful economic reforms such as labor legislation, liberalization, cutting redundancy government payments by more than 40 percent, and freeing small businesses and employers from collective bargaining contractual obligations, Portugal was able to get partial access to financial markets by October 2012 when it started selling bond series with 3-years maturity. In January 2013 Portugal was able to sell 5-year maturity bonds, and finally, by May 2013, it started issuing 10-year maturity bond series gaining complete access to lending financial market access. By May 2014 Portugal left the EU bailout program without additional assistance and was able to issue successfully 10-year government bonds with a rate as low as 3.59%. Despite the government debt in 2014 and 2015 was around 130% of GDP it was considered sustainable as far as it was a slow but steady path of economic growth.

Spain. Spain was able to avoid the major downturn of the 2008 crisis during its first years, but when housing bubble bursts, Spain spent hefty amounts of money received by increased tax revenue to help banks on bailouts. In May 2012 major Spanish banks received €19 billion in the bailout and in December 2012 the government estimated that Spanish banks needed at least 59 billion euro in supplementary capital to compensate the losses from real estate investments. In the June of the same year (2012) the interest of Spain's 10-year bonds reached as high as the 7% level and created complications in accessing bond markets, therefore the EU decided to grant Spain financial support for about 100 billion euro which will be used mainly for bank recapitalization. The negative growth rate of Spain reached 1.7% and unemployment raised to 25% in 2012 which caused the ECB to step in by announcing that it will start an unlimited bond-buying plan for Spanish bonds. The introduction of a number of reforms in 2012-13 in the labor market, pension sector, and the liberalization of regulated professions raised the investor confidence. At the beginning of 2014, Spain officially exited the bailout EU/IMF mechanism and had full lending access on financial markets.

Cyprus. The small island of Cyprus with a population of 840 000 people was another EU country hit by the financial crisis. In 2012 the main Cypriot banks were exposed with 22 billion euro to Greek sovereign debt which triggered the downgrading of the Cypriot economy by international rating agencies into junk status. In June 2012 the Cypriot Government, to support the banking system due to Greek debt exposure made a formal request to the *European Financial Stability Facility* (EFSF) and the *European Stability Mechanism* for financial assistance. The European Commission, IMF and ECB (Troika) agreed on bailout terms upon implementation of substantial reforms and austerity measures such as reducing government salaries, social benefits, cutting pensions and increasing taxes on tobacco, alcohol, fuel and introducing some healthcare charges. Part of the agreement bailout was the closing and subsequent liquidation of the Laika Bank, recapitalization of the financial sector, starting of the privatization programs, and the fiscal consolidation to reduce the budget deficit. On March 2013 Cyprus got from Troika an overall bailout package consisting of 10 billion euro which was considered appropriate to recover from the financial crisis. By June 2014 Cyprus was able to get access to private lending market and later in April 2015 Cypriot government issued 1 billion euro 7-year bonds with a reasonable 4.0 % yield, which marked the end of the bailout financial support.

The Brexit Case

The term Brexit was hardly known before June of 2016 when the United Kingdom voted with a referendum to leave the European Union after more than five decades of membership. UK was admitted in the European Communities (EC) in 1973 and confirmed its membership in a 1975 referendum. The Brexit vote came as a surprise to all kind of people and businesses and the international markets penalized the UK by quickly devaluating its currency right after the referendum. After a long debate in the House of Commons, the UK government has started the withdrawal process in 2017 that will eventually be concluded by 2019.

On the other side Scotland, which is part of the United Kingdom, threatens to hold a referendum for independence from the United Kingdom in April 2019 and remain in the European Union. It must also be said that the UK was never 'married' completely to the European Union as it was never part of the Eurozone or EMU (European Monetary Union) and has always maintained its own currency, pound sterling, which was always considered a core currency since 18th century, and part of the SDR (Special Drawing Rights) basket at IMF. This will make the separation softer as it does not have to go back to the old currency.

The reasons why the UK left the European Union are many and go decades back in the early 1990'. The critical point came in 2015 when the Conservative Party won the 2015 general election and introduced the *European Union*

Referendum Act 2015, which enabled the referendum if the renegotiation with the European Union was not possible in four key points:

1) exemption of the UK from an "ever-close-union",
2) restricting EU immigration (due to Syrian crisis),
3) protection of the single market for non-EMU countries like UK, and
4) increasing competitiveness by setting a target for the reduction of the burden of red tape.

The result of the referendum in June 2016 regarding in-out referendum on EU membership closed every possibility for renegotiation with the European Union in the four key points that the ruling Conservative Party was hoping to work on with the EU. There are different opinions regarding the economic effects of the UK divorce from the EU. The supporters of remaining in the EU believe that being in the EU has a strong positive effect on trade and businesses which means that the UK's trade would worse off if it left the single market of EU. On the other side, the supporters of withdrawal from the EU believe that the termination of the yearly UK's net contribution to the EU would allow the British government to cut taxes or pour the money in government spending and infrastructure.

Other effects could be the relocation of businesses and banks outside the UK in any EU country to benefit from the single EU market and the reduction of financial services provided in the UK since they have benefitted from the EU-wide 'passporting' for financial products which by some estimations could result in the loss of thousands of jobs and billions of dollars in revenue loss in financial sector. However, these are only estimated of the real effects of the UK withdrawal from the EU are still unknown.

Despite Brexit, the other members of the European Union or EMU were not willing to follow the case of UK, but rather be part of a bigger community called Eurozone reigned by a single common currency, called euro and a single market called the European Union. It is beyond the scope of this book to analyze the effects of the Brexit as there are still uncertain and unknown answers at the current stage.

Global Monetary Influence Areas. Two or Three Monetary Blocks?

An interesting thing about optimum currency areas and monetary unions are that for the first time since the world moved to a system of flexible exchange rates back in 1973, was possible to establish a single dominant currency for large currency areas such as Europe, the United States, and possibly for the rest of the world. Euro — since its creation on January 1, 1999 — has established a large zone of monetary stability in western, central and east Europe and also in its periphery. According to McKinnon, the best-near-term strategy is a hand-off, *laissez faire* policy over a wide range of values for the dollar/euro exchange rate (McKinnon 2001, 417).

The introduction of Euro has created as a matter of fact two powerful monetary blocks, euro and dollar. Mundell, instead, considers three monetary blocks: dollar, euro and yen, and in some of his recent writings has emphasized that the volatility of the rates between the major blocks (dollar, euro and yen) would be eliminated if there is an agreement among nations for the creation of the G-3 Monetary Union or a G-3 block (Mundell R. A. and Friedman M., 2000). Rather than having unstable exchange rates among the three major currencies the rest of the world would choose to anchor its own currencies in relation with the G-3 block. Therefore, for Mundell, the consequence of creating a monetary union between the dollar, euro and yen would produce stability in the international exchange rates system eliminating a good part of a currency crisis. Furthermore, the cooperation between currency areas - according to Mundell- will drive countries ultimately, at least in theory, to a more efficient solution such as for example the creation of a world currency.

In reality, the yen currency belongs to the strongest economic power in Asia, Japan, but is not the dominant currency. This was demonstrated by the Southeast Asian currency crisis in 1997. There were few rapid growth countries involved in the crisis. It was a currency crisis for Malaysia, Indonesia, Thailand and South Korea, but not for the fast-growing and many stable economies of China, Japan, Hong Kong and Taiwan, although indirectly the outcome of the crisis influenced the whole Southeast Asia. The Japan economy and yen currency were not able to arrange the Asian crisis. The Bank of Japan was unable to fight this currency crisis and recession by lessening monetary policy as it was caught in low-interest-rate trap and yen/dollar exchange rate-imposed. Even after the crisis in 1999-2000, the Bank of Japan in order to avoid other market repercussions tried to keep as much as possible the exchange rate below 105 yen per dollar in fear of yen being appreciated with respect to the dollar and its exports being less competitive.

Differently should have been the reaction if the crisis was concentrated in Europe or in North America where the existence of two large monetary blocks would have created a different approach to handle the crisis. Unfortunately, there has never been a political activist in Japan or in other East Asian countries to save the whole area in case of a currency crisis, as it happened in 1997. Most of East Asian economies for a long time has been anchored to the

US dollar and not yen. The East Asian area lacks a strong political and economic association or community to prevent asymmetric shocks and currency crisis. East Asia region is not as regulated and immune as the eurozone.

Even when the Eurozone was hit by the 2008-9 debt crisis, it was able to absorb the shock thanks to the reorganization of the European banking system in order to oversee the systematic financial risk at the EU level. Eurozone is largely integrated (economically and politically), and fluctuations in the euro/dollar exchange rate have had a modest impact on European price indexes, and there is a moderate range in exchange rates against the dollar. Differently from Eurozone, the East Asian countries use mainly USD currency for import/export invoicing for much of their foreign trade making them vulnerable to dollar oscillations.

The US dollar is still largely used as an international vehicle currency, despite the introduction of euro, which means that USD is used as invoice currency for most of the manufactured and raw material exports in the developing countries in Asia, Latin America, Africa and elsewhere. As a result, the price levels of all the East Asian countries are much more affected by fluctuations in their separate exchange rates against the US dollar than against each other. Economic recovery in East Asia requires different and strong intervention and what is more important cooperation between major players that are at the same time competitors such as China, Korea, Japan, Singapore, Thailand and Taiwan in order for them to fairly peg their currencies to dollar and not allow any gain from depreciation of their respective currencies (with respect to dollar) which undermines competitiveness in the region. According to McKinnon, given that there is no region-wide "Asian euro", the dollar is the only plausible anchor for creating an East Asian zone of monetary stability in price levels and exchange rates (McKinnon, 2001, 417).

The rise of China as a new monetary influence area

The rising of Chinese economy at the second position in the 2010s only after the US economy has created the premises for a new monetary power in East Asia and the world as a whole. China's rapid growth at the beginning of the 21st century has redesigned the world economy, creating an influential driver of corporate strategies, financial markets and geopolitical decisions. China appeared to have a momentum that would provide a stable source of profit and capital. This momentum started in the early 90s of the 20th century and has continued for decades to present day where prices for iron ore has increased steadily, the main ingredient in making steel, as new high rising buildings, roads highways, bridges, rail lines and other infrastructure were built across China. In 2014 alone, a multinational company such as BHP Billiton transported sufficient iron ore each day to China to fill the Empire State Building.

Because of the rising power of China in the global market as a global player the Executive Board of Directors of the IMF on November 2015 concluded that Chinese Renminbi (currency) will be included as a fifth currency effective October 2016 alongside with the US dollar, euro, Japanese yen, and pound sterling in the SDR (Special Drawing Rights) basket. The SDR as per definition is an international reserve asset created by International Monetary Fund in 1969 to supplement its 188 member countries' official reserves. Technically, the SDRs are exchangeable for actual currencies with their value based on the basket of underlying curries. The weighting of Chinese renminbi (yuan) in the basket of SDR will be assigned at 10.92 percent higher which is higher than yen, 8.33 percent and the pound, 8. 09 percent. Most of the new weighting in the SDR valuation basket come at the expense of the euro, whose portion will drop to 30.93 percent from 37.4 percent. The almighty US dollar will remain at the same level at 41.73 percent.

Joining the SDR basket has been a top priority for Chinese government since the early 2000s. China is keen to exercise more power in global financial affairs, counter US dominance and appeal more international capital. China has moved to make its once firmly controlled currency more accessible and tradable at a time when capital has been flowing out of the country, and its reserves have been shrinking. IMF in 2015 has recognized the progress Chinese authorities have made in the past years in reforming China's monetary and financial system. The Chinese government, among other measures, has removed some limitations on access to the domestic bond market for foreign central banks and other reserve-holding institutions. At the same time, it is issuing more debt to surge liquidity and is increasing the currency-trading hours. The continuation and expanding of the monetary reforms in China will bring about a more vigorous international monetary and financial system, which in turn will support growth and stability in China and the global economy.

China has still to do more homework to be accepted as a new monetary influence area by foreign capital, comparable to US dollar, euro, yen or British pound. In fact, the factors that are considered important for central banks and investors in determining whether to hold yuan (Chinese) assets have to do with liquidity, steady return, and depth. China's debt market has a large gap between government and private bond market. The government bond market is large but has a low turnover meanwhile, the corporate bond market is small but has a high turnover. Policy makers in China direct more companies and local government toward increased debt issuance and away from bank loans. China authorities have been relaxing its monetary policy over the tight control of the yuan for a while, and China's central bank has come under huge pressure to be more transparent, vigilant and improve its way of communicating with international monetary organizations and global capital markets.

Actually, there isn't any strategy of creating an optimum currency area or a monetary union of Eurozone style in East Asia. The absence of an economic, political, social, military and cultural integration in East Asia is the major hindrance to creating an Asian-monetary-zone. For this region, the dollar currency remains the anchored or the referred currency but not the common monetary standard or the common currency. The case for an East Asian monetary union is less likely to be realized.

The only strongest economy among the industrialized countries that has arisen after the 2008-9 deep recession is, without doubt, the US economy. The US economy took a huge toll during the financial crisis however it learned the lesson how to avoid the crisis and even invented new monetary tools such quantitative easing and used exceptional bailout programs to keep the money flowing and restart the wounded economy. The strong North American demand after 2013 has kept the US dollar currency at the top of the performing currencies in the world. A strong US dollar has helped to rebalance the global economic growth by sharing the U.S. demand with the rest of the world.

The US dollar steady climb made the U.S. exports to decrease in the first quarter of 2015. In few words, U.S. exporters earned less on contracts that had in place losing business because international competitors had currency advantage. The international trade which in 2011-12 helped pull the United States economy out of the recession when the dollar was weak, became a hindrance to growth as the business cycle started to mature later in 2014-15. However, thanks to the flexible exchange rates the system adjusted itself. In fact, the United States economy started to share its demand with the rest of the world readjusting at the same time its own economy. It became apparent that the United States was no longer getting a boost from international trade, due to a strong dollar, but rather from the new orders coming from the huge domestic market. This helped the US dollar grow stronger and stronger and gave foreign investors a free hand to invest more in the US economy and buy safer US bonds. From this perspective, the US dollar as the most powerful global monetary influence area was never put in doubts.

Some Conclusions about the Optimum Currency Areas and Monetary Unions

This chapter has considered the evolution of the OCA theory from the sixties to our days. At the beginning, there were different criteria for determining an OCA which later swiftly evolved with the creation of eurozone. We have seen that the main criteria for determining an OCA are factor mobility (capital and labour mobility), the "openness" of the economy or inter-sector factor mobility and the criteria of production or the similarities in the goods produced by the regions belonging to an OCA. We have also seen that factor mobility, one of the most important criteria of defining an OCA - emphasized by Mundell- is different in EU and in the U.S. In EU the labor mobility is somehow limited between different countries, while in the US the mobility of this factor between regions is greater and help on adjusting the consequences of region-specific shocks which tend to be large.

A single currency is more suitable for some areas of the world than for others. There are always economic benefits from having a single currency in one area than a multitude of currencies. Monetary integration produces more net benefits for a large number of countries that meet most of the OCA properties. Most parts of benefits of a single currency consist of savings the transaction costs of currency exchanges, hedging and so on. There can be offsetting costs if a single currency stands in the way of economic adjustments that may be initiated or assisted by monetary policy. Many empirical studies have confirmed the relationship between countries in an OCA between openness and the level of growth of real income. The countries which have a common currency need less monetary reserves to face the external shocks, than those who act separately. An OCA is said to be an asymmetric shock absorber. For the EMU members, the single currency has brought considerable benefits but also has required a long period of several decades. The progress towards the European Union has not been easy and linear but has required several stages of economic and monetary integration. The European experience has shown that heterogeneity of institutions, policy preferences, economic structures, cultural and social determinants diminish only gradually over years and decades.

There are still some unresolved problems regarding Optimum Currency Areas particularly in the case of EMU. The success of the eurozone seems to depend from the credibility of the European Central Bank (ECB) to hit its principal objective to "the maintenance of price stability". The ECB has still to resolve its own big puzzle; the technical question of deciding which variable it will target in order to preserve price stability.

Two alternative monetary policy strategies are available to the ECB. The first alternative is to target the rate of inflation directly, with the interest rate being pegged at the level necessary to secure price stability. So interest rates are expected to change in response to inflationary trends. This approach has been followed by Bank of England since 1992 when sterling was forced out of the ERM. The difficulty in this approach is that the empirical studies specify that changes in interest rates (supposed to be affected by changing the supply of money) only influence the underlying rate of inflation after a time lag estimated at two years (Scott, 1999). So there is no agreement among economists that changes in the money supply in the OCA influences interest rates in the short term.

The second alternative for ECB is to control inflation by controlling the money supply. This approach involves the selection of an appropriate aggregate measure of the supply of money in circulation. The growth of money supply, in this case, is restricted to the underlying rate of economic growth for the EU as a whole.

The Bundesbank for a long time has preferred the second approach to control the inflation. Monetary aggregates regarding the measure of the money supply have the advantage of being readily measurable, and differences between the targeted and the actual rate of monetary growth can be quickly detected and corrected. The same approach is also followed by the ECB. By considering this method, the problem remains unresolved if we take into consideration the transmission mechanism that links changes in money supply to the subsequent changes in the inflation rate at the level of the euro-zone. The monetary model that envisages a given change in the supply of money will produce a particular change in the rate of inflation is based on the assumption that the underlying demand for money is basically stable, or that it changes only slowly over relatively long periods.

The monetarist approach (second alternative) is based on the idea that inflation is directly, and proportionately, attributable to the rate of growth of the money supply exceeding the economy-wide rate of economic growth. While many studies have been conducted into the demand for money function within a country, there is very little or nothing known about the demand for money function at the level of an OCA, and in our case, at the level of the euro-zone. Given that there is very little known at present about the transmission mechanism that links changes in money supply to changes in the inflation rate at the level of the euro-zone, the monetarist model "link money supply/inflation" seems to be no more appropriate to an OCA unless further studies prove otherwise.

We have also seen that the introduction of a single currency in two OCAs, the United States (two centuries ago) and Europe in 1999 produced both economic benefits and economic costs. On average, the net economic benefits for a society should exceed the costs. Consequently, economic adjustments must be made in one of three ways. First, labour must be mobile so workers can move from an area suffering from recession to one that is enjoying an economic boom. Second, wages and prices must be flexible in order for the economy to respond to changes in supply and demand. Third, there must be some way of transferring resources (federal transfers in the US) to the country or region which is in bad economic straits in order to help it recovers from its recession. Given these three criteria, it is unlikely that the United States and Europe would fit Mundell's definition of an optimum currency area.

The national sovereign default for European nations sharing a common currency in the monetary union has become an issue of great concern, especially regarding the contagion to other nations, since the last financial and debt crisis of the 2008-9. The unilateral sovereign default of an individual member of the EU has no economic reason to leave the union as the debt can still be restructured if there is a willing by other members to financially support the debt.

From the debt, crisis perspective is obvious that a minimal fiscal Euro-zone with a mutual fiscal agreement between EU members and governing bodies of the EU is required to compensate the loss of the national monetary policy and be used as a sovereign default prevention mechanism. Another instrument that can be used for the European Union to well-function and survive is the European Stability Mechanism (ESM) which could recapitalize the important cross-border financial institutions in distress by allowing them to continue operating and recover from financial difficulties or in the worst-case-scenario to liquidate them without high social costs.

This chapter has also put some thoughts on the Eurozone macro-structure after the latest developments of the 2008 deep financial crisis and the Greece debt crisis which was considered by some analysts as the breaking point of the European Union. Fortunately, this did not happen thanks to the political will to keep the union together by reorganizing the European banking system and using unprecedented bailout programs to keep Greece inside the union and save the euro.

The European Monetary Union currently composed of 19 countries has been the most successful case of a monetary union with a common currency, despite its diverse national economies and the recent debt crisis as a result of 2008 financial crisis. Although, it is much to do in the future in particular in the field of centralized fiscal policy, regional federal taxation and federal transfers. Truly and unfortunately we do not see another monetary union case. The case for a North American, an East Asian, an Australian, a Latin America and even an African monetary union is unlikely to be realized.

Chapter 5

Financial Crisis and Unconventional Monetary Policies

Introduction

The financial crisis of 2007-8 put in place a number of big challenges for monetary authorities and central banks in the developed countries not seen since the global recession of the 1930s. Unfortunately, the conventional monetary policy that was supposed to keep inflation stable and low did not stop market bubbles from happening. In general, a conventional monetary policy conducted by a central bank would focus on short-term interest rates through open market operations.

But this policy seemed not to work on the 2008 financial crisis, therefore new monetary policies called unconventional monetary policies were introduced to deal with on influencing interest rates rather than the usual short-term interest rates. The main aspect of the new policy consists of the central bank buying or selling high or low-risk securities from the banking system to influence the level of reserves the banks hold in the system. Different from the conventional monetary policy, where buying and selling assets normally short-term debt has the objective to influence the interest rates, the unconventional monetary policy has as target the level of purchases on reserves which would have a spill-over effect on the economy by raising the price of assets and eliminating the deflationary forces.

This eccentric and unconventional monetary policy is often called the quantitative easing (QE). The goal of this policy is to speed the economic recovery and to stabilize inflation at levels considered consistent with price stability, steady market demand and sustainable employment. The objective of this chapter is to reconsider briefly the recent financial crisis and some of the unconventional monetary policies used by central banks to ease the effects of the financial crisis.

The New Banking Era and Financial Crisis

In modern times, the definition of banking liability is the creation of short-term trading or transaction securities backed by longer-term assets, such as chequing accounts (demand deposit), etc. Bank's trading securities are short-term liabilities and need not be renewed. The short-term bank liabilities, which we are focused on are the "repo" ones. These are short repurchase agreements where the dealer or the holder of the securities sells the securities to a lender and agrees to repurchase them at an agreed future date at an agreed price. In this agreement, the cash lender is commonly remunerated in the form of a repo rate, which is basically an interest on the gross value of the transaction.

The repo market is not insured. Short-term bank liabilities are designed to be safe, as they are redeemable and backed by collateral in the form of bank assets. However, in practice, they have always been exposed to panic in the sale and repurchase market, which means repo market especially during the financial crisis of 2008.

Since the early 1980s, there has been a change in the form and quantity of bank liabilities that have involved the combination of securitization with the repo market. This change was made possible because of the traditional banking system was becoming unprofitable. In fact, in the 1980s traditional banks lost market share to money market mutual funds which replaced demand deposits and high-yield, high-risk securities, called junk bonds which took market share from lending. For traditional banks, it was becoming unprofitable to keep passive cash flows on the balance sheet from loans when credit decision was already made. The national regulators that supervise the banking system can make banks hold more capital, but they cannot prevent banks to exit from investments or portfolios if they become unprofitable. This process led to securitization, which consists of selling cash flow made of loans to increase the gross margin. Thus, the securitization is the selling of portfolios of loans. The process of securitization for a traditional bank is a risky one, as the bank keeps the residual or equity portion of the securitized loans and earns fees for servicing these loans.

The motive the banks sells loans is the profitability. Securitization was a significant financial innovation that happened in the last two decades of the 20th century and allowed commercial banks to increase profitability. According to Pennacchi (1988), the securitization process was going to have a significant impact on the commercial banking business. Securitization process allows banks and other non-financial companies to acquire liquidity from assets that otherwise cannot be sold in liquid markets and make a profit. An example of securitization is when banks can issue a covered bond referenced to a mortgage or even to a portfolio of mortgages rather than holding them in a balance sheet for their entire maturity, let say 25-30 years.

Another example of securitization is when banks can sell the mortgage portfolio to another company or to a company created as a *special purpose vehicle* (SPV) that funds the transaction selling mortgage-based bonds to other institutions or retail investors. Based on this transaction, the banks could use the proceeds of the mortgages to cover the interest of the mortgage-based securities, or the bank might decide to get rid of the credit risk embedded in the mortgage subject to deliver or not a credit improvement to the SPV in which the bank assumes a certain level of shared losses in the mortgage-backed securities. Covered bonds and asset-backed securities (ABS) are other categories of securities that have different risk premiums for investors buying them.

With the new funds raised by securitization, the banks transform into liquidity assets that could have been sitting in balance sheet until their maturity and at the same time increase lending. Banks also, thanks to securitization, have the possibility to transfer risk right after the loan has been granted, by putting it into a bundle of other mortgages, and giving a risk assessment by rating agencies and finally selling out the bundle as asset-backed security (ABS). In this type of operation, the main proceeds for banks come from the fees they earn creating and packaging loan vanishing the traditional relationship with the customer.

For banks, transferring risk to other investors using securitization could have been easy if there were no issues, as it was intended to be when securitization was invented. In reality, there are two main concerns. The first one is that the lender has to accurately screen and monitor borrowers, as it is going to transfer the credit risk to other buyers or investors. The second concern is that the bank selling loans must continue to persuade loan buyers of its obligation to appraise the credit quality of borrowers by maintaining a percentage of the loan's risk. This commitment makes asset securitization incentive compatible. However, in practice, some loan originators might have transferred the whole credit risk in a loan securitization rather than keeping a portion of it creating a lack of confidence from investors buying the ABS.

Due to these concerns, the banking supervising authorities were involved in 1999 in a thorough revision of the current capital regulatory framework that ended up creating the new bank regulations which were included in the so-called Basel II framework, where the capital requirements for each commercial bank has to be aligned with the risk profile of their portfolios.

Thanks to Basel II capital regulations banks were required to hold a higher level of capital for loans granted to high-risk borrowers. Despite the Basel II regulations, it was still possible through securitization process for banks to sell a part of those loans (the loans of better quality) to investors and with the proceeds, lend in a second moment new loans to riskier borrowers in order to increase the expected returns of their portfolio with no modification in capital requirement for risky loans. The loans of better quality assets were securitized and sold to investors without problem meanwhile poorer quality assets were subsidised with deposits under asymmetric information and without government intervention (Greenbaum and Thakor, 1987).

Securitization process has helped many lenders ease the regulatory burden despite the risk associated with it. During the 2007-8 financial crisis, structured finance markets came to a halt after almost a decade of remarkable growth. The main victims were the mortgage-backed securities (MBS), and collateral debt obligation (CDO) that saw their reputation go down after their risk re-assessment by rating agencies was downgraded to the lowest levels, and major banks amounted theirs loses. Market professionals and the academic world blamed securitization for encouraging risky lending and being in part responsible for the 2007-8 crisis. In fact, a number of empirical studies computed during this period indicated that securitization laid in lower lending standards, as never seen before, which resulted to adverse selection in the collateral pools underlying these products (Drucker and Puri 2009, and Keys, Mukherjee, Seru and Vig 2010).

The main difference between the corporate loans and mortgage securitization is based on the fact that corporate loans are only partially securitized. The corporate loans are significantly larger than mortgages and are syndicated, which means that at origination, the loans are funded by a group of banks and institutional investors. The banks that originated the loans usually retains a portion of the loan on its balance sheet, and each underlying loan is rated. On the other side, subprime mortgages are commonly sold in one piece to MBS issuers with little to no risk retention by the originator.

The dissimilarity between corporate and mortgage loans securitization regarding the securitization process and consequent collateral performance have created implications for the future of the securitized assets which has broad to new legislation in financial derivatives. In order to reduce agency problems with securitization process in 2010 in the U.S. government introduced Section 941 of the Dodd-Frank Wall Street Reform and Consumer Protection Act which requires federal agencies to develop credit risk retention requirements for securitizers and originators in structured and non-structured financial markets. During the 2008 financial crisis, many mortgage-based securities (MBS) and collateralized loan obligations (CLO) were downgraded or placed on negative credit watch. Many CLOs were downgraded partly due to the deterioration in the credit quality of corporate borrowers, and partly due to the aggressive adjustments to rating agency methodologies. Despite widespread downgrades, there were few defaults on CLO tranches (less than 1%) compared to MBS.

Mortgage securitization which is referred to the securitization process for nonconforming mortgages, such as jumbo, alt-A, and subprime, do not meet the criteria for securitization by government-sponsored enterprises. Technically speaking, after origination a subprime mortgage (around $150 000 - $190-000 on average) is normally sold by the originating lender as a part of a pool of other investors. The mortgage pool would be used as part of the collateral held by SPV (Special Purpose Vehicle company), and none of the individual mortgages will be split into parts, as it is only one direct claim that will be used against the borrower who took the original mortgage. On the other hand, the loans held by CLOs are syndicated, which means at origination each loan (about $522 million on average) is funded by a group of lenders, where each syndicate participant holds a direct pro rata claim against the borrower.

The syndicated loans contain certain mechanisms that the lead bank retain a share of the loan on its balance sheet that could reach up to 27% of a loan, which made this shared loans to function properly prior to the 2008 crisis. However, during the 2004-7 period, lead banks were not conducting due diligence and monitoring borrowers properly due to broader syndication resulting from large CLO demand. In fact, the research done by Ivashina and Scharfstein (2010) concluded that the average share of loans retained by lead banks fell rapidly during the 2004-2007 credit expansion.

The outstanding amount of subprime bonds was not large enough to cause the financial crisis of 2008 and the losses that were experienced at that time. Subprime mortgages started to worsen in January 2007, at least 8 months before the financial panic that hit the financial markets in August 2008. Government and federal regularity policies allowed some changes in the reserve requirements of U.S. banks which combined with the creation in 1994 of a special "sweep" account to connect commercial checking and investment accounts allowing banks greater liquidity to be used for more loans.

In addition to that, from 2001 to 2002, in the wake of high tech crash, the Federal Reserve Funds Rate was reduced from 6 percent to 1.24 percent, leading to comparable rate decreases in the London Interbank Offered Rate that banks typically uses to set some of the ARM (Adjustable-Rate Mortgage) rates. The decrease in ARM rates in the U.S. meant that for the prospective homebuyers the monthly payment of a mortgage on a $400,000 home had fallen to about a monthly cost of a mortgage on a $200, 000 home purchased

2-3 years earlier. This sent the demand for "cheap" or "discounted" mortgages to the highest levels never seen before.

The period between 2004 and 2006 was dominated by risky mortgage products and lax of lending standards in the United States. In fact, for some of the high-risk loan options like ARM and interest only loans the lending standards were relaxed so much that in some cases the borrowers did not have to provide documentation to substantiate the income stated on the application to finance home purchase and no stress test was done if they were able to pay the loan if interest rates increased. In other cases, the lenders offered new incentives for home buyers by using a new invention called "teaser rate". A "teaser rate" was a low but temporary introductory prime rate that would increase after the initial period and in some cases doubling the monthly payment. About one-third of ARMs originated between 2004 and 2006 had "teaser rates" below four percent. There were also programs called *Downpayment Assistance Programs* (DPA) in which a seller gives money to a charitable organization that then gives money to buyers. During the 2000-2006 period, more than 650 000 homebuyers in the U.S. got their down payments via non-profit organizations through DPA. Later, in October 2007, the Internal Revenue Service and the Department of Housing and Urban Development banned the DPA for non-profit status because of the doubtful circular nature of the cash flow used to sell and buy homes.

Bank experts believe that the mortgage standard in the United States became lax because of a "moral hazard" where each link in the mortgage chain made a profit while believing it was passing on a risk. This process helped deteriorate the quality of the mortgages. In fact, mortgage denial rates for regular home purchase loans, according to Home Mortgage Disclosure Act, dropped from 29 percent in 1998, to 14 percent in period 2002-3. Mortgage Brokers was another factor that determined the quality of the mortgage loans in the U.S. In 2004 alone, more than 68 percent of all home purchase loans in the United States with sub-prime and Alt-A loans were originated by mortgage brokers, which didn't do enough to determine if borrowers were able to repay the loans by following standard parameters, leaving lenders/banks with a large number of defaults. Another 40 percent of subprime loans in 2007 were generated by 'automated' underwriting requiring minimal documentation and much faster decisions avoiding in many cases the standard requirements of a full set of documentation.

The securitization of mortgage-backed securities (MBS), those passed to third-party investors, as a result of higher ratings given by credit rating agencies increased from 54 percent in 2001 to 75 percent in 2006. The growth of subprime industry in the United States brought the first problems of foreclosure on properties starting from the second half of 2006. What the frequency of subprime lenders foreclose on properties was much higher than on the conventional banks. The subprime mortgage industry started to show sign of collapse by January 2007. A large part of homeowners fell behind on their mortgage payments, and the foreclosures continued to increase which left the subprime lenders unable to finance new loans. As result of the subprime mortgage collapse, the Ameriquest, one of the largest subprime lenders in the U.S., filed for bankruptcy and laid off 3800 employees.

The collapse of the subprime market in the United States affected the global market. The stock markets around the globe plunged on January 21, 2008. In fact, on the same day, the stock prices fell 5.5 percent in Britain, 5.1 percent in India, 7 percent in Germany and 3.9 percent in Japan. The markets simple tumbled in their worst decline since September 11, 2001, because the fear spread quickly as the massive losses on loans made to U.S. home buyers would cascade through the world financial system.

Monetary Unions, Debt Crisis and Slow Growth

Although a large public debt is never a good thing it has always co-existed in the economy since the birth of capitalism. The government needs money to run its business but collecting taxes is never enough, so borrowing money from the public by paying them interest is another form to raise funds that help run the economy. It is very interesting to see how public debt builds up.

Debts in war times are less problematic for the government and health of the economy than debts accumulated in peacetime. High wartime public debts to finance the war will come to an end as peace returns, and the economy starts running at its regular growth pace. Differently, debts accumulated during peacetime reflects the unstable political conditions and external and internal shocks that can last for some time. In the peacetime a financial crisis can trigger a debt crisis. A number of disparities can be created between countries of a monetary union in terms of current accounts, public finances, competitiveness and evolution of property prices.

The financial crisis that started in 2008 in the US hit European countries with dramatic fall in demand. The reduction in demand eroded the revenue bases of the government despite the efforts to use discretionary fiscal measures to stimulate economic growth. The depression suddenly increased some government expenditure categories like unemployment benefits and the cost of supporting the financial crisis with the bailouts of certain important financial institutions mainly in the US and Europe which put pressure on yearly fiscal budgets. In addition, the pricing of government bonds in different countries hit by the crisis started reflecting the risk associated with the fragile public finances and a steep decline in competitiveness.

The uncertainty about the capability of some countries to service their debts led to negative spiral between banks and European governments. The financial integration of a monetary union such as Europe meant the crisis would spread rapidly from one country to another as it happened in 2010 where the financial crisis was so critical for Greece that it became contagious for other countries with financial difficulties such as Ireland, Portugal and Spain. In fact, in these countries, the government bond yields rose to very high levels which led to a serious of urgent support measures from the EU and International Monetary Fund.

A quick view of the financial crisis, made many economists think that the main responsibility for coming to the financial crisis lies with the long-term problems that countries had in the past, such as the management of the high level of public debt. The development of the public debts is very responsive to interest rate levels, to the improvement of fiscal policy and the rate of growth in the short and long term. The combination of these three factors despite contradictory among them, as in the case of fiscal policy contraction and growth, would in theory and eventually in reality launch a credible plan for the sustainability of public finances.

Table 5.1 shows the dimension of the fiscal problem among the developed countries during the 2008-9 financial crisis. The table illustrates that only a handful of developed countries were in a good fiscal-financial shape in 2009. This group includes a number of countries that historically have had best results on fiscal commitments. Some of them are Australia, New Zealand, Denmark, Norway, Sweden, Finland and Switzerland. Other countries such as Austria, Canada, Germany and the Netherlands, are considered traditionally to have good fiscal-financial conditions only if compared with other similar countries that are in poorer conditions. Greece in 2009, with almost 115% of gross government debt and 15% budget deficit of GDP, represents the greatest fear of the Eurozone. The numbers of the Euro Area are in a certain sense more sustainable if compared with the fiscal situation of the Japan, US and UK.

Percentage of 2009 Nominal GDP

Country	Gross Debt % of Nominal GDP	Net Debt % Nominal of GDP	Budget Deficit Balance %	Structural Balance %	Cyclically Adj. Primary Balance
Australia	15.9	-5.7	-4.5	-3.3	-2.5
Canada	82.8	28.6	-4.8	-3.2	-2.3
Czech Republic	42.0	-1.0	-5.8	4.6	-3.7
Denmark	51.8	-5.1	-2.8	0.1	0.7
EuroArea	**81.8**	51.7	-6.3	-3.6	-1.2
Austria	66.5	37.2	-4.1	-2.4	-0.4
Belgium	96.7	80.7	-5.6	-2.8	0.4
Finland	44.0	-63.2	-2.7	1.1	0.6
France	77.6	50.6	-7.6	-5.7	-3.7
Germany	73.2	48.3	-3.1	-1.4	0.8
Greece	115.1	87.0	-15.6	-11.7	-7.1
Ireland	64.0	27.2	-13.9	-9.9	-8.2
Italy	115.8	101.0	-5.4	-2.7	1.5
Luxembourg	14.5		-0.8	-4.5	-0.2
Netherlands	60.9	28.5	-5.6	-0.8	-3.0
Norway	43.7	-153.4	10.6	-7.4	-3.8
Portugal	76.8	57.9	-10.2	-7.3	-4.7
Slovak Republic	35.7	12.4	-8.0		
Slovenia	35.9		-6.0		
Spain	53.2	34.8	-11.2	-8.3	-7.1
Hungary	84.0	58.0	-4.5	-1.6	2.2
Iceland	122.7	41.0	-10.0	-7.4	-5.0
Japan	189.3	96.5	-8.8	-5.5	-4.5
Korea	34.9	-31.0	-1.1		
New Zealand	35.0	-8.1	-2.6	-1.4	-2.3
Poland	58.4	22.3	-7.4	-7.3	-5.3
Sweden	51.8	-23.4	-1.0	2.3	2.6
Switzerland		5.5	0.8	1.3	1.7
United Kingdom	72.3	43.5	-10.9	-8.6	-7.0
Unites States	83.9	56.4	-11.9	-9.0	-7.6

Table 5.1 Fiscal Data, the year 2009 for some industrialized countries. ***Source*: Eurostat, European Commission and OECD 2010.**

Furthermore, the recent IMF Fiscal Monitor publication in October 2012 considers the situation where growth in many parts of the world is weakening, and the fiscal policy remains challenging for many governments. Nevertheless, substantial progress has been made in consolidating the fiscal accounts in the period 2010-13 following the deterioration in 2008-9. There are at last two schools of economic thought regarding budget deficit.

The Keynesian school believes that governments should run deficits spending during recession periods and high unemployment to sustain demand and growth in the presence of a sluggish private sector demand. Only during periods of strong growth and full employment the government should be able to balance the budget. In fact, based on this Keynesian thought some economists believe that the stimulus program following the 2008 economic crisis has increased the budget deficit beyond any forecast but at least has helped the economies to escape a dangerous and vicious "Great Depression".

On the other side, there is a large number of economists who believe in austerity programs that serve to reduce the deficit by cutting government spending in order to match government revenue generated mainly by taxes. At the beginning of the 2008 crisis, many world leaders used the Keynesian economic theories to put in place huge stimulus packages in several countries to find the recession. But two years later, in the first months of 2010 as a result of mounting deficits and market turmoil, governments started calling for heavy cuts in public expenditures. Some countries in the Euro area with the highest deficits, such as Greece, Cyprus, Ireland, Italy, Spain and Portugal had to do substantial short-term spending cuts to avoid the default which sparked rising unemployment and widespread malcontent among people. Table 5.2 illustrates the government deficit/surplus as a percentage of GDP for OECD countries in the period 2007-2014.

Countries	2007	2008	2009	2010	2011	2012	2013	2014
Australia	1.8	-0.8	-4.5	-4.7	-4.0	-2.8	0.0	0.5
Austria	-1.0	-1.0	-4.1	-4.5	-2.5	-3.1	-2.7	-2.1
Belgium	-0.1	-1.1	-5.6	-3.9	-3.9	-2.8	-2.3	-1.7
Canada	1.4	-0.4	-4.8	-5.4	-4.3	-3.5	-3.0	-2.5
Czech Republic	-0.7	-2.2	-5.8	-4.8	-3.2	-3.3	-3.3	-2.7
Denmark	4.8	3.3	-2.8	-2.7	-2.0	-4.1	-2.1	-1.7
Estonia	2.4	-2.9	-2.0	0.2	1.2	-1.0	-0.3	0.2
Finland	5.3	4.3	-2.7	-2.8	-0.9	-1.4	-1.0	-0.4
France	-2.7	-3.3	-7.6	-7.1	-5.2	-4.5	-3.4	-2.9
Germany	0.2	-0.1	-3.1	-4.2	-0.8	-0.2	-0.4	-0.7
Greece	-6.8	-9.9	-15.6	-10.8	-9.5	-6.9	-5.6	-4.6
Hungary	-5.1	-3.7	-4.5	-4.5	4.3	-3.0	-2.7	-2.7
Iceland	5.4	-13.5	-10.0	-10.1	-5.4	-1.8	-0.4	0.7
Ireland	0.1	-7.4	-13.9	-30.9	-13.3	-8.1	-7.5	-5.3
Israel	-1.6	-4.0	-6.7	-4.8	-4.4	-4.7	-4.1	-4.0
Italy	-1.6	-2.7	-5.4	-4.3	-3.8	-3.0	-2.9	-3.4
Japan	-2.1	-1.9	-8.8	-8.4	-9.3	-9.9	-10.1	-7.9
Korea	4.7	3.0	-1.1	1.3	0.5	0.9	1.6	1.7
Luxembourg	3.7	3.2	-0.8	0.8	-0.3	-2.0	-1.7	-0.9
Netherlands	0.2	0.5	-5.6	-5.0	-4.4	-3.8	-3.0	-2.5
New Zealand	4.5	0.4	-2.6	-3.8	-7.9	-4.3	-3.6	-2.1
Norway	17.3	18.8	10.6	11.2	13.7	15.2	16.0	16.8
Poland	-1.9	-3.7	-7.4	-7.9	-5.0	-3.5	-2.9	-2.3
Portugal	-3.2	-3.7	-10.2	-9.8	-4.4	-5.2	-4.9	-2.9
Slovak Republic	-1.8	-2.1	-8.0	-7.7	-4.9	-4.6	-2.9	-2.4
Slovenia	0.0	-1.9	-6.0	-5.7	-6.4	-4.3	-3.6	-3.0
Spain	1.9	-4.5	-11.2	-9.7	-9.4	-8.1	-6.3	-5.9
Sweden	3.6	2.2	-1.0	0.0	0.2	-0.3	-0.8	-0.2
Switzerland	1.0	2.0	0.8	0.3	0.5	0.7	0.5	0.4
United Kingdom	-2.8	-5.0	-10.9	-10.1	-8.3	-6.6	-6.9	-6.0
United States	-2.9	-6.6	-11.9	-11.4	-10.2	-8.5	-6.8	-5.2
Euro area(15 countries)	-0.7	-2.1	-6.3	-6.2	-4.1	-3.3	-2.8	-2.6
Major seven-G7	-2.2	-4.3	-9.4	-9.0	-7.9	-6.8	-5.9	-4.8
OECD-Total	-1.3	-3.4	-8.2	-7.7	-6.5	-5.5	-4.6	-3.6
Brazil	-2.8	-2.0	-3.3	-2.5	-2.6	-2.2	-1.7	-2.0
China	2.0	0.9	-1.1	-0.7	0.1	-2.0	-2.2	-1.7
India	-4.0	-7.1	-9.7	-7.4	-7.9	-8.4	-8.3	-7.6

Indonesia	-1.3	-0.1	-1.6	-0.7	-1.1	-2.0	-1.8	-1.6
Russian Federation	5.6	7.3	-4.3	-3.5	1.6	0.5	0.1	0.0
South Africa	-0.6	-1.7	-4.9	-6.0	-5.2	-5.0	-4.7	-4.0

Table 5.2. Government Deficit/Surplus as a percentage of GDP. *Source*: OECD Economic Outlook No.92 (database). OECD 2012 (years 2013 and 2014 are estimates).

Most of the OECD countries, starting from the early 1990's to the beginning of 2000, had substantial deficits but by 2007 half of them had improved the government spending reducing the deficit or even turning deficit in surplus. In fact, that year from Table 5.2, we can see that the total deficit for OECD countries was as low as -1.3% of total GDP. During the 2008 and in 2009 because of the deep crisis and as a consequence of the stimulus programs many OECD countries faced rising budget deficits. And by 2012 the overall OECD deficit grew up to 5.5 percentages. For the year 2012, table 5.2 shows that the government deficit was still high for some OECD countries and low for others. It ranged from a surplus of 15.2 % for Norway, 0.9% for Korea and 0.7% for Switzerland to large deficits in Ireland (8.1% of GDP), Japan (9.9%), United States (8.5%), Spain (8.1%), Greece (6.9%), United Kingdom (6.6%) and Portugal (5.2%). By the year 2014-16 the government budget of most of the OECD was forecasted to restore to their pre-crisis value. In fact, deficits were estimated to be reduced for Ireland, Japan. United States, Spain, Greece and Portugal, by 1-3 percent of the value they had in 2012, putting them in line with more fiscal disciplined countries. Table 5.3, instead, illustrates the GDP growth (and forecast) as a percentage of GDP for the OECD countries during the 2007-14 period.

Countries	2007	2008	2009	2010	2011	2012	2013	2014
Australia	4.89	2.24	1.48	2.38	2.25	3.7	3.0	3.17
Austria	3.67	1.06	-3.48	2.23	2.69	0.6	0.78	1.84
Belgium	2.86	0.95	-2.75	2.42	1.81	-0.13	0.53	1.58
Canada	2.09	1.10	-2.8	3.17	2.57	2.04	1.82	2.41
Czech Republic	5.74	3.10	-4.51	2.49	1.89	-0.92	0.76	4.43
Denmark	1.58	-0.78	-5.67	1.58	1.10	0.24	1.39	1.73
Estonia	7.49	-4.15	-14.07	3.33	8.28	3.15	3.75	3.44
Finland	5.34	0.29	-8.54	3.32	2.74	0.67	1.14	2.16
France	2.25	-0.19	-3.05	1.57	1.70	0.17	0.33	1.26
Germany	3.39	0.80	-5.07	4.02	3.10	0.94	0.56	1.94
Greece	3.54	-0.21	-3.14	-4.94	-7.10	-6.27	-4.55	-1.27
Hungary	0.11	0.89	-6.77	1.32	1.65	-1.57	-0.13	1.16
Iceland	5.98	1.19	-6.58	-4.01	2.56	2.53	2.73	2.67
Ireland	5.43	-2.14	-5.47	-0.78	1.42	0.48	1.34	2.19
Israel	5.90	4.11	1.11	4.98	4.60	3.13	2.90	3.90
Italy	1.55	-1.16	-5.50	1.77	0.56	-2.16	-0.98	0.55
Japan	2.19	-1.04	-5.53	4.53	-0.75	1.64	0.65	0.76
Korea	5.11	2.30	0.32	6.32	3.63	2.24	3.05	4.42
Luxembourg	6.56	-0.75	-4.08	2.89	1.66	0.57	1.19	1.98
Netherlands	3.91	1.77	-3.66	1.57	1.07	-0.86	0.19	1.46
New Zealand	3.38	-0.65	-0.20	0.91	0.52	1.64	2.38	2.91
Norway	2.65	0.04	-1.67	0.68	1.45	3.32	2.51	2.02
Poland	6.83	4.99	1.65	3.85	4.32	2.48	1.58	2.55
Portugal	2.37	-0.01	-2.91	1.40	-1.67	-3.09	-1.75	0.91
Slovak Republic	10.49	5.75	-4.94	4.38	3.23	2.64	1.95	3.38
Slovenia	6.96	3.38	-7.84	1.24	0.60	-2.37	-2.08	1.08
Spain	3.48	0.89	-3.74	-0.32	0.42	-1.29	-1.42	0.54
Sweden	3.43	-0.77	-4.98	6.27	3.94	1.20	1.88	3.03
Switzerland	3.85	2.16	-1.94	3.03	1.93	0.84	1.08	2.29
Turkey	4.67	0.66	-4.83	9.16	8.50	2.86	4.11	5.16
United Kingdom	3.63	-0.97	-3.97	1.80	0.87	-0.14	0.90	1.55
United States	1.91	-0.34	-3.07	2.39	1.81	2.24	2.01	2.81
Euro area(15 countries)	2.99	0.25	-4.35	1.94	1.49	-0.41	0.09	1.31
Major-seven-G7	2.25	-0.35	-3.86	2.75	1.44	1.39	1.27	2.08
OECD-Total	2.79	0.16	-3.60	2.96	1.85	1.40	1.41	2.31

Non-OECD members								
Brazil	6.08	5.17	-0.31	7.55	2.74	1.53	4.04	4.06
China	14.20	9.60	9.21	10.45	9.29	7.54	8.53	8.88
India	9.96	6.01	5.22	10.46	7.79	4.52	5.92	7.04
Indonesia	6.35	6.01	4.63	6.20	6.46	6.23	6.34	6.53
Russian Federation	8.54	5.25	-7.82	4.34	4.34	3.44	3.78	4.08
South Africa	5.55	3.62	-1.54	2.89	3.12	2.62	3.25	4.05

Table 5.3. GDP yearly growth (volume) as a percentage of GDP. *Source*: OECD Economic Outlook No.92 (database). OECD 2012 (estimation for years 2013 and 2014).

Based on the figures in Table 5.3 all OECD and non-OECD countries were experiencing growth in 2007. It was business as usual when things suddenly changed with the 2008-9 financial crisis. In 2009 when the crisis hit hard all the OECD members with very few exemptions (Australia, Israel, and Poland) had negative growth rates.

Three years later in 2012, the majority of the OECD countries were recovering and showing modest growth except for few of them such as Ireland, Spain and Portugal that were hampered by the substantial cost to rescue domestic banks in the wake of crashing housing markets, which led to the deteriorating of public finances. Greece was a special case of the Euro area as its finances were fragile when the crisis started and became even weaker later on, and in 2012 it was still showing a deep negative growth figure (-6.27), the highest of all the OECD countries. Italy was another case of the G7 countries showing substantial negative growth rate despite the efforts of a transitional government to sparkle growth through a combination stimulus programs. Some of the countries having negative or trivial growth rates in 2012 such as Greece (-6.7), Ireland (0.48), Spain (-1.29) and Portugal (-3.09) have also experienced large deficits in the same year as shown in Table 5.2.

The European Union has been hit by large deficit every year from 2008 when the crisis started to 2012 and beyond (including the forecast), but the growth rates have been mostly on rising although at a slow rate, thanks to the growth rates of the big European horsepower such as Germany and France and the increased demand for commodities exported to Asia. The United States is another exemption because with high government deficit in 2012 (8.5%) was able to reach a staggering growth rate of 2.24 percent transmitting confidence and stability to international markets. Broadly speaking, during the period 2008-2012 the gross public debt in several countries increased to worrying levels, despite the mild signs of growth, and the financial crisis turned into a debt crisis.

In 2010, two well-known Harvard economists, Carmen Reinhart and Kenneth Rogoff published a scholarly paper emphasizing the public spending cuts and austerity measures as efficient tools to control deficit and ignite growth. The scope of the authors was to suggest, by using a number of "stylized facts", that there is a relationship between public debt and GDP growth. The main result of their research indicates that across a range of countries and periods, economic growth is relatively weak when country's level public debt goes beyond 90 percent of GDP.

Based on a sample of 20 industrialized countries in the post-war period, the average of annual GDP growth vary between 3 and 4 percent when the ratio of public debt to GDP is below 90 percent, but the median growth rates drop to -0.1 percent when the ratio of the public debt increases above 90 percent threshold. In addition, Reinhart and Rogoff (2010) observed the experience of 44 countries straddling up to two centuries of data on public debt, inflation and growth and found that developed and developing countries with high debt/GDP levels of 90 percent and above are related to lower growth rates compared to countries with lower levels of public debt/GDP for example at 60 percent where the growth rates are much favourable for advanced countries than for emerging economies. These findings served as the basis to support austerity programs by many high-rank politicians in the U.S., Europe and elsewhere.

The widespread results of the article published by Reinhart and Rogoff about public debt and growth could have gone further had not three researchers of economics from the University of Massachusetts reviewed the findings of Reinhart and Rogoff and published three years later their own conclusions. Thomas Herndon, Michael Ash and Robert Pollin issued in April 2013 their own working paper finding fault with Reinhart and Rogoff (2010) conclusions. According to Herndon, Ash and Pollin (2013), the Reinhart and Rogoff (2010) research was based on data errors and unsound statistical techniques which reduced the measured average GDP growth of advanced countries in high public debt category, transforming the reality that countries carrying high public debts will inevitably require drops in GDP growth.

After re-computing the calculations, Herndon, Ash and Pollin (2013) using the same Reinhart/Rogoff data realized that when countries' debt-to-GDP ratio goes over 90 percent, the average growth is 2.2 percent and not -0.1 percent as claimed by Reinhart and Rogoff (2010). Reaching the threshold of 90 percent public debt-to-GDP ratio does not mean the countries will go right into a recession, but it only tells that these countries have to be cautious about the dimension of the public debt and to serve the debt. Another finding of Herndon, Ash and Pollin was that the average GDP growth rate for all those countries exceeding the threshold of 90 percent public debt was close to or even higher than those countries whose public debt ratios are between 30 percent and 60 percent as the inflation and interest rates tend to be kept at lower levels.

When Europe and U.S. were hit hard during the 2008-2009 financial crisis, and as a result of private sector collapse they went into recession, deficit government spending was the most efficient way to increase demand and fight unemployment in order to put the economy back in track. The increases in deficit and public debt were large for all the countries going into the downturn. Therefore, the public debt was not the cause of the growth decline. All supporters of austerity programs and government spending cuts who consistently argued that high debt will lead to high inflation and interest rates proved to be not true as confirmed by the work of Herndon, Ash and Pollin. As a matter of fact, since 2009 the U.S. government's interest payments to serve the U.S. public debt have been at historically low levels despite the surging level of the debt, as shown in Table 5.4 because the U.S. Treasury was able to borrow at low rates. Table 5.4 illustrates the gross government debt[1] as a percentage of GDP for a number of OECD countries.

[1]Public debt is normally called the amount of money that a government owns to holders of treasury securities. The securities issued by a government consist on treasury bills, notes, bonds, TIPS and saving bonds. Gross debt, instead, is usually referred to the public debt plus intergovernmental debt obligations or eventually debts held by trust funds.

Countries	2007	2008	2009	2010	2011	2012	2013	2014
Australia	14.54	13.83	19.38	23.51	26.66	29.26	28.91	28.02
Austria	63.42	68.58	74.09	78.03	79.78	83.12	85.16	86.01
Belgium	87.88	92.72	99.80	99.53	101.93	103.16	102.86	101.90
Canada	64.97	69.25	81.52	83.01	83.46	85.81	85.49	85.98
Czech Republic	31.00	34.39	40.86	45.11	47.96	51.28	54.47	56.89
Denmark	34.34	41.44	51.29	54.58	61.54	61.01	60.97	60.68
Estonia	7.31	8.50	12.77	12.48	9.83	14.48	16.05	15.73
Finland	41.41	40.33	51.83	57.87	57.98	62.34	65.50	67.71
France	72.96	79.26	91.22	95.48	99.97	105.13	108.16	109.72
Germany	65.61	69.87	77.8	86.27	86.43	87.60	86.18	85.12
Greece	115.21	118.53	134.35	153.01	175.19	181.35	193.26	199.91
Hungary	73.56	77.12	86.69	87.53	86.14	87.43	86.43	86.72
Iceland	53.28	102.08	119.97	125.23	128.36	124.65	120.61	115.43
Ireland	28.70	49.72	70.72	98.08	112.25	123.16	127.72	127.85
Israel	78.49	77.13	79.52	76.04	74.01	73.51	73.11	71.83
Italy	112.40	114.86	128.04	126.74	119.84	127.03	129.56	131.41
Japan	162.40	171.13	188.74	192.75	205.31	214.29	224.31	230.04
Korea	28.77	30.47	33.50	34.32	36.11	36.43	36.44	36.74
Luxembourg	11.27	19.27	19.01	25.76	25.81	29.84	32.57	34.41
Netherlands	51.47	64.78	67.60	71.62	75.89	82.52	83.55	84.00
New Zealand	25.63	28.81	34.62	39.62	48.35	51.31	54.29	55.59
Norway	56.82	54.28	48.92	49.61	33.85	44.67	43.97	42.89
Poland	51.75	54.42	58.39	62.26	63.34	64.15	65.19	65.36
Portugal	75.53	80.78	93.49	103.91	118.15	125.58	133.11	134.63
Slovak Republic	33.50	32.20	40.35	45.86	48.05	56.98	59.66	60.94
Slovenia	30.65	30.39	44.00	48.17	55.54	59.94	63.55	66.15
Spain	42.39	47.73	62.89	67.72	76.93	93.76	100.23	105.32
Sweden	49.77	49.96	52.20	49.31	49.23	48.56	47.95	47.25
Switzerland	45.17	41.86	41.09	40.63	40.18	39.46	38.96	38.62
United Kingdom	46.96	56.15	72.04	85.59	99.91	105.32	110.38	113.87
United States	66.48	75.37	88.79	97.81	102.17	109.78	113.01	114.14

Table 5.4 General government gross financial liabilities, as a percentage of GDP. *Source*: OECD Economic Outlook No.92 (database). OECD 2012 (years 2013 and 2014 are estimates).

Taking into consideration the gross debts as a percentage of GDP for different advanced countries in Table 5.4 and comparing them with growth rates in Table 5.3 we can easily highlight that some big size countries such as Germany, France, United Kingdom, United States, Canada and even Belgium whose gross government debt go close to or beyond 80-90 per cent of GDP during the period 2010 -2012 were able to sustain growth (Table 5.3) between in the range of 1-4 per cent with very few exceptions of moderate or negative growth which confirms the Herndon, Ash and Pollin (2013) thesis. Despite the fact that there is no proven positive or negative correlation between government debt, growth and government deficit, the governments are still required to maintain fiscal discipline to prevent using temporary high tax revenues for permanent increases in expenditure. Government revenues should match the expenditures otherwise the government has to reduce the spending to keep fiscal discipline and reduce the deficit.

In 2011, the EU decided that reforms are urgently needed as the previous structure has not prevented the two main causes of the debt crisis: macroeconomic imbalances between centre and periphery in the euro area and high level of debt in several countries. The reforms were included on the "Six-Pack" which came in force in December 2011 consisting of five regulations and one directive having the scope to adjust and strengthen fiscal policy amid EU members. These regulations and the directive are supposed to have an impact on fiscal policy and macroeconomic imbalances.

The three regulations and the directive on fiscal policy are as follows: i) the First Regulation of the European Parliament and the Council (EC) No 1466/97 regards the increase of budget supervision and synchronization of economic policies. ii) the Second Council Regulation (EC) No 1467/97 considers any clarification regarding the implementation of the excessive deficit. iii) the Third Regulation of the European Parliament and Council Directive has to do with the effective enforcement of budget examination in the euro area. iv) meanwhile, the Directive of the Council (Council Directive 2011/85/EU) is based on the requirements for the control of the fiscal agenda of the Member States (Commission report 2013). The fourth and the fifth regulations have to do with macroeconomic imbalances. The fourth regulation of the European Parliament and the Council deals with the prevention and correction of macroeconomic imbalances. The fifth regulation arranges the enforcement action to correct excessive macroeconomic imbalances in the euro area. The fiscal policy regulations are the main fiscal instruments of the Six-Pack created to strengthen the "Stability and Growth Pact" among the member of the European Union that entered into force in the late 1990s.

The regulations have the power to enforce fiscal discipline in the countries of the euro area, as they come into force earlier and are more consistent. For instance, if a member of the EU has an excessive deficit procedure opened and fails to comply with necessary measures to eliminate the deficit, it is obliged to make an interest-bearing deposit of 0.2% of GDP, which can be converted into a fine if the deficit is not reduced. It will also be easier for the EU to impose sanctions at an earlier phase than before, prior to the stage when the country members are subject to so-called Excessive Deficit

Procedure. If is found that the country has reported false data to hide the excessive deficit another fine is imposed, and automatic sanctions are triggered based on the decision taken by the Council of the EU. The two last regulations of the Six-Pack regarding the macroeconomic imbalances aim to control excessive macroeconomic imbalances like those that have occurred in Greece, Ireland, Italy, Portugal and Spain. It will be possible to use correction mechanisms by imposing sanctions on EU members if they fail to correct the imbalances.

The introduction of the *European Systematic Risk Board* (ESRB) on December 2010 in response to the financial crisis was done to oversee the systematic financial risk at the EU level. The ESRB is an independent EU body that does not have binding tools at its disposal but acts by issuing warnings and public recommendations to different parties and on the macro-prudential mandate of national authorities. Later, on June 16, 2012, the EU leaders had plans for the European Central Bank to become a bank regulator and to form a deposit insurance program for respective national programs.

The same year, on September 6, 2012, the ECB pronounced the launch of a program called *Outright Monetary Transactions* (OMT) to offer financial support using the yield-lowered bond purchases for all Eurozone countries engaged in sovereign state bailout program from EFSF *(European Financial Stability Facility* created in 2010). An EU member country could have assistance from this program if it were in a situation to suffer from stressed bond yields at excessive levels after agreeing to meet all the terms signed Memorandum of Understanding.

Another condition required by EU countries to have access to this program was to have complete market access which could happen only after having received the last scheduled bailout disbursement (similar to what happened in Greece, Portugal and Ireland). This OMT program was also considered as a pre-bailout rather than a sovereign bailout and was extended to Eurozone countries suffering from stressed interest rates on its government bonds as well. The financial markets took notice of OMT program and started lowering the short-term and long-term interest rates in all EU countries which helped unlock the frozen liquidities.

In addition, the creation of a permanent rescue mechanism, the *European Stability Mechanism* (ESM) on October 8th, 2012, had the main objective to preserve stability and provided instant access to financial assistance programs for EU members in financial distress and had a maximum lending capacity of €500 billion. The 19 members of the EU were supposed to contribute to 90 percent of its capital based on the treaty establishing the ESM. The ESM which replaced EFSF (*European Financial Stability Facility* founded in May 2010) is now the only permanent mechanism to respond to new requests for financial assistance to EU members by issuing bonds and other debt instruments on capital markets and using the proceeds of the issues to lent loans to EU governments or finance the recapitalization of large financial institutions under a recovery program.

The debt crisis of 2008-9 caused serious challenges not only to single members of the EU but to the Eurozone itself and showed to policymakers that the centralized European monetary policy requires new aspects of economic policy to avoid excessive macroeconomic imbalances between member states. As a result of the financial and debt crisis the individual countries of the EU begun to implement different reforms and reduce inequities among themselves, reform monetary policy and discipline the fiscal policy in all aspects especially by matching expenses with revenues not only in the short-run but also in the long-run.

Quantitative Easing and the Financial Market Impact

The global financial crisis that followed the collapse of real estate securities and Lehman Brothers in the fall of 2008 led central banks around the western world to introduce a wide range of monetary policies intended on stabilizing financial conditions and sustain the aggregate demand. The 2008 recession was deeper than any financial crisis since the end of WWII, and full recovery was put in the discussion by economists as it was slow, fragile and incomplete. A consistent number of central banks in industrialized countries were somehow forced to pursue unconventional monetary policies such a quantitative easing and escape from balance sheet recession.

The main tool of the monetary policy is the interest rate on overnight loans between banks which in normal business days is relatively sensitive to the quantity of excess reserves. Nevertheless, since winter of 2008 the Federal Reserves' target for the federal funds has been practically zero and the level of reserves, which in normal times before the crisis was around $10 billion, has been increased to 1 trillion dollars. The standard monetary policy of trying to lower the short-term interest rate or increase the volume of reserves offered little if not no solution to boost the aggregate demand. Considered that when the short-term interest rates get close to zero an open-market purchase of short-term Treasury securities could be characterized as an exchange of equivalent assets.

With over 1 trillion dollars in excess reserves the Federal Reserve has well past the satiation point and on November 25, 2008 announced that it would purchase up to $100 billion of government-sponsored enterprise (GSE) debts and up to $500 billion in mortgage-backed securities (MBS) from US government-sponsored housing agencies to reduce risk spreads on GSE debt and help alleviate the housing market credits hit hard by the crisis. A few months later, on March 18, 2009, the Federal Reserve announced that would purchase an additional $750 billion in MBS, an extra $ 100 billion in debt from MBS agency and $300 billion of long-term Treasury securities (representing only 8% of the market). These large purchases by the government are often called "large-scale asset purchase" (LSAP), a term that was introduced in 2009 by Kohn.

The logic behind these LSAP purchases was the reduction on yields on securities which would help reduce the borrowing cost for private borrowers. In total, the LSAP amounted to 1.7 trillion dollars over a period of 15 months during the 2008-9 crisis. This was so far the largest government intervention in the financial-market history, but not the only one. In the early 1960s the Federal Reserve, in a smaller scale, attempted to decrease the long-term yields relative to short-term yields by simply selling the short-term Treasury debt and purchasing the long-term debt. This operation was called, "Operation Twist". The study of Modigliani and Sutch (1966) found that the "Operation Twist" was able to reduce long-term rates successfully because the purchases for that time were incredibly large and were offset by new Treasury issuance (Hakim and Rashidian, 2000). The Federal Reserve purchases of securities during the Operation Twist were relatively of minor volume and were quickly offset by Treasury issuance of long-term debt.

Turning back to the LSAP during the 2008-9 crisis we have that the Federal Reserve has to meet its objectives to provide liquidity and improve the market functioning by increasing the flow of the credit to business and households by reducing the level of interest rates. The monetary authorities, despite the unique and unconventional nature of monetary policy the weak theoretical direction and inadequate proof on the possible effects of LSAP purchases on asset prices, expressed reservations about the effects of the large securities purchases. A number of articles published during this period offered hints on asset purchase programs. Stroebel and Taylor (2012) discussed time series methods to prove that Federal Reserve's purchases produced little or insignificant effects on mortgage-Treasury spreads but not yields. Gagnon (2011a and 2011b), and Meyer and Bomfim (2010) suggested that when Federal Reserve announced LSAP it reduced that U.S. long-term yields. Hamilton and Wu (2012) studied the LSAP impact on the market of securities by using a structural model that forecasts the effects of changes in the maturity structure of U.S. debt from asset purchases.

Vayanos and Vila (2009) and then Greenwood and Vayanos (2010) created a model and presented empirical evidence where investors based on the preferred-habitat theories (introduced by Modigliani and Sutch 1966) have preferenced over a particular segment of the yield curve where the supply of bonds affects yields when there is an arbitrage condition. Valente (2009) observes how short-term interest rates in two countries with a dynamic economy such as Hong Kong and Singapore, responded to the unforeseen U.S. federal funds target announcements.

Berkmen (2012) in his study examines whether quantitative easing and other unconventional monetary easing measures have effects in the real economy. His analysis shows some indication that between 2008 and 2010 monetary easing has been weak on supporting economic activity and growth with low than expected average inflation rates. Berkmen (2012), as in the previous study of Lam (2011) over Japan experience, suggests that QE handled by Federal Reserve in the US had no statistically significant impact on inflation expectations while the demand was weak, but it was more effective during the 2008-10 period than the previous experience in Japan due in part to the improvements in the banking sector and corporate system.

The question posed by many researchers and economists was if the changes in the stock of Treasuries during the LSAP program were large enough to affect the yields on Treasuries themselves. By using time series regressions, and connecting risk premium to the LSAP announcement in order to measure the supply of government debt it has been found that LSAPs reduced the 10-year term premium by an estimated 30 to 100 basis points overall.

A number of recent studies have established that the Federal Reserve's LSAP1 asset purchases in the United States were somehow successful in reducing medium and long-term interest rates more than expected. A list of these studies includes D'Amico and King (2010), Krishnamurthy and Vissing-Jorgensen (2011), Hamilton and Wu (2012) and Baumeister and Benati (2013). In order to see these effects on yields, based on D'Amico and King (2010, 7-11) analysis, we consider a hypothetical market with risk-neutral traders where short-term risk-free rate progresses based on the exogenous stochastic process. The risk-free rate of maturity *n* at time *t* is given by

$$r_t^n = \frac{1}{n} \int_0^n E_t r_{t+s}^0 dt \qquad (5.1)$$

where *Et* is the expectation hypothesis. The condition in equation (5.1) is satisfied because any movement of the rate *r* greater than the integral on the right or on the left will put in place situations where the arbitrageur could profit by selling short-term debt and buying long-term debt. The arbitrage could trigger the rate to go down or up until equality is reinstated. There is no fluctuation in the outstanding of long-term debt as the fluctuations do not stimulate the movements of risk-free trade. In addition, we have that the short-term rate follows the Ornstein-Uhlenbeck (O-U) process[2] of the Brownian motion used widely for modelling a mean reverting process and is given as,

$$dr_t^0 \;=\; \lambda(\mu \;-\; r_t^0)dt \;+\; \sigma dB_t \tag{5.2}$$

where *Bt* is the Brownian motion, λ measures the speed of mean reversion, μ is the 'long run mean', to which the process tends to revert and σ measure of the process volatility. Equation (5.1) can be reduced to a simple linear function of the time t-short-term debt given as,

$$r_t^n \;=\; a(n) \;+\; b(n)r_t^0 \tag{5.3}$$

where b(n)=(1-exp(-λn)/λn, and a(n)= μ(1-b(n). The expectations hypothesis condition tells us that asset purchases do not affect yields as they do not appear somewhere in equation (5.3) (D'Amico and King (2010, 8).We assume now that the risk-neutrality assumption is eliminated and with it the expectations hypothesis, therefore the market traders choose to purchase the maturities of zero-coupon bonds to maximize a risk-return objective function, *max It (n),* over an direct investment horizon. This condition for investors is given as,

$$I_t(n) \;=\; E_t\left[\frac{dp_t^n}{p_t^n}\right] \;-\; \alpha \, \mathrm{var}_t\left[\frac{dp_t^n}{p_t^n}\right] \tag{5.4}$$

where $p_t^n \;=\; \exp(-nr_t^n)$ is the price of zero-coupon bond with maturity *n* and $\alpha \geq 0$ is a risk-aversion parameter. Using the mean reverting process in equation (5.2), equation (5.4) has a solution similar to equation (5.3) using same functions *a(n)* and *b(n)* which are determined by parameters σ and α. Despite in equation (5.4) there is no risk-sensitive term the quantity of debt outstanding is not able to influence securities prices. Even by integrating a preference for specific maturities in the objective function is not enough for quantity variations to matter. In fact, if the objective function takes the following form,

---

[2] Mean reverting Ornstein-Uhlenbeck (O-U) processes introduced by Ornstein-Uhlenbeck in the early 1930s are very often used to model commodity prices as they represent the economic condition under which when prices are 'too high', demand will fall and supply will increase, producing a counter-balancing effect, and when prices are 'too low' the opposite will occur, pushing prices back up towards a long term mean. Mean reverting processes are also used on creating economic models for other observed and unobserved processes, such as interest rates or effects on yields, etc.

$$I_t(n) = E_t\left[\frac{dp_t^n}{p_t^n}\right] - \alpha \operatorname{var}_t\left[\frac{dp_t^n}{p_t^n}\right] - \beta(n - n')^2 \tag{5.5}$$

where β is an incorporated parameter that punish all the traders who want to take risk and invest far away from the maturity n'. Fluctuating the supply at these maturities does not generate departures from equilibrium interest rates in this model.

Some other researchers such as Greenwood and Vayanos (2008) and Vayanos and Vila (2009), have developed theoretical models whereby altering the relative bond supply it affects pricing. These models use friction that has a restriction on arbitrage across different types of financial assets. In fact, risk-averse arbitrageurs do not have the capability to reduce price differentials because they focus on possible adverse price movements in certain conditions during the arbitrage transactions. But if certain investors have preferences over specific security maturities the demand can be transformed into price differences that would violate no-arbitrage conditions. Based on these preferences the Vayanos-Vila model (2009) produces a solution simplified as,

$$r_t^n = a(n) + b(n)r_t^0 + c(n)\theta_t \tag{5.6}$$

where θt is the demand factor that measures in the yield curve the quantities purchased by a group of investors called preferred-habitat investors, that take the risk for holding particular maturities of Treasures. Therefore, the LSAP purchases could be considered as shifts in θt. Discontinuing the Treasury supply of the LSAP purchases would certainly affect the level, and slope of the yield curve and the risk-averse arbitragers could not influence the effects of demand factors on the yield curve in the short-term.

According to D'Amico and King (2010, 10), if preferred-habitat investors are interested in spot prices and not on expectations of possible returns, spot prices will be affected once the Treasury supply is not available which could trigger what is called a 'flow-effect' mechanism of LSAP purchases. 'Flow-effects' program consists on when LSAP purchases have effects on Treasury prices around the times when purchases have been completed. Since the LSAP purchases were not known beforehand to the traders, it would have created yield differentials based on the days of purchases between those that are purchased and those that are not.

Yield differentials could have been caused even by market illiquidity and other not measured technical factors. Given a variety of maturity sectors where securities are supposed to be purchased, it is suspected that the securities purchased within those sectors have responded differently to other securities purchased outside the purchased sectors. Securities purchased within the expected purchase sectors are called 'eligible' securities, and securities purchased outside these sectors are called 'ineligible' securities. The effects of purchases are normally analysed not the same day but the day after they incur. A regression will give us the returns on the days after purchases have taken place. The regression takes the form as,

$$\frac{\Delta op_{it+1}}{op_{it}} = \alpha_i + \theta_t + \beta q_{it} + \sum_{j=1}^{n} \lambda_j s_{ijt} + \varepsilon_t \qquad (5.7)$$

where Δop is the change in the price of Treasury security i in period t, and β is a parameter that shows the price elasticity of Treasury securities, meanwhile λ is another parameter that gives the cross-elasticities of Treasury security prices with respect to other Treasury securities. Table 5.5 illustrates the data of the LSAP program that befell during the first half period (March 25 – July 6) and those that occurred during the second half (July 7 – October 29) in 2009.

	Eligible		Ineligible	
	Mar. 25-Jul.6, 2009	Jul. 7-Oct. 29, 2009	Mar. 25-Jul.6, 2009	Jul.7-Oct. 29, 2009
Own Response (β)	0.3442*** (0.094)	0.2975*** (0.089)	----	----
Cross Responses (λj)				
Near Substitutes (within 2 years)	0.2863*** (0.086)	0.3038*** (0.083)	-0.127*** (0.025)	0.3844*** (0.031)
Mid Substitutes (2 to 6 years away)	0.1989*** (0.082)	0.2037** (0.073)	-0.1426*** (0.0150	0.2021*** (0.0170
Far Substitutes (6 to 14 years away)	----	------	-0.153*** (0.014)	0.0925*** (0.011)
Number of Obs.	563	360	4529	3479
Number of CUSIPS	131	121	167	172
Adjustment R	0.42	0.27	0.38	0.53

Table 5.5 Flow effects on the day of purchase, by sub-period (maturity <15 years). Asterisks indicate the statistical significance at the 10% (*), 5 %(**), and 1% (***) levels. Standard errors are shown in parenthesis. In this table, only days when LSAP purchases are completed are included. The dependent variable is the daily % price change in each CUSIP. *Source:* D'Amico and King (2010, 28).

The second half period has better liquidity in the Treasury market than the first half period. The second half period was better than expected regarding eligible securities within expected purchase sector given the price reaction to LSAP purchases due to obstacles in the market clearing and poor market performance. The other securities that were ineligible for purchase have negative coefficients in the first half of the sample and positive in the second half. These coefficients in the second half on the near and mid substitute purchases get close to the eligible security purchases. It looks like the security dealers have sold more to Federal Reserve than they had planned to sell. Therefore, they sold another type of securities, including those ineligible after LSAP operations to keep the portfolio target (D'Amico and King (2010, 16-18).

The 'stock effects' explains the process by which LSAP program had a relatively considerable influence on yields by permanently reducing the amount of Treasury securities available for purchase by the public. As soon as the market became alert of the LSAP program announcement, the expectations of 'stock effects' have already been embedded into Treasury prices affecting the stock prices which got reduced in average by 25 to 50 basis point drop in Treasury yields. The expectation effects are important prior to the conclusion of the program, but once the total amount of LSAP purchase have been disclosed the expectations will become not any more relevant for any difference in security price changes.

The study of D'Amico and King (2010) suggests that both flow and stock effects of unprecedented Federal Reserve program in 2009 to purchase $300 billion of nominal Treasure coupon securities, were statistically and economically significant. The average LSAP purchase operation reduced yields by 3.5 basis points, and when the program started in 2009, it moved down yield curve by up to 50 basis points. For stock effects, the differences between LSAP purchases and substitute purchases are larger in less-liquid segments of the market, and for flow effects, the results during 2009 suggested that they did not depend mostly on the liquidity. It is estimated (Gurkaynak and Wright 2010) that the augmented risk aversion during the financial crisis of 2008-9 could have reduced the arbitrage activity eventually and led to greater segmentation.

The Effects of Quantitative Easing on Interest and Exchange Rates

The main purpose of large assets purposes was to lower the long-term interest rates given that the short-term interest rates get close to zero and to impact the inflation expectations. Different studies have pointed out that there is a consistent relationship between macroeconomic variables and stock prices.

Interest rates have no impact on stock prices, but exchange rates do affect them. For short periods of time (6-12 months), an expansionary monetary policy designed to reduce interest rates will also increase interest-sensitive spending in physical capital by companies, residential investments and consumer-durable spending, and it will put pressure on exchange rates, depreciating the domestic currency causing in this way the exports to rise and imports to decrease. Interest-Sensitive spending eventually resulting in an increase in general spending in the economy will depend partly on the unemployment rate and the response of inflation rate. In many developed economies, it has been observed that in the long run an increase in the monetary base and credit has been offset by a more rapid rate of inflation growth, having little or no impact on real GDP and employment.

During the 2008 financial crisis and beyond by taking into consideration a long-run period (with contracts over 1-2 years) the standard relationship between money growth and inflation has not been held giving rise to a paradoxical behaviour. There are two explanations for the paradoxical behaviour. First, in the short period, the system of contracts in place make it impossible to adjust prices and wages in reaction to rapid growth of money and credit. Second, the expectations are slow to adjust to the long-run period as a result of changes in monetary policy, which adds rigidities to wages and prices. Due to the rigidities, changes in the growth of money and credit expansion would have a hefty initial effect on output and unemployment in the short-run (6-8 quarters) until the economy get adjusted to the new monetary policy.

Fiscal and monetary policy can be used to affect the domestic spending in the economy. Monetary policy can change quicker than the fiscal policy in some developed countries such as U.S., England, Canada, etc. Central banks like FED in the U.S. meets every 6 weeks to take into consideration changes in interest rates. But changes in fiscal policy normally take at least a year to occur upon approval by respective governments and parliaments. Right after the central banks have decided to changes interest rates it will affect immediately interests for loans granted to business and homes in the short period compared to the effects of yearly fiscal policy.

Regarding fiscal policy, there are political restrictions related to budget deficits even during the recession periods, despite the fact that budget deficits and increased government spending have been more popular than austerity measures. In fact, the economy of U.S. has been continuously in deficit for over 50 years since 1961, except for 5 years, which has led to a federal debt accumulation giving less room for a vigorous expansionary fiscal policy. The long period consequences of fiscal and monetary policy differ considerably. Expansionary fiscal policy will create debt that must be serviced paying interest on the debt by future generations. It can be owned by residents of the country or by foreign investors. The government is supposed to issue controlled debt as the investors (domestic and foreigners) need to believe that the debt will be honoured although the conditions may require running deep in the budget deficit in order to make a quick recovery of the economy.

Monetary policy, instead, does not affect generational equity but requires a different level of interest rates that may affect lenders and borrowers differently. A monetary policy based on lowering interest rates would cause capital to flow in foreign markets where the rates of return are higher. There are cases when the economy is getting close to recession stage, and any kind of monetary policy may lose part of its effectiveness. Lowering interest rates continuously will make interest-sensitive spending not responsive to other rate cuts. The monetary policy is limited to lows interest rates close to zero and this limit is called "zero lower bound". The only effective policy in this situation should be the fiscal policy which is managed by government and not central bank.

The independence of central bank from the government in industrialized countries put the chosen monetary policy in a non-coordination-mode with the fiscal policy. If the central bank and government were to choose harmonious fiscal and monetary policies, respectively, the economic effect could have been more powerful than each policy implemented separately. It may take time to reassess the balance between monetary and fiscal policy and provide a more focused fiscal rather than monetary stimulus. In the case of large size countries like U.S.A, Canada, EMU, Australia, Brazil, etc., the federal or central government cannot fully implement the fiscal stimulus push without the participation of regional and state prospects across the country. The fiscal policy should target those areas, regions or sector where is more needed. Targeted fiscal programs that can boost particular hit sectors such as construction sector using a home renovation tax credit (introduced in Canada during 2009 recession) could be very effective against recession in that particular sector and beyond. Specific infrastructure projects of middle-large scale and central government/provincial/state loans could be used to successfully increase job creation and boost activity in those industries with local supply chains.

It's interesting to understand how the monetary policy in the biggest economy in the world, the United States of America, was done prior to the 2008 financial crisis. Between 2001 and 2003 the US had a short recession resulting in increased rate of unemployment for which the Federal Reserve was willing to take action. The Federal Reserve lowered the federal fund's interest rates from 6.5% to as low as 1% by mid of 2003 but after the economic expansion took place in this year and more than expected inflation increase was registered the federal funds slowly increased to 5.25% in 2006. The Federal Reserve took an expansionary monetary policy approach by keeping short-term interest rates too low to make sure the ongoing economic expansion continue without interruption. This policy stimulated easy credits for banks to make loans. The low short-term rates caused an increase in the demand for housing and the move from fixed to variable rate mortgages with also loose lending standards made the housing sector particularly vulnerable that resulted in a price bubble.

As a matter of fact, by 2006, the rates, unfortunately, moved up to 5.25% which lowered the demand and increased the monthly payments for adjustable rate mortgages. This caused the housing bubble to burst which led to a financial crisis that affected the depository institutions and other segments of financial sector related to the process of lending money for housing. As a result of high rates of home mortgage defaults, financial firms exposed to mortgage market suffered capital losses and were not able to access to liquidity. This process affected other types of loans and spilt over in the US whole economy as the lack of credit affected the manufacturing sector and the aggregate demand negatively.

In December 2007 and the beginning of 2008, the US economy entered a recessions phase, which had spillover effects on the global market. The Federal Reserve in the United States responded quickly to the recession by reducing federal funds target rate from 5.25% in 2007 to a range between 0% and 0.25% in December 2008. It was the first time that Federal Reserve has to lower the interest rates close to zero to provide a stimulus. This reduction was called the *zero lower bound* to indicate that when federal funds rate is at a lowest level close to zero open markets operations cannot be used to generate an incentive to the economy.

The traditional monetary policy to provide liquidity to the broader economy and the system, in general, was not functioning properly because the liquidity provided to banking system was not getting to other parts of the financial system to finance the real economy as the federal fund has reached the zero bound limit. To resolve this problem, the Federal Reserve decided to use non-conventional monetary tools to provide additional money into the system. The Federal Reserve introduced a number of emergency credit facilities to input liquidity directly to financial institutions and non-financial institutions. The scope of these credit facilities was to close the gap as much as possible between open market operations and discount window, providing short-term loans backed by collateral exceeding the value of the loan.

During the 2007-08 the Federal Reserve started providing assistance through emergency liquidity facilities helping directly two institutions that were on the brink of bankruptcy, American International Group (AIG) and Bear Stearns.

On August 2007 the assistance of Federal Reserve provided to financial and non- financial institutions through liquidity facilities was about $234 billion and reached nearly $1.6 trillion on December 2008, and after that, it fell gradually to $100 billion on February 2010 where many liquidity facilities were allowed to expire. The Federal Reserve has sterilized the effects of lending to the system by letting the assets on its balance sheet to grow and selling an offsetting amount of treasury securities. The Federal Reserve's balance sheet more than doubled between September 2007 and November 2008, increasing from $1 trillion to over $2 trillion.

As mentioned on the previous segment the Federal Reserve in the United States introduced an unconventional monetary policy to boost the liquidity in the system by using a tool called large-scale asset purchases (LSAP) or quantitative easing (QE). The first LSAP or the quantity easing called simply QE1 increased the assets holdings of securities on Federal Reserve's balance sheet from $500 billion in November 2008 to over $2 trillion in November 2010. The second round of LSAP or differently called QE2 started in November 2010 and increased the Federal Reserve's balance sheet from $2.3 trillion to $2.9 trillion in July 2011. The third and the last round of LSAP called QE3 started in October 2012 and ended in October 2014 where the Federal Reserve's holding of securities in balance sheet increased to a record figure of 4.5 trillion dollars. The assets increase on Federal Reserve's balance sheet should be matched by an equivalent increase of liabilities in the form of currency, bank reserves and cash deposited by the U.S. Treasury to Federal Reserve. The three rounds of quantitative easing (QE1, QE2 and QE3) increased the bank reserves (liabilities of Federal Reserve) from $46 billion in 2008 to over $2.8 trillion in 2014. The increase in bank reserves is seen as financing the Federal Reserve's asset purchases and loan programs (crediting the proceeds to the receivers' reserve accounts at the Federal Reserve).

Federal Reserve Bank and Interest Rates in the U.S.A.

It's a strong believing among people and investors who care about an economy that the Central Bank of the U.S. called the Federal Reserve Bank (the central banking system composed of 12 Federal Reserve banks) set the interest's rates that matter to the stock market. That it's not the case. The Federal Reserve (Fed) controls directly only the Federal Reserve Funds rate where the commercial banks lend each other reserves overnight and not the long-term rates. There may be a relationship between the Fed funds rate and another short-term rate, but the connection disappears as we moved to long-term rates that determine the investing decisions. The most important long-term interest rates are not controlled by the Federal Reserve. These rates reveal the state of the economy and are affected by mainly two factors: the expected inflation and the expected economic growth which can closely foresee the ten year government bond rate.

Given that these two factors determine the interest rates the natural question that rise is why so much attention is when Feds announces the changes on Fed funds interest rates.

It looks that the Fed announcements about interest rates are based on mythology and gives to all of us a sense of control over the economy. If interest rates are high, the Fed can lower them, and if they are too low close to zero the Fed can raise them. Many analysts and investors are induced to believe that the stock-market boom of past few years was motivated by low-interest rates. Federal Reserve during the financial crisis had to use unconventional monetary policies such as Quantitative Easing consisting on buying a huge amount of government-backed bonds to induce the lowering of interest rates and convince investors that low rates are good for bargain-basement deals during a recession or slow economic growth.

If the Federal Reserve raises the Fed funds interest rates it signals that there is confidence on a stronger economy, but still for the long-interest rates to rise it needs to sum the two factors; the expected inflation to rise and expectation that the growth rate of the economy will continue to be steady with employment rising. A move away from near-zero rates will be respectable for the economy as it will allow investors to be more realistic about the inflation and economic growth. It also will help Federal Reserve move away from an unconventional monetary policy of quantitative easing to a more traditional monetary policy of managing interest rates. This is what happened in December 2015 when Federal Reserve increased interest rates for the first time since 2006 by 0.25 points because of the confidence in the American economy (unemployment rate went down to 4.5%, and inflation went up).

Regarding the stock prices, companies can generate enough cash flow to return to investors that drives the stock price up combined with the capacity to nurture earnings over the same period. The flow of cash in U.S. companies could be receding if the U.S. dollar goes too high and if the Chinese economy continues to stay weak. This will cut profits and the amount of cash returning to investors affecting at the same time the stock price. And this will take place no matter if the interest rates sit high or low. However, a higher inflation rate, a healthy prospect of growth and increasing rate of employment will return the cash flow to investors and drive up the stock prices.

The main purpose of Quantitative Easing (QE) was to put pressure on long-term interest rates by reducing the rates of long-term Treasury securities and MBS. By reducing the long-term interest rates, the financing process will feed the private sector with cheap borrowing money in order to stimulate spending on durables goods such housing, cars, business investments in equipment and plants. Before determining if the QE has lowered interest rates should also be wise to consider other factors such as the fragile economy as a result of recession which normally tends to reduce the interest rates and interest-sensitive spending.

Another phenomenon observed during the Quantitative Easing policy was the increase of the Federal Reserve's balance sheet that was potentially seen as inflationary because the bank reserves, also considered as the monetary base (part of monetary supply), was increased exponentially fast. The increase in the monetary base (monetary supply) during 2008-9 did not ignite higher inflation because the bank reserves have, for most of the time, remained deposited at the Federal Reserve. Therefore, the banks could not provide increased lending to the public or even asset purchase.

The exit strategy for Quantitative Easing (QE) started in October 2014, when the Federal Reserve in the United States announced that it would stop making large-scale asset purchases. The Federal Reserve plan was to continue making monetary policy by setting a target range for the federal funds rate instead of setting a point target when the rates during the crisis touched the zero bound. But the Federal Reserve was unable to change the federal funds rate by altering the reserve levels because the Quantitative Easing policy had filled the market with excess bank reserves of more than $2 trillion, therefore the only option was to eliminate excess reserves by reducing the balance sheet through asset sales or by ceasing to roll over mortgage-backed securities (MBS) as they mature.

The ultimate goal of Federal Reserve was to eventually reduce the balance sheet to the level of not holding more securities so it can start implementing monetary policy in a more traditional and efficient way. The table below shows the Federal Reserve purchases of MBS each year from 2009 to 2014. Each year from 2009 to 2014 the Fed purchased in the secondary market from primary dealers more MBS that were issued on net apart from for one year in 2011.

Years	2009	2010	2011	2012	2013	2014
In billions of dollars/percentage	Treasury Securities	Treasury Securities	Treasury Securities	Treasury Securities	Treasury Securities	Treasury Securities
Net Purchase by Fed	$300.8	$244.9	$642.0	$2.7	$542.6	$252.6
Net Issuance	$1,443.7	$1,579.6	$1,066.8	$1,140.6	$759.5	$670.5
Net Purchased/Net Issuance	20.8%	15.5%	60.2%	0.2%	71.4%	37.7%
	Agency MBS					
Net Purchase by Fed	$908.4	$83.8	-$154.5	$89.0	$563.5	$248.2
Net Issuance	$506.8	-$107.3	$16.0	$71.9	$152.3	$90.1
Net Purchase/Net Issuance	1792%	NA	NA	123.8%	370%	275.5%

Table 5.6. Treasury and Agency Mortgage-Backed Securities (MBS) issuances and Fed purchases since 2009. *Source*: Labonte M. 2015, p.16.

The Federal Reserve believed that could control the federal fund rates by raising the rate it pays banks on reserves held at the Federal Reserve. The US Congress in 2008 approved the Emergency Economic Stabilization Act (P.L. 110-343) which among others allowed the Fed (Federal Reserve banks) to pay interest on reserves. Banks normally can earn interest on excess reserves by lending them to federal funds market or simply by depositing them at the Federal Reserve. Paying interest on reserves would permit Fed to keep excess liquidity, so the banks would not use the extra liquidity to finance activity in the real economy.

Federal Reserve also uses another monetary tool to accomplish additional monetary stimulus at the zero bound. This tool is the federal fund's rate which is normally lower than the interest rate on federal reserves. By keeping the federal fund's rate low for a prolonged period of time, which has been called *forward commitment*, will stimulate the economy as the consumers would be more willing to take on long-term investment commitment if they are assured rates will be low for the life of the loan. But the low federal fund's rate was not supposed to last forever. In fact, in August 2011 and later in December 2012 the Fed set an economic threshold for which it pledges to maintain low federal funds rate if at least the unemployment rate is above 6.5% and inflation is low.

The economic condition in the United States quickly evolved, especially during 2013-14, where the unemployment rate constantly fell below 6.5%, despite there was no significant improvement in the labor market or the general economic conditions. Unfortunately, the inflation rate was still low below the average, which made Fed get more concerned, even though the economy was operating near 6.5% which was the threshold for the mandate-consistent level of quasi-full employment. As a result of these conditions at the job market, the Fed decided to continue keeping low the federal fund's rate as it viewed the low inflation as a greater risk than the higher inflation.

The impact of quantitative easing on inflation and exchange rates is mixed rather than a direct relationship. There is a short and medium-term evolution of interest, exchange and inflation rates during the QE transactions, which certainly can be seen in the expansion of balance sheet. For example, for Japan, the quantitative easing is characterized more like a quickening of asset purchases rather than a new monetary policy or an unconventional monetary policy instrument. During the QE operations in Japan, the exchange rate had appreciated and then depreciated abruptly when the pace of asset purchases accelerated in 2012. It has been formed the impression among analysts that a QE operations of large size can have a strong impact on the exchange rate of yen versus US dollar.

In the case of the United States is even harder to determine the impact of QE on exchange rate or inflation. The US dollar was depreciated rapidly before the event of QE1 and then appreciated after the massive security purchases under the QE1 program. The US dollar was running high in 2008 following a weak performance on the exchange rate that coincided with QE2 until 2011 and then appreciated under the QE3 program. Also, the impact of QE on inflation is not very clear as it fell down for almost two years after the QE1 was implemented in 2008, it changed course when the QE2 started in 2010, but then the inflation went downwards after the QE3 was introduced in September 2012.

In the case of England, the exchange rate of the pound depreciated swiftly before the QE1 started in March of 2009 and then after the start of QE2 in October 2011 seems to be no relations on the exchange rate depreciation or appreciation. Regarding inflation, there is an increase in inflation after the QE1 was implemented in England and afterwards a quick fall right after the QE2 was applied. In the Eurozone, despite the recession started since 2008-9, the European Central Bank (ECB) did not start the QE until March 2015, so the ECB was able to influence the size of its balance sheet only indirectly via long-term lending to banks at favorable rates. The table below shows the impact of quantitative easing programs on interest rates.

	Long-term Interest Rate in %			
	Before	**At Start**	**After**	**Change**
Euro Area				
PSPP (Mar2015)	1.6			
United Kingdom				
QE1 (Mar. 2009)	4.2	3.5	3.6	-0.6
QE2 (Oct. 2011)	2.9	2.3	2.2	-0.6
United States				
QE1(Nov. 2008)	3.9	3.3	2.7	-1.1
QE2(Nov. 2010)	2.8	2.9	3.5	0.7
Twist(Sept.2011)	3.2	2.4	2.0	-1.2
QE3(Sept. 2012)	1.8	1.6	1.7	-0.1
Japan				
QQE(Apr.2013)	0.6	0.8	0.7	

Table 5.7. Impact of QE programs on interest rates. ***Source:*** **Gros, Alcidi, and De Groen 2015 (OECD), p.15.**

Table 5.7 shows the data before, at the start and after of the QE program respectively to the quarterly averages for the quarter before the start, the quarter in which the program started and the quarter the after the program started. Long-term interest rates represent the average government bonds maturing in ten years published by OECD. The last column 'change' illustrates the variance between the long-term interest rates one quarter before the start of the QE program and the rate one quarter after the start of the QE program.

The figures in 'change' column describe a combination of the announcement effect and the impact of the initial implementation of QE program after one-quarter period. Given that five out of seven entries in the 'change' column are negative, we can state that in most of the cases asset purchase program did have an impact on the long-term interest rates. Despite this, the impact on long-term interest rates is challenging because there was a global trend towards lower interest rates and a high degree of movements across main currency areas. As a matter of fact, in the US, QE program was believed to have contributed to the fall of interest rates, but rates have also dropped as much in the Eurozone even before the start of QE program. Therefore, the studies about the QE should take into consideration the global trend on interest rates that was global and could somehow occur in a different degree even without the stimulus program (QE).

The impact of QE program on the exchange rate is illustrated in table 5.8.

	Nominal effective Exchange rate (index 2010=100)			
	Before	At Start	After	Change
Euro Area				
PSPP (Mar 2015)	100.3			
United Kingdom				
QE1 (Mar. 2009)	104.5	97.2	101.4	-3.1
QE2 (Oct. 2011)	98.4	100.0	101.0	2.6
Unites States				
QE1 (Nov. 2008)	95.8	106.0	108.8	13.0
QE2 (Nov. 2010)	100.7	97.4	96.1	-4.6
Twist (Sept. 2012)	93.6	94.2	97.8	4.3
QE3 (Sept. 2012)	99.0	98.9	97.5	-1.5
Japan				
QQE (Apr. 2013)	91.7	86.1	86.5	-5.1

Table 5.8 Impact of QE programs on exchange rates. Source: Gros, Alcidi, and De Groen 2015 (OECD), p.16.

In table 5.8 there are three columns that demonstrate nominal effective exchange rates before, at the start and after the initiation of QE programs in four major areas and countries. The nominal effective exchange rates are considered to be the three-month averages of the BIS effective exchange rate indices (BIS stands for 'Bank for International Settlements' which is an international financial institution that has 60 member central banks).

The last column named 'change' gives us the difference between the nominal effective exchange rate one quarter before and one quarter after the start of the asset purchases. In this column, there are three indexes with positive signs (UK, QE2; and US, QE1, Twist) that indicates that the exchange rate has been appreciated (instead of resulting on depreciation as we would normally expect) and these entries with positive signs are larger in absolute value compared to negative signs. The US dollar got depreciated before the start of QE1 and appreciated quickly right after the start of the QE1 program reaching a peak of change index of 13.

Another point about the QE programs is that we should be looking not only at the effects of these programs on domestic markets but also on international financial markets. Long-term interest rates typically follow the long-term trend across major currency areas in the advanced economies. Meanwhile, short-term interest rates follow the national boundaries as they are determined by national central banks and can fluctuate strongly if the policy position is different. Since the start of QE program in 2008, the long-term interest rates (10-year) have fluctuated following a downward trend, but the short-term interest rates have been almost equal to zero in the US and Eurozone.

According to Gros, Alcidi and De Groen (2015, 17-20), the efficiency of large asset purchases by the Federal Reserve in the United States should be measured by a fluctuation in the interest rate differential between the major international markets such as the US and the Eurozone, rather than the domestic market. The table below illustrates the development of the long-term (10 years) interest-rate differential between the US and the euro area. In table 5.9, the column 'change' shows the changes in interest rates are calibrated subtracting the average interest rate in the quarter after the start minus the average of the quarter before the start.

	Long-term interest rate (in %)	
	Change (T+1q –T-1q)	**Compared to Eurozone**
United Kingdom		
QE1 (Mar. 2009)	-0.57	-0.40
QE2 (Oct. 2009)	-0.65	-0.22
United States		
QE1 (Nov. 2008)	-1.13	0.06
QE2 (Nov. 2010)	0.67	-0.05
Twist (Sept. 2011)	-1.16	0.00
QE3 (Sept. 2012)	-0.12	-0.07
Japan		
QQE (Apr. 2013)	0.08	-0.18

Table 5.9 Impact of QE programs on long-term interest rates. Source: *Source: Gros, Alcidi, and De Groen 2015 (OECD), p.18.*

Table 5.9 indicates that most of the QE period rates have decreased in those areas that QE was not undertaken. For the US, the change in the interest rate differential is not more than 0.1%. Only for the United Kingdom, there is a case when the change in the differential reaches 0.4% compared to the euro area. Despite this significant change in interest rates (0.4%) for the UK in 2009, the pound has had a trend to follow the US dollar. The long-term interest US rates (referred to average government bonds maturing in 10 years) have resulted in slight rising compared to the euro-area rates. These rates increased from QE1 to January 2014, long before that European Central Bank (ECB) could get engaged in large-scale purchases of government bonds. The ECB was criticized for not having commenced QE program earlier than 2015. One of the main reason for this is that Eurozone is made of 19 members who use same currency but different fiscal systems and political governments, that need to agree before deciding a significant change on monetary policy. ECB did take other monetary policy operations by delivering more liquidity to the banking system.

Based on cross-reference statistics and empirical research the US Quantitative Easing did have little impact on interest rate differentials especially US Dollar vs. Euro and vs. British pound. This explains that asset purchases had little impact on exchange rates because the interest rates had fallen before the QE programs were activated. The major central banks started the asset purchases only when they comprehended that the recession started in 2008 could have been much longer than anticipated. Long-term rates controlled by markets were swiftly revised and started falling because of dim expectations and slow growth even before the Federal Reserve and other central banks started buying assets, which exclude the assumption of QE impact on exchange rates.

Regarding the Federal Reserve funds interest rates we can state that there is wide confidence among investors and public, the U.S. economy is getting stronger and healthier, and the unemployment rate continues to decline which will make the Federal Reserve raise the Fed funds interest rates. But this time it signals the U.S. rate hikes (higher than 0.25) could have a greater global impact than in the past and have consequences in the eurozone more in some respects than the domestic market. In addition, a Federal Reserve rate increase would have a larger impact worldwide because emerging markets, particularly China, South Korea, etc., are more integrated into the global economy than before.

In fact, emerging markets and all countries, in general, are more interlinked in production, cross-border capital flows have increased, and forward guidance has become a vital monetary policy instrument. The major first global impact of a Fed interest rate increase will be through capital markets, and secondly through international trade. German yields recently had followed the change of U.S. yields in response to Fed tightening by more than one third. Overall, there is suggestion that spillovers from U.S. monetary policy might be greater (on the euro area) than the domestic effects in the U.S. There has been a continuing US dollar's rise, since the end of the financial crisis, in international capital markets and given that markets are more integrated than before, there's no institution large enough to handle extreme stress and it is a mistake to think central banks can solve all problems.

There is an enormous amount of debt in U.S. dollars created around the world without liquidity backstops, and we are still in a situation where there is no a global lender of last resort adequate for an integrated global modern market of capitals and commodities.

Furthermore, there is another hurdle of aftermath financial crisis of 2008. Most of the central banks of industrialized countries do not have direct experience in raising interest rates from an extended period at zero, so they will have to learn through practice, without a full understanding of how economies and markets may respond and act quickly to keep economies running in positive territories.

Quantitative Easing and the Real Economy

The impact of quantitative easing (QE) on the real economy differs considerably across countries and regions and depends on the time and its scale of application. Quantifying the macroeconomic effects of unconventional monetary policies such as QE is particularly puzzling. There is a lag involved before the effects of QE get entirely conveyed to domestic output, and inflation and analysis normally have to rely on constructing model-based policy and no-policy counterfactuals which was made difficult by the severity of the financial crisis in 2008. There is a basis for ambiguity when studies are undertaken to estimate the effects of QE program in the economy. When the QE programs were launched was difficult to isolate the effects of unconventional monetary policy from financial markets and macroeconomic conditions. There was a slight historical precedent on these unconventional monetary policies compared to conventional monetary or fiscal policies which means that the results have to be comprehensively qualified.

The four countries or currency areas that experienced the impact of QE were Japan which started a serious QE program in 2001, US and UK started their own massive QE programs during the 2008 crisis and Eurozone in 2015. It emerges that Japan's QE programs during the 2001-2013 period were not effective in the real economy or they have a small effect on demand and none on inflation or the exchange rate. Regarding the US, the first QE1 in 2008 was the most effective as it has a good impact on unemployment and inflation, while QE2 in 2010 was less effective. In the UK the QE impact in the real economy seems to be more complex and uncertain. By looking at the experience of different countries, we are able to have a general idea of the impact of QE in the real economy.

The impact of QE in Japan

Japan was one the first countries to introduce the quantitative easing to boost its economy. After a continues recession and deflation for more than ten years, Japan performed an aggressive fiscal policy, and the Bank of Japan (BOJ) decided to introduce in 2001 a new round of the QE1 program. When the Japanese economy was hit by a negative shock during 1999-2001, the BOJ was following a zero-interest-rate policy which increased the risk of deflation. The Bank of Japan responded with a QE program by purchasing Japanese government bonds to increase the reserves of financial institutions. The QE1 for Japan ended in March 2006 as there were signs that deflation was fading and the economy recovering. The Bank of Japan purchased directly only a limited amount of government bonds as the biggest amount was bought by Japan postal offices which were owned by the government. The main purpose of BOJ's policy using QE was to influence the stock price by buying risky assets in an effort to reduce term and risk premium. The second round of QE in Japan started in 2013 to relaunch the slowing Japanese economy. There have been mixed results regarding the effectiveness of QE1 and QE2 in the real economy.

An empirical study, published by Ugai in 2007 right after the end of QE1, suggested that there is evidence QE1 helped to reduce yields in Japan but its impact on the wide economy and inflation was considered to be relatively small. The Bank of Japan committed to sustaining the QE shaped expectations close to zero interest rate, helping in this way to lower the yield curve. According to Kurihara (2006), there was a relationship between exchange rate and stock prices during the quantitative easing policy in Japan during the QE1 (2001-6). Based on his research the exchange rate has influenced Japanese stock prices, and quantitative easing has influenced the stock prices. In addition, the U.S. stock prices have also influenced the Japanese stock prices recommending a dependent correlation between the U.S. and Japanese economies.

The QE impact on Japan's economy through transmissions channels has shaped an accommodative environment of corporate financing by containing financial institutions' funding costs. Hausken and Ncube (2013) and Ueada (2011) revisit the QE and non-conventional monetary policy measures in Japan case and show evidence that QE, in general, has supported weakly the economic activity and to a lesser extent the inflation. Although the impact of QE on demand was weak the QE program was more effective than previous intervention, probably due to improvements in banking and corporate sectors. It looks that the monetary policy transmission mechanism was reinforced, but unfortunately Japan's steady inflation expectations and quite a flat Phillips curve (the curve that defines the relationship between inflation and unemployment) has kept the effect of monetary policies of low impact on the real economy.

The Impact of QE on the US economy

It is well known the fact that between December 2008 and March 2010 the Federal Reserve started the LSAP (large-scale asset purchase) program also called QE1 by purchasing more than $1.7 trillion in assets, representing almost 22% of the $7.7 trillion stock of long-term agency debt, MBS agency securities and other Treasury securities outstanding. The year 2010 was a very active for Federal Reserve as by the end of this year, and exactly by November 2010 Fed declared the start of the QE2 program consisting on purchasing of $600 billion of long-term Treasury securities to give a big push to economic growth and increase employment rate.

Chung et al. (2012) examined the impact of Fed's LSAPs in the US economy by using a simulation of a combination of macroeconomic models and a model of portfolio balance effects reducing the long-term interest rate by 50 basis point. The past and the expected expansion of Federal Reserve's securities holdings from 2008 to 2012 are approximately 300 basis-point reductions in policy interest rates. Based on the research of Chung et al. (2012) computed on model simulations the QE has kept the unemployment rate at a lower level, by 0.5 percentage points in 2012, than it was supposed to be without the LSAP purchases preventing the US economy from hitting a further deflation.

The empirical work of Liu and Mumtaz (2013) considers a change-point VAR model to observe the transmission mechanism of macroeconomic shocks during the 2008 financial crisis for the U.S. economy. The model examines the relationship between the 10-year interest rate spread and macroeconomic and asset price variables and whether the transmission mechanism of macroeconomic shocks has changed under the Fed's unconventional monetary policy during the crisis. The authors of this research found that the US economy responded to key macroeconomic shocks in the same way during the crisis compared to the years prior to the crisis. Using a simulated scenario, they estimated the Fed's LSAPs program helped reduced the 10-year interest rate spread by an average of 90 basis points during the crisis period which helped to reduce the unemployment rate by 0.7 % and inflation increased by 1%. If the LSAP program did not put pressure on the spread shock, the unemployment rate could have hit 10.6% in December 2009 rather than 10%, and the inflation rate could have been at around 2% in July 2009 rather than about 1%.

The effects of the second LSAP program (QE2) in the US are analyzed in the study of Chen et al. (2012) which used a simulation in an estimated medium-scale DSGE model and found that the effects this program (QE2) had on the United States GDP growth and inflation were modest but with a durable impact on the level of GDP. The authors of this study agree that the large purchase asset programs are more effective at stimulating the economy than previously believed because there are limits to arbitrage and market segmentation between short-term and long-term government bonds. During the QE2 program there was no high financial volatility that could lead to financial market segmentation, therefore the effects of QE2 on GDP growth were estimated not to exceed 0.5%, and the inflationary effects on asset purchase programs were even smaller.

The impact of QE programs on GDP growth and inflation rises considerably if it is associated with a commitment to keep interest rates low for a longer period of time, which indicates that the degree of LSAP effects depends prominently on expectations of interest-rate policy. This strongly indicates that when Federal Reserve decides to raise the federal-funds rates, it will have a significant impact, rather than guidance, on the perception of the economy's health among investors, public and policymakers.

The research study of Gagnon et al. (2011b) demonstrates that LSAP in the US diminished in a certain way the net supply of assets with long duration to the private sector and boosted the supply of assets of bank reserves with zero duration by affecting the risk premium of the assets being purchased and generating a portfolio reallocation. The reduction of 10-year term premium as a result of LSAPs in the US was between 30 and 100 basis points. The effects of LSAP were extensive including a wide range of Treasury securities, corporate bonds, interest-rate swaps and especially the purchases of MBS and agency debt by Federal Reserve at a time when liquidity was scarce, and Treasury yields were remarkably wide and helped to improve market liquidity. In fact, the LSAPs helped to narrow yields relative to Treasury yields and improved the mortgage market and long-term interest rates on agency debt and MBS. It removed the assets with high prepayment risk from private portfolios and restored credibility to the market.

The analysis of Baumeister and Benati (2013) is focused on the macroeconomic effects in both output growth and inflation of a spread compression at the zero lower bound generated by the Federal Reserve as a result of LSAPs. The macroeconomic simulations indicated that in the absence of Federal Reserve policy interventions the US economy could have been affected by deflation and severe recession until 2009: in fact, the simulation showed that the Q3 annualized based inflation rates could have gone as low as -1%; the GDP contraction would have been -0.9%, and unemployment rate would have been increased by 0.75% reaching the level of 10.6% in the fourth quarter of 2009.

The impact of QE in the UK

A number of studies and published articles have looked at the macroeconomic effects of Bank of England policy intervention following the QE program that started in the first quarter of 2009. Over a year the Bank of England purchased more than £200 billion of assets mainly in government securities. The QE program in the UK did not have separated rounds of QE as in the United States, but in October 2011 the program was prolonged after one year of maintenance. The work of Kapetanios et al. (2012) scrutinizes the effects of QE asset purchases on GDP and inflation in the United Kingdom during the financial crisis of 2008. Kapetanios (2012) uses three VAR (vector auto-regressive) models integrating structural change used to produce counterfactual estimates evaluating the impact of QE on 10-years gilt yield spreads.

The peak impact of QE in the UK on 10-year gilt yields was estimated at 100 basis points higher than actual outturns of the no-policy scenario. This is interpreted as the QE had a peak effect of 1.5% on the level of real GDP and a peak effect of 1-1.25% points on annual CPI inflation in the United Kingdom. Different econometric analysis indicates that the QE effects in the UK are approximately in the range that might have been expected. There was a portfolio balancing effect induced by quantitative easing that suggested asset prices recovery which was translated into higher demand to have wider effect in the economy by increased GDP at least one percentage point.

In another study, Joyce at al. (2011) investigate the impact of Bank of England's QE on UK asset prices. The response to six QE announcement in the UK had the sterling investment-grade corporate bond yields drop by 70 bases points, with no changes on spreads. Meanwhile, sterling non-investing-grade corporate bond yields fell by 150 basis points, with spreads closing by 75 basis points. Over the same period, the US dollar and euro-denominated investment-grade bond yields dropped by 23 basis points and 11 basis points correspondingly, 50 basis points lower than sterling-denominated bonds, resulting in a specific-country effect for the United Kingdom. Joyce's research reaches the same conclusion as Kapetanios (2012) where the QE purchases financed by using the central bank reserves may have depressed medium to long-term government yields by almost 100 basis points with a large part of stimulus coming directly through a portfolio balance effect.

The Impact of Policy Intervention in the European Union

The Quantitative Easing in the Euro Zone started much later than the United States, UK and Japan, only in March 2015, but before that, during the financial crisis of 2008, the European Central Bank (ECB) began a policy intervention called the *enhanced credit support*. This policy consisted of allowing financial institutions to obtain unlimited liquidity for extended periods using a fixed-rate full allotment policy. The work of Lenza *et al.* (2010) explores the ECB's policy through changing money market spreads. In this research, they use a Bayesian VAR model to calculate a policy projection conditional on actual money market rates with a different no-policy estimate conditional on a path for money market rates that would have succeeded if the European Central Bank had not implemented unconventional monetary policy. The effects of ECB's unconventional monetary policies resulted in the solidification of spreads and had an analogous impact to a standard monetary policy shock in normal times. This policy deeply affected the loans and interest rates, increasing the volume of real activities and inflation rate.

Fahr *at al.* (2010) and Peersman (2011) indicated that the ECB's unconventional monetary policies during the financial crisis of 2008 were effective in supporting the Eurozone economy. Contrarily, to economies where securities markets have an important role in the funding the private sector in Eurozone borrowing and lending take place through the intermediation of the banking sector. Bank loans in Euro area have accounted for about 85% of the total external financing of the private sector. The scope of the unconventional monetary policy in the EU was to fuel the banking system with liquidity. The use of this policy in Eurozone contributed the interest rate not to hit the zero lower bound.

The influx of liquidity influenced the rise of credit supply by banks, which resulted in reducing the lending rates and therefore the interest rate spread charged by banks. The drop in the interest rate spread was indirectly imposed for the first month, but it looks that continued for more than two years. Even the credit multiplier used by banks dropped substantially in the short run, but it gradually returned to its previous level after one year. Thus, the increase in the monetary base is purely uniformly transmitted to the volume of bank lending in the long run, contrarily to the case of monetary policy easing where the traditional innovation to the policy rate results in a considerable increase of interest rate spread charged by banks. The interest rate drop of the ECB is conveyed on to bank lending rates, but less proportionally than using conventional monetary policy. The reduction in bank lending rates and the rise of interest rate spreads equivalently increase credit demand and supply which is transmitted quickly to economic activity and inflation. This mechanism does not impact the credit multiplier and does not have any effect on the volume of liquidity available in the short run.

Peersman (2011), by using a VAR model covering the turbulent years of financial crisis, examined the effects of 2008 crisis in Eurozone and concluded that the transmission mechanism turned out to be dissimilar compared to traditional interest rate innovations. Interest rate spreads charged by banks tend to decline insistently after a rise in the monetary base, meanwhile spreads rise considerably after a fall in the policy rate. Based on the analysis of Peersman (2011) it is worth to say that there is no substantial short-run liquidity impact after an interest rate innovation which means that additional bank loans are generated by a greater credit multiplier. In addition, a credit multiplier can drop significantly after an expansion of the Eurozone's balance sheet.

The analysis of Giannone *et al.* (2012) provides the impact of unconventional monetary policy taken by ECB by using a new data on bank balance sheets that contains the volumes of interbank lending and loans in the Eurozone bank system. The authors of this study used a Bayesian VAR model composed of macro and financial variables to generate forecasts for lending banks over crisis period and find that ECB lending to the banking system in Eurozone was much higher than previously assumed. The VAR model was used to evaluate the impact of the ECB monetary intervention policy in the euro area economy and was found that it has positive effects in the Eurozone industrial production sector by increasing it at a 2% rate and reducing the unemployment rate at 0.6%. Without the ECB intervention, the 2008 financial crisis in the Euro-area could have been much worse.

In September 2015 the inflation rate unexpectedly turned negative after six months, and consumer prices in the 19 countries of the Eurozone fell 0.1% compared to same period of (September) 2014, meanwhile, the unemployment rate remained at the same level at 11%. Based on the market analysis it is believed that the decreasing prices are largely a consequence of cheaper energy as a result of cheap oil in 2015 which fell almost 40% compared to 2014. Therefore, policymakers including the ECB President Mario Draghi indicated that could expand the Euro quantitative easing to prevent further deflation well beyond September 2016, most likely until mid of 2018 and the program could reach a record of 2.4 trillion euros.

Quantitative Easing and Fiscal Policy

The purpose of Quantitative Easing (QE) was to support aggregate demand because the function of QE is to reduce the maturity structure of debt instruments that private investors have to hold. This means that the Central Bank is using unconventional monetary policy to manage debt. In normal conditions, the central bank and Treasury of a sovereign country can be consolidated for fiscal purposes. In fact, any gain or losses from the central bank are transferred to an account to the national Treasury of that particular country, which brings us to the situation that monetary and fiscal policy cannot be completely separated.

In the Eurozone, there is a special fund created to save Euro governments from insolvency called Emergency Liquidity Assistance (ELA) which is granted by national banks and all losses or gains from ELA operations remain with the national bank that has granted it and are not transferred to European Central Bank (ECB). In addition, all the ELA purchases have to remain in the books of individual national banks and will be entirely for the national bonds.

At the beginning of April 2015, all the securities purchased under the Public Sector Purchase Program (PSPP) in Eurozone were offered for security lending by a number of national central banks. The goal of security lending was to support the bond and repurchase government securities agreements (repos) without improperly limiting normal repo market activity. The aim of Eurozone policy was to target the market participants with market making obligations. It was decided that 80% of the asset purchases under PSPP would be accepted under the national central banks' responsibility which will affect of reducing the duration of the existing national public debt.

The public debt held by national central banks has a zero duration. If, for example, one national central bank such as Bundesbank buys German government bonds with residual maturity of 10 years will reduce the maturity of that particular part of the German public debt from 10 years to zero.

A rise of short-term interest rate will have the effect of a loss of Bundesbank's investment which will be offset against the gain of the German Treasury (German Ministry of Finance) by selling the bond. If the Bundesbank is planning to buy about one-quarter to one-fifth of all publicly traded German Federal debt over the lifetime of the PSPP, then the shortening of the duration of government debt could be considerable. Given that the average maturity of purchases of the biggest and most powerful national central bank in Europe, the Bundesbank, is about six years then the current duration of tradable German Federal debt would be reduced significantly by 1.2 to 1.5 years.

In another study conducted by Greenwood *at al.* (2014), we have that the monetary and fiscal policies in the United States have been following opposite directions following the financial crisis with debt management policies partly counterpoising the impact in monetary policy. The authors suggest that regarding the QE policies, the Federal Reserve has focused mostly on the effects the LSAPs program were excepted to have on long-term interest rates and the economy as a whole. Nevertheless, the Federal Reserve has completely ignored any impact on the fiscal policy, despite any Federal Reserve's gain or loss is remitted to US Treasury.

The 2008-2009 financial crisis had an extensive impact on the U.S. economy and worldwide. It has been the impression of academics and policymakers that the Federal Reserve's dual objectives of low inflation and full employment were not in conflict with the goal of managing federal debt by limiting fiscal risk at the U.S. Treasury. It was thought that the Federal Reserve

and the Treasury could independently achieve their respective policy objectives without formal coordination. It has not always been the case of synchronization between these two organizations. Before the 1970s the coordination between Federal Reserve and Treasury has been through official communications and eventually converging monetary policies. Attempts have been made to increase the correlation between maturity structure of federal debt and the maturity structure of Treasury holdings on the Fed's balance sheet.

The highest level of cooperation between Federal Reserve and Treasury was many decades ago when the United States entered the World War II where the Fed and the Treasury agreed to fix the entire yield curve of Treasury securities to finance the government spending and war efforts. In fact, during this period the Fed was able to buy or sell all the treasury securities in order to maintain the sloped yield curve positively. After the WWII the independence of Federal Reserve was restored by the 1951 *Treasury-Federal Reserve Accord* where the debt management and monetary policies were perceived as two separate strategies trying to finance the US Government but at the same time to minimize the monetization of the public debt.

Another cooperation between Fed and US Treasury was during the Operation Twist program of 1961 where the Fed wanted to achieve a more accommodative policy and was unwilling to drop the short-term interest rates because that could affect the nation's balance of payments and result in gold outflows under the Bretton Woods system. Therefore, the Fed and US Treasury started the cooperation by lowering long-term interest rates and by reducing the term premium on long-term bonds while holding short-term interest rate constant.

The Federal Reserve agreed to buy longer-term securities whereas the US Treasury would sell mainly short-term securities. The study of Swanson (2011) using a high-frequent event methodology analysis found that the Operation Twist program of 1961 had a significant impact in the economy different from the study of Modigliano and Sutch (1966) which stated that the program was only able to reduce the long-term interests.

Recently and especially during the 2008-2014 period the U.S. monetary policy and debt management have changed the path in reaction to the events of the financial and economic crisis, dragging the government balance sheet in opposite directions. The Federal Reserve's balance sheet grew five times over a six years period (2008-14) to $1.8 trillion of long-term Treasuries and

$1.8 trillion of mortgage-backed securities (MBS) financed by an increase in interest-bearing reserves (introduced by the Emergency Economic Stabilization Act of 2008). The portfolio of Federal Reserve holding Treasury securities increased the duration from 3.3 years to 7.8 years, meanwhile the Treasury debt outstanding increased from 31% of GDP in 2007 to 70% of GDP in 2014. In addition, the duration of outstanding Treasury debt rose from 3.9 years to 4.6 years. The $600 LSAP by Federal Reserve lowered the ten year-term premium by 20 basis points (bps), therefore the aggregate impact of QE has been to lower the term premium by 137 bps, meantime Treasury's maturity extension increased the term premium by 48 bps (Williams 2014). These calculations highlight the dissimilarities and inconsistency between the Federal Reserve and Treasury debt management policy.

The constructive impact of QE on long-term yields has been acknowledged by (Gagnon, Raskin, Remach and Sack 2011a) but also the positive effect of QE on stock prices, exchange rates and foreign asset prices has been recognized by a series of studies such as Neely (2012), Bauer and Neely (2014), Glick and Leduc (2013), etc. There is confidence among economists that Fed asset purchases (QE) have a downward effect on the long-term interest rates through portfolio balance channel. This policy has increased substantially rather than reduced the quantity of long-term government debt held by private investors. The Fed's LSAP announcement has moved the expectations component of long-term interest rates by helping as an implicit form of forwarding direction about the trail of future short-term interest rates.

The direct supply impact of QE has been counterbalanced by the huge expansion in outstanding government debt and the Treasury's decision to prolong the debt maturity (Bauer and Rudebusch 2014). Fed announcements have twice the impact as Treasury announcements of the same size. The Federal Reserve's actions with QE programs have the effect of reducing the duration of the debt held by the public at a time when the Treasury is sustaining the thesis that it's in taxpayers' interest to prolong the duration of the debt at a rapid pace.

The goal of Federal Reserve LSAP purchases was to lower the long-term interest rates by reducing the supply of longer-dated government bonds to the public. However, the large US federal deficits had managed to follow the direction of large increases in the supply of longer-dated federal securities bonds, given that the main portion of the debt issued by the US Treasury is always in the longer-term paper. Nevertheless, the decision of the US debt management office to extend the average maturities of the newly issued securities to the public had strengthened the outstanding amount of longer-term US federal debt securities. Despite this, about one-half of the increase in longer-dated US federal securities has been offset by the LSAP rounds of the

Federal Reserve which was used to decrease the long-term interest rates. The combination of these two policies has resulted in a considerable increase of the longer-term securities held by the public.

The fiscal deficits integrated with the expansion of maturity by the debt management office could have had effects of increasing the supply measured in the equivalents of 10-years bonds by about 30%, but due to the different LSAP of asset purchases by Federal Reserve, it removed about 15% of GDP from the market. In addition, the weighted-average duration of federal debt securities issued by US Treasury has jumped from almost 4 years in 2008 to 4.6 years at the end of 2014. By combining the US Treasury and Federal Reserve, the weighted-average duration of debt securities has fallen to 2.9 years.

The lower effective average maturity of the US federal debt might be more significant if the Federal Reserve increases the interest rates because it will lead to a higher cost of debt service much faster than if the duration of the public debt was at 4.6 years. Government is not the only entity that can issue short-term debt as there are also financial intermediaries which can issue short-term debt that is collateralized by risky long-term assets increasing the liquidity premium as Treasury does with the T-bills (Gorton and Metrick, 2012).

The government has always tried to regulate the issuance of short-term debts by shortening the maturity structure. By increasing the T-bill supply, the Treasury tries to lower the premium on short-term money-like debt and diminish the capability and attraction of private financial intermediaries to issue short. The public debt management by the government with a short maturity is supposed to have a comparative advantage over the private sector in the creation of money-like short-term debt. The suggestion in favor of a short-term debt seems to be better than the argument in favor of long-term debt. Despite this, there is not much to know which is the best-weighted maturity debt, 3 months, 4 months, 6 months or 9 months. Taking into considerations the equation of the debt in terms of primary deficit we have,

$$Debt_t \;=\; Debt_{t-1} \;+\; \Pr\ imDef_t \;+\; Int._t \qquad (5.8)$$

where *Debtt* is the public debt held at the end of the fiscal year t, *PrimDeft* is the primary deficit and *Int.t* is the interest paid counting bonds, imputed interest on Treasury bills, coupons on notes, etc. (Greenwood *at al.* (2014, 37-8). A counterfactual study of time series from year 1952 to 2012 in the United States shows that interest payments average 1.8% of GPD per year which reveals an average effective nominal interest rate paid of 4.97% with a standard deviation of 0.72%. By using the 3 months Treasury bills and assuming the short-interest rates have been dominant since 1952 we compute the effective annual interest rate using the counterfactual interest payment given as,

$$Int_t^{counterfactual} = Debt_{t-1}^{Counterfactual} x R_t^{Counterfactual} \qquad (5.9)$$

By combining equations 5.8 and 5.9, we have that the counterfactual debt stock is given as,

$$Debt_t^{Counterfactual} = Debt_{t-1}^{Counterfactual} + \Pr imDef_t + Interest_t^{Counterfactual} \qquad (5.10)$$

Quantity Easing and Transmitting Channels

The quantitative easing (QE) works through several operating channels. A wide discussion of the operating channels will give more insights on how the QE is supposed to operate. A research study completed by Krishnamurthy and Jorgensen in 2011 give us insights about the effects on quantitative easing on interest rates through operating channels. An important operating channel is a signaling channel, which reveals the market gathering information from QE announcement about future Federal Funds rates. The signaling channel has impact on all bond market interest rates, depending on bond maturity, because lower yields (lower future Federal Funds Rates) will influence all interest rates. This channel is typically measured by using changes in the prices of the federal fund's futures contract as a monitor to market prospects of future federal funds rates. The signaling channel has a big influence on reducing intermediate maturity rates rather than long maturity rates since once the economy recovers from the crisis, the Federal Reserve can sell the assets right away (Krishnamurthy and Jorgensen 2011, 5).

Another operating channel used during the QE process is the duration risk channel. The one-factor model introduced by Vayanos and Vila (2009) has a risk premium on a bond maturity *t* based on the duration of a maturity *t* bond and the price of duration risk given as a function of the duration risk transmitted by the marginal bond market investor who is risk aversion. The Vayanos -Vila (2009) model demonstrates that the duration risk premium results are assumptions where a group of investors have preferences for bonds of specific maturities (preferred habitat demand) and another group of investors who consider themselves as arbitrators but change their approach and become marginal investors for pricing duration risk. If the duration risk channel model on QE applies to a broad class of fixed income, it has two main expectations: i.) QE reduces the yield on all long-term nominal assets such as Agency bonds, Treasuries, MBS and corporate bonds. ii.) for longer duration assets the effects have a bigger impact.

The liquidity channel instead consists of purchasing long-term securities by Federal Reserve during the QE process to increase reserve balances. Given that reserve balances are more liquid than long-term securities, the Federal Reserve will increase the liquidity in the hands of investors and therefore reduce the liquidity premium on the most liquid bonds and at the same time increase Treasury yields. The Treasury bond premiums have been relatively high during the acutest periods of the crisis. Hence, the liquidity channel normally raises Treasury yields compared to other less liquid assets and is very accommodating during the financial crisis and deep recessions.

The safety channel is another evidence suggesting that there are investors disposed to pay an additional premium for assets with low default risk so the expected default rate could be even lower. The safety channel is a deviance from the risk premium of a standard asset pricing model because of the particular clientele demand. The Treasury and Agency bonds in the United States are evidently safe as they offer certain nominal payments, nevertheless, Agency MBS (Mortgage-Backed Securities) have substantial prepayment risks which means that it might not meet the investor's safety demands.

Therefore, the safety channel foresees that during the QE process the yields of safe assets such as Treasuries, Agencies and high-level corporate bonds are reasonably lower compared to less safe assets such as low-grade corporate bonds or even some bonds with prepayment risk such as MBS. The *Aaa* rated bonds are normally high-grade bonds that meet the safety clientele demands. If there are fewer long-term Treasuries, which means there are not as much of long-term safe assets to meet the preferred habitat of investors or the clientele demand, the spread between *Baa* and *Aaa* rated bonds rises. In addition, the mortgage prepayment risk conveys a positive risk premium which depends on the quantity of prepayment risk tolerated by mortgage investors (Krishnamurthy and Jorgensen 2011, 6-8). The safety channel on prepayment risk premium is primary evident during the QE1 where MBS purchases reduced the MBS yields in relation to other bonds market yields.

Default rick channel is another channel used during the QE operations where the lower grade bonds such as *Baa* rated bonds have greater default risk than Treasury bonds rated as *Aaa*. If the MBS yields are lowered during the MBS purchases in QE, then we can assume that the default risk of corporate bonds will fall and the *Baa* rates will drop. This means that the QE has been successful in stimulating the recovering of the economy, which indicates a lower default risk premium. A useful financial tool to measure the default risk channel is a financial derivative called the credit-default swap

(CDS) which is used to hedge against default by a firm. It consists of measuring the percentage of face-value that must be paid as an annual insurance premium to ensure against default on corporate bonds.

Another channel called Inflation Channel increases inflation expectations which implies an impact on interest rates. There is always the risk that in a situation where the investors are uncertain about the effects of policy on inflation may lead to greater insecurity over inflation consequences. Regarding interest rate option, we have that an increase in inflation uncertainty will reasonably lead to a rise in interest rate uncertainty and implicit volatility. Therefore, the inflation channel envisages two situations, first, the quantitative easing raises the rate on inflation swaps as well as inflation prospect measured by the difference between nominal bond yields and TIPS (Treasury Inflation-Protected Securities). Second, the quantitative easing may help to increase or decrease interest rate insecurity calculated by the implicit volatility in swaptions (Krishnamurthy and Jorgensen 2011, 9).

TIPS are a noteworthy way to eliminate one of the most important risks to fixed income investment- inflation risk – whereas providing a real rate of return guaranteed by the U.S. Government. A zero-coupon inflation swap is a financial tool used to hedge against an increase in inflation. The swap consists of a contract between a "fixed rate payor" and a "floating rate payor" that decides a one-time payment of cash at the maturity of the contract. The realized cumulative inflation over the life of a swap measured using the CPI index is paid by the "floating rate payor". Meanwhile, the fixed rate payer makes a fixed payment upon agreement at the beginning of the swap agreement. The market is efficient if the fixed rate payment measures the expected inflation rate over the life of the swap. A swaption is another financial derivative based on interest rate, where the buyer of a call swaption earns a profit when the interest rate rises compared to the strike of the swaption. The expected volatility of interest rates implies the current market prices of swaptions.

An interest rate or a variety of different interest rates would be impacted by QE by a range of channels in different ways. In fact, the transmitting channels during the QE is summarized by an equation where a real yield on long-term and risky corporate bond, *r*, are given as,

$$r = E\left[i_{safe,liq,st}\right] - \pi^{e} + Dur.\times P_{Dur.Risk} + Illiq\times P_{liq.} + Saf.\times P_{saf.} + Def.Risk\times P_{DefaultRis} + \text{Prep}.Risk\times P_{\text{PrepRisk}} \tag{5.11}$$

where E is the expected average interest rate over the next t years on short-term safe and liquid bonds and п is the expected inflation during the same period. Each term of the equation above reflects a transmitting channel previously discussed. As a matter of fact, the second term indicates the duration risk premium that is a function of duration and the price of duration risk. The third term points out the illiquidity premium that is a function of liquidity and market price liquidity. The same thing we can say for the fourth term that reflects the safety premium and for the fifth and sixth terms that show the default risk and a premium on the prepayment risk, respectively.

Using the empirical methodology through channels to explain the quantitative easing we have that quantitative easing is a difference-in-difference approach to estimate the liquidity, safety, duration risk premium and prepayment risk channels (Krishnamurthy and Jorgensen 2011, 11). The difference-in-difference approach is also used for derivative prices of a singular channel, say liquidity, to isolate the effects of another channel, say duration risk premium. For example, if two type of bonds, such as the Treasury bond and the Agency bond have the same duration, safety and default risk except for the yield spread (over the QE events) then the difference between these two bonds is based only on the liquidity channel. In fact, the Treasury bond is more liquid than the Agency (MBS) bond.

The research of Krishnamurthy and Jorgensen (2011) - different from other studies about QE in the United States, such as D'Amico and King (2010), Hamilton and Wu (2012), Gagnon et al. (2011a and 2011b) - focuses on the channels for which QE has an impact on interest rates. Based on this research, there are at least three channels having an effect on QE1 and QE2 during the massive American QE program. First, the signaling channel which has evidence in QE1 and QE2 has the capability to drive down the yield on a large range of bonds. Second, the safety channel can put down the yields on medium and long maturity safe bonds because of an existing clientele for safe nominal assets. Third, the inflation channel indicates that expected inflation has increased which suggest larger declines in real than nominal rates, with evidence from inflation swaps rates and TIPS (Treasury Inflation-Protected Securities). In addition, there were more channels for QE1 during the 2008-2009 period in the US, such as the risk premium channel which reduced yields on MBS, a default risk premium channel which lowered yields on corporate bonds and a liquidity channel which was financed by reserves (through QE1) increasing yields mostly on liquid bonds.

A policy implication used during QE2 in 2010-2011 was that Treasuries-only policies had impact principally through a signaling channel where the market reduces the expectation of future federal funds rates. There is also the portfolio balance channel where assets held by investors are a substitute for those which the Fed purchases in terms of duration risk, safety and liquidity. In the Fed has the intention of buying a lot of assets, private investors offer a higher price on the remaining of low-default-risk securities which imply lower yields on these assets. This brings us back to the safety channel which considers the substitutability of assets or securities with low default-risk and is a preferred-habitat for certain maturities of the same class of low-default risk assets. As a conclusion, it is proved that the Quantitative Easing affects interest rates through a wide range of channels.

The Concept of Balance Sheet Recession during Financial Crisis

The concept of Balance Sheet Recession has been introduced by the Taiwanese-American economist Richard C. Koo who is specialized in balance sheet recessions and debt crisis.

His book entitled *The Escape from Balance Sheet Recession and the QE Trap* published at the end of 2014 uncovers risks and vulnerabilities still remaining as the world economy was gradually recovering from the financial crisis or as he calls it the "balance sheet recession" of 2008. Richard Koo, in his work, enlightens the political and economic difficulties that stand in the way of recovery from this unique type of recession not seen since the end of WWII that was mostly ignored by economists.

The particular 2008 recession known as "balance sheet recession" was new to many researchers and analysts and was never studied or taught in schools. The Koo's work explains how history was somehow repeating itself in Europe while the United States, which learnt from the Japanese experience in the 1990s and early 2000s, was doing much better by avoiding the fiscal disaster. The government of the countries facing the recession must explain to people that the government must borrow the unborrowed savings in the private sector in order to prevent the economy from collapsing and to provide income to the private sector so that it can repair its balance sheet.

The government will do the fiscal consolidation only after the private sector has completed repairing its balance sheet and is ready to borrow money again at established interest rates in the market. But because the quantitative easing was already applied, the United States, the United Kingdom, the Eurozone and Japan would aspect a non-easy path to normality in what Koo calls the QE Trap. According to him, understanding the balance sheet recession will help resolve the EU crisis and escape from recession.

In the real world, the financial sector has the duty to ensure that saved funds are borrowed and spent to those that can make best use of the funds and the tool that equates savings and investment is the interest rate. The interest rate will rise if they are too many borrowers and will drop if they are few borrowers and the demand is meek. Nevertheless, if the private sector since the 2008 crisis is saving money at near interest rate, it means that the savings generated by the private sector will not find borrowers. If the interest rates cannot go lower, the private savings are stuck in the financial sector incapable of entering the real economy to help with investment and spending. If the unborrowed funds are left unused the economy will hit a deflationary gap that will reduce the aggregate demand corresponding to the saved but unborrowed amounts.

Therefore, government spending and spending becomes crucial in relaunching the economy and helping the private sector to recover from the recession. The government has to expand the current expense and borrow the unborrowed savings in the private sector to keep the economy away from the deflationary spiral. By performing more spending to keep the GDP from decreasing the government makes certain that the private sector has the needed income to repair the balance sheet. When the private sector balance sheet is restored, and the private sector can start borrowing money again the government should try to reduce the deficit spending in order to repair its own balance sheet.

The purpose of deficit spending by the government is to help preserve the flow of money supply from decreasing when the private sector is minimizing debt due to paying down the debt. The commercial banks are not capable of lending out money once the private sector pays back to them because the entire private sector is decreasing its financial leverage and not thinking of borrowing money again in the short-run. In fact, this is what happened in the United States during the Great Depression from 1929 to 1933 when the US money supply decreased by 30 percent mostly related to deleveraging (around 85 percent) and in a smaller portion related to bank failures and withdrew (about 15 percent). At that time, during the gold standard regime, there were not enough monetary tools to reverse the trend and ease the financial crisis as they were in the first decade of the twenty-first century.

According to the Koo (Koo. R.C. 2014, 60-63) fiscal and especially monetary policy are not so effective in those economic conditions where the private sector is trying to minimize the debt compared to the economic situation where the private sector is trying to maximize profits. This, according to Koo, indicates that there are at least two stages of macroeconomics, 1) the normal or the healthy world and 2) the world of balance sheet recessions, called Yang and Yin respectively. In the Yang stage or the Yang economy, the private sector balance sheets are strong with assets dominating liabilities and businesses striving to maximize profits. In the Yang economy, the monetary policy should be the main tool used by policymakers.

The things are different in the Yin economy where the private sector companies have suffered impairment to their balance sheet because of the financial crisis that has resulted in a decrease of the asset prices. Therefore, the main concern of the Yin economy is concentrated on improving the balance sheets of the firms by reducing liabilities and debts and improving some accounting ratios such as current ratio (current assets/current liabilities), quick test ratio (cash, securities, net receivables/current liabilities), current cash debt coverage (net cash/ average current liabilities), etc. If a large number of private companies are trying to minimize debts and lean their organizational structure, the economy as a whole will be directed toward a contractionary equilibrium known as a recession.

In this stage, any monetary policy conducted by the central bank will be ineffective as firms are struggling to pay down their debts and the private sector demand becomes flat eliminating any possibility of growth in the short-run. In this phase, the role of government is crucial, as it has to borrow and spend the savings generated by the private sector so the corporate debt repayments and household savings can be returned to the economy again to support growth. The fiscal policy based on large government spending to keep the economy afloat plays a fundamental role in the economy.

The difference between Yin and Yang stages, according to Koo (2014, 60-63), is the stability of the private sector. In the Yang economy, the private sector balance sheets have more than enough assets to pay up the liabilities. So asset prices are high, and there is a strong credit rating for businesses, which drive firms to take more risks and invest in new operations to maximize profit. In the Yin economy, the private sector is in difficulties, and it needs the help of the government in the form of expansive fiscal spending to put back into the economy the unborrowed private-sector savings. The government might have to match the needs of the Yin economy in recession by applying an appropriate fiscal stimulus in order for the economy to grow.

The time-frame period for an economy to move from the recession phase to the steady growth path will depend on conditions in which private sector will manage to repair its balance sheet and how fast the households and businesses will cope to overcome their aversion to debt. The previous historical realities tell us that, for example, during the 1929 financial crisis it took the US interest rates almost 30 years until 1959 to get back to the average level of the pre-crisis. This historical fact recommends that the aversion to debt can carry on for an extended period of time. In the early thirties, under Roosevelt presidency, the United States started the public works projects under the New Deal which ignited a speedy recovery of the economy. Unfortunately, in 1937 Roosevelt had to change course due to enormous government spending and announced a fiscal contraction which quickly turned into another recession. During a balance sheet recession such as that of 1929 monetary policy is ineffective but fiscal policy is more effective for the recovery of the economy and the launch of a growth path.

In the post-1990 recession in Japan and post-2008 recession in the Western world, the financial crisis was caused mainly by the shortage of borrowers and not lenders. The banks were ready to lend money to households and business, but the borrowers were concerned that they wouldn't be able to pay back the loans because of the recession, so they decided not to borrow, but rather pay back the old debts. The policymakers of the Japanese economy in the 1990s and of Western economies in 2008 were wide-open to severe flaws in the analytical framework of Keynes theory which failed to consider the balance sheet theory and minimized debt process during a financial crisis. Keynes always assumed that firms have to maximize profits, but it was the deterioration of the marginal efficiency of capital that prompted corporations to stop the investments in extra production capacities.

Keynes, like postwar monetarists and neoclassical economists, neglected the point that businesses could be minimizing debt instead of maximizing profits. Monetary policy, according to Keynes, was ineffective at low-interest rates during the recession because people will prefer to keep cash rather than corporate bonds and this is called the *liquidity preference.* Keynesians and monetarists missed the point that the liquidity trap was a borrowers' occurrence, not lenders' one. Despite this, the Keynesians had the solution for economic downturn by using deficit spending and the logic used by them was in terms of the multiplier and marginal disutility of labor for the long-term unemployment. For Keynes using deficit spending as a counterbalance to private sector debt minimization was off the table and out of the discussion. In fact, his postwar followers had even less reason to get concerned about the balance sheet problems because no economy in the postwar period had stumbled upon a balance sheet crisis until Japan in 1990 and the US in 2008. The private sector debt minimization is the dynamic force behind the economic problem of the economy in recession, and it was the missing argument of the micro foundation of Keynesian macroeconomics.

The lack of debt minimization foundation has forced even the New Keynesian School that arose in the early 1990s to believe that wage and price rigidities can cause unemployment and recession. According to Koo (2014), if firms are minimizing debt no wage or price rigidities are needed to create protracted unemployment and recessions, since the outflow of income stream in private sector which try to minimize debt will continue to reduce aggregate demand until it reaches the point where firms are able to repair their balance sheets, and private sector is capable of reinvesting the savings in new activities or start borrowing again.

Stimulus Programs and Failed Investments

An Economic Stimulus package is normally referred to efforts done by a government to enhance economic growth and lead the economy out of a recession or economic downturn.

Generally speaking, there are at least three considerations in developing a stimulus package:

- The stimulus program must have a rapid impact on economy
- It must increase the economy's productivity capacity by raising long-term growth outlook
- It must help ease the adjustment in areas most negatively affected by economic slowdown and commodity price declines.

A stimulus package in principle has to provide tax rebates and increase spending through diverse types of investment in different sectors, as spending increases demand, which leads to a rise in employment rate which in turn increases income and wealth (GDP) of the economy.

The stimulus package can be achieved by using few options.

One option could be to introduce tax rebates to lower-income households, which means that households can spend the increased tax-income-returns amounts from the government. Despite this option, past spending patterns show that only a portion of amounts returned from taxes would be spent, not enough to generate a path of growth in the economy.

For example, during the deep recession that started in 2008 in the United States, the role of American Government was focused on tax and benefit policy in protecting family incomes. The majority of American middle-income families were affected by tax cuts and higher government benefits which compensated almost 90 percent of the market income losses triggered by the recession. Between 2008 and 2010 millions of Americans were laid off which worsen their financial situation and reduced spending. However, income replacement through permanent tax and transfer system plus temporary measures helped improve families' spendable incomes which was government intended goal. The American Government reached the poor and moderate-income families in America to replace their wage and capital losses caused by the recession with tax cuts and benefit increases so they could keep spending in the same way as before the recession. Families with an unemployed householder received government transfer payments and unemployment benefits.

The extraordinary measures to boost spending of middle-class families consisted on passing through the Congress some transitory measures regarding the weekly payments and the duration of benefits. Government benefits were able to compensate up to $2,800 or 47 percent of the average loss in market income sustained by middle-quintile families erasing the negative effects of the recession partly. Spending for middle-class families kept flowing thanks to the lower federal taxes and higher public benefits.

Another stimulus option is the time-limited tax credits to boost investment in capital goods. This type of stimulus option could encourage investment in the current year which will help increase investment in long-term growth, whereas generating a direct increase in demand.

Infrastructure spending is another alternative option of the stimulus package. By identifying investments to put on new and easily implementable projects to increase demand in a period that goes from 6 to 18 months will help raise productivity and employment rate. All investments or projects should be sorted out to ensure that they are economically feasible and incremental to current investment plans. The infrastructure spending could be oriented to meet the needs of the areas or regions most affected by low commodities prices, on the condition that projects are of economic significance and could be largely completed within the estimated time.

Approximately, one percent of GDP spending in infrastructure in any advanced or developing country would provide a relatively quick boost to economic activity, reduce excess capacity and lay the foundation for stronger growth over the long term. This kind of stimulus package would significantly increase the current fiscal deficit, but for advanced countries that have low net debt-to-GDP, good credit rating and sufficient cost fund would not be a problem as they normally maintain fiscal credibility. It will be a concern for those countries that have a high debt-to-GDP ratio, not decent credit ratings and high-cost fund.

The key ingredient of the government's fiscal strategy should be to achieve a declining debt-to-ratio once the economy is in no need of policy support. The international markets will take into consideration a well-designed stimulus package for a given economy unless the new expenditures are unproductive and wasteful. A carefully planned stimulus package has the potential of helping the economy in recession to reach its growth objectives and achieve escape velocity from slow growth or stagnation.

Based on classical macroeconomic and monetary textbooks there are at least two main ways for stimulating the economy: the expansionary monetary policy and expansionary fiscal policy.

The first way to stimulate the economy by using fiscal policy implicates government spending or taxation to impact the aggregate demand and boost the GDP. This policy normally involves tax cut and spending increases.

Reducing or cutting income taxes will increase the amount of income available after taxes that will help household spend more than before. This fiscal policy is more effective for low incomes because by reducing taxes for low-income earners will have a higher marginal propensity to consume. The government has the capability to increases public spending by injecting big amounts of money into the economy to build infrastructure such as highways, hospitals, schools, railways, ports, etc., that will boost employment rate, domestic consumption and the Aggregate demand.

On the other hand, increased public spending will cause higher government deficit and higher government borrowing. As a result, more resources might be committed to paying for the service of government borrowing. Fiscal policy may sometimes cause an undesired effect called as 'crowding out', which means that increased spending in public sector may drive down or eliminate the private sector spending. By definition, this is a situation when increased interest rates will result in private investment spending reduction that diminishes the initial increase in total investment spending.

The second way to stimulate the economy is the monetary policy. If the central bank cuts the interest rates, the effects will be to increase consumer spending and rise investments. In fact, lower interest rates will reduce the cost of borrowing for enterprises and will reduce the mortgage interest payments for householders and increase their disposable income. It will reduce the incentive to save and stimulate the investment.

There is, of course, a number of factors that determine the success of monetary policy.

1) **The accuracy of inflation forecast** is crucial for healthy monetary policy to try to reduce the inflationary pressures before they occur. For example, if the inflation is higher than predicted then interest rates will be too low to control inflation and they need to rise. On the other hand, if inflation is too low, means that the demand for goods and services is too low and the interest rates could be too high for the economy, thus they need to be lowered so money could be cheaper to borrow.
2) **The time lag** is also important for the achievement of monetary policy. Interest rate changes can normally take up to 18 months to have their full effects. If the interest rates rise, the current project will continue, however, future projects may be deferred. In the same way, if the demand is slow and the projects are put on hold, the central

bank will lower interest rates, but it will take about 12-18 months to identify the right projects to invest given the cheap borrowing money.

3) **Interest Elasticity of Demand** measures the reaction of the demand to changes in interest rates. For instance, if the demand is good and the consumer confidence is high, then increasing interest rates may not discourage consumer spending. In the same way, if the demand for consumer confidence is very low, even lower interest rates close to zero may not encourage consumer spending, as it happens in the aftermath of the 2008 crisis.
4) **Other variables** that are affected by interest rates in the economy. Higher interest rate normally increases the value of the domestic currency (through hot money flows), which causes problems to exporters and may worsen current account. Lower interest rates, may not devalue or revalue the domestic currency of a developed country (such as U.S., U.K., Canada, EU, Japan, Australia, etc.) but it may cause a disproportionate effect on the volatile housing market of the advanced countries. In the less developed countries, the changing of interest rates affects the economy but must be taken into consideration other factors such as the risk of investing in these countries, political and social factors related to the stability of the country, etc.

In some cases, the tools to boost economic growth may also fail. In fact, there is also the possibility of failed investments and failed stimulus plans in some sectors of the economy that reflect the downturn of the economy. Low commodities prices may not be enough to spur economic growth. For instance, in the energy sector, a drop of oil and natural gas prices for almost 50-60% in 2015-16 compared to 2009-2014 are supposed to have greater benefits for consumers. In addition to that, low-interest rates must be able to revive the economy.

This is not happening as expected by analysts and policymakers in some countries where energy sector counts for 20 percent or more of the economy. The situation in the oil industry is the result of overinvestment by companies that miscalculated the growth of global economy. They simply failed to take into consideration that many of their competitors were correspondingly over-investing in the same sector, and underestimated the speed at which innovation could render their own investment unprofitable.

Overinvestment in a sector might be considered wasteful or non-productive if there is a diminishing return on productivity on that particular sector, but is considered productive if invested in other sectors where there is more probability of an increasing return. If low oil prices are the result of investments that should not have been made, there is an indication of a redolent problem and the economy could have been better off if scarce resources had been invested in sound projects that didn't lead to falling prices. Of course, the failures and successes are part of capitalism, but in the end, the successes have to outset the failures so the economy can grow. Otherwise, entrepreneurs and investors have wasted resources more than they have contributed to increasing the health of the society.

Generally speaking, when prices of real estate, wages, oil and capital are low because of the overinvestment using the same technology, rather than using innovation and productivity improvements, there is a signal of failure and waste not an indication of success and improvement. For example, in 2015-16 if the prices of the oil had remained high or at the same level as in previous years, it would have suggested that past investments in the oil industry were necessary. However, with the collapsing of oil prices from $90-100 in previous years to $35-45 per barrel in 2015-16 and extensive bankruptcies, there is compelling evidence that some of the investments in the oil industry were a terrible idea. With discovery of cheaper, heavy-oil and more accessible oil from massive shale deposits in North America at the beginning of 2000s, called shale revolution, made possible thanks to large investments aimed at extracting large volumes of barrels of oil per day and shipped directly to the nearest market to maximize profit per oil-barrel when the price was above average.

The innovation and technological advancement in the early 2000s have made finding and producing oil in shale and tight rock formations significantly more affordable, but not as cheap as drilling oil in Saudi Arabia and other OPEC countries.

The OPEC meeting in November 2014 decided not to cut oil production to keep the price falling, so the shale-oil produces could lose market share. Generous profit from shale oil deposits was not anymore guaranteed. Resources injected into developing oil sands projects would have found a better use in other sectors.

A good part of investors squandered precious financial resources in three successive bubbles over a relatively short period. Technology in the late 1990s, real estate in the mid-2000s, and commodities and energy over the last few years. These bubbles were not beneficial to growth and acted as a big hindrance to investor's confidence. This confidence loss describes why worldwide credit conditions, especially in the aftermath of the 2008 crisis and the steep drop of oil and mineral prices, are getting tighter and tighter despite the expansive global monetary policies.

The future growth may deteriorate if investors remain diffident due to poor investment track record and loss of confidence that needs to be reversed for things to improve and confidence to be restored. Assuming that Central Bank uses all conventional monetary tools available such as lowering near-zero interest rates, quantitative easing, or bailouts programs but to no avail, as these interventions are making things worse for the economy, then what are the other options? Challenged by growing evidence that monetary stimulus is inadequate, and adding up the failing investments in the past, many analysts may favor the aggressive fiscal policies. If the interest rate is near to zero and animal spirits are at their lowest, policymakers have no choice but to recall the old Keynesian policies.

The Keynesian recipes might work if public infrastructure programs are done well-planned. If public infrastructure programs of Keynesian type will succeed in restoring global investor's confidence to borrow at interest rates high enough to invest in sound investment that yields respectable returns, then this is the only path to sustainable growth if other monetary policy tools fail.

Some Notes on Global Debt

Concerns about sovereign debt have always been around since European nations foremost used this instrument as a fairly cheap way of meeting the high cost of waging wars and under-taking other expensive projects. In the seventeenth century, and exactly in 1694 when Bank of England was founded it started soon issuing bonds and the government debt within four years went from £1.25 million to £16 million. This was considered an easy, low-cost way to finance anything that government needed at that time; from roads, canals for navigation, government buildings, infrastructure, to wars for colonial expansion, etc.

Coming back to modern times of the 21st century, the global financial crisis of 2008 was ignited by the desire to accumulate excessive debt and leverage in developed economies, predominantly in the household and financial sectors. The recent financial crisis created new conditions for raising the volume of sovereign debt across the world for countries that were looking to finance growth and recover from the recession. By the second quarter of 2014, the government related debt around the globe was estimated to have increased by USD 58 trillion a 76 percent increase since the 4th quarter of 2007 reaching $ 199 trillion and raising the ratio of all debt to GDP by 17 percentage points to a staggering 286 percent. If we consider one example; China's debt alone has risen four times since 2007 reaching an astounding amount of $28 trillion, which represents almost 37 percent of the growth in global debt (McKinsey

Global Institute, 2015, 12-15). At the beginning of the recession in 2008, the government debt in most of the countries accounted for a smaller portion of debt pie than corporate, household or financial debt. The government debt increase in the industrialized countries after 2008 explains at least one-third of the overall growth, due in part to the decreasing tax revenue and the high cost of financing bailouts (through public borrowing). Meanwhile, the debt of developing countries has counted for half of the growth during the same period.

With interest rates near at zero (2014-16), the central banks around the globe have tried to get as much debt as a possible increase at all time high the indebtedness of governments. The role of central banks such as Federal Reserve (Fed), European Central Bank (ECB), Bank of Japan, Bank of England was to make sure that there was confidence in their quantitative purchasing programs otherwise the investors in the capital markets will begin a stampede out of stock and bonds putting in jeopardy the global economic recovery.

Of course, the government cannot all be put in the same pot and stir with the same debt brush. Some governments such Japan have had little or no distress managing high level of debt for such long time sustained by strong demand and relatively low financing costs. The British government announced in fall 2014 that it would redeem £218 million worth of bond obligations coming from the First World War with other old debts dating back to the beginning of the 19th century during the Napoleonic wars. This means that the British government would leave around £2 billion of Britain's First World War in the hands of almost 120 000 investors accumulating about 3.5 percent interest per year. This is still manageable for the British government but for other more troubled and fiscally challenged countries such as Greece and Ukraine cannot make their payments in time without receiving a lifeline from international organizations such as IMF and ECB.

Despite the high level of debt, governments do not face the same constraints and limitations as households or businesses when it comes to debt. The simple reason is that governments can always levy taxes or can still print their own currency to finance debt.

Global government debt alone (debt of central and local governments) has risen $25 trillion between 2007 and second quarter of 2014. In a series of advanced countries that have faced severe recession, such as Greece, Italy, Spain, Ireland, Portugal and the United Kingdom, the government debt has grown quickly as a share of GDP. The growth in government spending and debt has been seen by some analysts as welcome policy to stimulate growth and finance infrastructures vital for job growth thanks to the borrowing costs that are at historic lows. The assessment whether a government is using its debt-raising capacity prudently depends on its ability to translate the borrowed money into economic growth without raising inflation at high levels that will reduce household's standard of living.

The rise of debt in public sector, in a number of advanced economies (such as Germany, United States, Spain and the United Kingdom), has been offset by a decrease of household and non-financial corporation debt relative to GDP since 2008. In other developed countries this trend has not been seen, on contrary, private sector, debt has grown in some cases more than 25 percentage points of GDP since 2008. The question is not if the debt is too high but if the resources have been maximized available for the private sector to restart the recovery. Emerging market debt has grown faster than the debt of the advanced economies, despite is only 121 percent of GDP compared to 280 percent of GDP in 2014 of developed economies because the developing countries have started from very low levels of debt in 2007 (McKinsey Global Institute, 2015, 21-22).

Advanced Countries	Household	Non-Financial corporation	Govern-ment	Total	Develo-ping countries	Household	Non-financial Corp.	Govern-ment	Total
Japan	65	101	234	400	Hungary	29	114	83	226
Ireland	85	189	115	390	Malaysia	76	91	55	222
Singapore	76	201	105	382	China	38	125	55	218
Belgium	56	136	135	327	Thailand	76	65	46	187
Netherlands	115	127	83	325	Israel	38	73	67	178
Greece	65	68	183	316	Chile	36	86	15	137
Spain	73	108	132	313	Poland	35	42	57	134
Denmark	129	114	60	303	South Africa	39	49	45	133
Sweden	82	165	42	289	Czech Republic	33	49	47	129
Italy	43	77	139	259	Brazil	25	38	65	128
United Kingdom	86	74	92	252	India	9	45	66	120
United States	77	67	89	233	Turkey	22	47	35	104
South Korea	81	105	44	230	Romania	19	47	38	104
Canada	92	60	70	222	Indonesia	20	46	22	88
Australia	113	69	31	213	Mexico	1	22	44	73
Germany	54	54	80	188	Russia	16	40	9	65

Table 5.10. Debt-to-GDP ratio as a percentage in Q2, 2014 for advanced and developing economies. (*Source:* McKinsey Global Institute, 2015, Exhibit 6, p.22.)

Debt-to-ratio of advanced and developed countries in the second quarter of 2014, which includes the household, non-financial corporate and government debt is given by table 5.10. In the top of the list for advanced countries is Japan, Ireland and Singapore with a debt-to-ratio of around 382-400 percent.

Japan has the highest government debt in the world of around 235 percent (in Q2, 2014) and still, nobody puts it on the same basket as Greece, Ireland, or Spain when it comes to sovereign risk. It has been a concern for Japan's massive public debt that decreasing demographics and aging population make it particularly vulnerable to an internal or even external shock. In addition, a reduction on savings rate and given that insurers and pension funds are in search of higher yields to cover government expenses, the government cannot count anymore on domestic institutions only to buy the bulk of its bonds at close-to-zero interest rates. That role for now is done by the Bank of Japan which holds more than one-third of the government's 10 year-bonds, but in the future the Japanese's government may have to use international markets for financing, which will come with a string of tough reforms.

Regarding the developing economies, we have seen a rapid growth in emerging-market debt which reflects the rapid urbanization and industrialization and the building of much-needed infrastructure as a result of fast population growth, which has generated substantial demand for credit and other forms of financing. A large part of households and companies in developing countries have now access to domestic formal banking systems which they can obtain loans with favorable terms, to foreign creditors and in some countries the corporate bond market has emerged.

According to macroeconomics and monetary theory, governments, in order to reduce the debt-to-GDP ratios, need to either run fiscal surpluses large enough to repay the debt or raise nominal GDP growth. The growth of this ratio is given by an equation which describes the relationship between a country's primary balance, the interest rate it pays on debt and the growth rate of nominal GDP. Country's primary balance or the fiscal balance normally excludes the interest payment, and the growth rate of nominal GDP depends on the inflation rate and real GDP growth of rate. Therefore, the government debt-to-GDP ratio is given as,

$$D_t = \left(\left[\frac{1+i_t}{1+g_t} \right] D_{t-1} \right) - \mathrm{Pr}im_t \qquad (5.12)$$

where *Dt* is the projected government debt-to-GDP ratio for the next period, *it* is the interest rate on a government bond, *g* is the nominal GDP growth forecast, *Dt-1* is the current government debt-to-GDP ratio, and *Primt* is the primary balance. The equation above emphasizes the role of interest rates in managing the government debt. Fortunately, since the start of the 2008 financial crisis, the governments around the world have profited from very low-interest rates, as never seen before.

Hence, even if the government debt has grown relatively, interest payments have gone down which has given governments a powerful tool to scoop up cheap capital. For example, in March 2015 a small country like Slovenia sold €1-billion of 20-year debt to investors at a low yield of around 1.6 percent. Another country in the EU, Bulgaria, issued Eurobonds with a yield of 2.3 percent for 7-year maturity and 3.4 percent for 20 years. Even Armenia, another small country with low-bond rating by international rating agencies was able to issue 10-year U.S. dollar bonds with a yield of just 8 percent.

The cheap capital situation will be reversed if interest rates begin to rise quickly possibly accelerating the growth of government debt, which suggests that is necessary to take steps to reduce debt before this happens. Reducing government debt ratios will involve at least four possible paths: 1) make fiscal adjustments to reduce fiscal deficits, 2) increase GDP growth through productivity improvements, 3) raise inflation targets and 4) restructure sovereign debt (Stiglitz J, 2014).

The first path which considers making fiscal adjustments to repay debt requires the government to maintain significant fiscal surpluses to cover debt service for long periods of time. The required fiscal surpluses became very different and hard to achieve especially after the 2008 financial crisis. For example, a country moving from a fiscal deficit of 2.5 percent of GDP to a surplus of at least 2 percent of GDP would require a shift of 4.5 percent of GDP. This achievement would require tough choices about taxes and spending. It will eventually raise taxes and cut government spending to reduce the current fiscal deficit or simply keep the government debt ratios to more sustainable levels. Even if the level of fiscal contraction is achieved, it may have created unwanted consequences of slowing GDP growth, making the reduction in government debt ratios much harder to achieve. Other options to achieve fiscal adjustments could be the sale of public sector assets to generate cash or the partial or full privatization of state-owned companies.

The second path of reducing government debt ratios is the increase of real GDP growth through productivity improvements. Countries need to generate enough growth to begin reducing government debt ratios, especially in the most indebted nations where growth is required at higher levels than normally planned. For example, for countries like Italy, Spain, Portugal, Ireland, Greece, etc., the GDP has to grow by two percentage points faster than the projected growth of 1-2 percent to reach at least growth rates of 2.5-4.0 percent a year to start seeing a reduction on government debt ratio.

Meanwhile, an indebted advanced country like Japan (government debt was about 234 percent in 2014) based on classic monetary theory needs at least 3 percent growth per year to reduce its debt. In reality, such growth is almost unbearable to achieve given the still weak economy of the advanced countries after the 2008 financial crisis. Some of the heavy indebted countries have ageing populations that will drag the GDP down given the slow growth of the labor force. On the other hand, high rates of unemployment among the long-term employees in countries such as Greece, Spain, Portugal and Italy have reduced but not eliminated the potential GDP growth rates. The delayed structural reforms is another setback on productivity gain which will affect the GDP growth.

The third path of raising inflation to boost nominal GDP growth is considered by market analysts and economists as another way to increase nominal GDP growth which is part of the denominator of equation 5.12, to reduce debt ratio. In theory, this path is available only for advanced countries where debt is held in the local currency which are considered strong currencies. But in practice, this path could be applied to any advanced or developing economy as far as the local currency is widely used by the local population (instead of foreign currency) as a way of payment for goods and services. If the government debt is held in local currency, a rising inflation will reduce the amount government has to pay back to investors. So far, in recent years the inflation has remained at low levels despite the fact that interest rates were at a record low and the use of unconventional monetary policies such as quantitative easing. The injection of a large amount of liquidity in the system through quantitative easing programs in some countries did not translate into inflation, as it was hoped because the demand was depressed and rational people decided to save rather than go for spending especially on the aftermath of the disastrous 2008 financial crisis.

The forth path to reduce government debt ratios consists of restructuring the sovereign debt. Many researchers in sovereign debt field think that restructuring sovereign debt is hard and painful as much as doing nothing to restructure it, which could be even more painful. In fact, non-restructuring sovereign debt or doing nothing about it could result in sovereign default. Sovereign default is considered as improbable for many economies in recent years, however, a variety of debt restructuring has occurred over the past years after the 2008 financial crisis, in some cases with unilateral default as the extreme form. As mentioned in chapter 3 there was a lot of monetary crisis that happened in the 1990s and early 2000s in several countries in Asia, Europe and Latin America. From the exchange mechanism (ERM) crisis in Europe during the 1992-93 period to the Mexican crisis in 1994, Turkish crisis in 1994, Russia crisis in 1998, and the South-Asian crisis in 1997-1998 moved again back to Latin America (Brazil) crisis in 1998-1999, and the Argentina crisis in 2001-2002. In the recent years, another massive sovereign debt restructuring was done in 2012 in Greece (and later in 2015), which involved write-downs of bonds held by private sector creditors but not public sector bonds.

We know that government debt restructuring comes with major costs and if a unilateral default has occurred, it has generated financial crisis and consequently deep recession, therefore a default is considered a last resort. Given the high level of government debt in recent years, the absence of political will to continue with austerity in many countries, and the incapability to recover from the crisis and restart a path of growth, some countries may have no options but to think of new tools of restructuring sovereign debt.

A staff report study published by IMF in 2014 suggests a number of reforms to enable sovereign debt restructuring to progress more efficiently (IMF staff report, 2014, 1-48). The International Monetary Fund report recognizes contractual reforms intended to address collective action problems through CAC (Collective Agreement Clauses) in those countries that are facing a sovereign debt restructuring. Given that all decision related to contractual provisions are made by the sovereign issuer and its creditors, it is the IMF's main role to smooth agreement on the design and use of the provisions. The IMF in the past years has contributed and encouraged the use of Collective Agreement Clauses (CAC) and concentrated on legal enforcement of contractual provisions in international sovereign bonds governed by the laws of New York and England, which represent roughly 48 percent and 40 percent respectively of the outstanding stock of international sovereign bonds.

Some Conclusions about Unconventional Monetary Policies

The low-interest rates combined with simulative QE introduced in some economies during the global financial crisis of 2008 created a buffer against a far worse outcome. Despite the years of heavy quantitative easing (QE) and ultra-low interest rates, the global economy has not been able to reach full capacity steady growth. The institution of large-scale assets purchases managed by central banks has directed the focus towards the quantity of money as well as the price of money.

The main idea of infusing more money into the economy was to increase spending and help the MPC to bring inflation back to target (around 2%) in the medium and long term, so the economies can grow again. The stimulus plans through QEs were designed to occur through a number of channels, and the responses of those who receive the additional money balances will be the key to success and effectiveness. In fact, the more the households and organizations use the new money to buy goods, services, equipment and assets the more will increase spending. In addition, if the banks use their superfluous reserves to expand their lending, the impact on the economy could be even stronger.

But there is still a considerable ambiguity about the strength and timing of the QE effects.

The first thing is that if the QE has been effective in boosting the economy and starting a growth path, the recovery still remains brittle and has not completely solved the problem of a slow economy after a financial crisis, despite it has helped to mitigate the recession partially. It suggests increasing the scale of QE so it can have a higher macroeconomic effect in the future, even though there is not too much proof of whether QE could be facing diminishing returns.

The second thing or concern is that what might be the cost of the unconventional monetary policy and if the central bank purchases of government bonds will help reduce the unsustainable levels of government debt in those countries where QE policy has been applied. Or if a high level of bank reserves could reduce interbank lending and knock the interbank interest rate, managed by the central bank, out of conventional monetary policy.

There is also vagueness over the magnitude and duration of the effect and specific channel through which QE works, despite this could be seen as predictable given the short historical period available and the severe nature of the recession which makes QE very challenging. Although the unconventional monetary policy embedded in QE has been found to work even though its positive effects have not been sufficient to compensate the negative forces of a banking sector crisis and economic downturn. This implies that the role of central bank and financial regulators should be focused on improving the framework of the financial and banking system, refining the loan lending process to avoid large-scale defaults, so that the unconventional monetary policy (QE) does not need to be involved so deeply in the future to boost the spending and restore economic growth.

Chapter 6

Approaches to New Exchange Rate Theories

Introduction

There is no doubt that in the global market economy the exchange rates are an important factor that affects the trade of goods, services and capitals. The economics of exchange rates is an important field of economics because it helps understand the determinants of exchange rates and the capability to accurately predict the future exchange rates.

Forecasting future exchange rates helps investment and hedging decisions for investment especially for those who hold international portfolios. It also helps estimate the country's foreign reserves and foreign denominated debt payment. Forecasting exchange rates help evaluate the import and export prices. The economics of exchange rates have been surrounded by some theoretical dilemmas, such as the difficulties to find a link between exchange rates and macroeconomic variables like output and inflation. It has been found little evidence that the determinants of exchange rates, such as monetary policy and determinants of real income and inflation can explain the exchange rate movements in the short and long term.

The uncovered interest parity (UIP) condition also has not been able to predict the exchange rates trend. The UIP condition suggests that the forward exchange rate is an unbiased forecaster of future spot rates. The currencies that have high-interest rates tend to appreciate which means that they convey trade strategies to the markets and tend to yield positive returns on average ensuing "forward premium puzzle". The exchange rate mechanism by its nature is speculative. The forex markets are, most of the time speculative markets, differently from rational expectations theories and the concept of efficient markets.

The overall value of tradable goods, capital values and their expected returns depend on the exchange rates. The foreign exchange markets on which exchange rates are established are not quite stable and often appear mysterious and unpredictable. Generally speaking, there is no stable equilibrium and most of the times is hard to understand and determine the current exchange rate.

Exchange rate theory is in a continues evolution mode. However, the prevalent opinion among economists and what is taught in textbooks still rest on the traditions of purchasing power parity theory, monetary exchange rate theory, and the theories of covered and uncovered interest parties. All the new theories or recent empirical studies in the exchange rate are considered as deviations from the standard theories as they try to interpret exogenous shocks that are unpredictable. The empirical studies have shown that observed shocks are not normally distributed, and the fundamental factors play a small role in exchange rate determination. On the other side, the expectations of foreign exchange rate dealers are indicated as significant but cannot be measured, and empirical evidence can do little to measure them. It implies that the irrational expectations prevail in the short run and the rational expectations prevail in the long run which leads to more balanced fundamentals-based exchange rates that are normally captured by standard exchange rate theories.

Exchange rates are not predictable as they depend on a lot of factors such as the choice of predictor, forecast horizon, sample period, model and forecast evaluation method. Exchange rate fluctuations are tough to predict when we use only economic models, however by using a 'random walk' there is a much higher probability of forecasting exchange rates. This chapter will take into consideration the recent approaches to some of the new exchange theories.

Some Critiques on the Exchange Rate Models

After the collapse of the Bretton Woods system in 1973, there was an explosion of a vast pool of theories and economic models that were trying to explain the exchange rate fluctuations. The economic literature at that time was full of models devoted to clarifying the implications of the exchange rate oscillations in the open economies. Two young economists working at IMF, Meese and Rogoff, in 1983 published a study that aimed to determine which of the existent exchange rate models were able to generate the best forecast. Unfortunately, all the models tested in the study were shown to perform poorly in out-of-sample empirical studies. The tested exchange rate models could not outperform the simple assumption that today's spot price is a predictor of tomorrow's spot price.

Most of the models were unsound or partial because foreign exchange markets have been modeled as stand-alone processes rather than being designed as part of the complete self-sustained economic system. These models were incorrect because they have used, in a neoclassical context, short-term forecasting abilities that were fundamentally long-term processes. Economists started studying and testing currency market characteristics and different case scenarios that were close to the reality of exchange rates rather than complete models of foreign exchange rate determination. In addition, the assumption of rationality and efficiency of the exchange rate models using short-run forecasting tool were questioned.

The undeniable results found by Meese-Rogoff (1983, 1988) were confirmed by Rossi (2013) that for at least one to two years exchange rates forecast seem no better than a random walk. The purchase power parities determine exchange rates in the long-run and hence the equilibrium on the foreign exchange markets, but as we know the long-run is not well defined, and the switch from short term to long term is not explained. The decades that followed the early results found by Meese and Rogoff (1983) helped develop a lot of testing in the incoming years involving exchange market expectations. The most popular tests in foreign exchange markets were those devoted to rationality and efficiency of spot currency data. The rational expectations are tested by using spot currency data and a set of currency forecast. For example, the rational expectation can be tested using the following equation,

$$FX_{t+n} = \beta + \delta E_t(FX)_{t+n} + \varepsilon_{t+n} \qquad (6.1)$$

where *FXt+n* is the spot price of foreign currency in period *t+n*, *E(FX)t+n* is the forecast in period t of the spot rate for period *t+n*, and ε is a random error term used in the calculation of rational expectation. The forecast of the spot price of foreign currency is unbiased if $\beta = 0$ and $\delta = 1$. The above test of market participants' rational expectation process can be extended by expressing it using $\varepsilon t+n$ from equation (6.1),

$$\varepsilon_{t+n} = \alpha + \lambda I_t + \psi_{t+n} \qquad (6.2)$$

where *It* is the information available in time t, and $\psi t+n$ is the random error term. Equation (6.2) implies that if the market is efficient, there should be no connection between the forecast error term given by $\psi t+n$ and the information available at the time period taken into consideration. This will bring $\alpha = \lambda = 0$. The number of tests computed for rational expectations has shown evidence that short-term forecasts are unreliable and biased, which means that markets are inefficient. The agents' prediction regarding the spot price of foreign currency holds persistent errors that can be eliminated or reduced if they use the available information. The empirical evidence is limited which means that rational expectations prevail in the long-term which can lead to balanced and fundamentals-based exchange rates.

Chartists vs. Fundamentalists

In order to simply the way in which agents in the market create expectations on future exchange rate movements, we take into considerations an approach that defines two types of economic agents that use simple forecasting rules to form expectations about exchange rate movements.

The so-called chartist-fundamentalist models of exchange rates for different types of agents were introduced by Frankel and Froot (1987). The fundamentalist agents or the traders of the first type will normally trade in a way that will put pressure on the exchange rate to return to the exogenously fundamental rates. The fundamentalist agents forecast currency prices using the exchange rate models. The chartist agents or the traders of the second type are those that forecast currency prices by relying exclusively on autoregressive technical trading rules. A chartist principally looks for well-known patterns in securities so as to trade them more profitably. Chartists can operate their trade in all markets where financial instruments are normally traded such as -equities, currencies, commodities and bonds. Chartists are often recognized as technical analysts. For chartists, the price movements in a stock are not random but can be projected through a study of past trends and other more complex technical analysis. There is also a third type of agents called, portfolio managers, who buy and sell foreign assets based on the combination of the expectations of both chartists and fundamentals.

The fundamental analysis basically helps to decide which stock to buy or sell meanwhile the deep use of technical analysis is to decide when is the right time to buy or sell a stock. The chartist agents can also be considered as being trend-following speculators who try to raise the price up after an initial price increase and try to push it down right after there is an initial price decrease. The trend-following behavior used by chartists may also cause financial bubbles as the agents rely on the chart and technical analysis. Based on the Frankel-Froot (1987) model, the process that determines exchange rates are assumed to be as,

$$FX_t = c\Delta FX_{t+1} + f_t \tag{6.3}$$

where FXt is the spot exchange rate, $\Delta FXt+1$ is the rate of depreciation that portfolio managers expect to happen, and ft indicates other current determinants that represent fundamentals that are supposed to drive the currency prices.

The fundamentalist agents' expectations can be expressed as,

$$fdFX_t = -\mu(FX_{t-1} - eFX^*) \tag{6.4}$$

where $fdFXt$ is the fundamentalist agent's expected exchange rate at time t, μ is a parameter that indicates the speed of convergence of fundamental exchange rate, $FXt\text{-}1$ is the usual exchange rate at time $t\text{-}1$ and eFX' is the exogenously determined fundamental exchange rate, which means the rate towards which the fundamentalists expect the exchange rate should converge.

Meanwhile, the chartist's exchange rate expectations are expressed by the following equation,

$$cdFX_t = \beta dFX_{t-1} \qquad (6.5)$$

where cdFXt is the chartist trader's expected exchange rate at time t, β is a parameter managing the scale of the autoregressive process, and dFXt-1 is the exchange rate at time t-1. As it normally happens in the exchange currency market, it is assumed that market expectations about future rate movements are basically a weighted average of both types of traders, chartists and fundamentalists, who make up the speculative segment of the foreign exchange market.

The combined expectations of chartists and fundamentalists that make up the market expectations of future exchange rate movements are given by the following equation,

$$dFX_t = w_c cdFX_t + w_f fdFX_t \qquad (6.6)$$

or combining equations (6.4) and (6.5), we can have equation (6.6) rewritten as follows,

$$dFX_t = w_c \beta dFX_{t-1} - w_f \mu (FX_{t-1} - eFX') \qquad (6.7)$$

where $dFXt$ is the market's expected change of exchange rate at time t, wc is a proportion chartist in the speculative segment, and wf indicates the proportion of fundamentalists in the speculative segment of the foreign exchange market. Equation (6.7) specifies that chartists and fundamentalists are not expecting their expectations in foreign exchange market to be far away from each-other. In fact, if the exchange rate is moving downwards/ upwards but is above/below the fundamental rate, both chartists and fundamentalists traders, are expecting the exchange rate to decrease/increase. Assuming also, that if the exchange rate is moving upwards/downwards and above/below the fundamental rate, the market expectations of future exchange rate movements will depend on the size of last upward/downward move on the difference of the exchange rate value from the fundamental value, for a given set of β, μ, wc and wf parameters. The exchange rate value may move further from its fundamental value which will increase the fundamentalist's expectation relative to that of the foreign exchange market until the movement in exchange rate reverses its course. Any movement of exchange rates caused by the exchange rate market that goes above the fundamental rate driven by chartists will continue upward until the fundamentalists' belief will start putting downward pressure on the market expected to get the exchange rate back to the level of fundamental rate.

Chartists normally try to dominate the market with their trend-following behavior, which in return generates its own kind of risk for the other type of traders, fundamentalists. When in time, the exchange rate misalignment becomes more and more clear, the relative desirability of fundamentalism increases and more market participants follow fundamentals. This process limits the power of chartism and reduces the deviation of exchange rates from their fundamental equilibrium rate and at the same time motivates foreign exchange interventions (Beine, De Grauwe, and Grimaldi, 2009). There is a common principal often assumed by chartist-fundamentalist models that chartists base their forecasts on prevailing market trends by following these trends. Despite this, there is a number of ways to build a technical trading rule so that the focus on trend-following strategies is less than obvious.

An important component of chartist-fundamentalist models in foreign exchange is the dynamics between groups. As suggested by Brock and Hommes model (1998) there is a switching mechanism where agents alter their strategy when they realize an alternative strategy has performed better than their original one. In the economics of exchange rate modeling, all traders know both technical and fundamental trading rules and choose the one that is based on the expected future performance rather than the ex-post performance. Based on this logic the agents tend to move from chartist to fundamental strategies when the deviation between fundamental value and exchange rate becomes large. The trend for chartists is to shift positions more recurrently than fundamentalists between appreciation and devaluation expectations, when they show instability behavior, as they try to estimate alternative strategies on the basis of their ex-post profitability.

Most of the studies on assessing chartists' performance have been focused on analyzing the simulated trading rules without attempting to calculate the real-world returns of the trading in the exchange rate markets. An interesting study conducted by Dick and Menkhoff in 2012 at the Centre for European Economic Research (ZEW) in Mannheim, Germany consists on a real financial market survey among several hundred professional forecasters working in foreign exchange market about their individual US-dollar/Euro expectations. The study consisted of the information received from professional forecasters about their self-assessment of the use of charts and fundamentals on forecasting the exchange rate. The survey was started on January 1999 and concluded on September 2011 and the sample involved about 100 professional forecasters in Germany and Austria which provided a panel of more than 30 000 observations covering a period of 153 months. The exchange rate forecasters were characterized in three main categories: chartists, fundamentalists and others called intermediaries.

By analyzing the large data of observations, Dick and Menkhoff (2012) were able to make use of three behaviors: the forecasting behavior, forecasting dynamics and forecasting performance for chartists and fundamentalists. Regarding forecasting behavior, they found that chartists as in an earlier model (Menkhoff and Taylor 2007) tend to follow tendencies more regularly than fundamentalists. Regarding the second behavior - the forecasting dynamics - chartists tend to change the direction of their exchange forecast more often than fundamentalists also based on a recurrent assumption in heterogeneous agents' models such as the model of Farmer and Joshi 2002. The forecasting dynamics is based on forecasting tools subjective to recent experiences of the forecasters. If the exchange rates follow some trends, chartists and fundamentalists quickly move towards chartism. Meanwhile, when the exchange rate moves away from the long-term average of the purchase power parity chartists and fundamentalists move away from chartism.

Regarding the third behavior - forecasting performance - chartists will stay in the competitive foreign exchange markets if they perform well, otherwise, they will lose their ex-post profitability.

Chartists and fundamentalists have different exchange rate expectations with chartists following the trend while fundamentalists considering main exchange rate models. Chartists lean towards changing their expectations more frequently in the short-run creating a certain degree of instability, but in the long-run, both chartists and fundamentalists have common changes in expectations when the exchange rates depart substantially from the market average. Chartists' exchange rate expectations, in general, follow the market average, and at this point, their expectations are as good as fundamentalists', however, in the short-run, the chartists perform better than fundamentalists.

There are also forecasting errors computed by chartists and fundamentalists. At least two main errors where forecasters can be mistaken: i) the forecasters make a small error when they predict an unchanged variable when the result is an increase; ii) the forecasters make a big error when they predict a decline when the outcome is an increase. These errors can be taken into considerations by computing absolute forecast errors given as |E|i, t+n=|Xi,t,t+n – Xt,t+n| and the values taken on are 2 for a severe error, 1 for a small error and 0 for a correct prediction by chartists and fundamentalists. The table below based on the empirical research of Dick and Menkhoff (2012) indicates the average absolute forecast errors made by individual forecasters for the group of chartists, intermediates and fundamentalists on different horizons (1, 2, 3 or more months).

Average absolute forecast error	1 month	2 months	3 months	6 months	12 months	24 months	36 months
Fundamentalists	0.92	0.90	0.88	0.81	0.83	0.70	0.67
Intermediates	0.88	0.87	0.86	0.84	0.83	0.74	0.71
Chartists	0.87	0.86	0.86	0.82	0.81	0.75	0.71
t-values fund. vs. chart.	**2.10	1.46	0.60	0.10	0.55	1.12	1.00

Table 6.1 Average absolute forecast errors by groups. *Source.* Dick and Menkhoff (2012), p. 45.

The table shows that in short horizons, such a 1, 2, 3, 6, months there are differences in the value of errors between chartists and fundamentalists. The last row in the table presents the results of t-statistics, with *Ho* assuming equal means between chartists and fundamentalists (with *** 1%, **5%, * 10% significance level). In fact, fundamentalists make more errors in short horizons (in 1 month, 0.92 vs. 0.87 and t-value = ** 2.1 as severe error) compared to chartists, but on longer horizons (such as 6 months, 0.81 vs. 0.82 and t-value =0.10 as a very small error) there are no substantial differences between chartists and fundamentalists when the forecasts are read with respect to their predictability.

Generally speaking, chartists are likewise good forecasters as fundamentalists. However, on forecasting horizons, chartists perform fairly better on short horizons meanwhile fundamentalists perform relatively well on longer horizons. Shifting between chartists and fundamentalists is considered mainly an opportunistic way to switch the weight the forecasters give to exchange rate expectations, although the general preferences for chartists or fundamentalists are quite steady over time as both forecaster groups are profitable in long-run.

The New Open Economy Macroeconomic Models

The new open economy macroeconomic models (NOEM) are a class of models that emphasizes on optimizing the behavior of agents combined with the behavior of producers who set their own prices one period in advance in their own currency. The producers operate in a monopolistic regime where prices exceed the marginal cost and wherein the short-run the producers are able to supply the needed output for increased demand. Obstfeld and Rogoff had first developed the NOEM approach in 1995 when they used a two-country redux exchange rate model, which was essentially an alternative version of the Mundell-Fleming-Dournbusch model where optimizing individuals using prices preset operate in an imperfectly competitive market.

The two-country model of the redux model indicates that each country has a continuum of consumer-producer that produces different goods in the domestic market and for the foreign market. The Obstfeld-Rogoff base-line model also assumes that the agents operate as monopolists by charging a price above the marginal cost. This means that the output produced is less than the socially optimum level and hence an expansionary monetary policy can be used to increase output and employment.

There are different variants of the base-line NOEM models, in which exporter's invoice is in the currency of the importer's currency at the local currency pricing rather than using their domestic currency to invoice their products. In few words, the pricing policy is to use the prices of the importer's (buyers) currency, which is referred as local currency pricing (LCP) with sticky prices in the short run.

Two economists in the nineties, Betts and Devereux (1996) have analyzed the implications of the Pricing-to-Market (PTM) for real exchange rate variability using a different variant of the NOEM model. In this model, each of the *m* goods is assumed to be sold solely by price-setting firms. Each firm operate by using a standard linear production technology given as,

$$Y(x) = AL(x) \tag{6.8}$$

where Y(x) is the total output of the firm taken into consideration, L(x) is the employment, and A is a constant. For firms working under Price-to-market (PTM) total output is shared between output sold in the domestic market, d(x), and output exported and sold abroad, m(x). The firms operating under PTM choose domestic price p(x) and foreign currency price f(x) to maximize the profit function,

$$\pi(x) = p(x)d(x) + sf(x)m(x) - (W / A)(d(x) + m(x) \tag{6.9}$$

where firms have a constant-elasticity demand curve for the output sold to the market as

$$c(x) = \left[\frac{h(x)}{P}\right]^{\omega} C \tag{6.10}$$

where c(x) is consumption and h(x) is equal to domestic currency price p(x) or foreign currency price f(x). The markup price for both domestic currency market and foreign currency market is given as,

$$p(x) = sf(x) = \frac{\omega}{\omega - 1}\frac{W}{A} \quad (6.11)$$

where *s* is the exchange rate and *(ω/ω-1)* is the markup price in the equation above. Given that elasticities of demand are the same in both domestic and foreign markets, the law-of-one-price (LOOP) and purchase price parity (PPP) must hold for all the price-to-market goods (MacDonald R., 2007, ch.11). Nevertheless, the determination of price-to-market can influence the set of prices if they are set one period in advance. The domestic and foreign price indices, *P'* and *P"*, assumed the prices stays sticky are given as,

$$P' = (1\text{-}m)(1\text{-}h)s' \quad (6.12)$$

$$P'' = \text{-}m(1\text{-}v)s' \quad (6.13)$$

The reaction of aggregate price indices to exchange rate fluctuations, when prices are sticky, is lower or higher depending on the share of goods, *m*, subject to price-to-market. Using the money balances (M'-M") in the utility function combined with log-linear money demand equations, we obtain the long-run exchange rate relationship given as,

$$S' = (1 - h) = M'\text{–}M'\,' - \frac{1}{\varepsilon}(C'\text{–}C'\,') \quad (6.14)$$

where *1/ε* is the consumption elasticity of money demand and *h* determines the scale of deviations from PPP. The exchange rate relationship may be derived as,

$$s' = \frac{C'\text{–}C'\,'}{(1 - h)(\omega - 1) + h} \quad (6.15)$$

The equation of the exchange rate above shows that a depreciation or appreciation of the exchange rate allows the domestic consumption to be above or below foreign consumption, having no effect on relative prices which increases/decreases the earnings of the domestic firms using domestic currency and reduces/increases the earnings of the foreign firms using foreign currency. The depreciation of domestic currency reallocates the income distribution by allowing the home country to consume more compared to its trading partner. Combining equations (6.14) and (6.15), we get a new form of exchange rate relationship as follows,

$$s' = \frac{(M'-M^{*}{}')}{(1 - h)(\varepsilon + \omega - 1) + h} \qquad (6.16)$$

Equation (6.16) indicates that an increase in h will raise the response of the exchange rate when

$\varepsilon > \omega$-1. And for the condition, ω >1, we have that PTM will increase the instability of exchange rate as long as the consumption elasticity of demand, given as ε, will not rise too high. On the other side, when consumption elasticity of demand is below one (unity) in the presence of PTM, the exchange rate will increase its volatility quickly eventually generating an exchange rate overshooting.

The study of Bergin and Feenstra (2001) focus likewise on analyzing the price-to-market in the context of NOEM model. Differently, from Betts and Devereux (1996), they introduce intermediate goods into production process and firms have the capability to set prices by themselves any time rather than the standard one-period in advance assumption. There is a high degree of perseverance and unpredictability regarding the real exchange rate data. Bergin and Feenstra (2001) examine a class of preferences that are trans-login which show the property that the elasticity of demand is not constant but is essential for generating pricing-to-market (PTM) behavior in price-setting firms and facilitating staggered contracts to generate endogenous persistence.

Bergin (2004) has tested the NOEM models by using a two-country version of NOEM, where the two countries are the US versus a pool of other G7 countries. The variables used in the two country model are the exchange rate, current account, output growth, inflation and interest rate deviations, whereas the data used covers a period from 1973 first quarter to 2000, fourth quarter. The results of this research show that the forecast for the exchange rate and the current account are capable of beating a random walk but not the predictions from a standard VAR model (Vector Auto-regression). VAR is an econometric model used to identify the linear interdependencies among multivariate time series. Each variable in the structure of a VAR model is a linear function of past lags of itself and past lags of the other variables). Bergin (2004) also finds out that studying the local currency pricing will help explain the current exchange rate movements in the data set taken into consideration and that the elasticity of substitution between domestic and foreign goods is close to unity (one) as often assumed in theoretical NOEM models.

The persistence of real exchange rate can increase the volatility of the exchange rate which leads to exchange rate overshooting. Even when monetary shocks have persistent effects on real exchange rates the firms are hesitant to change the prices of their goods if other firms keep their prices fixed to avoid losing market share. In addition, their total marginal cost does not changes or adopts quickly enough to real exchange rates fluctuations given the price of intermediate goods fixed. The variable of markup price over marginal cost deviates persistently from the Law-of-one-price (LOOP) which produces a substantial accumulation of net foreign assets during adjustment period that is affected by the permanent impact of real exchange rate volatility.

It has been recognized by several studies that there is a significant correlation between net foreign assets and the real exchange rates of the industrialized countries. Lane (2001) for example, has proved these findings in his research that even temporary disturbances or fluctuations can have persistent effects because current account imbalances can modify net foreign assets which can generate enduring real effects.

Purchase Power Parity and Exchange Rates

Purchase power parity (PPP) is one of the most important concepts in international finance as it has been widely used to measure the equilibrium values of different currencies. The PPP proposition states that national price levels should equal when expressed in a common currency. A large number of studies have tried to examine the validity of PPP empirically over a long-period by testing if nominal exchange rates and relatives prices in different countries move together in the same direction or if exchange rate tends to return to a steady level over time. If the nominal exchange rate move towards a stable equilibrium level over time than the real exchange rate may well be defined as the nominal exchange rate adjusted for relative national price levels (Sarno 2008).

Estimates of PPP are regularly used to determine the incorrect arrangement of the nominal exchange rate and the appreciate policy response, the setting of exchange rate parities and the international comparison of national income levels. Sometimes the literature mentions the difficulties faced to find strong evidence in favor of PPP as the " PPP puzzle" (Rogoff 1996) which distresses the reconciliation of the high short-term volatility of the real exchange rate with the slow mean reversion speed of the real exchange rate. In fact, if PPP does not hold it will be regarded as an abnormality given that economists lean towards believing that the PPP must guide the long-run relationship between exchange rates and relative prices. If real exchange rate adjustment tends towards the PPP, then the equilibrium is determined by arbitrage in international goods markets where there is a need to use the applicable price index in order to implement PPP correctly.

Sarno and Valente (2006) in the empirical study use a long-run data of the five most industrialized countries across different exchange regimes from gold standard, to the Bretton Woods period and then to the floating regime since 1970s in an attempt to find any pattern of deviations that is stable over time at the extension of the full sample considered. Their results support the long-run PPP for each of the major exchange rates examined. Under fixed exchange rate regimes such as gold standard or Bretton Woods, relative prices adjust to restore deviations from long-run equilibrium, while under flexible exchange rate regimes the nominal exchange rates endure most of the burden of adjustment.

The Purchase Power Parity (PPP) can be defined as a relationship between price indices such as consumer price index (CPI) or producer price index (PPI) on one side and the exchange rate on the other side. A simple description of the PPP is that the common currency price of an identical bundle of goods is given in log levels as,

$$h_t = p_t - p_t^{*} \quad (6.17)$$

where *Log h* is the nominal exchange rate expressed in units of domestic currency *pt*, per foreign currency *pt'*, and *p* is the log price level that corresponds to a bundle of goods. There is a direct relationship between the deviation from PPP and the real exchange rate which can be expressed as

$$d_t = h_t - p_t + p_t^{*} \quad (6.18)$$

where *dt* measures in home units the domestic basket of goods required to purchase a single basket of foreign goods. In terms of PPP, we can state that if relative PPP holds then the (log) real exchange rate should be constant, and if absolute PPP holds then the (log) real exchange rate should be zero. Considering price indexes rather than prices of bundles of goods we can decompose the general price index into tradable and non-tradable goods. Therefore, the general price index can be written as,

$$p_t = \beta p_t^N + (1 - \beta) p_t^T \quad (6.19)$$

where N indicates the non-tradables and T tradables and β is a constant. The real exchange rate can be expressed in terms of tradables and non-tradables as,

$$d_t = d_t^T + \beta(p_t^N - p_t^T) \tag{6.20}$$

where $d_t^T = h_t - p_t^T + p_t^{T'}$. Based on equation (6.20) we have that the real exchange rate diverges from zero if tradables prices differ or if the relative price of non-tradables versus tradables differs across countries taken into consideration.

The definition of Law-of-One-Price (LOP) is that identical goods should sell for the same price across differential international locations once the domestic prices are converted into a common currency. The LOP compares identical or similar products or services sold in two different countries but with a different origin of production and dissimilar pricing currency for which prices should be very close after taking into considerations transaction costs because of competition in the international goods markets. The LOP in its absolute version, ignoring the transaction costs can be written as,

$$P_{i,t} = H_t P'_{i,t} \tag{6.21}$$

where *Pi,t* indicates the price of good *i* in terms of the home currency at time *t*, and *P'i,t* is the price of good *i* in terms of the foreign currency at time t. and *Ht* is the nominal exchange rate expressed at the home price of the foreign currency at time *t*. The absolute value of PPP can be obtained if we add up all the traded goods in each country and is given as,

$$\sum_{i=1}^{N} \alpha_i P_{i,t} = H_t \sum_{i=1}^{N} \alpha_i P'_{i,t} \tag{6.22}$$

where the weight of the traded goods satisfies. In the same way, if we consider the price indices using the geometric index, then the weighted sum using logarithms takes the form as,

$$\sum_{i=1}^{N} \lambda_i p_{i,t} = h_t + \sum_{i=1}^{N} \lambda_i p'_{i,t} \tag{6.23}$$

where the geometric weights λi, satisfies the sum, $\sum_{i=1}^{N} \lambda_i = 1$. It is often assumed that PPP should hold roughly using the price indices of each country, so the geometric index from equation (6.23) can be rearranged as,

$$\sum_{i=1}^{N} \lambda_i p_{i,t} = h_t + \sum_{i=1}^{N} \lambda'_i p'_{i,t} + \sum_{i=1}^{N} (\lambda_i - \lambda'_i) p'_{i,t} \tag{6.24}$$

where $\lambda' I$ indicates the weights in the foreign price index. Equation (6.24) can also be arranged in a shorter form as,

$$\sum_{i=1}^{N} \lambda_i p_{i,t} = h_t + \sum_{i=1}^{N} \lambda'_{i=1} p'_{i,t} + \mu_t \qquad (6.25)$$

where μt represents disparity between the national price indices from PPP even when LOP is valid for single goods. If geometric price indices are homogeneous of degree one, then any differences in weights between different countries will not be so important because price changes will impact all goods and services by the same proportion. For example, if a z percent increase in the prices of the foreign country leads to a z percent increase in the foreign price level, then the right side of equation (6.25) will be increased by z and the change in term μt will be zero. Therefore, if the prices are constant, then a z percent appreciation of the domestic currency is needed to re-establish equilibrium.

PPP also has its own weaknesses related to the difficulties to find a comparable basket of goods to measure the purchasing power in different countries. In fact, if two countries trade different baskets of goods it is not rational to use the LOP to build PPP as it will be impossible to arrive precisely at the same price level by aggregating baskets of different goods. In addition, people in different countries consume a different basket of goods and the purchasing patterns and goods and services available are different in each country.

However, the arguments to support the notions of LOP and PPP continue to be useful as they help in calculating the approximations to long-run exchange rate behaviour. Regarding the assumption of identical goods, it is apparent that the theoretical concept of identical goods is not very representative when thinking about the LOP in practice and that it is more logical to think about similar goods. Similar goods are those goods that serve to satisfy the same specific consumer needs. The specific consumption needs consists of an "intrinsic price" which is embedded in the wholesale and consumer price of that particular good in international markets.

The intrinsic price is theoretically the one that would be used to determine the LOP and PPP, but in reality, it is not observable. The total price instead will include a number of factors such as the quality, size, etc., which differs among goods and in different export markets any good will have different prices because of the transactions and transport costs, tariffs, taxes, etc.

Regarding the relationship between nominal exchange rate and PPP, it is a common ground among economists that nominal exchange rate moves in the short-run in reaction to a large number of factors, some of which are unrelated to economic fundamentals, but in the long-run, there appears to converge towards PPP. This suggests that PPP is a reasonable assumption for long-horizon forecasting of the real exchange rate. Deviations from the LOP are transitory, and hence the LOP holds in the long-run among a broad range of tradable goods and currencies.

A number authors, such as Sarno, Taylor and Chowdhury (2004), Blavy and Juvenal (2009), have delivered evidence of nonlinear reversion towards the LOP in a large number of sectorial exchange rate after the Bretton Woods period, and evidence of stickiness and heterogeneity across goods and currencies. Based on the empirical evidence the LOP is a good approximation of the link between exchange rates and goods prices across countries.

There is also clear support of the PPP as a valid international parity condition. If PPP holds for a basket of tradable goods, long-term returns from diversified portfolios are mostly unaffected by exchange rate risk. This means that any decision to invest in currency markets should be directed by the motivation to obtain a risk premium that is different from that generated by equities or bonds. There is normally a risk premium associated with foreign exchange due to the fact that medium-high-interest currencies tend to appreciate over time strong enough to offset interest rate differentials.

Behavioral Finance and Exchange Rates

Behavioral finance has its starting point on criticizing the assumption of rational, consisting of agents maximizing their profit or utility conducted by rational expectations that lead to efficient markets. The behavioral finance, differently from predominant macroeconomic literature, has recognized that the rational expectations assumption cannot always explain the basic stylized facts of financial markets. Based on this school of thought (behavioral finance) individuals do not behave in the way described by the rational agent paradigm.

Therefore, alternative expectations models are used some of the facts of the financial markets. Some authors such as De Grauwe and Grimaldi (2006), Hommes (2006) etc. have applied these theories to foreign exchange markets and exchange rate formation. They criticize the theories of financial market analysis, such as the theory of rational expectations and the efficient market hypothesis, namely as the Rational Expectations and Efficient Markets Model (REEM). Based on behavioral finance, in the rational agent model the individual's preferences are not affected by the particular way a choice is presented, but rather the agent's preferences are pretty much influenced by the way a choice is framed.

The basic assumptions regarding the behavioral finance theory consist of the way the markets agents financially behave. Market agents look for simple rules, whose appropriateness is frequently checked and their actions are mostly determined by trial and errors based on their behavior to act rationally as a result of their experience and rational predictions. In other words, market agents recognized that they are not able of understanding and handling the complexity of the information provided, so as a result, they use simple rules to forecast the exchange rates. None of the rules used by market agents to forecast the exchange rates is rational in the technical sense, yet they behave rationally within the context of indecision they face continuously. The market agents are looking for the profitability of the forecasting rule all the time and decide to reject the rule if they see that it is less profitable than the competing rules. Therefore, the agents use trial and error strategies until they find the forecasting rule that fits their margin of profitability.

The pioneering work De Grauwe and Grimaldi (2006) is explained by the studies based on model simulations. The behavioral finance model of De Grauwe and Grimaldi is based on two types of equilibria having as main players chartist and fundamentalist agents.

The first type of equilibrium consists of the exchange rate converging to its fundamental value and is often called the fundamental equilibrium.

The second type of equilibrium is when the exchange rate converges to a bubble equilibrium based on the extrapolative forecasting by chartists. When the second type of equilibrium is simulated in a stochastic environment, it generates a complex scenario of bubbles and crashes. When market agents react swiftly to changing relative profitabilities of different forecasting rules, the frequency of the bubbles increases much faster than expected. Under these conditions, chartists will make hefty profits and will tend to dominate the market by ruling out the fundamentalists who have poor forecasting data and make substantial losses. Therefore, the market is dominated by chartists, and it is quite rational to be a chartist.

The market expectations are often considered a function of fundamentalist and chartists expectations and depend on the relative weight each group has on the market. Therefore, two sources of volatility would be considered in the market; the feedback between real and foreign exchange markets through the nominal exchange rate e, and the endogenous market expectations created by the interaction of various market agents.

We consider the behavioral expectations in the financial markets with heterogeneous agents. The trades of foreign bonds are separated into two large groups; fundamentalists and chartists. The fundamentalist agents have high expectations in the markets, as they expect capital gains in the foreign exchange market, πf, to converge back to their steady-state position (zero in our case) with speed αf. Meanwhile, chartist agents implement a simple adaptive mechanism to forecast the evolution of capital gains in the foreign exchange markets πc, which is transmitted with a speed αc to the chartists' expectation formation. The capital gain expectations for fundamentalists and chartists are given as,

$$\pi'_f = \alpha_f (0 - \pi_{ef}) \qquad (6.26)$$

$$\pi'_c = \alpha_c (e' - \pi_{ec}) \qquad (6.27)$$

Market agents, normally have diverse expectations and is hard to determine a priori, what the market expectations would be, as behavioral expectations do not follow the standard equilibrium models with efficient markets. However, assuming that chartists and fundamentalists that form the population shares of market agents are constant (Assenza, et al. (2012) and indicated respectively as, νc and $(1\text{-}\nu c)$, then we can state that the market gain expectation is the weighted average of the expectations of chartists and fundamentalists, given as,

$$\pi'_e = \nu_c \pi'_c + (1 - \nu_c)\pi_{ef} \qquad (6.28)$$

where $\pi' e$ represents the market expectations that reflect what both chartists and fundamentalists think when the process of aggregation of chartists and fundamentalists expectations will emerge. In few words, the market expectations reflect the market agent's view about their "average" opinion.

The exchange rate is determined by the expectations or the forecasts of the market agents about the future exchange rate and weighted by their respective variances. As mentioned in previous paragraphs, individual market agents are overcome with the amount and complexity of information provided to them, therefore they try to use simple rules to make forecasts. Forecast rules, as well, are of two types, fundamentalist and "technical trading" or chartist forecast rules. In the fundamentalist forecast rule, the forecast is based on the comparison between the market and fundamental exchange rate in the future. The speed of return to the fundamental value of the market exchange rate is presumed to be determined by the speed of adjustment in the goods market that contains the information set of the fundamentalists. The forecasting rule of the fundamentalist can be expressed as,

$$E_f(\Delta s_{t+1}) = \varphi(s_{t-1} - s'_{t-1}) \quad (6.29)$$

where *Ef* indicates the forecasting rule for fundamentalist, *s* is the fundamental exchange rate at time t, which follows a random walk and φ is a parameter ($0 < \varphi < \infty$). The value of the fundamental exchange rate equilibrates the current account and is exogenous.

On the other hand, the "technical trading analysts" or the chartist agents forecast the future exchange rate by extrapolating the exchange rate movements from the past periods. The chartist's forecasting rule can be written as,

$$E_c(\Delta s_{t+1}) = \delta \sum\nolimits_{i=1}^{T} \alpha_i \Delta s_{t-i} \quad (6.30)$$

Equation (6.30) shows that chartists analyze the past exchange rate changes and extrapolate them into the future exchange rate change. Parameter δ in the equation above indicates the degree of extrapolation. Chartist agents do not ignore the fundamental exchange rate, but they take it into account indirectly through the exchange rate itself. Both chartist and fundamentalist agents use partial information or when they have the available more complex information they are similar in understanding the complexity of the information and none of them can be considered to be superior with respect to each other. Both agents evaluate their risk of portfolio by using variances $\sigma_{i,t}$ which are defined as the weighted average of the squared forecasting errors made by chartists and fundamentalists, given by the following equation,

$$\sigma_{i,t} = \sum_{k=1}^{\infty} \psi_k \left[E^i_{t-k}(s_{t-k+1}) - s_{t-k+1}\right]^2 \quad (6.31)$$

where ψ_k define the geometrically declining weights of both chartists and fundamentalists.

In the study of De Grauwe and Grimaldi (2004) we have that for any small early disturbance in the market the chartists' weight can reach as high as 50 percent of the market and when the exchange rate converges to the fundamental rate the weight of both chartists and fundamentalists is equally split at 50 percent. But, when the initial disturbances are large in the market the chartists' weight tend to converge to 1 (100 percent), and the chartists take over the whole market converging the exchange rate to a bubble. The number of fundamentalists has become relatively small having no power to bring back the exchange rate to its fundamental value. The exchange rate bubbles are fixed point solutions reaching equilibria, meaning that exchange rate will be constant once the point solutions reach the equilibria state.

Once the chartists reach the market domination, their expectations based on the past movement extrapolations are more consistent (no changes in the forecast), leaving no choice to fundamentalist agents but to abandon the exchange rate market. Therefore, we have two categories of equilibria: first one, called a fundamental equilibrium where chartists and fundamentalists co-exist sharing the market equally: and a second one, called a bubble equilibrium dominated by chartists that have ousted the fundamentalists. The fundamental equilibrium is locally stable as it can be reached by different initial conditions and the system returns to the main fundamental values. Meanwhile, the bubble equilibrium has only one initial condition reaching the exchange rate bubble solution in an exchange rate market ruled by chartists. Small or large disturbances in the exchange rate market can lead to either a fundamental or a bubble equilibrium.

Lavoie and Daigle (2011) are in favor of using stock-flow consistent models that include stocks of internationally-traded assets and flow of trade, income and output. Stock-consistent models, different from traditional mainstream economics assumptions that are based on rational expectations hypothesis, use a compressive accounting framework that is perfect for the behavioral finance models. The authors try to put in a behavioral finance model the expectations of chartists and the fundamentalists which they label as "conventionalists". The chartists have the tendency to follow the adaptive expectations of the preceding period, while conventionalists follow the equilibrium of the exchange rate that is not feasible with the current account equilibrium.

The extensive empirical simulations done by Lavoie and Daigle (2011) have determined that exchange rate expectations have a substantial impact on exchange rate movements and trade account balances in steady states. In a monetary regime dominated by flexible exchange rates, import and export elasticities with respect to relative prices are appropriately high compared to the elasticity of terms of trade delivering stabilizing properties as long as the exchange rate market is not dominated by chartist agents only. But if chartists dominate fundamentalist agents then any shock in the exchange rate market will provoke cyclical changes of greater scale and the exchange rates will take more time to return to their steady-state values.

In a real world where the exchange rate markets are very sensitive to rumors and news, the "judgement" of fundamentalist agents about the "fundamental" value of the exchange rate will frequently be fluctuating which will affect the changes in the steady-value of the economy. At the same time, the number of market agents setting their expectations as chartists and behaving as chartists will influence the foreign exchange market in the short run putting it in an unstable mode. The combined effect of chartists and fundamentalists' behavior in the foreign exchange market put the economy running forever between short and the medium run, never reaching the long run equilibrium, consequently always exposed to the effects of exchange rate expectations.

Taylor Rules Fundamentals for a Monetary Policy

Another branch of macroeconomic based models has involved the incorporation of central bank reaction functions into exchange rates models, improving the exchange rate forecasting, by proposing the Taylor rule for monetary policy. Engel and West (2005) and then Molodtsova and Papell (2009) were the first economists to incorporate Taylor rule fundamentals in a derivation model of exchange rates. The Taylor rule was based on Taylor (1993) study that the monetary authority sets the interest real interest rate as a function of how inflation differs from its target level. By analyzing, let say dollar exchange rate, Taylor rule can be used for the US dollar and an interest rate targeting rule for the foreign currency that incorporates an exchange rate gap, where the foreign currency targets a PPP value of the nominal exchange rate.

Engel and West (2005) were able to evaluate the model of exchange rates by assessing the correlation between the change in the exchange rates and the change in constructed fundamentals by using either univariate regressions or bivariate VARs (two variable vector autoregression analysis) with discount factors. If the correlations were positive, then the exchange rates model using Taylor's rule was valid.

Taylor (1993), in his pivotal study, bases his Taylor-rule fundamental model of exchange rates by considering two economies where their bilateral exchange rate reflect their relative interest rates and as a result their output gaps their inflation levels. The interest rate using the Taylor-rule fundamental model is given as,

$$r_{t+1} = \lambda(\pi_t - \pi_{tar}) + \tau y_{gap} + r_{tar} \quad (6.32)$$

where *rt+1* is the real interest rate defined as the difference between the nominal interest rate, *it+1* and the inflation rate *πt+1*, πt is the inflation rate, πtar is the target rate of inflation, *ygap* is the output gap and *rtar* is the equilibrium real interest rate. Molodtsova and Papell (2009) improved the Taylor rule by taking into account more facts. First, it is in the benefit of Central Bank to maintain the nominal exchange rate as close as possible at its purchasing power parity. Second, interest rate changes are very slow especially when Central Banks put to achieve their targets. A modified Taylor rule can be expressed as,

$$i'_{t+1} = (1 - \rho)(\mu + \theta\pi_{t+1} + \tau y_{gap(t+1)} + \delta q_t) + \rho i_t + v_{t+1} \tag{6.33}$$

where *vt+1* is the monetary policy shock. The foreign and domestic country in the modified Taylor rule can be identified by using asterisk and non-asterisk respectively,

$$i^*_{t+1} = (1 - \rho^*)(\mu^* + \theta^*\pi^*_t + \tau y^*_{gap} + \delta^* q_t) + \rho^* i_t + v^*_{t+1} \tag{6.34}$$

$$i_{t+1} = (1 - \rho)(\mu + \theta\pi_{t+1} + \tau y_{gap(t+1)}) + \rho i_t + v_{t+1} \tag{6.35}$$

The Taylor rule can be further redefined by taking the difference of the above two equations (6.34 and 6.35) based on Molodtsova and Papell (2009) is given as,

$$E_{t+1} = \mu + \delta q_t + \phi * \pi^*_t + \tau^* y^*_{gap} + \lambda\pi_t + \gamma y_{gap} + \rho i_t - \rho^* i^*_t \tag{6.36}$$

Equation (6.36) is also called the “asymmetric” Taylor rule, which can be simplified and converted into a symmetric form showing the difference between inflation rate and the target rate of inflation and the output gap differences, given as,

$$E_{t+1} = \mu' + \phi * (\pi_t - \pi^*_t) + \gamma(y_{gap} - y^*_{gap}) \tag{6.34}$$

Equation (6.34) indicates that forecast exchange rates out-of-sample are much better than the random walk tested for several countries (Molodtsova and Papell, 2009). It tells also that interest rates and exchange rates move in response to inflation and output gaps. In fact, if the inflation gap rises in the domestic country (e.s. U.S.A.) relative to the foreign country (United Kingdom), then the Central Bank (Fed) will have the option to raise the interest rate, which in turn will appreciate the domestic currency. By incorporating the Taylor rule variables will help with out-of-sample forecasting at short horizon which will improve upon conventional interest rate, purchasing power parity, and monetary models. The exchange rates of core currencies allow the coefficient on the gap terms to vary across countries, and the exchange rate gap to enter, works well in out-of-sample forecasting exercises, at the one quarter horizon, which is statistically significant, using some tests.

Chinn (2008) explores that in the sample, output and inflation gaps enter in with an expected sign and usually with statistical significance for the dollar/euro exchange rate period taken into consideration (1999-2007). But for longer periods using dollar/euro exchange rates and other variables, there are more complications in term of implementation since the output gap is directly noticeable and measurable by the use of production function based approaches. The coefficient on the exchange rate gap sometimes is not statistically significant because this variable depends on two respective central bank reaction functions that assign different weights on the exchange rate.

Taylor rules are considered to be a good indication of monetary policy in the eighties, nineties and the beginning of 2000s, nevertheless, the monetary policy changed rapidly during the 2008 crisis adapting to the new reality. Further study in the Taylor rule to include the post 2008 crisis years were completed by Molodtsova and Papell (2012) analyzing the exchange rate forecasting during the recent financial crisis including some new indicators of financial stress such as the Libor-OIS/Euribor-OIS differential and TED spread differential which show positive evidence for most of the advanced countries and half of the developing countries.

In addition, they found that analyzing the bilateral exchange rates (for example, USD/Euro) the specification imposing common coefficients, and omitting the exchange rate, and omitting the interest rate smoothing work better in out-of-sample forecasting in one-month horizon and up to one year longer horizons.

Some of the exchange rate models that have as primary scope to investigate predictability of exchange rates have incorporated the Taylor rule fundamentals by using heterogeneous coefficients and interest rate smoothing. These models have proved that evidence of predictability is much robust with Taylor rule models than with the conventional interest rate, purchasing power parity or other monetary models.

Foreign Exchange Market Psychology

In an exchange rate market, portfolio capital flows are the primary drivers of currency prices and agents' forecasts are the main determinants of the capital flows, therefore highly developed models of expectations formation are crucial to understanding foreign exchange rate determination. The dynamic nature of these processes involves the use of schematic and psychological models rather than standard general equilibrium models.

There are at least three reasons that agents purchase foreign currency: importation of foreign goods and services, direct foreign investments, and foreign portfolio foreign management. The perception of these three reasons by agents that operate in the exchange rate market is what forms their mental model and therefore their expectations. In fact, agents tend to normally generate only two sets of expectations: short-term and medium-term. The medium-term expectations usually become the main anchor where agents through which try to filter inputs regarding expectations for exchange rates.

Market agents may have specific expectations of the exchange rate in mind when performing medium-term expectations, however it is best if we take into consideration all three values with respect to a particular currency they are dealing with: bullish (pro the currency in question), bearish (anti the currency in question), or neutral. If medium-term expectations are bullish, then the consequence of the events that would lead to currency appreciation will be magnified, and the consequence of the events that would lead to an end in depreciation will be discounted. Bearishness, given the trend to be anti the currency in question, has a similar impact as bullish, meanwhile neutral has no particular attraction to medium-term currency expectations.

For instance, if the Central Bank announces that interest rates are going to rise soon, the market agents see this as an indicator of currency appreciation and the agents' medium-term expectations (which are also called "attractors") with respect to that exchange rate are currently bullish, and a large increase in the value of the currency is likely to take place. But, if the medium-term expectations have been bearish, then the Central Bank's announcement would have less impact and might even be ignored by market agents. Agent' medium-term expectations or the attractor is normally a function of a moving average of the variables driving the short-term expectations.

The short-term forecast responds relatively quickly in the exchange rate market to inputs that come from all sources, meanwhile the medium-term or the attractor reacts only after a trend has emerged. For this reason, the medium-term expectation is considered as an exogenous variable that is affected by a moving average of the short-term forecast (Harvey 2009, 82-89).

There are at least three facts that regard the short-term forecast, medium-term forecast and the factors that influence them. The first fact is that expectations are related to the object variable that they determine. Second, expectations of the future impact in a way or other influence the spot price directly and the scale of this effect is measured by a function of the difference between the expected and spot rates and the agents' confidence in the forecast. Third, if the expectations heavily impact the currency prices then the market could be moved by whatever agents decide is important to influence the market (e.s. changes in GDP, unemployment rate, inflation rate, etc.).

The currency market agents, based on the three reasons (mentioned above) to purchase foreign currency, form their own exchange rate market psychology, therefore their mental models which base their short-term and medium-term expectations. In the mental model of the agents that operate in the exchange rate market, the three reasons to purchase foreign currency will be assumed to create three determinants which in turn will create a certain demand for domestic currency, let say US dollar. Let's assume *(X-M)e* the expected net exports, *DFIe* the expected net direct foreign investment into US and *PFIe* is the net expected a portfolio of foreign investment into the US. *$/FX* also indicates the exchange rate expectation of the mental model and is linked to the three determinants which represent the three processes listed above (Harvey 2009, 84-90).

If the three determinants above create a net demand for the domestic currency, USD, then we will have a dollar appreciation (fall in $/FX) resulting in a negative link between the three processes and the forecast. If we have a rise in any of determinants that describe the three processes *(X-M)e, DFIe* and *PFIe* then $/FX will decrease and vice versa. The realized figures of expected net exports, net direct foreign investments, and net expected a portfolio of foreign investment are important for forecast purpose but are not very reliable as they will be not known for at least few weeks after the events have taken place and after the estimates have finally been realized.

The mental model also considers three base factors upon which the three processes above depend. The three base factors are (rd-rfx)e, the expected relative interest rates (domestic less foreign); *(Yd-Yfx)e,* expected macroeconomic growth; *(Pd-Pfx)e,* the expected price (domestic less foreign) and the expected liquidity denominated as *$.* The relations between the base factors and processes are considered when the expectation of rising (relative) prices effects negatively on market agents' forecast of the net domestic exports as imports would become cheaper and exports more expensive. Price rise will also impact negatively the foreign direct investment, *DFIe,* given that they are discouraged by increasing input costs. Regarding the expected price *(Pd-Pfx)e,* any changes in the prices of food and services will have no direct influence on portfolio investment.

Any expectations of rising macro growth would cause market agents to forecast a fall in next exports, an increased income which will lead to more imports, an increase in net *DFIe,* and an increase in net *PFIe.* The mental or psychology model that describes the foreign exchange market psychology is given in figure 6.1 as created by Harvey (2009, ch.5) and is composed of base factors on the left side respectively given as: (rd-rfx)e, the expected relative interest rates: *(Yd-Yfx)e,* expected macroeconomic growth; and *(Pd-Pfx)e,* the expected price, and processes on the right side respectively given as: *(X-M)e,* the expected net exports, *DFIe,* the expected net direct foreign investment and

PFIe the net expected portfolio of foreign investments. The base factors are related to each of the processes influencing them negatively (negative sign -) or positively (positive sign +). The three processes/determinants impact negatively the domestic currency (negative sign -), which is transmitted as dollar appreciation (fall in $/FX) in $/FX forecast.

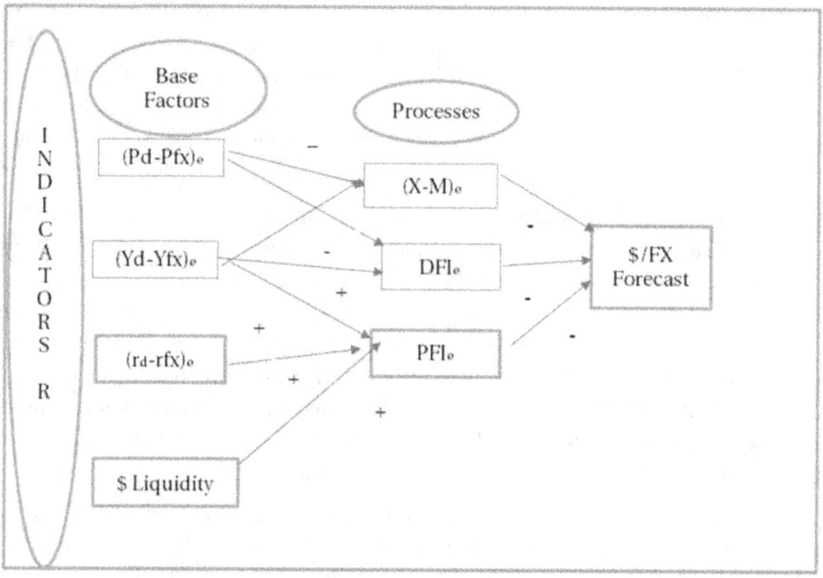

Figure 6.1: Mental model of an exchange rate market.

Market agents use the mental model described in figure 6.1 to elaborate their forecast. They start their analysis by picking up different clues and macroeconomic indicators or variables from the market and economy such as interest rates, unemployment rate, rate of growth, inflation, etc. and use them to predict the movements of the base factors, which are fed into the forecast of the processes and finally to the exchange rate itself. For example, a macroeconomic indicator such as the trade of balance (X-M) which is reported monthly can be fed directly into the forecast of next month's trade balance (X-M)e which affects the forecast of the $/FX.

There are also other case scenarios where market agents, rather than entering the mental model as close to $/FX forecast possible, will prefer to use variables and indicators that are frequently reported and pretty straightforward to interpret. One of the variables that plays a pivotal role in the expectation formation is the interest rate. The interest rate variable allows for some shortcut of the mental model and is reported continuously. Any change of interest rates by Central Bank will affect lenders, borrowers and portfolio investment of domestic and foreign investors. Another direct indicator that enters the mental model on the far left is the unemployment rate which is reported monthly, easy to interpret and influence in the way or other the portfolio investment through macroeconomic growth and stability.

The four core macroeconomic variables (interest rates, unemployment rate, trade balance, and inflation), form the core of indicators that affect base factors and processes in the mental model that feeds the expectations of market agents in forming their forecast regarding the exchange rate market. For short-term horizons, a technical analysis that help creates trading rules (created in real time) are appropriately taken into consideration as well.

Despite the efforts to optimize the forecast of the exchange rate market there are always forecast errors done by agents at some point during the process of creating the expectations. Forecast errors often provide the motivation for a re-valuation of the core macroeconomic indicators and variables. However, despite the forecast errors done by some agents, the average expectation is supposed to be always right because there is an immediate currency price adjustment in the forecast direction towards the correct direction of the magnitude.

Therefore, the community of those agents operating in the foreign exchange rate market has a distinctive subculture with its habits and patterns. These agents, using their foreign exchange market psychology and their mental model, often dominate the market and whatever they think is true becomes fact as it moves the market and reduces the uncertain interpretations.

Financialisation of Exchange Rates

The modern foreign exchange rate theories depart from classical exchange theories, such as the purchasing power parity and are focused on showing the transition from short to long-term equilibrium and the explanation for the exchange rate volatility. The recent exchange rate markets have evolved to handle the very high volume of financial flows compared to the flows for goods transactions, which bring us to the new term used as financialisation of exchange rates.

The financialisation has different aspects. One of the aspects of financialisation is that foreign currency is used a medium of exchange for the purchase of foreign financial assets and as a store value such as an asset which profit can be realized through the increased value of the asset such as currency appreciation. Keeping the foreign currency as a medium of exchange rate increases the trade of the short-term foreign assets such as portfolio investments, meanwhile keeping the foreign currency as a store value helps creates a buffer or hedging against currency speculation that frequently happens in the market (appreciation or depreciation of other currencies).

In the case of the flexible exchange rate, the currency risk is much higher as there is more speculation on depreciation and appreciation. In fact, in this case, the prices of all foreign assets purchased by residents of a country become more volatile when they are the rate in domestic currency. Because of the volatility, the short-term investments are preferred, as the investors can exit from investments in a much shorter time to minimize the currency risk. At the same time the hedge currency risk increases which drives the growth of currency derivatives used by investors to protect their investment in foreign currencies. In some case scenarios, the protection psychology of hedge currency used by investors and market agents will make them take higher risks which generate more speculation. In addition, taking higher risk increases the probability of market assets to be wrongly underestimated or overestimated, resulting in high or low-risk aversion when bears or bulls[1] occur favoring a driving force to speculation. Figure 6.2 shows the interconnection aspects of the financialisation of exchange rates.

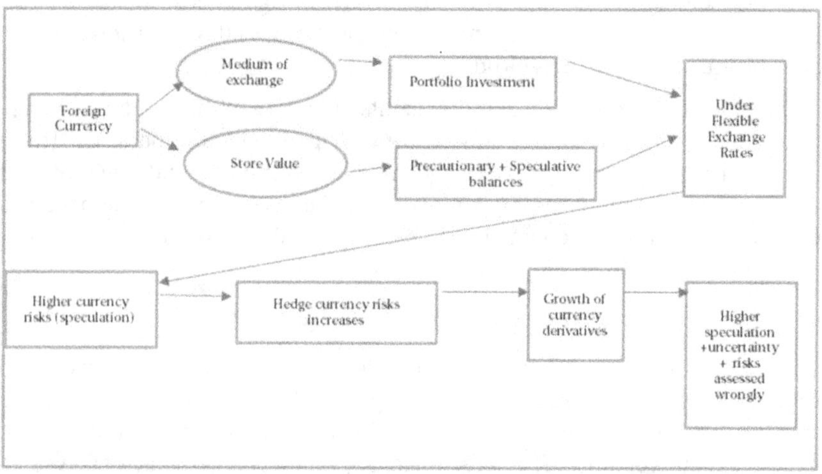

Figure 6.2. Interconnection aspects of the financialisation of exchange rates.

[1] A bull market is when market is showing confidence with prices going up, which means that the prices of market indices are going up too resulting on increased number of share traded in the exchange market. A market running bullish for days will be labeled as bullish market. A bull market is on rise in value of the market of at least 20%.

A bear market is when the market shows lack of confidence, where price go down, indices fall and volumes of shares traded decreases. If the market falls more than 20% than we have entered a bear market.

The basic idea to make money in the stocks market is when you buy low and sell high so it can give you a profit. Any agents that want to make money has to buy stocks in a bear market and sell stocks in a bull market when stock prices are high. But, knowing when it is the best time to buy and sell stocks is not simple.

Getting back to the foreign exchange rates, we have that the short-term business of currency traders is flourishing with different kind of trends, trials and errors. On the short-term, the foreign exchange markets in the industrialized countries do not influence the central banks or governments and they are free to follow the trend of chartists or fundamentalists. Only in times of crises, when the currency valuations become very volatile and threaten the core macroeconomic indicators, the central banks will intervene pushing the currency traders to change the direction (sign) of the speculation.

Foreign exchange agents or traders (forex traders) to some extent operate on both sides of the transactions. They are agents of both sides of those who supply and demand a foreign exchange. More specifically, foreign exchange agents supply in one side and demand on the other side foreign exchange to investors and asset owners who want to structure and diversify their portfolio internationally. In this case, there is a theory called 'portfolio theory of exchange rates' that tries to explain the investment on portfolio diversification (which will not be discussed here). Investors and asset owners tend to invest in all kind of asset classes but their time horizon is not as short as that of forex traders operating in high-frequency trading. The trading in ultra-time horizon often used by forex traders brings currency speculation affecting the investment of asset owners, and the portfolio theory of exchange rates has little significance.

The frequent movement of exchange rate increases the fluctuation of the value of foreign assets calculated in domestic currency. Securities held in foreign currency, enhanced by price increases, could get easily inflated by the revaluation of the foreign currency and in the case of devaluation speculation securities could get easily deflated and fall in value. The speculation brings us to the use of hedging that has the scope of limiting the fluctuation of exchange rates and asset prices volatility, which in turn decreases speculative profits and losses.

With the hedging system in place, it depends on the degree of risk aversion that investors are about to take to reach a high yield. Normally, when investors go for high-risk aversion they also go for high liquidity preference in a core currency or reserve currency such as US dollar or Euro. If the investors decide to go for low-risk aversion, it means that they have low liquidity preferences and are ready to switch currencies. At this point, the fundamentals conducted by PPP, have a small role on financialized currency markets, as they are no

PPP with same or similar financial products denominated in different currencies despite the fact that expected returns on capital could be equal. But, there are estimates of foreign financial assets due to exchange rate risks that investors and assets owners in different countries must take into consideration.

Foreign exchange markets are often called “flex-price-markets” as they are normally cleared due to flexible prices, and they are mostly in a general equilibrium which is composed of a combination of ultra-short equilibriums. The exchange rate determined in the market is a result of very large, medium or small currency transactions which affect the price of goods and assets in foreign currency. There is a constant change in the system of relative prices to find new equilibria although the foreign exchange markets are continuously in ultra-short equilibrium.

The market agents and all actors involved in foreign currency transactions are under constant stress to adapt to follow the exchange market trends. Therefore, a higher degree of price flexibility is essential to adopt to the difference between the exchange rate movements and changes in goods and factor prices.

Some Conclusions on the New Exchange Rate Theories

The literature on the new exchange rate theories has split into several directions over the past few decades with greater confidence on certain types of models in certain macroeconomic areas. Greater importance has been placed on modeling exchange rates in perspective of general equilibrium models. However, the empirical work of new exchange rate theories has been derived from either the application of new econometric models to existing based approaches (such as monetary approach), or time series models integrating reaction functions like the Taylor Rule, or simple balance sheet variables.

The Taylor rule fundamentals approach has been no doubt of great impact on this field because the data is easy to obtain and elaborate to reach conclusions. The Taylor Rule approach and net foreign assets fundamentals have more out-of-sample predictive content than traditional fundamentals (like interest rate, inflation, output growth, money differential, etc.). At long time horizons, monetary fundamentals, and at short horizons interest rate differentials have the capability to display some reasonable forecasting data.

The selection of data can substantially affect the predictive ability and explain the differences in results among different studies. At longer horizons, the forecasting ability of the monetary models is much weaker when estimating the co-integration parameters. The predictive abilities depend also on the choice of the country, the frequency of the data, the sample period and forecast evaluation method chosen.

The behavioral equilibrium exchange rate models is another macroeconomic phenomenon that could be a good fit in assessing exchange currency fair values. In addition, the foreign exchange market are analyzed using the market psychology of the agents who use their mental model to elaborate their forecast. Of the economic models, purchasing power parity and interest rate parity do equally well, perhaps due to the prudence of the specifications given that IRP requires no parameter estimation.

The critics of exchange rate theories complain that currency traders do not take seriously into consideration the fundamental data, especially in the case of strong deviations from presumed fundamental equilibria. In fact, if there is a large fluctuation in exchange rates, fundamental data appears to play a principal role and fundamentals have a role in the normal currency trading of chartists. Ultra-short-horizon speculation in exchange rates have effects on both sides of the market players. Those who speculate appreciation require another player or dealer on the other side that receives a contrary position as depreciation, which mostly refers to different expectations regarding the degree of appreciation/depreciation.

Overall Conclusions about the Monetary Debate on Fixed vs. Flexible Exchange Rates

Let me conclude by emphasizing that the debate about fixed and flexible exchange rates is still open, the literature is growing substantially and is not easy to say which of them is better. However, I would like to make some final considerations.

This work has taken into consideration extensively the monetary debate on fixed versus flexible exchange rates from the fifties to present, or exactly from the "case for a flexible exchange rate" to the creation of "optimum currency areas" and monetary unions.

There are good reasons for fixing exchange rates or for allowing them to float, depending on the structure of an economy and its trade orientation and pattern. Decisions regarding the choice of future exchange rate regimes, however, require being internally and logically consistent. If fixed exchange rates have a major preference over flexible exchange rates, this choice necessarily implies giving up monetary autonomy. There is a lot of confidence in the fixed exchange rates, thanks to the fact that their effective mechanism is in part composed of coordinated macro policies to keep the domestic currency stable. Given the slowness of wages and prices adjustment, a system of fixed exchange rates would compel the adjustment onto domestic quantities rather than prices which will create greater volatility of employment and output.

A floating exchange rate system is supposed, in some cases and mostly for advanced countries perform better than a fixed rate system when the dominant shocks are real because under a floating rate system the exchange rate can adjust following real shocks, rather than requiring prices levels changes. The beauty of a system of flexible exchange rates is that it is self-adjusting.

On the other hand, a floating exchange system for developing and underdeveloped countries have produced financial imbalances and wild currency gyrations rather than stability and growth. The flexible exchange system in these countries has not been self-adjusting or able to absorb internal and external real shocks. Besides, very often markets were providing to be neither stable nor rational. It was required that domestic monetary authorities, government and international intervention to bring markets back to stability. International Monetary Fund (IMF) has urged developing countries to loosen currency controls and allow devaluation.

For example, if a developing country such as Nigeria has pegged its domestic currency, *naira*, to an official rate of about 197 to the U.S. dollar, even though it is trading at approximately 300 to the dollar on the informal markets, due to heavy pressure from international market because of the massive fall in oil prices in 2016 (Nigeria is heavily dependent on oil production), the IMF recipe is to allow *naira* to devaluate and adjust its value to the informal market value, as this market shows the real value of *naira*. Loosening currency control and adopting a more flexible exchange rate will be more beneficial and less painful in the long-term for developing countries than trying to keep their currencies at any cost pegged to the U.S. dollar. In fact, if oil-dependent countries such Azerbaijan, Angola and Nigeria which heavily depend on oil revenues, require international financial assistance from World Bank and IMF because of the oil price drop, the first requirement from both international lending organizations to receive potential loan deals will be to relax domestic currency controls and let the local currency devaluate.

The success of the Euro and the creation of new international institutions such as European Central Bank have opened new perspectives on the integration of the international monetary system. So far the Eurozone accomplishment has shown that the stability of a common currency area for the members of the union which have pegged their exchange rates to each other (or use the same currency) is more guaranteed in the event of external shocks (unless the external shocks are too big to drag out the whole monetary area) than if they have to float their currencies against each other.

The recent events after the 2008 financial crisis have demonstrated that Eurozone can absorb any internal and external shock if there is the political will to keep the union together even in the case when one member is close to default. The currency crisis of 2008 helped the union put more warning monetary and fiscal instruments to protect from future shocks. As a matter of fact, in 2015 another country, Lithuania joined the European monetary union and more are scheduled to join in the future. If the European monetary union was at the breaking point, there was no reason to ask new countries to join it. However, the Brexit case (Exit of Britain) from the EU should be considered as a particular case that had seen British politics heavily involved (with little public consultation) to the option for independent not-sharing EU policies with economic and monetary consequences still unknown at this stage. There are no other countries in the Eurozone planning to follow the Brexit case.

The latest debate raging across Europe is that if wealthy countries are demanding budget-slashing measures as a precondition for continuing to bail out poorer neighbors, even though doing so will cause many Eurozone economies to shrink making it harder for them to pay out debt.

The answer to this debate is that it is worth making there extra efforts by rich European countries to help weaker neighbors of the European Union. Saving a big monetary union such as EU and keeping all the EU members inside the Eurozone is considered a paramount priority by most of the advanced and developing countries, in Europe, North-America, Asia, Latin America and Africa as it keeps steady the global market stability and help perform well the system of core global currencies that have been dominant in international markets in the last decades. In a dynamic global economy, the creation of large currency areas or monetary unions would provide competition, and what is more desirable a long-lasting monetary stability.

And lastly, the predictability of exchange rate models change over time, so economists are always looking for ways to exploit instabilities and improve exchange rate forecasts. Despite all efforts, remains the fact that exchange rates are poorly forecasted by economic models due to different elements like sampling errors, model misspecification, wrong forecast methodologies, incorrect evaluation methods and instabilities.

Bibliography

ACIR (Advisory Commission on Intergovernmental Relations), 1989, *Significant Features of Fiscal Federalism,* US Government Press, Washington DC.

Aghion P., Bacchetta P. and Banerjee, A. 2000. "A Simple Model of Monetary Policy and Currency Crisis," *European Economic Review,* 44 (4-6), 728-38.

———., ———. and ———. 2001. "Currency Crisis and Monetary Policy in an Economy with Credit Constraints," *European Economic Review,* 45 (7), 1121-50.

———., ———. and ———. 2004. "A Corporate Balance-Sheet Approach to Currency Crisis, *Journal of Economic Theory,* 119(1), 6-30.

Aizenman J., and **Flood P., 1993.** " A Theory of Optimum Currency Areas: Revisited", *Greek Economic Review,* Issue Year. 1993.

Alesina A. and Wagner A., 2003. "Choosing (and Reneging on) Exchange Rate Regimes," *NBER Working Papers* No. 9809, Cambridge, Massachusetts, National Bureau of Economic Research.

Alesina A., Barro R., and **Tenreyro S.,** (2002). "Optimal Currency Areas", *NBER working papers,* Macroeconomic Annuals, v. 17, Issue 1, 300-45.

Aliber R.Z., 1972 "Uncertainty, Currency Areas and the Exchange Rate System", *Economica,* New Series, 39 (15), 432-441.

Assenza, T., Brock, W.A., and Hommes, C, H., 2012. "Animal Spirits, Heterogeneous Expectations and the Amplification and Duration of Crisis", *Working Paper, CeDEF,* University of Amsterdam.

Atkenson A. and Bayoumi T., 1993. "Do Private Markets Insure against Regional Shocks in a Common Currency Area? Evidence from the US", *Open Economies Review,* 4, 303-24.

Barajas A., Erickson L. and Steiner R., 2008. "*Fear of Declaring: Do Markets Care What Countries say about their Exchange Rate Policies?* IMF Staff Papers, Vol. 55. No. 3, 445-480.

Barro J.R. and Gordon B. D., 1983, "A Positive Theory of Monetary Policy in a Natural Rate Model", *The Journal of Political Economy,* Vol. 91 (4), 589-610.

Barro, J. R., 1979. "Money and the Price Level Under Gold Standard", *Economic Journal,* 89, 12-33.

Baumeister, C. and Benati, L. (2013) "Unconventional Monetary Policy and the Great Recession: Estimating the Macroeconomic Effects of a Spread Compression at the Zero Lower Bound", *International Journal of Central Banking,* June, pp. 165-212.

Bauer, M, D., and Neely. C, J., 2014. "International Channels of Fed's Unconventional Monetary Policy", *Working Paper 2012-028, Federal Reserve Bank of St. Louis.*

Bauer, M, D., and **Rudebusch, G. D.,** 2014. "The Signaling Channel for Federal Reserve Bond Purchases." *International Journal of Central Banking,* 10(3), 233-289.

Bayoumi T., 1994. "A Formal Model of Optimum Currency Area," *Staff Papers, International Monetary Fund,* Vol. 41, No. 4, pp. 537-54.

Bayoumi, T., and Masson P. R., 1995. "Fiscal flows in the United States and Canada: Lessons for monetary union in Europe," *European Economic Review, Elsevier,* 39(2), 253-274.

Bayoumi T. and **Eichengreen B.,** 1993. "Shocking Aspects of European Monetary Unification," in F. Giavazzi and F. Torres, (eds.) *The Transition to Economic and Monetary Union in Europe,* Cambridge University Press, New York, pp. 193-229.

———. 1994. "One Money or Many? Analyzing the Prospects for Monetary Unification in Various Parts of the World." *Princeton Studies in International Finance, 76, Princeton, NJ: Princeton University Press.*

———. 1996. *"Operationalising the Theory of Optimum Currency Areas,"* paper presented at the CEPR's conference on Regional Integration in La Coruna, Spain.

Bayoumi, T., and **Taylor P. M.,** 1995. "Macro-Economic-Shocks, the ERM, and the Tri-Polarity", *The Review of Economics and Statistic,* 77 (2), 321-31.

Beine, M., De Grauwe, P., and Grimaldi, M. 2009. "The Impact of FX Central Bank Intervention in a Noise Trading Framework," *Journal of Banking and Finance,* 33(7), pp. 1187– 1195.

Bergsten F., and **Subramanian A**., 2009. "American Cannot Resolve the Global Imbalances on its own", Financial Times, August 20, 2009.

Berkmen, S.P. (2012), "Bank of Japan's Quantitative and Credit Easing: Are They Now More Effective?", *IMF Working Paper 12/2,* International Monetary Fund, Washington, D.C.

Bergin, P., 1995. "Mundell-Fleming revisited: Monetary and Fiscal policies in a Two-Country dynamic General Equilibrium Model with Wage Contracts". *Unpublished Manuscript,* Yale University, New Haven, Connecticut.

Bergin, P. and Feenstra, R. C., 2001. "Pricing-to-Market, Staggered Contracts, and Real Exchange Rate Persistence", *Journal of International Economics,* 54 (2), pp. 333-359.

Bergin, P., Glick R., and Taylor, A.M., 2004. "Productivity, Tradability and the Long-run Price Puzzle", *NBER Working Paper* No. 10569, pp.1-32.

Betts, C. and Devereux, M., 1996. "The Exchange Rate in a Model of Pricing to Market", *European Economic Review,* 40, 1007–21.

Betts C., and Devereux M. 1997. "The International Monetary Transmission Mechanism: A model of Real Exchange Rate Adjustment Under Pricing to Market", *Mimeographed, Unpublished Manuscript,* University of British Columbia, Vancouver.

Bickerdike, C. F., 1920. "The Instability of Foreign Exchanges", *Economic Journal,* 117 (30), pp. 118-122.

Blanchard, O. and Quah D., 1989. "The Dynamic Effects of Aggregate Demand and Supply Disturbances", *American Economic Review,* 79, 655-73.

Blanchard, O. and Katz L.F., 1992. "Regional Evolutions", *Brooking Papers on Economic Activity*, Washington D.C.

Blavy, R., and Juvenal, L., 2009. "Mexico's Integration into NAFTA Markets: A View from Sectorial Real Exchange Rates", *Federal Reserve Bank of St. Louise Review*, 91, pp. 441-64.

Blustein, P., 2015. 'Laid Low: The IMF, the Euro Zone and the First Rescue of Greece', *CIGI Papers Series*, N. 61 p. 1-32.

Blyth, M. 2013., "Austerity: The History of a Dangerous Idea", *Oxford University Press*, New York.

Bordo, M. D. and **Kydland, F. E.**, 1996. "The Gold Standard as a Commitment Mechanism", in Tamin Bayoumi, Barry Eichengreen and Mark Taylor (eds.), *Modern Perspectives on the Gold Standard*, Cambridge University Press.

Broda, Ch., 2001. "Coping with Terms-of-Trade Shocks: Peg versus Float", *American Economic Review Papers and Proceedings*, 91 (2), 376-80.

Brock, W., and C. Hommes. 1998. "Heterogeneous Beliefs and Routes to Chaos in a Simple Asset Pricing Model," *Journal of Economic Dynamics and Control*, 22(8-9), pp. 1235–1274.

Buiter, W., 2014, "The Fed's Bad Manners Risk Offending Foreigners", *Financial Times*, February 4.

Calvo, G., and Reinhart C. M., 2002. "Fear of Floating", *Quarterly Journal of Economics, 117 (2), 379-408.*

Candel-Sanchez, F., and Campoy-Minarro C. J., 2004, "Is the Walsh Contract Really Optimal?" *Public Choice*, 120, pp. 29-39.

Canzoneri M., Vallés J., and Viñals J., 1996. "Do Exchange Rate Move to Address International Macroeconomic Imbalances?" CEPR Discussion Paper no, 1948, October.

Camdessus M., 1996. in an interview about "Global Monetary Policy", see www.imf.org.

Carr L. J. and Floyd E. J., 2002. "Real and Monetary Shocks to the Canadian Dollar: Do Canada and the United States form an Optimal Currency Area?" North American Journal of Economic and Finance, 13, 21-39.

Chinn, M., 2008. "Nonlinearities, Business Cycles and Exchange Rates," *Economic Notes*, 37 (3), pp. 219-239.

Chiodo A. J. and **Owyang M. T.**, 2002. "A Case Study of a Currency Crisis: The Russian Default of 1998", *The Federal Reserve Bank of St. Louis, Working Paper* Nov./Dec. *2002 , pp. 7-17.*

Chen, H., Curdia, V., and **Ferrero, A.,** 2012. "The Macroeconomic Effects of Large-Scale Asset Purchase Programs", *Federal Reserve Bank of San Francisco.* Working Paper 2012-22, Oct.

Chung, H., Laforte, J.P., Reifschneider, D., and William, J.C. 2012. "Have we underestimated the Likelihood and Severity of Zero Lower Bound events?" *Journal of Money, Credit an Banking*, v.44 (sup), pp. 47-82.

Cohen D. and **Wyplosz C.,** 1989 "The European Monetary Union: An Agnostic Evaluation," in R. C. Bryant, D. A. Currie, J.A. Frenkel, P.R. Masson, and R. Portes (eds.), *Macroeconomic Policies in an Interdependent World*, Washington, D.C.: IMF, pp.311-37.

Coleman A.M.G., 2001. "Three Perspectives on an Australasian Monetary Union," pp.156-188 in Gruen D. And Simon J. (eds.), "*Future Directions for Monetary Policies in East Asia,*" Sydney, Reserve Bank of Australia.

Corcoran T. 2001. A Couple of Prima Donnas: Managing Friedman-Mundell, *Policy Options* (May), 1-9.

Corden W. M., 1972. "Monetary Integration", *Essays in International Finance* 93, Princeton, New Jersey, *International Finance Section*, Princeton University.

Combes J. L., Minea A., and Sow M., 2012. "Crises and Exchange Rate Regimes: Time to break down the bipolar view?", *Workshop papers* Oct. 2012, The Graduate Institute, Geneva, 1-26.

Commission of the European Communities, 1990. "One Market, One Money", *European Economy*, Brussels, 44, 63-178.

Commission Report: Interim progress report on implementation of Council Directive 2011/85/EU on requirements for budgetary frameworks of the Member States" *29th Report of Session 2012-13 - European Scrutiny Committee Contents: 18 Economic governance.* Parliament.uk. 30 January 2013.

Council Directive 2011/85/EU. 2011, "On the Requirements for Budgetary Frameworks of the Member States", *Official Journal of the European Union.* L306, 41-47.

Council Regulation (EC) No 1467/97. 2005. "On Speeding up and Clarifying the Implementation of the Excessive deficit procedure", *Official Journal of the European Union*, L209, 1-10.

Davidson, P., 1992. *International Money and the Real World*, Second Edition, New York: St. Martin's Press,

———. 2002, *Financial Markets, Money and the Real World*, Edward Elgar, Cheltenham, UK and Northhampton, MA.

D'Amico, S. and **King, T.B.**, 2010. "Flow and Stock Effects of Large-scale Treasury Purchases", *Finance and Economics Discussions Series*, No. 2010-52, 1-38.

De Grauwe, P., and Grimaldi, M., 2004. "Bubbles and crashes in a behavioural finance model", *Sveriges Riksbank, Working Paper Series*, No.164, pp.1-42.

De Grauwe, P., and Grimaldi, M., 2006. "The Exchange Rate in Behavioural Finance Framework", *Princeton University Press*, Princeton and Oxford.

Delors J., (Chairman), 1989. Committee for the Study of Economic and Monetary Union. "Report on Economic and Monetary Union in the European Community. "European Commission, Report and Collection of Papers, Catalogue No. CB-56-89-401-EN-C, 1-38.

Demertzis M., Hughes A., Rummel O., 2000. "Is the European Union a Natural Currency Area, or it is held together by Policy Makers? " Weltwirtschaftliches Achieve, Vol. 136 (4), 657-79.

Dick D. C., and Menkhoff L., 2012. "Exchange Rate Expectations of Chartists and Fundamentalists Christian", *Centre for European Economic Research, ZEW*, Paper No. 12-026, pp.1-47.

Dornbusch R., 1976. "Expectations and Exchange Rate Dynamics", *Journal of Political Economy* 84, 1161-76.

Dornbusch R., and Krugman P., 1976. "Flexible Exchange Rates in the Short Run", *Brookings Papers on Economic Activity*, No.3, 537-584.

Dornbusch, R., and Park, Y. C., 1999. "Flexibility or Nominal Anchors?", in *Exchange Rate Policies in Emerging Asian Economies*. Eds, S. Collignon, J. Pisani-Ferry, and Y.C. Park, New York: Routledge.

Drabek Z. and Brada. J. C., 1998. "Exchange Rate Regimes and the Stability of Trade Policy in Transition Economies" in *The Impact of Exchange Rate Regimes on the Stability of Trade Policy.* World Trade Organization (WTO), Economic Research and Analysis Division, Geneva, Switzerland.

Drucker, S., and **Puri M.**, 2009. "On Loans Sales, Loan Contracting and Lending Relationships," *Review of Financial Studies*, 22, 2635-2677.

Economic Outlook 2012, No.92 (database) OECD, December 2012.

Edwards S. and Levy Yeyati E., 2005. "Flexible Exchange Rates as Shock Absorbers", *European Economic Review*, 49, 2079-2105.

Ellsworth P.T., 1961. "Gold and the Dollar Crisis. Review authors", *The American Economic Review*, 1 (51) 210-12.

Eichengreen B., 1985. " Editor's Introduction." In Barry Eichengreen (eds.) *The Gold Standard in Theory and History*, London, Methuen.

Eichengreen B., 1990. "One Money for Europe? Lessons from the U.S. Currency and Customs Union," *Economic Policy*, 10, 117-187.

Eichengreen B., 1997. "European Monetary Unification: Theory, Practice, and Analysis", MIT Press, Cambridge, MA.

Eichengreen B., 2009. "Out of the Box Thoughts about the International Financial Architecture", *IMF Working Paper*, May 2009, WP/09/116, p. 1-26.

Eichengreen B., 2014. "The Dollar and the Damage Done", *Project Syndicate*, February 2014.

Eichengreen B. and **Bayoumi T.** 1996. "Operationalizing the Theory of Optimum Currency Areas," *CEPR Discussion Papers* 1484, C.E.P.R. Discussion Papers

Eichengreen B., Rose A., and Wyplosz C., 1996. "Contagious Currency Crisis", *CEPR Discussion Paper 1453.*

Eichengreen B. and Haussman R., 1999. "Exchange Rates and Financial Fragility", NBE Working Paper No. 7418.

Emerson, M., Gros D., Italianer A., Pisani-Ferry J. and Reichenbach H., 1992, "One Market, One Money: An Evaluation of the Potential Benefits and Costs of Forming an Economic and Monetary Union", Oxford; New York, Oxford University Press.

Engel, C., and West, D. K., 2005. "Exchange Rates and Fundamentals", *Journal of Political Economy*, 113 (3), pp. 485-517.

Eurostat., 2014. "Compact Guides, Basic Figures on the EU", *Statistical Office of the European Union*, Luxembourg.

———., 2015. "Compact Guides, Basic Figures on the EU", *Statistical Office of the European Union*, Luxembourg, p. 1-6.

Farrell M. J., 1966. "Profitable Speculation", *Economica*, 33, 183-93.

Farmer, J., and S. Joshi., 2002. "The Price Dynamics of Common Trading Strategies," *Journal of Economic Behavior and Organization*, 49(2), 149–171.

Fahr, S., Motto, R., Rostagno, M., Smets, F., and **Tristani, O.,** 2010. "Lessons for Monetary Policy Strategies from Recent Past", *ECB Working Paper Series,* No. 1336.

Frankel, J. A., and Froot, K. A. (1987): "Using Survey Data to Test Standard Propositions Regarding Exchange Rate Expectations," *American Economic Review,* 77(1), 133–153.

Feldstein M., 1997. "The Political Economy of the European Economic and Monetary Union: Political Sources of an Economic Liability," *The Journal of Economic Perspectives,* 11 (4), 23-42.

———., 2000. "The European Central Bank and the Euro: The first Year", *National Bureau of Economic Research Working Paper* 7517.

Fellner W., Machlup F., and Triffin R., 1966. *Maintaining and Restoring Balance in International Payments,* Princeton, N.J., Princeton University Press.

Findlay, R., and Rodriguez Alfredo C., 1977. "Intermediate Imports and Macroeconomics Policy under Flexible Exchange Rates", *The Canadian Journal of Economics,* 10(2), 208-217.

Fisher. I., 1922. *The Purchasing Power of Money.* Augustus M. Kelly, New York.

Flandreau, M. 1996. "The French Crime of 1873: An Essay on the Emergence of the International Gold Standard,1870-1880." Journal of Economic History, 51, No. 4, 862-897.

Fleming, M. 1962. "Domestic Financial Policies Under Fixed and Under Floating Exchange Rates", *IMF Staff Papers* 9(3), 369-79. Reprinted in Cooper, Richard N., ed. (1969). *International Finance.* New York: Penguin Books.

———. 1971 "Essays in International Economics" *Cambridge, Mass. Harvard University Press.*

Flood, R. P. and Garber, P. M. 1984. "Collapsing Exchange Rate Regimes: Some Linear Examples", *Journal of International Economics,* 17(1-2), 1-13.

Forni, M. and Reichlin, L., 1997. "National Policies and Local Economies: Europe and the United States", *CEPR Discussions Paper,* No. 1632.

Frankel, J. and Rose, A., 1997. "Is EMU more justifiable ex post than ex ante?", *European Economic Review,* 41, 753-760.

Friedman M., 1953. "The Case for Flexible Exchange Rates", in Friedman M. (ed.) *Essays in Positive Economics,* University of Chicago Press, Chicago, 157-203.

———., 1998. *A primer on exchange rates,* Forbes, November 2nd, 1998.

Frankel J.A. and Rose A.K., 1997. "Economic Structure and the Decision to adopt a Common Currency", *Institute for International Studies, Stockholm University, Seminar Papers,* No. 611.

Gagnon, J.E., Raskin, M., Remache, J., and **Sack, B.P.**, 2011a. "The Financial Market Effects of the Federal Reserve's large-scale asset purchases", *International Journal of Central Banking,* 7 (1), 3-43.

———., 2011b. "Large-Scale Asset Purchases by the Federal Reserve: did they work?" *Federal Reserve Bank of New York Economic Policy Review,* 17 (1), 41-59.

Ghosh A. R., and **Wolf D., (1994).** " How Many Monies? A Genetic Approach to Finding Optimum Currency Areas," *NBER Working Paper No. 4805.*

Giannone, D., Lenza, M., Pill, H., and Reichlin, L., 2012. "The ECB and the Interbank Market", *Economic Journal.* v. 122 (564), pp. F467-86.

Glick, R., and Leduc, S., 2013. "Unconventional Monetary Policy and Dollar." FRBSF, Economic Letter, no 2013-09, April.

Goodhart, C. A. E., 1998. "The two Concepts of Money: implication for the analysis of Optimal Currency Areas", *European Journal of Political Economy,* 14, 407-432.

Gorton, G. B., and **Metrick A.**, 2012. "Who Ran on Repo?" *NBER Working Papers* 18455, National Bureau of Economic Research, Inc.

Greek Ministry of Finance, 2010. "Update of the Hellenic Stability and Growth Program", *European Commission. 15 January 2010.*

Greenbaum, S. and **Thakor, A.** 1987. "Bank Funding Modes: Securitization versus Deposits". *Journal of Banking and Finance,* 11, 379-401.

Greenwood, R. and **Vayanos, D.** 2008. "Bond Supply and Excess Bond Returns", *NBER Working Paper,* 13806.

———.,. 2010. "Price Pressure in the Government Bond Market", *American Economic Review, Papers and Proceedings,* 585-590.

Greenwood, R., Hanson, G. S., Rudolph, J., and **Summers, L.**, 2014. "Government Debt Management at the Zero Lower Bound", *Hutchins Center on Fiscal and Monetary Policy at Brookings,* Working Paper No. 5, Brookings Institution, Washington, D.C., pp. 1-55.

Grimes A., Holmes F., and **Bowden R.**, 2000. "An ANZAC Dollar? Currency Union and Business Development"

Gros D., Alcidi C., and **De Groen W.P.**, 2015. "Lessons from Quantitative Easing: Much ado about so little?" *CEPS, No. 330. March 2015.*

Grubel H. G., 1970. "The Theory of Optimum Currency Areas", *The Canadian Journal of Economics,* 3 (2), 318-214.

Grubel H. G., 1973. "The Theory of Optimum Regional Associations" paper presented at the Optimum Currency Areas Conference in Madrid, March 1970. Reprinted in *The Economics of Common Currencies,* (eds. H. Johnson and A. Swoboda). London: George Allen and Unwin Ltd, 1973. pp. 99-113.

———. 1999. "The Case for the Amero: The Economics and Politics of a North American Monetary Union", *Critical Issues Bulletin,* The Fraser Institute, Vancouver, 1-48.

Gunsel N. R., Tursoy T., and Rjoub H., 2010. "An Empirical Analysis of Currency Crisis, Fundamentals and Speculative Pressure", *African Journal of Business Management,* 4(6), 972-78.

Gurkaynak, R. and **Wright, J. 2010.** "Macroeconomics and the Term Structure", *Mimeo,* April 2010.

Hagen J von. , 1992. "Fiscal Arrangement in a Monetary Union: Evidence from the US", in Fair E. D. and Boissieu de C. (eds), *Fiscal Policy, Taxation, and Financial System in an Increasingly Integrated Europe,* Dordrecht, Netherlands and Boston, Kluwer Academic Publishers, 337-59.

Hagen J von. and Neumann M. J. M., 1994 "Real Exchange Rates Within and Between Currency Areas: How Far Away is EMU?", *The Review of Economics and Statistics*, 76 (2), 236-244.

Hahn F.H., 1954. Review Authors "Essay in Positive Economics", *Econometrica*, Vol. 22, No.3. 399-401.

Hakim, S.R. and **Rashidian**, M., 2000. "Testing for Segmentation in the Term Structure: Operation Twist Revisited", *Quarterly Journal of Business and Economics*, 39 (1), 3-21.

Hamilton, J.D. and **Wu,** J.C., 2012. "The Effectiveness of Alternative Monetary Policy tools in a Zero Lower Bound Environment", *Journal of Money, Credit and Banking*, vol. 44, (Supplement), 3-46.

Harberger A. C., 1950. "Currency Depreciation, Income and the Balance of Trade", *The Journal of Political Economy*, 58 (1), 47-60.

Harrod R., 1965. *Reforming the World's Money*, London-New York, MacMillan.

Harris, R.G., 2000. "The Case for North American Monetary Union", *Isuma, Canadian Journal of Policy Research*, Spring, 1 (1), 93-96.

Hassan Sh., 2006. "Currency Crisis and Monetary Policy in an Economy with Credit Constraints: The Case for Low Interest Rates Restored." *University of Cape Town, Working Paper No. 14.*

Harvey, T, J., 2009. "Currencies, Capital Flows, and Crises: A Post Keynesian Analysis of Exchange Rate Determination", *Routledge, Taylor& Francis Group*, London and New York.

Hause J. C., 1966 "The Welfare Costs of Disequilibrium Exchange Rates," *Journal of Political Economy*, 74, 333-52.

Hausken, K. and **Ncube M.**, 2013. "Quantitative Easing and Its Impact in the US, Japan, the UK and Europe". London: Springer.

Herndon T., **Ash M.**, and **Pollin R.**, 2013. "Does High Public Debt Consistently Stifle Economic Growth? A Critique of Reinhart and Rogoff", *Working Paper No. 322, Political Economy Research Institute*, University of Massachusetts, Amherst, MA, 1-25.

Holmes J. M., 1972. "The Experience of Capital Flows, Fixed and Flexible Exchange Rates and Full Employment", *The Canadian Journal of Economics*, 5(2), 215-226.

Hommes, C., (2006). "Heterogeneous Agent Models in Economics and Finance", in *Handbook of Computational Economics*, Vol.2, Agent-based Computational Economics, eds. Tesfatsion, L., and Judd, K.L., pp. 1109-1186. Amsterdam, North-Holland.

Johnson H. G., 1963 "Equilibrium under Fixed Exchanges", *The American Economic Review*, 53 (2), 112-119.

———. 1966. "Some Aspects the Theory of Economic Policy in a World of Capital

Mobility", in *Essays in Honour of Marco Fanno*, ed. T. Bagiotti, Padova.

———. 1976. "Elasticity, absorption, Keynesian multiplier, Keynesian policy, and monetary approaches to devaluation theory: a simple geometric exposition", *American Economic Review*, 66, 448-52.

Jones, R. W., 1968. "Monetary and Fiscal Policy for an Economy with Fixed Exchange Rates," *The Journal of Political Economy*, 76, 921-43.

Joyce, M., Tong, M., and **Woods, R.**, 2011. "The United Kingdom's Quantitative Easing Policy: Design, Operation and Impact", *Bank of England Quarterly Bulletin*, Q3, vol. 51(3), pp. 200-12

IMF staff reports; 2008. IMF, *World Economic Outlook Database and IMF staff estimates*, April 31, 2008.

IMF Fiscal Monitor, 2012, IMF, *Taking Stock: A Progress Report on Fiscal Adjustment*, Oct. 2012, Washington D.C.

IMF staff report, 2014. "Strengthening the Contractual Framework to Address Collective Action Problems in Sovereign Debt Restructuring", *staff paper*, Sept. 2014, 1.48.

Ingram, J.C., (1962), "Regional Payments Mechanisms: The Case of Puerto Rico", University of North Carolina Press, North Caroline.

Ishiyama Y., 1975. "The Theory of Optimum Currency Areas: A Survey", *IMF Staff Papers*, 22, 344-383.

Ivashina, V. and **Scharfstein, D.,** 2010. "Loan Syndication and Credit Cycles", *American Economic Review*, 100, 57-61.

Kapetanios, G., Mumtaz, H., Stevens, I., and **Theodoridis, K.,** 2012. "Assessing the economy-wide effects of Quantitative Easing", *Economic Journal*, vol. 122 (564), pp. F316-47.

Kawai, M., 1987 "Optimum Currency Areas." In Eatwell J., Milgate M., and Newman P., (ed) *The New Palgrave: A Dictionary of Economics*. Vol. 3, p: 740-742. New York: The Stockton Press.

Kemp, M. C., 1962. "The rate of Exchange, the Terms of Trade and the Balance of Payment in fully Employed Economies," *International Economic Review*, 3 (3), 314-327.

Kenen, P. B., 1969. "The Theory of Optimum Currency Area: An Eclectic View", in *Monetary Problems of International Economy*, Mundell and Swoboda (eds.), University of Chicago Press, Chicago, Il.

Keys, B., Mukherjee, T., Seru, A., and Vig, V., 2010 " Did Securitization lead to lax Screening? Evidence from Subprime Loans", *Quarterly Journal of Economics*, 125, 307-362.

Kohn, D.L. 2009. "Monetary Policy Research and the Financial Crisis: Strengths and Shortcomings", Speech delivered at the Federal Reserve Conference on Key Developments in Monetary Policy, Washington D.C.

Kollman, R. 1996. "The Exchange Rate in a Dynamic Optimizing Current Account Model with Nominal Rigidities: A Quantitative Analysis", *Mimeographed, Unpublished Manuscrip*, University of Montreal, Montreal.

Koo. C. R., 2014. "The Escape from Balance Sheet Recession and the QE Trap: A Hazardous Road for the World Economy". *John Wiley & Sons Singapore Pte. Ltd*, 1st Edition.

Krishnamurthy, A. and **Vissing-Jogersen, A.**, 2011. "The Effects of Quantitative Easing on Interest Rates: Channels and Implications for Policy", *National Bureau of Economic Research*, Cambridge. MA., Working Paper 17555, 1-46.

Krueger, A. O., 1965. "The Impact of Alternative Government Policies Under Varying Exchange Systems", *The Quarterly Journal of Economics,* 79 (2), 195-208.

———. 1969. "Balance-of-Payments Theory", *Journal of Economic Literature,* 7(1), 1-26.

Krugman, P. 1979. "A Model of Balance-of-Payment Crises." *Journal of Money, Credit and Banking,* 11 (3), 311-25.

———. 1983. *Oil Shocks and Exchange Rate Dynamics,* in "Exchange Rates and International Economics", Jacob A. Frenkel, ed., University Chicago Press, 259-284.

———.1991, "Target Zones and Exchange Rate Dynamics", *Quarterly Journal of Economics,* 106(3), 669-682.

———.1993. "Lessons from Massachusetts for EMU" in Torres F. and & Giavazzi F. (editors) *Adjustment and Growth in the European Monetary Union,* London: CEPR and Cambridge University Press, Cambridge, 241-261.

———. 1996. "Are Currency Crisis Self-fulfilling?" *NBER Macroeconomics Annual.*

———. 1999. "Balance Sheets, the Transfer Problem, and Financial Crisis, *International Tax and Public Finance,* 6(4), 459-72.

Kurihara, Y., 2006. "The Relationship between Exchange Rate and Stock Prices during the Quantitative Easing Policy in Japan", *International Journal of Business,* 11 (4), 376-86.

Kydland F. E. and Prescott C. E., 1977, " Rules Rather than Discretion: The Inconsistency of Optimal Plans", *The Journal of Political Economy,* Vol. 85 (3), 473-92.

Labonte M., 2015. "Monetary Policy and the Federal Reserve: Current Policy and Issues for Congress", *Congressional Research Service,* 7-5700, RL30354.

Laidler, D. 2005. "Inflation Targets versus International Monetary Integration: a Canadian Perspective," *Structural Change and Economics Dynamics,* 16, 35-64.

Laidler, D., and **Poschmann, F.**, 2000 "Leaving Well Enough Alone: Canada's Monetary Order in a Changing International Environment", *C.D. Howe Institute Commentary,* Toronto, May, No. 142.

Lam, R.W., 2011. "Bank of Japan's Monetary Easing Measures: Are They Powerful and Comprehensive?", *IMF Working Paper 11/264,* International Monetary Fund, Washington, D.C.

Lane, P.R., 2001. 'The New Open Economy Macroeconomics: A Survey", *Journal of International Economics,* 54 (2), pp. 235–66.

Lane, R. P., 2000.Money Shocks and the Current Account, In *Money, Capital Mobility and Trade: Essays in Honor of Robert Mundell,* ed. Calvo A. G., Dornbusch R., and Obstfeld M., MIT Press, Cambridge, Massachusetts, London, England, 385-411.

Lavoie, M., and Daigle, G., 2011. "A Behavioural Finance Model of Exchange Rate Expectations within a Stock-Flow Consistent Framework." In: *Metroeconomica,* Vol. 62:3, pp. 434-458.

Laursen S., (1955), "Productivity, Wages and the Balance of Payments", *The Review of Economics and Statistics,* 37(2), 180-188.

Laursen S., and Metzler L.A. 1950. "Flexible Exchange Rate and the Theory of Employment", *The Review of Economics and Statistics*, 32 (4), 281-299.

Leaven L., and **Valencia F.**, 2010. "Resolution of Banking Crises: the Good, the Bad and the Ugly", *IMF Working Papers*, 10, 146.

Lenza, M., Pill, H., and **Reichlin, L.**, 2010. "Monetary Policy in Exceptional Times", *Economic Policy*, v.62, 295-339.

Levy-Yeyati, E., and **Sturzenegger F.**, 2003. "To Float or to Fix: Evidence on the Impact of Exchange Rate Regimes on Growth", *American Economic Review*, 93(4), 1173-93.

Levy-Yeyati E. and **Sturzenegger F.**, 2005. Classifying Exchange Rate Regimes: Deeds vs. Words. European Economic Review, 49, 1603-35.

Licchetta M., 2009. "Common Determinants of Currency Crisis: Role of External Balance Sheet Variables", *Bank of England, Working Paper*, pp. 366-69.

Liu, P. and Mumtaz, H., 2013. "Changing Macroeconomic Dynamics at the Zero Lower Bound", Bank of England working paper, work-in-progress, Bank of England, London.

MacDougall D., 1977. "Report on the Study Group on the Role of Public Finance in European Integration," *Commission of the European Communities*, Brussels, vol.1.

MacDonald, R., 2007. "Exchange Rate Economics: Theories and Evidence", *Routledge*, London and New York.

Marston, R. C.,1984. "Exchange Rate Union as an Alternative to Flexible Exchange Rates: The Effect of Real and Monetary Disturbances, in Bilson J.F.O. and Marston R.C. (eds.), in *Exchange Rate Theory and Practice*, Chicago: University of Chicago Press.

McKinnon R. I.,1963. "Optimum Currency Areas", *American Economic Review*, 53 (4), 517-525.

———. 1971. "Exchange-Rate Flexibility and Monetary Policy," *Journal of Money, Credit and Banking*, 3 (2), 339-55.

McKinnon R.I., 2001. "Euroland and East Asia in Dollar-Based International Monetary System: Mundell Revised", in *Money, Capital Mobility and Trade*, (ed. Calvo A. G., Dornbusch R., and Obstfeld M.), MIT Press, 413-429.

McKinsey Global Institute, 2015, "Debt and (not much) Deleveraging", *McKinsey& Company* publications, London, San Francisco & Shanghai, p.1-124.

Meade, J. E. 1951. *The Theory of International Economic Policy. The Balance of Payments* (Vol. one), Oxford University Press.

———. 1957. The balance-of-payments problems of a European Free-Trade Area, *The Economic Journal*. 67: 379–396.

Meese, R and Rogoff, K., 1983. "Empirical Exchange Rate Models of the Seventies: Do They Fit Out of Sample?" *Journal of International Economics*, 14(1-2), pp. 3-24.

Meese, R.A., Rogoff. K.S. 1988. "Was It Real? The Exchange Rate–Interest Differential Relation over the Modern Floating-Rate Period." *Journal of Finance*, 43 (4): pp. 933–48.

Mèlitz, J. 1996. "The Theory of Optimum Currency Areas, Trade and Adjustment and Trade", *Open Economies Review*, 7(2), 99-116.

Melvin, R.J. 1968. "Capital Flows and Employment under Flexible Exchange Rates", *The Canadian Journal of Economics*, 1(2), 318-333.

Meltzer A. H., 1986. "Size, Persistence and Interrelation of Nominal and Real Shocks," *Journal of Monetary Economics*, 17 (1), 161-194.

Menkhoff, L., and Taylor M. P., 2007. "The Obstinate Passion of Foreign Exchange Professionals: Technical Analysis," *Journal of Economic Literature*, 45, 936–972.

Meyer, L.H. and **Bomfim, A.N.**, 2010. "Quantifying the Effects of Fed Asset Purchases on Treasury Yields", *Monetary Policy Insights: Fixed Income Focus*.

Minford, P., 1995. "Other People's Money: Cash in Advance Microfoundations for Optimal Currency Areas," *Journal of International Money and Finance*, Vol. 14, 427-440.

Modigliani, F and **Sutch, R**. 1966. "Innovations in Interest Rate Policy", *The American Economic Review*, 56 (1-2), 178-97.

Molodtsova, T., and Papell, D. H. 2009. "Out-of-Sample Exchange Rate Predictability with Taylor Rule Fundamentals," *Journal of International Economics*, 77 (2), pp. 167-180.

Molodtsova, T., and Papell, D. H. 2012. "Taylor Rule Exchange Rate Forecasting During the Financial Crisis." *NBER, International Seminar on Macroeconomics*.

Mundell R. A., 1960. "The Monetary Dynamics of International Adjustment under Fixed and Flexible Exchange Rates", *Quarterly Journal of Economics*, 74, 227-57.

———. 1961a. "Flexible Exchange Rates and Employment Policy", *Canadian Journal of Economics and Political Science*, 27(4), 509-517.

———. 1961b. "A Theory of Optimum Currency Areas." *The American Economic Review*, 51, (4), 657-665.

———. 1963. "Capital Mobility and Stabilization Policy Under Fixed and Flexible Exchange Rates", *Canadian Journal of Economics and Political Science, 29(4), 475-485.*

———. 1968. *International Economics*, New York: Macmillan, 1968.

———. "A Plan for a European Currency". Paper presented at the Optimum Currency Areas Conference in Madrid, March 1970, reprinted in *The Economics of Common Currencies* (eds. H. Johnson and A. Swoboda). London: George Allen & Unwin Ltd. 1973: 143-173

———. 1973. "Uncommon Arguments for Common Currencies", in Johnson H.G. and Swoboda A.K. (eds.), *The Economics of Common Currencies*, George Allen and Unwin Ltd, London, pp. 114-32.

———. 1997. "The European Monetary System 50 Years after Bretton Woods: A comparison between Two Systems". *Columbia University.* (Paper presented at Project Europe 1985-95, the tenth edition of the "Incontri di Rocca Salimbeni", meetings, in Siena, 25 November 1994).

———. 1998. The Case for Euro, Part I and II, "*The Wall Street Journal*", March 24-25.

———. 2000. "A Talk with a Father of the Euro." Interview with Mundell in *Business Week* (November 13th, 2000).

———. 2001. "The Internationally Monetary System at the New Millennium", *Rivista di Economia Politica* (Third Angela Costa Lecture), 7-39.

Mundell, R. A. and **Friedman, M.**, 2000. Mundell Robert and Friedman Milton debate the virtues – or not – of fixed exchange rates, gold, and a world currency, "One World, One Money", *The Canadian Financial Post,* articles published between November 14th and December 14th, 2000, conceived and organized by editor-in-Chief Terence Corcoran.

Mundell, R.A. and **Friedman M.**, 2001. "One World, One Money", *Policy Options* (May), 10-30.

Mussa M., 1986. "Nominal Exchange Rate Regimes and the Behaviour of Real Exchange Rates: Evidence and Implications," in *Real Business Cycle, Real Exchange Rates and Actual Policies, Cornegie-Rochester Conference Series* 25, North Holland, Amsterdam.

Neary, J.P. and **Purvis, D.D.**. 1982. "Sectoral Shocks in a Dependent Economy: Short-run Accommodations and Long-Run Adjustment". *Scandinavian Journal of Economics,* 84, 229-53.

———. 1983. "Real Adjustment and Exchange Rate Dynamics", in *Exchange Rates and International Macroeconomics* (ed.) Jacob A. Frenkel, University of Chicago Press.

Neely, C, J., 2012." Large-Scale Asset Purchases had Large International Effects." *Federal Reserve Bank of St. Louis,* Working Paper, no. 2010-018c.

Obstfeld, M., 1980. "Intermediate Imports, the Terms of Trade, and the Dynamics of the Exchange Rate and Current Account," *Journal of International Economics,* 10(4), 461-480.

———. 1994. The Logic Currency Crisis, *NBER Working Paper No. 4640.*

———. 1996. Models of Currency Crisis with Self-Fulfilling Features. *European Economic Review,* 40, 366-69.

Obstfeld, M. and Rogoff, K. 1995a. "Exchange Rate Dynamics Redux", *Journal of Political Economy,* 103, pp. 624–60.

Obstfeld, M. and **Rogoff, K.** 1995b. "The Intertemporal Approach to the Current Account". In *Handbook of International Economics,* (eds. Grossman G. and Rogoff K)., 1731-99, vol. 3, Amsterdam: North-Holland.

Obstfeld, M. and **Rogoff, K.**, 2002. "Global Implications of Self-Oriented National Monetary Rules, " *The Quarterly Journal of Economics,* v. 117(2), 503-535.

Ornstein, L. S., and **Uhlenbeck, G. E.** 1930. "On the Theory of the Brownian Motion". *Physical Review,* 36, no. 5: 823. doi:10.1103.

———. F*oundations of International Macroeconomics,* Cambridge, Mass.: MITT Press, 1996.

Oppers, S., 1996. "Was the Worldwide Shift to Gold Inevitable? An Analysis of the End of Bimetallism", Journal of Monetary Economics, 37, 143-162.

Peersman, G., 2011. "The Macroeconomic Effects of Unconventional Monetary Policy in the Euro Area", *ECB Working Paper Series,* NO. 1397, pp.1-33.

Pennacchi G. G., 1988. “Loan sales and the cost of bank capital”, *The Journal of Finance,* Vol. XLIII, No. 2, 375-396.

Penner, G. R., 1962. “The Inflow of Long Term Capital and the Canadian Business Cycle 1950-1960,” *Canadian Journal of Economics and Political Science,* 28 (4), 527-42.

Persson T. and **Tabellini G.,** 1993. “Designing Institutions for Monetary Stability”. *Carnegie-Rochester Conference Series on Public Policy,* 39, 53-84.

Reinhart C.M., 2000. “The mirage of Floating Exchange Rates”, *American Economic Review, 90 (2),* 65-70.

Reinhart C. M. and **Rogoff, K. S**., 2010. "Growth in a Time of Debt", *American Economic Review: Paper & Proceedings,* 100 (2), 1-6.

———. 2011. “From Financial Crash to Debt Crisis”, *American Economic Review,* 101 (5), 1676-1706.

Rhomberg, R.R., (1964). “A Model of the Canadian Economy under Fixed and Fluctuating Exchange Rates”, *Journal of Political Economy,* 72 (1), 1-31.

Ricci L. A., (2008). “A Model of an Optimum Currency Area,” *IMF, Special Issue,* Vol. 2, 2008-8, pp. 1-31.

Rogoff, K. S., 1996. “The Purchasing Power Parity Puzzle”, Journal *of Economic Literature* 34, 647-68.

———. 1985. “The Optimal Degree of Commitment to a Monetary Target”, *Quarterly Journal of Economics,* 100, 1169-90.

Rose A. K., 1994. "Exchange Rate Volatility, Monetary Policy, and Capital Mobility: Empirical Evidence on the Holy Trinity", *NBER Working Paper* No. 4630, Cambridge, Ma.

———. 2007. “A Stable International Monetary System Emerges: Inflation Targeting is Bretton Woods, Reserved,” *Journal of International Money and Finance,* 26 (5), 663-81.

Rossi, B. 2013. “Exchange Rate Predictability.” *Journal of Economic Perspectives,* 51 (4), pp. 1063–1119.

Sala-i-Martin X. and Sachs J., 1992."Fiscal Federalism and Optimum Currency Areas: Evidence for Europe from the United States," CEPR Discussion Papers 632, C.E.P.R. Discussion Papers.

Samuelson P.A., (1947). *Foundations of Economic Analysis,* Cambridge, Massachusetts. Harvard University Press.

Sarno, L., 2008. “Purchasing Power Parity” in Durlauf, Steven N., and Lawrence E. Blume (eds.) *The New Palgrave Dictionary of Economics,* 2nd edition, Palgrave MacMillan, London.

Sarno, L., Taylor, M.P., and Chowdhury, I., 2004. “Nonlinear Dynamics in Deviations from the Law of One Price: A Broad-Based Empirical Study”, *Journal of International Money and Finance,* 23, pp. 1-25.

Sarno, L. and Valente, G. 2006. “Deviations from Purchasing Power Parity under Different Exchange Rate Regimes: Do They Revert and, If so, how?”, *Journal of Banking and Finance,* 30, pp. 3147-3169.

Scott, A. 1999. “The Macro-economic context of the Euro”, in Beaumont, P. and Walker, N. (eds.) *Legal Framework of the Single European Currency,* Oxford, Hart Publishing

Sohmen E., 1957. "Demand Elasticities and the Foreign-Exchange Market", *The Journal of Political Economy*, 65 (5), 431-436.

———. 1958. "The Effect of Devaluation on the Price Level", *Quarterly Journal of Economics*, 72, 273-283.

———. 1961. *Flexible Exchange Rates – Theory and Controversy*, Chicago: University of Chicago Press.

———. 1967. "Fiscal and Monetary Policies Under Alternative Exchange-Rate Systems", *The Quarterly Journal of Economics*, 81 (3), 515-523.

Stein L. J., 1961. "Destabilizing Speculative Activity Can be Profitable", *Review of Economics and Statistics*, 43, 301-302.

Stiglitz J. E., 2002. "Capital Market Liberalization and Exchange Rate Regimes: Risks without Reward", *Annals of the American Academy of Political and Social Science*, Vol. 579, 219-248.

———. 2014. "The World Needs a Sovereign Debt Restructuring Mechanism," *Emerging Markets.Org*, December 10, 2014.

Stroebel, J. C., and **Taylor, J.B.**, 2012. "Estimated Impact of the Fed's Mortgage-backed Securities Purchase Program", *International Journal of Central Banking*, 8 (2), 1-42.

Swanson, E. T., 2011. "Let's Twist Again: A High-Frequency Event Study Analysis of Operation Twist and Its Implications for QE2", *Brooking Papers on Economic Activity*, Vol. 42(1), 151-207.

Tarapore Committee. 1997. *Report of the Committee on Capital Account Convertibility*. Mumbai, Reserve Bank of India.

Taylor, J.B. 1993. "Discretion Versus Policy Rules in Practice," *Carnegie-Rochester Conference Series on Public Policy*, 39, pp. 195-214

Tian G. and **Huang K.** 2011. "Reputation and Optimal Contract for Central Bankers," *Macroeconomic Dynamics Theory*, 15. 441-464.

Tower E. 1973. "Commercial Policy Under Fixed and Flexible Exchange Rates", *Quarterly Journal of Economics*, 87(3), 436-454.

Tower E., and **Willett T.** 1976. "The Theory of Optimum Currency Areas and Exchange Rate Flexibility: A More General Framework", *Special Papers in International Economics*, 11, Princeton University.

Triffin R. 1960. "*Gold and the Dollar Crisis*", New Haven: Yale University Press.

———. 1966. "*The World Money Maze. National Currencies in International Payments*", New Haven, Connecticut and London, Yale University Press.

Tsiang C. 1961. "The Role of Money in Trade-Balance Stability: Synthesis of the Elasticity and Absorption Approaches", *American Economic Review*, 51, 912-936.

Ueada, K., 2011. "The Effectiveness of Non-Traditional Monetary Policy Measures: The Case of the Bank of Japan", *CARF Working Paper, CARF-F-252*, Centre for Advanced Research in Finance, University of Tokyo.

Ugai, H., 2007. "Effects of the Quantitative Easing Policy: A Survey of Empirical Analyses", *Monetary and Economic Studies*, March, vol. 25 (1), p.1-48.

Valente, G., 2009. "International Interest Rates and the U.S. Monetary Announcements: Evidence from Hong Kong and Singapore", *Journal of International Money and Finance,* 28 (6), 920-40.

Vauber R., 1978. "Real Exchange Rate Changes in the European Community: A new Approach to the Determination of Optimum Currency Areas", *Journal of International Economics,* 8, 319-339.

Vayanos, D. and **Vila, J.L. 2009.** "A Preferred-habitat model of the Term Structure of Interest Rates", *NBER Working Paper* No. 15487.

Walsh E. C., 1995. "Optimal Contracts for Central Bankers", *The American Economic Review,* Vol. 85 (1) 150-67.

Williams, J. H., 1953. Trade not aid: A program for World stability. *Cambridge, Massachusetts. Harvard University Press.*

———. 1965 "The Crawling Peg", in *Essays in International Finance,* No. 50, Princeton, N.J.: Princeton University Press.

———.1996. The Crawling Band as an Exchange Rate Regime: Lessons from Chile, Colombia, and Israel, Washington: *Institute for International Economics.*

———.1999. Crawling Bands or Monitoring Bands: How to Manage Exchange Rates in a World of Capital Mobility, *Policy Briefs, Peterson Institute for International Economics.*

———. 2000 "Designing a Middle Way between Fixes and Flexible Exchange Rates" *Institute for International Economics,* Paper presented to a conference on "Monetary and Exchange Rate Policies: Options for Egypt" *Egyptian Center for Economic Studies,* Cairo, Egypt, November 2000, p. 1-13.

Williams, J. C., 2014. "Monetary Policy at the Zero Lower Bound: Putting Theory into Practice", *The Brookings Institution,* Hutchins Center Working Papers no.3, January.

Index

A

B

C

D

E

F

G

H

I

J

K

L

M

N

O

P

Q

R

S

T

U

V

W

Z